3249996500

D1422558

WITHDRAWN

from

STIRLING UNIVERSITY LIBRARY

University of Stirling Library, FK9 4LA
Tel.   01786 – 467220

POPULAR LOAN

This item is likely to be in heavy demand.
Please RETURN or RENEW no later
than the last date stamped below

2 3 NOV 2001	2 4 MAR 2003	
1 8 FEB 2002	3 1 MAR 2003	
1 9 APR 2002	2 6 MAY 2003	
2 9 APR 2002		
2 7 MAY 2002		
2 7 MAY 2002		
2 7 MAY 2002		

WAR
AND THE
MEDIA

LP
4
HUD

WAR
AND THE
MEDIA

A Random Searchlight

'The light shone by the media is not the regular
sweep of the lighthouse, but a random searchlight
directed at the whim of its controllers.'

Douglas Hurd

POP

Miles Hudson
&
John Stanier

SUTTON PUBLISHING

58611
12/98

First published in 1997 by
Sutton Publishing Limited · Phoenix Mill
Thrupp · Stroud · Gloucestershire · GL5 2BU

Copyright © Miles Hudson and John Stanier, 1997

All rights reserved. No part of this publication may be reproduced, stored
in a retrieval system, or transmitted, in any form, or by any means,
electronic, mechanical, photocopying, recording or otherwise, without
the prior permission of the publisher and copyright holders.

The authors have asserted the moral right to be identified as the authors
of this work.

British Library Cataloguing in Publication Data
A catalogue record for this book is available from the British Library

ISBN 0 7509 1220 0

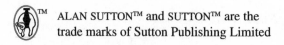
ALAN SUTTON™ and SUTTON™ are the
trade marks of Sutton Publishing Limited

Typeset in 10/13pt New Baskerville.
Typesetting and origination by
Sutton Publishing Limited
Printed in Great Britain by
MPG Books, Bodmin, Cornwall.

314705

Contents

List of Plates   vii
List of Sketch Maps   viii
Acknowledgements   ix
Introduction   xi

1   The Crimea, 1854–1856   1
2   Late Victoriana   23
3   The Great War, 1914–1918   39
4   The Second World War, 1939–1945   61
5   The Asian Connection: Korea and Vietnam   85
6   Suez, 1956   121
7   Ireland: The Longest Feud in Europe   141
8   The Falklands War, 1982   163
9   The Wounded Giant: The United States, 1980–1989   185
10   The Gulf War against Iraq, 1991   209
11   Somalia, 1992–1993   245
12   The Balkan Tragedy, 1991–1996 x   263
13   Conclusions   303

Select Bibliography   323
Index   329

List of Plates

Between pages 146 and 147

 1. Coldstream Guards, Crimea
 2. Balaklava Harbour, Crimea
 3. Lord Roberts of Kandahar in South Africa
 4. After the battle of Spion Kop, South Africa
 5. 'The British Empire', propaganda advert, First World War
 6. Coldstreamers on the Somme
 7. Raemaekers' cartoons, First World War
 8. Nazi mass rally
 9. Adolf Hitler
10. British propaganda leaflet, Second World War
11. Winston Churchill
12. 8th Hussars in Korea
13. Action in Vietnam
14. News headlines, Vietnam
15. British Navy in Port Said
16. El Gami Airfield, Port Said, Suez Crisis, 1956
17. Ulster headlines
18. Views on Internment
19. HMS *Sheffield*, Falklands War
20. Press briefing, Falklands War
21. The Americans in Grenada
22. Return from Grenada
23. The road to Basra, Gulf War
24. Kate Adie reporting the Gulf War
25. Douglas Hurd in Bosnia
26. International Force in Bosnia

List of Sketch Maps

1.	The Crimean War	4
2.	The Boer War	30
3.	The Korean War	88
4.	Vietnam	100
5.	The Falkland Islands	168
6.	Grenada	192
7.	The Gulf War	211
8.	Somalia	246
9.	Former Yugoslavia	264

Acknowledgements

We would like to express our gratitude to the many people who have helped us in our research for this book. In particular we must thank those who spared the time to meet us, to tell us of their own experiences and to discuss our ideas with us. These included:

Sir Antony Acland, Dr Jacqueline Beaumont, Field Marshal Lord Bramall, Rt Hon Lord Carrington, Rt Hon Lord Deedes, Professor David Dilks, Sir John Graham, Mr Brian Hanrahan, Mr Max Hastings, Rt Hon Lord Hurd of Westwell, Sir Bernard Ingham, Mr Simon Jenkins, Mr Iverach MacDonald, Lord Rees-Mogg, Sir Robin Renwick, General Sir Michael Rose, Hon Raymond Seitz, Mr Keith Simpson, MP, Mr John Simpson, Rt Hon Lady Thatcher, Mr Jeremy Varcoe, General Sir Michael Walker and Mr Hamish Wilson.

Many people have been kind enough to respond in writing to our enquiries and these include:

Admiral Sir Jeremy Black, Major General J.M.F.C. Hall, General Sir David Mostyn, General Sir David Ramsbotham, Major Colin Robins of the Crimean War Research Society, Mr Oren Root, Mr Gary Rudas and General Sir Harry Tuzo.

We are indebted to Major David Bennett for allowing us to publish extracts from a private letter.

We would also wish to acknowledge the help which we have received from Mr John Dekker, Lady (Penelope) Francis and Lieutenant General Sir Michael Gray.

Naturally, however, the views expressed in this book are those of the authors alone and should not be ascribed to others, save where they are quoted.

We would like to express our thanks for the help given to us by Miss Pam Bendall and the staff of the Library of the Army Staff College, of the Newspaper Library at Colindale and of the Imperial War Museum.

We are grateful to our agent, Mandy Little of Watson Little Ltd, for her help in launching our project and to Jonathan Falconer and Clare Bishop of Sutton Publishing for their encouragement. Without the help of Mrs Vikki Tate our book would never have seen the light of day.

Finally, we would like to thank our wives for their patience.

MMLH
JWS
Mattingley,
June 1997

Introduction

It is fashionable to say that we hate the media. Yet for something we profess to hate, we devote a great deal of time to it. We read the morning papers, we listen to the radio, we buy evening papers and weekly magazines and we watch the television avidly; most of us accept what the media tells us without question. After all, very few of us have any means of gauging its accuracy, particularly if the news it brings us comes from abroad. Why then should we say that we hate it? Usually because we disagree with something that is said. Few of us like to see our institutions challenged or demolished; few of us like to see the privacy of individuals intruded upon; few of us like to see our fellows openly derided. Yet when such news items do appear, they make intriguing reading or viewing, whetting our curiosity but at the same time exciting our distaste. Equally nobody likes to see the truth as they know it distorted or trivialized. When some event, of which we do have personal knowledge, is reported, it very seldom appears to have happened as we saw it, nor does it rate the importance that we might attach to it. Nobody likes to be told what they ought to be feeling: 'Fury at new tax!' says the headline. We probably don't like it, but are we really 'furious'? So we say 'we hate the media'. Nevertheless, despite our better inclinations, we find ourselves swept along on a tide of heady journalism, endlessly brought to us by the media in all its forms.

From the viewpoint of those who fashion the news for us, there is a ready argument: it is, they say, what the viewers, listeners and readers want. They want to be excited, shocked, amazed or horrified. Good news seldom sells papers; dull news never does. So, inevitably, our news is everlastingly sensationalized. The tabloid newspapers offer us short heavy headlines, the broadsheets write worthier prose, while the radio and television indulge in soundbites of varying lengths. That they should do so is no doubt our fault: you only have to look at the circulation figures to realize who likes what.

War is among the most horrific of activities pursued by mankind. Under a cloak of military splendour and the prospect of glory, war is cruel, bloody and destructive. Its reporting, however, makes brilliant news: it offers excitement, anxiety and horror and sometimes exultation or despair. The manner in which the news of war has reached its audiences has evolved remarkably over the past 150 years. The news of the victory at Waterloo in 1815 was brought by a young officer, still wearing his battle-stained uniform, who burst into the house in Grosvenor Square where the Prince Regent was being entertained to dinner. There he made his report, laying before the Prince the two Eagle standards captured from Napoleon's defeated Grande Armée. Wellington's despatches were not published in *The Times* until some days later. The changes since those days have been as sensational as the news itself. We have tried to discover how, as the means of transmitting news has changed, the reporting of events has influenced opinion and the policies of those in positions of power. We have tried to determine whether media reports over the years have provoked or prevented wars, have prolonged or curtailed them.

In our study, the mass of evidence is so great that we have had to be rigorously selective. We too have shone a random searchlight. It is little credit to mankind that in this century of so-called civilization, there have probably been more wars than in any other – certainly wars causing far greater slaughter and destruction. We have in the main confined ourselves to countries with a free press. Totalitarian regimes control their own media and our questions are not applicable; we have, however, made passing reference to the use of a controlled media by such men as Dr Goebbels and President Milošević. We have concerned ourselves primarily with Britain and the United States in some, but not all, of their forays into armed conflict. We pick and choose the types and organs of the media which we use to illustrate our points. No doubt we can be criticized in general and in detail for our choices, but to cover the whole field would be as impossible as it would be unsaleable.

We have tried to weigh the evidence before reaching our conclusions – a well-nigh impossible task in a subject so laden with prejudice. We have produced these conclusions in our last chapter, which we hope will provoke some new thinking in the minds of those who penetrate our pages.

Before we begin, we must acknowledge and admire the courage and dedication of the men and women who daily risk their lives to bring us reports of war from all quarters of the world. Our purpose is not to denigrate their achievement, but to follow the results of their reporting.

Many of these brave people have given their lives in the pursuit of their calling. They can in no way be compared to those evil photographers and journalists who earn their living by hounding the famous; our study does not touch on this despicable trade.

Finally we must remind our readers that our study, which gallops at a headlong pace through a catalogue of wars from the Crimea to Bosnia, is not a history. Every war of which we write has been fully documented elsewhere; our purpose is to study the manner of its reporting at the time and the results of that reporting. Our account of the wars themselves is often much simplified and merely provides a framework on which to hang our study.

We hope at least to have achieved some recognition of the complexities and of the importance of our subject.

CHAPTER ONE

The Crimea, 1854–1856

'The world is full of kindly people cutting each other's throats under a misapprehension. . . . The people enter war willingly, moved by generous passion to revenge injustice or protect the weak. The war must appear a battle between right and might, and the enemy becomes the personification of evil. As this regularly occurs on both sides it is unlikely that it often represents the situation accurately.'

Kingsley Martin, 1924[1]

If one defines 'the media' as the means of communication which stands between the event, projected or actual, and the people, then the impact of the media on conflict can be traced back to the beginning of recorded history. For our purposes, however, we will start with the Crimean War of 1854–6. This is, of course, an arbitrary date but it was important because it was this war, as far as Britain was concerned, in which appeared the first war correspondent really to have an impact on the course of events – William Russell. There had been others before him but his place as the first battlefield journalist with real influence is secure. Indeed, it is probably true to say that he was and is unique in his own, or any other, time.

This is not the place to explore in detail the labyrinthine diplomatic manoeuvrings of Britain, Russia, Turkey, France and Austria which culminated in the cruel and, many would say, senseless slaughter of the Crimean War. There are differing views, not surprisingly, as to the rights and wrongs of these matters. However, it is incontrovertible that the affair was far from straightforward and not to be explained by the soaring simplicities of journalists fuelling the prejudices of the time. The cartoon in *Punch* of Lord Aberdeen, the Prime Minister, blacking the Tsar's boots is an example of how, in its search for easily understandable short images, the media can distort truth and cruelly twist motives.

Indeed the approach to the Crimean War illustrates many of the themes concerning the media which we shall be covering in this book. There was a vast oversimplification of complex issues and an insistent and

1

irrational drive towards war derived not from an objective examination of the facts but from induced and often false emotion. There was a naïve polarization of the personalities and issues concerned; the Tsar was the devil and the Sultan of Turkey (a startlingly rapid transformation this) was the angel.

Here we are immediately confronted by a conundrum, central to much of this book: when we talk about 'public opinion', is this a euphemism for 'media opinion' or are the two separate, and perhaps conflicting? There can be no doubt that the 'public' in the Victorian era was greatly influenced by the media. Indeed on matters outside the country the information the public had on which to base any opinion at all came largely from the media. In the Victorian era there were many more public meetings at which politicians would attempt to persuade the public to their point of view, although this is now more than compensated for by television appearances. Also, the newspapers would publish political speeches at great length; few, if any, are covered at any length in the media nowadays. But the power of selection which all editors had, and have, and the impact of their editorials were of the utmost importance in leading public opinion, particularly if the press were all singing the same (or nearly the same) tune, and even more so if it was pandering to popular prejudice, a common fear or national *amour propre*. Of course, in the 1850s the newspaper reading public was comparatively small, although it increased dramatically when the newspaper tax was abolished in 1855. However, those who did read the newspapers were those who mattered in Victorian Britain, and it would be folly to disregard or play down the impact of the press on public opinion. Certainly the politicians of the time believed in the power of the press as they vied for support from editors and owners, Lord Palmerston outdoing all his colleagues in this respect.

The members of the Cabinet at the time, led by the moderate Lord Aberdeen, were reluctant warriors led step by step by 'public opinion' into a situation where they found themselves at war, together with their recent arch-enemy France, under Napoleon III, to protect the weak Islamic Turkish ruler against the Christian Tsar of Russia. There was indeed a fear that Russia might grab Constantinople from the ailing Ottoman Empire and this was seized on by the bellicose Lord Palmerston, of Don Pacifico fame,[2] who was in fact at the time the Home, not the Foreign, Secretary and the even more aggressive ambassador to Turkey, Lord Stratford. However, negotiations to prevent this development, if really it ever was a danger, were far from exhausted when war was declared. Indeed, the Tsar was evidently showing every sign of wanting a peaceful solution.

The press in England was originally divided, with the majority (including the *Morning Post*) pro-Palmerston, and the rest (including *The Times*) pro-Aberdeen. However, the moderates gradually, in some cases against their better judgement, succumbed to war fever, even *The Times* joining those baying for decisive action. To give an idea of the journalistic style of the day, when *The Times* was still arguing for peace, the *Morning Advertiser* declared on 10 August 1853: 'The Russian organ of Printing House Square yesterday returned to its vomit but it is rather too much for an English journal to profit both by Russian gold and English credit.' *Reynolds' Weekly*, a working-class journal, called the Tsar 'this fiend in human form'. Even the Crown was not immune. Prince Albert was attacked in the *Morning Advertiser* for 'traitorous communication with foreign courts'. The *Daily News* trumpeted that Prince Albert was 'part of a wider conspiracy . . . the avowed enemies of England and the subservient tools of Russian ambition'. Incidentally, Queen Victoria was so incensed that she threatened to refuse to open Parliament.

The dispute between Russia and Turkey had ostensibly been about protection of the holy places in Palestine and the treatment of the 12 million Orthodox Christians living in the Ottoman Empire. In response to a Russian move into the Danube Principalities, which the Russians claimed they were entitled to do under the Treaty of Adrianople of 1829, Turkey declared war on Russia in October 1853. The Russians then sank a large portion of the Turkish fleet at Sinope in the Black Sea on 30 November.

When Britain declared war on Russia on 27 March 1854 (France had done so the day before), there was an explosion of jingoistic enthusiasm in the streets of London. Anyone who was against the war was no patriot. War would 'sweep away at once', the Reverend Charles Kingsley said, 'the dyspeptic unbelief, the insincere bigotry, the effeminate frivolity which paralyses our poetry as much as it does our action.' The Queen told the King of the Belgians that 'the war was popular beyond belief'.[3]

The Times editorial on 29 March 1854 thundered:

No alternative is left to us; the decision has been taken out of our hands; and, unless we would submit, with our allies, to crouch under the insolent dictatorship of a barbaric Power, and see the liberties of

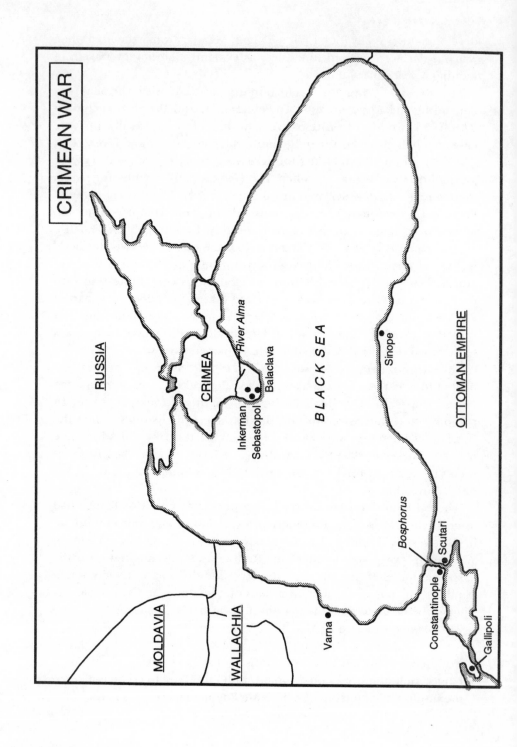

CRIMEAN WAR

RUSSIA

CRIMEA

River Alma

Inkerman
Sebastopol
Balaclava

BLACK SEA

Sinope

MOLDAVIA

WALLACHIA

Varna

Bosphorus

Constantinople
Scutari

Gallipoli

OTTOMAN EMPIRE

Europe disappear under the tramp of a Cossack, we had no other course.

The editorial went on, 'All England follows her sons to battle.'
The *Daily News* of 28 March 1854 delivered itself of the following:

In 1803 Great Britain went to war with a next-door neighbour, with the bravest and most intelligent nation in Europe, stimulated to preternatural energy by revolutionary enthusiasm and by a series of unprecedented military triumphs; in 1854 Great Britain, in firm and cordial alliance with that very power, is about to wage war against a remote power which can easily be locked up, in two inland areas, and which combines the weakness of a stereotyped corrupt mere routine framework of government, with the weakness of popular ignorance and serfdom.

At that time it was *The Times* which towered over the rest of the press (40,000 copies a day were sold in 1852 with its nearest rival selling only 7,000). It had been founded in 1785 by John Walter, a Lloyds underwriter, and under Thomas Barnes, its editor from 1817 until 1841, it had undoubtedly become the leading journal in Europe. John Walter's son had appointed John Delane as editor at the remarkably young age of twenty-three. He was to remain editor for thirty-six years. Delane was to have a marked effect on events in Britain, and in particular on the course of the Crimean War by his choice of William Russell as his special correspondent with the British army and by his support of him against the considerable pressures which were brought to bear.

With the plethora of media figures in the modern age, the power of any one editor is clearly diluted. However, in the 1850s, *The Times* was 'The Thunderer' and governments were very much in awe of it. Indeed it was *The Times'* change of attitude which had considerable impact on the decision to go to war. When Delane asked for facilities for Russell as a special correspondent, they were granted, in theory. In practice, in spite of a promised sea passage, Russell had to make his own way to Malta where the British army was assembling. Throughout the saga, from Gallipoli to Varna in Bulgaria and thence to the Crimea, he had to fend for himself.

The course of the war is easy to cover in bare outline. The British army had been sent to Malta before the outbreak of hostilities. It then went to

Gallipoli, to Scutari and thence to Varna in present-day Bulgaria in order to support the Turks in their dispute against the Russians who had occupied the principalities on the Danube, then a part of the Ottoman Empire. The Russians, however, withdrew before the British or the French, who were also at Varna, were able to take any part in the hostilities. With public opinion as it was at that stage it would have been impossible for the British Cabinet to call it a day even if the French had agreed, which must have been very doubtful. It was therefore decided to send the army across the Black Sea, to seize Sebastopol, the great Russian naval base on the Crimean peninsula on the northern edge of the Black Sea, in order to pre-empt any attempt by the Russians to threaten or indeed to seize Constantinople. When one thinks of the logistical problems which the landing and the consequent re-supply of two armies at the far end of the Black Sea must have implied and, as will be seen, the almost complete non-existence in Britain of a viable logistic organization, it is indeed surprising that this decision was taken with such apparent insouciance (the problems raised by the Falklands War were minor in comparison). In the event, the landings on the Crimean peninsula were unopposed. After a bloody battle on the River Alma, north of Sebastopol, the allies marched round that port and established themselves near the tiny port of Balaclava to its south. After two extremely bitterly fought battles at Balaclava and Inkerman, the winter of 1854 saw the British army still entrenched to the south of Sebastopol, suffering – as did the Russians – very greatly from the cold and the lack of almost all supplies.

The French, on the other hand, had a far superior Commissariat, and were not so badly affected. The British medical arrangements, both in the Crimea itself and at the base hospital in Scutari near Constantinople were horrifyingly inadequate. As we shall see, largely as a result of Russell's (and the other *Times* correspondent, Chenery's) reports from Constantinople, the condition of the British army vastly improved in the spring. Sebastopol was never, however, invested on all sides and the Russians were able to resupply it though they too had appalling problems in achieving this. A series of attacks on Sebastopol during the summer of 1855 failed, and it was not until 9 September 1855 that the Russians, succumbing to the British mortar bombardment and the French capture of the Malakov Tower – a key element of their defence – finally evacuated what remained of that city and naval base. After protracted negotiations, during which the British tried to insist on far harsher terms than the French who had become rather disillusioned by the whole affair (partly because many of their soldiers were drafted into the army, as opposed to the British all-volunteer force), peace was signed at Paris on 30 March 1856. The war had not achieved very much for the allies but, certainly, the Russian threat to Constantinople, if it had ever existed, was reduced almost to vanishing point.

Russell, a convivial Irishman with anti-imperial views, a friend of Dickens, Thackeray and later the Prince of Wales, was not the only special correspondent with the army. The *London Daily News* had sent Edwin Lawrence Godkin to Turkey 'for the hostilities'. *The Times* also had Thomas Chenery (later to become editor) as its correspondent in Constantinople. Russell's (and to a far lesser extent Chenery's) letters had an enormous effect on public opinion in Britain and hence on the political and military scene at home and in the Crimea. At no time was there any criticism of the declaration of war itself: it was accepted from the outset that the war was necessary and just. Neither was there the slightest hint of criticism of the British soldiery: indeed, the lower the rank the greater the praise. The management and the command structure, however, were different matters. Russell's reports took the form of letters to his editor. They were sometimes published as they stood; at other times they were used as the basis of leading articles and, occasionally, if thought too hot to handle, they were passed in secret to members of the Cabinet who Delane thought would be able to use them in order to improve conditions.

There was much to criticize. Very little, if anything, had been done to modernize the army since the Battle of Waterloo. It is true that the Minié rifle had been adopted, a vastly superior weapon to that used by the Russians, but the system of military administration was chaotic. The Secretary for War was assisted by a Secretary at War. The Commander-in-Chief at the Horse Guards was in command of all troops in Britain, but not those overseas, and his power derived from the monarch, not from Parliament. The Master General of the Ordnance, apparently virtually a free agent, was in charge of equipment, fortification and barracks, together with the raising, training, promotion, pay and discipline of the Royal Artillery and Engineers. A board of general officers was in charge of clothing, but some commanding officers clothed their own regiments. Transport and supplies were the responsibility of the Commissariat, a department of the Treasury. Wellington's baggage train, established during the Peninsula War, had been abolished. The Medical Department was financed by the Secretary at War who was also responsible for the pay and finance of the rest of the army, except the Artillery and Engineers. Overall control of the size and cost of the army was the responsibility of the Secretary of State for the Colonies.[4] The result, of course, was chaos, and Russell soon began to realize this. Even in Malta, at the beginning of the saga, he compared the British and French logistic arrangements greatly to the British disadvantage. On 28 November 1854 Lord Raglan had sent a requisition to England for 3,000 tents, 100 hospital marquees and several other items including 6,000 nosebags and various quantities of spades, shovels and pickaxes. On 4 April 1855 this requisition was still the subject of lengthy correspondence in Whitehall.[5] Cholera, soon to become the major killer in the Crimean War, began to take its toll and increased in severity until, eventually, by the winter of 1854, together with the other major deficiencies of supply and the effects of a violent storm and extreme cold, it had made the British army virtually non-combatant.

Russell did not pussyfoot. Even at Varna before going to the Crimea at all, he was pointing out the poor state of the British army.

The Brigade of Guards (three thousand of the flower of England) had to make two marches to cover ten miles. They had been so reduced by sickness, disease and a depressing climate that it was judged inexpedient to let them carry their own packs. . . . Think of this, and then judge whether these men are fit in their present state to go to Sebastopol, or to attempt any great operation of war.

(Letter of 19 August 1854)

It is now pouring rain – the skies are black as ink – the wind is howling over the staggering tents – the trenches have turned into dykes – in the tents the water is sometimes a foot deep – our men have not either warm or waterproof clothing – they are out for twelve hours a time in the trenches – they are plunged into the inevitable miseries of a winter campaign – and not a soul seems to care for their comfort, or even for their lives. These are hard truths, but the people of Britain must hear them.

(Before Sebastopol, 25 November 1854)

The army is suffering greatly; worn out by night work, by vigil in rain and storm, by hard labour in the trenches, they find themselves suddenly reduced to short allowance. . . . For nine days there has been, with very few exceptions, no issue of tea, coffee or sugar, to the troops. . . . The direct cause of this scarcity is the condition of the country which, saturated by heavy rains, has become quite unfit for the passage of carts . . . but though there is a cause, there is no excuse for the privations to which the men are exposed. . . . The fine weather was allowed to go by and the roads were left as the Tartar carts had made them, though the whole face of the country is covered thickly with small stones which seem expressly intended for road metal.

(1 December 1854)

It is clear, however, that neither afloat nor on shore is the medical staff nearly sufficient. I myself saw men dying on the beach, on the line of march and in bivouac without any medical assistance; and this within hail of a fleet of five hundred sail, and within sight of headquarters. We want more surgeons, both in the fleet and in the army. Often – too often – medical aid cannot be had at all; and frequently comes too late.

(16 December 1854)

A circumstance occurred in Balaclava today which I will state for the calm consideration of the public at home without one single word of comment. The *Charity*, an iron screw steamer, is at present in harbour for the reception of sick British soldiers, who are under the charge of a British medical officer. That officer went on shore today and made an application to the officer in charge of government stoves for two or three to put on board the ship to warm the men.

'Three of my men,' said he, 'died last night from choleraic symptoms, brought on in their present state from the extreme cold of the ship: and, I fear more will follow them from the same cause.'

'Oh!' said the guardian of the stoves, 'You must make your requisition in due form, send it up to headquarters, and get it signed properly and returned, and then I will let you have the stoves.'

'But my men may die meantime.'

'I can't help that: I must have the requisition.'

'It is my firm belief that there are men now in a dangerous condition whom another night will certainly kill.'

'I really can do nothing: I must have a requisition properly signed before I can give one of the stoves away.'

'For God's sake, then, lend me some; I'll be responsible for their safety.'

'I really can do nothing of the kind.'

'But consider, this requisition will take time to be filled up and signed and meantime these poor fellows will go.'

'I cannot help that.'

'I'll be responsible for anything you do.'

'Oh, no. That can't be done.'

'Will a requisition signed by the PMO of this place be of any use?'

'No.'

'Will it answer if he takes on himself the responsibility?'

'Certainly not.'

The surgeon went off in sorrow and disgust. Such are the 'Rules' of the service in the hands of incapable and careless men.

(25 January 1855)

Do people at home know how many bayonets the British army could number at this moment? Do they believe we have 25,000 after all our reinforcements? They may be told – nay, it may be proved to them by figures at home – that the British army here consists of 55,000 men. I warn the British public not to believe that, with all our reinforcements, they could reach *near* half that number. The grave and the hospital has swallowed them up by thousands. Just think of this 'fact' – that since the first day of December 1854, down to the 20th of January, 1855, 8,000 sick and wounded men have been sent down from camp to Balaclava, and thence on shipboard! Shall I tell you how many have returned? . . . The wretched boys sent out to us now are not even fit food for powder. They die away ere a shot is fired against them.

(Before Sebastopol, 27 January 1855)

Still basking in the then fading glory of Wellington and Waterloo, believing its army to be invincible, its generals superb and its military system omniscient, the British public was not prepared for the affront which Russell's letters, and *The Times*' leading articles, together with Chenery's remarks about the medical arrangements at Scutari, and Godkins' letters published in the *Daily News*, inflicted on its *amour propre*. The outcry was correspondingly intense. The Secretary at War, Sydney Herbert, a great friend of that remarkable woman Florence Nightingale, sent her out to the base hospital at Scutari with a team of nurses. She was appalled by what she found there, described by Lytton Strachey with perhaps some poetic licence in apocalyptic terms:

And in the hospital what did they find? . . . Want, neglect, confusion, misery – in every shape and in every degree of intensity – filled the endless corridors and the vast apartments of a gigantic barrack house which, without forethought or preparation, had hurriedly been set aside as the chief shelter for the victims of the war. The very building itself was radically defective. Huge sewers underlay it and cesspools loaded with filth wafted their poison into the upper rooms. The floors were in so rotten a condition that many of them could not be scrubbed; the walls were thick with dirt; incredible multitudes of vermin swarmed everywhere. As enormous as the building was, it was yet too small. It contained four miles of beds, crushed together so close that there was just room to pass between them. Under such conditions, the most elaborate system of ventilation might well have been at fault; but here there was no ventilation. The stench was indescribable. . . . The structural defects were equalled by the deficiencies in the commonest objects of hospital use. There were not enough bedsteads; the sheets were of canvas, and so coarse that the wounded men recoiled from them, begging to be left in their blankets; there was no bedroom furniture of any kind, and empty beer bottles were used for candlesticks. There were no basins, no towels, no soap, no brooms, no mops, no trays, no plates; there were neither slippers nor scissors, neither shoe brushes nor blacking; there were no knives or forks or spoons. The supply of fuel was constantly deficient. The cooking arrangements were preposterously inadequate, and the laundry was a farce. As for purely medical materials, the tale was no better. Stretchers, splints, bandages – all were lacking; and so were the most ordinary drugs.[6]

Florence Nightingale put it in even starker, simpler terms when she said that over the gateway of the Barrack Hospital should have been written: 'Abandon hope all ye that enter here'.

The authorities in London were apparently totally ignorant of the conditions at Scutari since Doctor Andrew Smith, the Head of the Army Medical Board, had, when Miss Nightingale asked if she should take anything with her, told her that 'nothing was needed'. The ladies, he assured her, would undoubtedly be a comfort to the men. Ladies had finer instincts; they might, for instance, see a spot on a sheet where a mere man might easily overlook it. As for medical duties – well, he did not think Miss Nightingale and her nurses could possibly go wrong in administering a nice soothing drink of capillary syrup to any man who seemed uncomfortable. She contemplated taking a quantity of stores, but he assured her stores were unnecessary. There was now a positive profusion of every kind of medical comfort at Scutari.[7]

The Times set up a fund which must have been one of the most successful relief funds in history. A considerable sum of money was put at Florence Nightingale's disposal and the situation at Scutari was greatly improved, the deaths there dropping from 3,168 in January 1854 to 582 in April. Several ships with comforts and supplies of all kinds, commissioned by *The Times*, appeared at Balaclava harbour. A railway was built from Balaclava to the front line which greatly improved the delivery of supplies, and by the winter of 1855 conditions in the British army were better than those in the French area.

> From hunger, unwholesome food, and comparative nakedness, the camp was plunged into a sea of abundance, filled with sheep and sheepskins, wooden huts, furs, comforters, mufflers, flannel shirts, tracts (*sic*), soups, preserved meats, potted game and spirits.[8]

There is some doubt about the figures of casualties in the Crimea. Those most commonly used come from the postwar medical history. These show that the total number of British deaths in the Crimea was 18,058. Of these, 1,761 died from enemy action, the remaining 16,297 from disease. Of those who died from disease, 13,150 died in the first nine months. The mortality rate in the Crimea during this period was 60 per cent. This was greater than the mortality rate had been in England during the Great Plague. The mortality rate in the Crimea in the second half of the war was lower on average than it was at home.[9]

However, perhaps the most remarkable result of Russell's despatches lay in the considerable part they undoubtedly played in the fall of the Aberdeen Government, which was defeated on a motion 'That a select committee be appointed to enquire into the conduct of those departments of Government whose duty it had been to minister to the wants of that army' on 6 February 1855.

Lord Aberdeen was succeeded as Prime Minister by the formidable Lord Palmerston, and the Duke of Newcastle as Secretary for War by Lord Panmure. A new organization, the War Office, was created under which were gathered all the previously disparate and often conflicting bodies which had sought to direct military affairs. Training camps were set up at the Curragh, Colchester and Aldershot. The Staff College, the School of Musketry at Hythe and the Gunnery School at Sheerness were established and, above all, the Army Medical Board was set up at Netley. Some of these changes had been set in train before the new Government took over and the new organization did not appear overnight. However, Russell's despatches and the resulting change of government undoubtedly lent impetus and direction to the upheaval. The press was largely responsible for all these vast improvements.

The Government having fallen, the supply situation having been improved and the medical organization transformed, *The Times* now turned its attention to the command structure in the field. Its leading articles began to attack Lord Raglan and his staff directly. A leader in *The Times* of 23 December 1854 said:

> the noblest army ever sent from these shores has been sacrificed to the grossest mismanagement. Incompetency, lethargy, aristocratic hauteur, official indifference, favour, routine, perverseness and stupidity reign, revel and riot in the camp before Sebastopol. . . . We say it with extreme reluctance: no-one sees or hears anything of the Commander-in-Chief.

The leader went on to speak of the soldiers dying in the mud and then of 'their aristocratic generals, their equally aristocratic staff viewing the scene of wreck and destruction with gentleman-like tranquility.' On 8 February *The Times* said:

> Lord Raglan, whiling away his time in ease and tranquility among the relics of his army, would soon return home with his well born staff and their horses, their plate and their china, the German (*sic*) cook and several tons worth of official returns, all in excellent order, and the announcement that the last British soldier being dead they had left our position to the care of their gallant allies.[10]

It would be foolish to argue that Lord Raglan was in any sense a great commander in the field or off it. He was shy, no self-publicist and lacking in the assertiveness necessary both in dealing with his subordinates and his allies. It would have taken a general of the highest possible calibre to have coped with the difficulties which confronted Lord Raglan and he was certainly not in that class or anything approaching it. Among other failings he relied too much on his staff and did not find enough out for himself. He was, however, calm, brave, kind and very hard-working – in fact much loved by all who knew him. The new Government did not feel itself able actually to demand his resignation, but it tried to insist that he got rid of many of his staff, notably Major Generals Airey and Estcourt and Commissary General Filder, which he resolutely refused to do. In an attempt to gather conclusive evidence of the failures of Lord Raglan's staff, the Government sent out Lieutenant General Simpson as Chief of Staff. However, General Simpson on his arrival, almost immediately, came to Lord Raglan's defence. He wrote:

> I consider Lord Raglan the most abused man I ever heard of!
> . . . The staff here at headquarters have, I am convinced, been very much vilified . . . nor have I any fault to find with Airey and Escourt .
> . . I see no staff officer objectionable in my opinion. There is not one of them incompetent . . . I must say I never served with an army where a higher feeling and sense of duty exists than I remark in the General Staff Officers of this army. It pervades all ranks, except among the low and grovelling correspondents of *The Times*.[11]

Having failed to secure the dismissal either of Lord Raglan or of any of his staff, *The Times* ended its campaign and turned to other less controversial matters. In fact, throughout, Lord Raglan had been complaining to his superiors in England of the lack of supplies and the chaotic medical situation. For instance, as early as 8 August 1854, he had told the Duke of Newcastle that he entertained grave doubts as to the possibility of wintering in Russia with the army's limited means of supply and subsistence.[12] But it had taken the articles of a war correspondent on the spot, whom he had himself shunned, to bring about any great improvements. This was an early example of the dire consequences as far as the army was concerned of deliberately rough treatment of the press. He could have enlisted Russell as his ally in his difficulties with Whitehall. He did not. He never even met him. Worn out by his own responsibilities and the criticism centred on him in England, Lord Raglan died on 25 June 1855, to be succeeded by General Simpson, who was himself succeeded by General Codrington on 10 November 1855.

In the Crimea were exemplified many of the dilemmas which have faced both war correspondents and those who deal with them over the years. First there is the whole question of censorship. The most obvious justification for preventing publication of reports about military affairs is to avoid giving the enemy information which he would not otherwise have. Wellington, as Sir Arthur Wellesley, when commanding the army in Spain, wrote to Lord Liverpool, the then Secretary for War, in the following terms:

I beg to draw your lordship's attention to the frequent paragraphs in the English newspapers, describing the position, the numbers, the objects, the means of attaining them possessed by the armies in Spain and Portugal. In some instances the English newspapers have accurately stated, not only the regiments occupying a position, but the number of men fit for duty of which each regiment was composed; and this intelligence must have reached the enemy at the same time as it did me, at a moment at which it was most important that he should not receive it.[13]

Lord Raglan raised the same problem in a letter to the Duke of Newcastle[14] complaining that Russell's letters describing the exact dispositions of the British troops must be invaluable to the Russians when telegraphed from London to Moscow. Although hotly denied by *The Times* which argued that the articles contained nothing that the Russians would not have learnt by other means, there may well have been some truth in this criticism. Indeed in a letter of 4 September (off Varna) Russell described in detail the entire British Order of Battle, the numbers and names of regiments and the names of the divisional and brigade commanders and their staffs. This must surely have helped the Russians when telegraphed to Moscow from London.

Lord Raglan went on to argue in a further letter to the Duke of Newcastle that:

on the 23rd October *The Times* in an article describing the condition and dispositions of the army – the number of its guns, the location of various regiments and its dearth of round shot, gabions and fascines gave also the exact position of a powder mill which some time later was the object of a heavy cannonade.

Here was the evidence that this sort of detailed information must be invaluable to the Russians:

I am quite satisfied that the object of the writer is simply to satisfy the anxiety and, I may say, the curiosity of the public and to do what he considered his duty by his employers and that it has never occurred to him that he is serving more essentially the cause of the Russians. The innocence of his intention did not, however, diminish the evil he inflicted; and something must be done to check so pernicious a system at once.[15]

It was not only Lord Raglan who complained of the result of press reports. In a book of letters called *The Story of the Highland Brigade in the Crimea*, Lieutenant Colonel Sterling who served in the Crimean War wrote:

The newspaper press of England was required by the nation to supply perpetual information about military movements, and perpetual gossip about the routine in the camp. The gentlemen sent for the purpose did supply all this, to the best of their ability; but unfortunately the British people could not receive this information and this gossip without providing it also for the use of the enemy and for the astonishment and ridicule of our continental neighbours. If the British nation chooses to have its army governed by the newspapers, the result must be that by degrees all the officers who reflect will, as it becomes possible, get out of the service. No army can succeed with such spies in its camp. No general can command when his character and conduct is canvassed openly by editors and while their remarks on both are soon broadcast among the soldiers. I do not believe that the outcry in the papers did any good. There is no doubt in my mind that the evils complained of would have been remedied as soon as possible whether the newspapers had taken up the question or not.

The Times and Russell himself took these strictures extremely seriously. Delane had already faced these problems when accused by Lord Derby of seeking to usurp the powers of statesmen without acknowledging their responsibilities. *The Times* spelt out its view of the press in successive leading articles:

The press lives by disclosures; whatsoever passes into its keeping becomes a part of the knowledge and history of our times; it is daily and forever appealing to the enlightened force of public opinion – anticipating, if possible, the march of events – standing upon the breach between the present and the future, and extending its survey to the horizon of the world.

(The Times, 6 February 1852)

It was the newspaper's purpose to seek out the earliest and most correct intelligence of the events of the time, and instantly, by disclosing them, to make them the common property of the nation.

(The Times, 7 February 1852)[16]

In his letter before Sebastopol of 25 November 1854 Russell wrote:

Although it may be dangerous to communicate facts likely to be of service to the Russians, it is certainly hazardous to conceal the truth from the British people. They must know, sooner or later, that the siege has been for many days practically suspended, that our batteries are used up and silent, and that our army are (*sic*) much exhausted by the effects of excessive labour and watching, and by the wet and storm to which they have been so incessantly exposed.

In his letter of 1 December 1854, Russell said:

No power on earth can now establish a censorship in England, or suppress or prevent the truth. Publicity must be accepted by our captains, generals, and men-at-arms, as the necessary condition of any grand operation of war: and the endeavour to destroy the evil will only give it fresh vigour, and develop its powers of mischief. The truth will reach home so distorted, that it will terrify and alarm far more than it would have done had it been allowed to appear freely and simply.

The most obvious method of censorship is to prevent special correspondents (or war correspondents as they came to be known) from appearing on the scene at all and to insist that the only news to reach the media is by official releases of one sort or another. This was the method used by Wellington after his unfortunate experience in the Peninsular War. However, as we have seen, such was the standing of *The Times* in 1854 that that particular method was not feasible. Nor was it possible in the

Crimea, for the same reason, to insist on actual censorship of a report before it was sent off. This was the method used, later, in the Boer War, and indeed by the French in the Crimean War. Another possible system was to make clear to the correspondents the effect on the course of the war if their reports gave information to the enemy which he would not otherwise have and to leave it to their consciences not to err in this way. In effect this was the method used by the British in the Crimea and it certainly did not succeed, in that much was reported to the express disapproval of Lord Raglan and other commanders.

The final, and perhaps least effective, form of censorship is to be obstructive to journalists trying to cover a conflict, not to give them interviews or facilities and generally to make life difficult for them in the hope that they will abandon the effort to see for themselves. Lord Raglan's treatment of Russell had precisely the opposite effect to that which was intended. Russell was incensed that Lord Raglan would not meet him, and the cruel nature of his attacks on that commander, at least partly unjustified, sprang from the ostrich-like attitude the Commander-in-Chief showed towards Russell and the other correspondents concerned. Russell was a convivial man with great persistence. He had many friends in the army and elsewhere and he used them. He had an editor in Delane who was determined to tell the truth to the people of Britain, come what may. He did not like using the new electric telegraph and nearly all his letters went by sea taking ten to fourteen days in the process, but his writing was so vivid and his strictures so severe that the delay did not seem to matter very much. In fact it was not possible to send material by telegraph to London direct from the Crimea except between April 1855, when a line was laid from Balaclava to Varna, and December of that year, when the line broke and was not repaired. Soon after the war began, the Allies had jointly financed, and the French built, a line from Bucharest to Varna which linked with Austria and the overland line to Paris and on to London.[17]

Russell was able to move around with astonishing ease in spite of his official ostracism. To our modern minds, it is astonishing how spectators seemed to be able to wander around battlefields at will (a classic fictional example of this is Tolstoy's depiction of Pierre at the Battle of Borodino). Some officers even had their wives with them. An example was evident in the journal of Mrs Henry Duberly, the wife of an officer in the 8th Hussars, which provides valuable first-hand evidence of the state of affairs in the Crimea during and after the winter of 1854. (Incidentally, battalions were allowed to take out with them six soldiers' wives per hundred men to help with domestic chores.)

It was almost certainly a result of the devastating effect of *The Times*' continued attacks on the conduct of the Crimean War that censorship was imposed in the Boer War, as we shall see. In fact, Sir William Codrington, who succeeded General Simpson as Commander-in-Chief, imposed a form of censorship on 25 February 1856 by ordering that any correspondent who published details of value to the enemy should be summarily sent home. It was, however, too late to have any effect.

Russell, who had already reported on the conflict over Schleswig–Holstein in 1850 and was subsequently to report on the Indian Mutiny, the American Civil War, the Franco-Prussian War of 1870/71 and the Zulu War of 1879, was knighted in 1895 and became a well-known establishment figure, a surprising culmination for such a radical man.

The Crimea also saw the arrival of the first war photographers, in particular Roger Fenton, a founder of the Royal Photographic Society, who was encouraged to go there by Prince Albert. His pictures, however, showed nothing of the enormous strains under which the army was operating and were not a factor in the formation of public opinion in Britain.

Judgements on the impact of the press on the Crimean War must, at this distance in time, be tentative. The press was, at least in part, responsible for the British involvement in the war at all, as a result of its stirring up bellicose patriotic emotions and its frenzied attack on the Tsar and his country. The two political giants of the second half of the nineteenth century, Gladstone and Disraeli, although opposed to each other on almost everything else, were both very lukewarm about the Crimean adventure. Gladstone was always ill at ease with it and opposed its continuation in 1855, which led to an attempt by the Duke of Beaufort to have him expelled from the Carlton Club (in those days an institution with catholic political tastes) – a sign of deep establishment disapproval.[18] Disraeli called the conflict 'a just but unnecessary war' and there probably is truth in at least the second if not the first part of that statement.[19]

Undoubtedly, Russell and Delane, his editor, exposed the chaotic nature of military administration in the Crimea and its medical support, bringing about much-needed changes, and leading to the fall of the Aberdeen Government. Although it is impossible to prove one way or another, this may have been at the expense of giving the Russians some militarily useful information and, by revealing the appalling physical situation of the British army in the winter of 1854, raising the morale of the Russian commanders, staff and soldiery. In some respects, *The Times* was unfair to Lord Raglan and his staff, and the tendency to hyperbole, which seems to be the hallmark of media coverage throughout the centuries, may have led to some ill-considered judgements. The outcome can perhaps be best described by Field Marshal Sir Evelyn Wood, who served in the Crimea as a young officer, when he said about Russell:

> He [Russell] incurred much enmity, but few unprejudiced men who were in the Crimea would now attempt to call in question the fact that by awakening the conscience of the British nation to the suffering of its troops, he saved the remnants of those grand battalions we landed in September.[20]

When he unveiled the memorial bust of Russell in St Paul's Cathedral on 10 February 1909 the Field Marshal, after paying tribute to Russell's personal qualities, went on to say:

> He 'showed up' the military mismanagement of the day when, in describing an interview with a lad who had been severely wounded at the assault on the Great Redan, he stated that the recruit had never fired his rifle because he had not been taught how to load it. On the other hand, Russell caused the heart of the nation to go out to its soldiers as it had never gone out before.

Another tribute came from Mrs Henry Duberly, already mentioned, who in her journal after the winter of 1854 said:

> I think the thanks of the army, or a handsome national testimonial, ought to be presented to Mr Russell, the eloquent and truthful correspondent in *The Times*, as being the mainspring of this happy change [the vast improvement of the situation of the British army by the spring of 1855].

She also gave credit to other newspapers: 'Our best general, our most unflinching leader has been the press.'

1. Kingsley Martin, *The Triumph of Lord Palmerston*, London, George Allen and Unwin, 1924, Introduction
2. In 1850 a Portuguese British subject, Don Pacifico, failed to receive compensation from the Government of Greece for property damaged by an Athenian mob. Palmerston, then Foreign Minister, reacted violently. British gunboats bombarded a Greek port and war with France and, possibly, Russia was narrowly averted. Palmerston defended his actions in a brilliant parliamentary speech
3. Christopher Hibbert, *The Destruction of Lord Raglan*, London, Longman, p. 25
4. Ibid., p. 7
5. Ibid., p. 215
6. Lytton Strachey, *Eminent Victorians*, London, Penguin, 1918, p. 141
7. Cecil Woodham Smith, *Florence Nightingale*, London, Constable, 1949, p. 146
8. Philip Warner, *The Crimean War – a Reappraisal*, London, Barker, 1972, p. 183
9. Ibid., p. 212
10. Hibbert, *The Destruction of Lord Raglan*, p. 223
11. Ibid., p. 258
12. Ibid., p. 210
13. Trevor Royle, *War Report*, London, Mainstream Publishing, 1987, p. 17
14. Hibbert, *The Destruction of Lord Raglan*, p. 158
15. Ibid., p. 158
16. Alan Hankinson, *Man of Wars*, London, Heinemann, p. 36
17. Major Colin Robins, Crimean War Research Society
18. Roy Jenkins, *Gladstone*, London, Macmillan, 1995, p. 143
19. Robert Blake, *Disraeli*, London, Eyre and Spottiswoode, 1966, p. 359
20. Royle, *War Report*, p. 26

CHAPTER TWO

Late Victoriana

'Get out of my way you drunken swabs.' •
Kitchener to War Correspondents in the Sudan, 1898

THE AMERICAN CIVIL WAR, 1861–1865

If the Crimean War had seen the emergence of the war correspondent as a major factor in the body politic, the American Civil War (1861–5), with its proliferation of correspondents (five hundred in the North alone), led to much blatant misrepresentation and skulduggery of every kind in the transmission of war news. Within America widespread use of the telegraph (almost 50,000 miles had been laid in the eastern states alone) meant that editors could get information from their correspondents for publication the day after the event. There was, therefore, an obsessive demand for the 'scoop', often resulting in instant as opposed to accurate news. Furthermore, the 1860s in America witnessed a frenzied circulation war as editors and owners vied with each other for readership. There had been no tradition of war reporting and the sudden need for numbers of correspondents led to many young and totally inexperienced men with very little idea of how to approach the task being taken on. As the editors saw it, it was vital to have as many 'stories' as possible, the more dramatic the better. If there was difficulty in finding them, they must be fabricated, even if it meant elevating rumour or gossip into truth. Wilbur Storey of the *Chicago Times* sent an order to one of his men: 'Telegraph fully all news you can get and when there is no news send rumour'.[1] Bribery of the military to obtain 'stories' was also undoubtedly rife. Furthermore, and this has echoes today, the need for correspondents to get their daily reports back to their editorial offices quickly meant that reporters were not necessarily where the news was, but that the news was often where the reporters were, within daily reach of a telegraph office – a haphazard affair indeed.

Both the North and the South saw the conflict as what we will later describe in another context as 'a war of national survival'. Editors and correspondents on both sides were, therefore, willing propagandists for their cause, often adding to the inaccuracy of the published reports of the war.

Edwin Godkin wrote of his American counterparts:

> Their communications are what you might expect from men of this stamp – a series of wild ravings about the roaring of the guns and the whizzing of the shells and the superhuman valour of the men, interspersed with fulsome puffs of some captain or colonel with whom they happened to spend the night.[2]

The establishment in Britain was broadly in favour of the South. There was a certain wry satisfaction in seeing their erstwhile colony break up and a great commercial interest in maintaining the supply of cotton from the South, a raw material vital to the highly important cotton industry in Britain. There was also, in some circles, support for what was seen as the aristocratic charms of the South against the brash, *nouveau riche* North. Against this, of course, was the deep dislike of slavery: Britain had been in the forefront of the campaign for its abolition.

Delane sent Russell to the United States as a disinterested observer: all correspondents there at the outbreak of war had inevitably already taken sides. A famous figure because of his reporting of the Crimean War, he was received with considerable ceremony by the leaderships in both North and South. He was particularly impressed by Abraham Lincoln.

Russell occasioned very great unpopularity in the North by his account of the defeat of the North in the first real action of the war at Bull Run, not far from Washington. He described the rout of the Northern army and its headlong and ignominious flight in his customary forthright and highly descriptive prose, filling up no fewer than nine columns of *The Times*. His article shocked many in the North who had been duped by their own propaganda. He became extremely unpopular and his life was threatened. He refused to change his methods and continued to report the truth as he saw it. He remained a force for moderation, advising against British involvement in the war. His reports undoubtedly calmed public opinion in Britain in the immediate aftermath of the *Trent* incident, when a Northern gunboat stopped a British mail packet at Havana and arrested four Southerners on their way to Britain to put the Southern case.[3] War with the North was narrowly averted when Lincoln released the prisoners.

THE BULGARIAN ATROCITIES, 1876

The impact of *The Times* and other newspapers on events in the American Civil War, however, was as nothing compared to the result of the reports by the American Januarius Aloysius McGahan, like Russell of Irish extraction, the correspondent sent by the *London Daily News* to investigate reports of Turkish atrocities in Southern Bulgaria in 1876:

> We were told there were three thousand people lying in this little churchyard alone . . . It was a fearful sight – a sight to haunt one through life. There were little curly heads there in their festering mass, crushed down by heavy stones; little feet not as long as your finger on which the flesh was dried hard; . . . little baby hands stretched out as if for help; babes that had died wondering at the bright gleam of sabres and the red hands of the fierce-eyed men who wielded them; children who had died shrinking with fright and terror; . . . mothers who died trying to shield their little ones with their own weak bodies, all lying there together festering in one horrid mass.[4]

These and other reports, notably by the American consul-general Eugene Schuyler, fired the formidable Gladstone:

> There is not a cannibal in the South Sea Islands whose indignation would not arise and over boil at the recital of that which has been done, which has too late been examined, but which remains unavenged: which has left behind all the foul and all the fierce passions that produced it, and which may again spring up in another murderous harvest from the soil soaked and reeking with blood, and in the air tainted with every imaginable deed of crime and shame . . . no Government ever has so sinned; none has proved itself so incorrigible or, which is the same, so impotent for reformation.[5]

Disraeli took the opposite view, in the first instance pooh-poohing the atrocities and supporting the Turks. The Eastern Question, with Gladstone anti-Turk and Disraeli anti-Russian, lurched on from crisis to crisis. War broke out between Russia and Turkey, and in 1878 Britain herself nearly became involved in war against Russia. Hostilities were, however, averted and a settlement was achieved, culminating at the

Congress of Berlin. It was during this period of apparently imminent war that the music hall song appeared which immortalized the word 'jingoism':

> We don't want to fight, but, by jingo if we do,
> We've got the ships, we've got the men, we've got the money too.
> We've fought the Bear before, and while Britons shall be true
> The Russians shall not have Constantinople.

McGahan's reports played a major part in inspiring Gladstone's oratory and a famous pamphlet he wrote which, in their turn, undoubtedly alerted the European powers to the appalling situation in Bulgaria. After many vicissitudes Bulgaria obtained her independence. Certainly, the independent Bulgaria believed that McGahan's reports were a crucial factor in this achievement and for many years an annual requiem mass was held in Bulgaria to commemorate his death.[6] Apart, perhaps, from Russell there can be few, if any, journalists other than McGahan who can be said to have changed the course of history. Not many masses can have been said for journalists in grateful thanks for anything at all, let alone for the achievement of a nation's freedom.

SUDAN, 1898

In contrast to the comparative freedom for war correspondents in the Crimean and American Civil Wars, and probably because of what was seen as the disastrous result of that freedom in the Crimea, the sixteen journalists who covered the final stages of the campaign in 1898 to reconquer the Sudan and avenge Gordon's death had to submit their despatches for censorship by a Major Wingate before they could be telegraphed to London from Wadi Halfa on the Nile. Winston Churchill who, through persistence and forceful use of his connections, had managed to get himself to the Sudan attached to the 21st Lancers in spite of Kitchener's initial refusals, would have none of this. He evaded censorship by sending letters rather than submitting copy to the telegraph. He tried to avoid obloquy by addressing these letters to a friend who happened to be Oliver Borthwick, the proprietor of the *Morning Post* (all his letters were prefaced 'My Dear' except for the last one when any need for concealment had passed). By the use of this subterfuge, Churchill apparently thought he could affect surprise when they duly appeared verbatim in that newspaper.[7]

Kitchener, Sirdar of the Egyptian army, had a dominating personality and a commanding presence: unlike Raglan in the Crimea, he towered over the proceedings. He did not think much of the press. He tried, first, to avoid having any war correspondents with his army at all. Then, when that failed, he tried to leave them at Wadi Halfa, while he proceeded down the Nile to Khartoum. And, finally, when that failed too, he attempted to freeze them out by ignoring them. However, in Britain there was intense interest in the campaign. The traumas of Gordon's death and the failure to rescue him lay deep in the national consciousness. There was a need for revenge, and a thirst for a renewal of national glory. Press correspondents were part of the apparatus expected to satisfy the need and slake the thirst. But what were they to report? That was the question. Kitchener need not have worried. The two leading war correspondents, Churchill and George Warrington Steevens, chosen by Alfred Harmsworth to represent the *Daily Mail*, (a newspaper he had started in 1896 which already had a readership of half a million), were far from being carping critics of Kitchener and his army. Churchill, thirsting for military action himself (he took part in the charge of the 21st Lancers at the Battle of Omdurman, 1 September 1898) took a romantic view of the glory of war while, somewhat paradoxically, acknowledging its tragedy and futility: 'War is but a dirty shoddy business which only a fool would play at' (letter to Borthwick, 18 September 1898). He did have reservations about the desecration of the Mahdi's tomb and the decapitation of the Mahdi's corpse, but his criticisms were comparatively muted. Steevens, later to die of enteric fever at Ladysmith, told his readers what they wanted to hear and even wrote an adulatory piece about Kitchener. The culminating overwhelming success of the Battle of Omdurman overcame any reservations anyone might have had about the campaign. Gordon had been avenged. God was in His Heaven and the British Empire reigned supreme.

It must be very difficult for the present generation of youth in Britain to comprehend the background of romantic imperial glory against which these events, including the subsequent Boer War, took place. A strong flavour of it can be tasted in Churchill's letter to the editor of the *Morning Post*, 12 September 1898 – Winston was twenty-four years old:

Consider, my dear, how strange and varied are the diversions of an Imperial people. Year after year, and stretching back to an indefinite horizon, we see the figures of the old and bizarre potentates against whom the British arms are continually turned. They pass in a long procession. The Akhund of Swat, Cetewayo brandishing an assegai as naked as himself, Kruger singing a Psalm of Victory, Osman Digna, the Immortal and the Irrepressible, Theebaw with his umbrella, the Mahdi with his banner, Lobengula gazing fondly at the pages of Truth, Prompeh abasing himself in the dust, the Mad Mullah on his white ass and, latest of all, the Khalifa in his Coach of State. It is like a pantomime scene at Drury Lane. These extraordinary foreign figures, each with his complete set of crimes, horrible customs and minor peculiarities march one by one from the dark wings of Barbarism up to the bright footlights of Civilization. For a space their names are on the wires of the world and the tongues of men. The Sovereign on his Throne, the Minister in his Cabinet, the General in his tent pronounce or mispronounce their styles and titles. A thousand compositors make the same combination of letters. The unusual syllables become household words. The street-boy bellows them in our ears. The artisan laughs over them at night in his cottage. The child in the nursery is cajoled into virtual silence by the repetition of the dread accents. And the world audience clap their hands, amused yet impatient, and the Potentates and their trains pass on, some to exile, some to prison, some to death – for it is a grim jest for them – and their conquerors, taking their possessions, forget even their names. Nor will history record such trash.

Perhaps the time will come when the supply will be exhausted and there will be no more royal freaks to conquer. In that gloomy period there will be no more of these nice little expeditions – 'The image of a European war without its guilt and only twenty-five per cent of its danger'; no more medals for the soldiers, no more peerages for the generals, no more copy for the journalists. The good old times will have passed away, and the most cynical philosopher will be forced to admit that though the world may not be much more prosperous it can scarcely be so merry.

THE BOER WAR, 1899–1902

As far as the South African war was concerned, however, matters were not so simple. The defeat of the British by the Boers in 1888 at Majuba Hill had led to self-government under British suzerainty of the Transvaal and the Orange Free State, to which the Boers had trekked in order to escape what they saw as heavy-handed British interference with their way of life. The discovery of gold in the Transvaal resulted in a considerable influx of non-Boer settlers from Cape Colony and Natal known by the Boers as Uitlanders (foreigners). Disputes arose as to their treatment and, in particular, as to whether and under what conditions they should obtain voting rights. A raid into the Transvaal by Dr Jameson, an associate of Cecil Rhodes, in an attempt to oust Kruger, the Transvaal President, failed with ignominy. This was followed by the appointment of Lord Milner, a powerful figure with strong imperialist convictions, as Governor of Cape Colony and High Commissioner for South Africa. Joseph Chamberlain, the Colonial Secretary in London, also had imperialist leanings, although he was more cautious than Milner in his policy towards South Africa. Negotiations between the two sides eventually broke down, certainly in part because of Milner's desire to establish British hegemony once and for all, if necessary by force of arms. The result of all this was a Boer ultimatum to Britain to withdraw her troops from the Transvaal border immediately and, when this was inevitably ignored, war broke out on 18 October 1899.

As is so often the case, a complicated series of events, of far greater complexity than is apparent in the short summary above, masked a simple problem: the Boers, a proud, tough, people with fundamentalist Christian beliefs, were determined on independence; the British, in their imperial heyday, were intent on ascendancy in the whole of South Africa.

Most of the press in England took a pro-Government and anti-Boer line, but there was some opposition: the *Manchester Guardian*, the *Morning Leader*, the *Star* and the *Daily Chronicle* (until its editor was sacked!) were inexorably opposed to the British action as was the well-known and influential journalist W.T. Stead. He had previously been a passionate imperialist, but he became a virulent critic of the war in his 'Review of Reviews' and, later, in his pamphlet 'Shall I Slay my Brother Boer?' Most newspapers, however, followed the imperialist line. The *Telegraph* said: 'Kruger's asked for war and war he must have.' *The Times* called the ultimatum 'an infatuated step by this petty republic'.

As with a number of other conflicts before and since there was a belief, indeed a near certainty, that the war would be over very quickly. How could a lightly armed, amateur collection of Boer farmers possibly stand up to the disciplined ranks of the highly experienced British army under the wise leadership of the British hero, General Sir Redvers Buller VC? *Punch* had a cartoon with two London urchins discussing the war. 'The

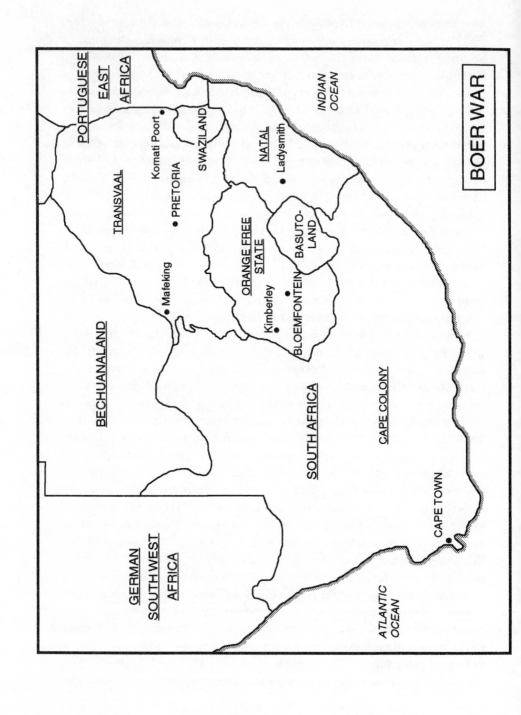

BOER WAR

PORTUGUESE EAST AFRICA

INDIAN OCEAN

Komati Poort

SWAZILAND

TRANSVAAL

PRETORIA

NATAL

Ladysmith

Mafeking

ORANGE FREE STATE

BASUTO-LAND

BECHUANALAND

Kimberley

BLOEMFONTEIN

SOUTH AFRICA

CAPE COLONY

GERMAN SOUTH WEST AFRICA

CAPE TOWN

ATLANTIC OCEAN

Boers will cop it now. Farfers gone to South Africa, an tooken 'is strap.' They were to be disillusioned as the war dragged on year after year.

There was a large number of war correspondents with the British army in South Africa, at one point up to three hundred, with *The Times* alone having up to twenty, coordinated by Leo Amery. He had been sent out to see what was going on and at one time reported from the Boer side until he became unwelcome there. As we have seen in the American Civil War, the telegraph had given a great boost to the provision of instant news. Russell, who was nearing the end of his life, greatly disapproved of the new press culture of 'the scoop', with speed often displacing accuracy and sensation ousting depth of analysis. Buller, in that way typical of generations of army leaders, vastly disapproved of the press and, on the journey out, forbade his officers even to talk to journalists at all. As was to be the case much later in the Falklands campaign, little, if any, thought had been given to public relations and there was controversy as to which journalists should be taken with the ships sailing to the theatre of war. Buller supervised this matter very carefully himself. He refused to take any foreign journalists, referring to them as 'spies'. Americans, however, were in his eyes not 'foreign', but 'relations'. When we saw her, Lady Thatcher made very similar remarks (less the accusation of spying) about journalists in the Falklands.

In the field, all letters and telegraphic messages were subject to censorship under rules which had been devised by Buller for a previous campaign. In essence, correspondents were allowed to report 'facts' provided these did not contain information of use to the enemy. They were not allowed to give 'opinions' since, it was argued, these might well have political implications. All journalists had to be officially accredited and also accepted by the commander of the force which they wished to join or accompany. In theory, once accepted they were supposed to be given facilities to do their work – but in practice the help they received varied greatly. Their reports were censored twice – once locally by an officer appointed for that purpose and once at formation headquarters. Telegrams went to England either by the eastern route via Aden or the western route via Cape Town. Some disappeared en route, to the great anger of the journalists who had sent them and who suspected ulterior motives. Journalists also complained that the telegraph companies charged even for words which had been censored out.

There was no censorship within Britain, and editorial criticisms abounded. The British army suffered a series of defeats largely the result of military incompetence and the difficulties of controlling and supplying a cumbersome military force. The force was not designed to operate in South African conditions or against the lightly armed, highly mobile Boer farmers operating in their own country. In fact their German Mauser rifles and field guns made by Krupp were superior to those used by the British and, of course, they were fighting, as they saw it, for their survival as a people. The British army was not used to fighting against such opposition: their almost routine triumphs in recent years had been against natives of a very different background and with very different equipment – spear and shield. Their casualties were considerable, 700 killed in the first few weeks with 3,000 wounded and 2,000 taken prisoner. The shock in Britain was considerable. No amount of censorship could hide the truth and things seemed to go from bad to worse. The *Manchester Guardian* published an article which talked about an 'acre of death' on Spion Kop. Winston Churchill had a similarly graphic account in the *Morning Post* and *The Times* erupted with unwonted fury. Buller refused to talk to journalists and his enemies among his subordinates spread disaffection widely. Even the initially pro-Government newspapers in Britain began to attack the Government and the military authorities, not about the fact of war, but about the way the war was being conducted. The anti-Government press continued their virulent attacks.

After some time it became clear to even the most optimistic jingoist that all was far from well. Buller was sidelined and later recalled. Roberts was appointed Commander-in-Chief with Kitchener as his Chief of Staff. The situation began to improve. Ladysmith, Kimberley and, later, Mafeking which had all been besieged, were relieved and Bloemfontein, the capital of the Orange Free State was captured, the first British into the town being three journalists from Reuters, *The Times* and the *Sydney Morning Herald* – an episode repeated many years later when journalists were the first to enter Port Stanley. On arrival at Bloemfontein Roberts organized the production of an English language newspaper – *The Friend of the Sovereignty and Bloemfontein Gazette* – which included articles by, among others, Rudyard Kipling. The first editorial was unequivocal. It proclaimed:

> The simple policy adhered to in these columns will be the maintenance of British supremacy in South Africa, equal rights for all white men without respect for race or creed, which principles in our opinion embody the establishment of sound government, the prosperity of the country and the happiness of the people.

The blacks were apparently to be ignored.

Roberts, a great self-publicist, had a very different attitude towards the press from that adopted by Buller. On arrival in South Africa he called a number of journalists together, told them that he was pleased to see them and asked how he could help. This, of course, made a tremendous impression. The journalists must have been utterly astonished and certainly many of them were encouraged to put the British army in general, and Roberts in particular, in the best possible light. Roberts was probably the first British general fully to realize the importance of public relations, even in one case delaying the entry of his soldiers into a town so that the media could film his triumphal entry. He himself wrote many of the reports sent home. Perhaps as a result of all this, he was not personally held responsible for the medical debacle which followed.

After the capture of Bloemfontein the medical situation deteriorated rapidly. Neglect of elementary sanitary arrangements led to a large-scale epidemic of typhoid. Again *The Times* came to the rescue. They sent out a Member of Parliament – W. Burdett Coutts – whose report was reminiscent of those from the Crimea:

> Hundreds of men to my knowledge were lying in the worst stages of typhoid with only a blanket and a thin waterproof sheet (not even the latter for many of them) between their aching bodies and the hard ground with no milk and hardly any medicines, without beds, stretchers or mattresses, without linen of any kind, without a single nurse among them, with only a few ordinary private soldiers to act as 'orderlies' . . . and with only three doctors to attend on 350 patients. In many of these tents there were ten typhoid cases lying closely packed together, the dying with the convalescent, the man in his crisis pressed against the man hastening to it.

Eventually matters improved and a Royal Commission was set up which, however, arrived after the worst had passed, partly because of the establishment of volunteer hospitals staffed by civilian doctors, including Dr Conan Doyle.

In spite of the reverses in the early stages of the war, public opinion remained broadly supportive of the British action. There was a need for heroes which was partially met by the rather spurious glory of the defence of Mafeking by Baden-Powell: its relief occasioned a display of hysterical rejoicing in Britain. Again Winston Churchill got in on the act, reporting for the *Morning Post* and adding to his burgeoning fame after his 'Boys' Own' escape from a Boer prison, an escapade which he reported with masterly relish for his long-suffering but grateful editor.

Apart from the telegraph which came into its own (long lines were trailed behind the advancing British columns), communications were difficult, particularly with the besieged Ladysmith. The heliograph was successfully used by the garrison to communicate with the relieving force when the sun shone: the large ones with 14.137 inch mirrors could be seen ninety miles away.[8] When there was no sun, messages were bounced off the clouds at night with a searchlight.

After the capture of Pretoria and of Komati Poort, to which the Boer leaders had retreated, in September 1900 it appeared that the war was over. Roberts returned to Britain and Kitchener was left to clear up any remaining problems. Army/press relations immediately deteriorated. Although he had a few press favourites, in South Africa notably H.A. Gwynne of Reuters (later editor of the *Daily Telegraph*), Kitchener, throughout his career, continued to maintain his disdain for journalists. This certainly did not help in the subsequent developments. The Boers were far from finished and began a series of raids by 'commando' columns throughout South Africa under the brilliant leadership of De Wet, Smuts and others. They were difficult to deal with. Kitchener decided on two methods of coping with the problem. He erected some 8,000 blockhouses connected by barbed wire along the railways, thereby attempting to corral the Boer commandoes into more manageable areas. He also attempted, eventually successfully, to remove the sources of the Boer columns' food and information – the farms – by burning them down. It was estimated that no fewer than 30,000 farms were burned and 3,600,000 sheep slaughtered.[9] Milner ordered the chief censor to cut out references to this from letters and telegrams, but eventually the truth came out in London and caused an uproar. The leader of the opposition, Campbell-Bannerman, called the practice 'methods of barbarism', and Churchill condemned it as a 'hateful folly'. There was much bad press publicity.

An even worse consequence of this policy, however, was that something had to be done about the women and children thus uprooted. Kitchener agreed to set up camps for these people where he thought they would be properly looked after. This was an appalling disaster as sanitary, medical and commissariat arrangements were vastly inadequate. The full story did not emerge until the daughter of a Cornish parson, Emily Hobhouse, decided to find out for herself, went out to South Africa, defied all the difficulties placed in her way and established the truth. On her return to Britain she went to see Broderick who was Minister for War. He was appalled by what he learnt but tried to limit the damage to the British reputation and did not publish her report. Determined that the truth should not be suppressed, Emily Hobhouse persisted. Her report was published in the radical press and caused a major uproar in Parliament.

The Government reacted by setting up a Commission to investigate – a time-honoured ploy used then and since by all governments when in severe difficulties. A Mrs Fawcett was chosen to lead it. This formidable lady, the widow of the blind Postmaster General, Professor Fawcett, and the author of a book on political economy, had recently published an article in the *Westminster Gazette* attacking Emily Hobhouse. It was, therefore, hoped that she would whitewash the affair. She did not. Mrs Fawcett's report, which was widely published, was damning and, belatedly, many improvements were made. The Bloemfontein Memorial, at the base of which Miss Emily Hobhouse lies buried, records its erection to the memory of 26,370 women and children who were said to have died in the camps (the exact number is a matter of dispute but is certainly more than 20,000). It is difficult to imagine any similar situation today which would not have been discovered by the press long before and blazoned to the world in strident tones. It took one of those remarkable Victorian women with their long skirts, tough boots and determined faces to unearth the scandal properly.

As always there was another side to the question. Lord Milner wrote a memorandum on the subject[10] in which he argued that the establishment of 'concentration camps', as they were called at the time (without the later infamous connotations), was an act of mercy:

> Humanity induced the British Commander to remove the inhabitants from their farms and assemble them in concentration camps where they have at all times received food similar to that provided for the British soldiers, as well as shelter and other comforts. . . . The high rate of mortality in these camps has been mainly due to the deplorable state of starvation and sickness in which great numbers of people arrived in the camps.

However, in a letter to Chamberlain on 17 December 1901 Milner admitted, 'The whole thing, I think now, has been a mistake.' Milner, a humane and socially liberal man with a strong conscience, undoubtedly deeply regretted the whole development and, when he knew about it, brought about much-needed and urgent improvements. Propaganda about the camps was used with devastating effect both in Europe and in the United States. The British reputation suffered greatly in many parts of the world. Kitchener appeared to be unmoved, seeing the episode as a necessary, if unfortunate, result of Boer actions.

Atrocities were reported on both sides. Indeed there were instances of the press reporting Boer atrocities which turned out to have no foundation at all; Edgar Wallace invented one notorious example.[11] The Boers, too, proved to be adept at propaganda. Allegations of atrocities by British soldiers were rife. Of course war is a cruel business and no doubt there were some unnecessary cruelties on both sides. However, in general, with the controversial exception of the concentration camps, this war was fought with surprisingly little bitterness on the ground, and there were many examples of chivalrous conduct by both sides. The British General Lord Methuen, for instance, after capture by the Boers was returned under safe conduct to hospital at Cape Town.

Advances in film technology, and in particular of the four-year-old cinematograph technology, led to enormous interest in Britain in pictures of the war. Many thousands of pictures of the British army in South Africa appeared in the press in Britain; indeed, some periodicals consisted of little else. The British army in South Africa was the largest ever to have left British shores for war, and the soldiers' relatives, particularly in traditional recruiting areas where almost everyone had a relative or friend serving there, clamoured for news of all kinds. Several of the news reels were faked, one notorious example being filmed on Hampstead Heath, but some were not. John Dickson of the London Biograph Company was particularly reliable, and his films were widely watched.

Although some pictures of the burning of farms and of the concentration camps did appear, as did graphic photographs of the carnage of the British defeat at Spion Kop, it would be overstating the case to argue that the course of the war was changed in any way because of the comparatively new phenomenon of the war photograph. The new technology heightened interest but actually changed nothing. Instant television, with all its implications, covered later in this book, was still years away.

On the whole and with some notable exceptions, the British press during the early stages of the South African war, mainly at its own volition, acted as a propaganda weapon to sustain the war effort and to keep up the patriotic fervour which was widespread at the time. Criticisms were made, but the majority of the press did not swerve from the belief that the war was just and that Britain had been right to fight it. After September 1900, when it appeared that the war was over and victory parades were held in London, the press and public began to lose interest. Many journalists came home – indeed many had already left. Other events were claiming attention, notably the Boxer rebellion in China and, of course, the general election of 1900.

When the war did not end and the Boers continued to fight, with their commando columns rampaging around the whole area, including Cape Colony, the press began to agitate, particularly when the news about the burning of farms and the deaths in the concentration camps began to circulate. Some newspapers became even more militant, calling for instant victory whatever the cost. Others which had believed that Britain should never have become involved in the first place called for instant peace, however apparently humiliating this might be.

Kitchener himself, eager to take up his post as Commander-in-Chief in India, was fed up with the continuation of these tiresome hostilities and, against Milner's opposition, pressed for lenient peace terms which the Boers could accept.

The eventual signing of a peace treaty on 31 May 1902 was the scene of one of the more ridiculous aspects of censorship. Edgar Wallace of the *Daily Mail* managed to scoop the rest of the press through the use of coded signals from a military clerk involving the use of coloured handkerchiefs waved at a passing train – red for stalemate, blue for progress and white for success.[12] A white handkerchief was eventually waved. The long nightmare was over.

Fervently believing in the role of the British people and Empire as a force for good in South Africa, Milner then turned his remarkable energies to the task of reconciliation and achieved a great deal before having to resign in 1905 on the issue of Chinese labourers in the mines. By the South Africa Act of 1909 the Union of South Africa came into being with a Boer majority. Botha was Prime Minister with Smuts in his cabinet.

It cannot be said that the media had much influence on the most remarkable aspect of this whole unhappy affair: Botha, the Boer Commander-in-Chief at the end of hostilities in 1902, became a fervent admirer of the British Empire and sat with Milner (by then the British Secretary for War) at the Versailles Peace Conference. Smuts, his wartime colleague, sat in Lloyd George's War Cabinet and, in spite of strong opposition by De Wet and others, South Africa fought with Britain in the First and Second World Wars. All this fourteen or so years after the burning of 30,000 farms and the death of over 20,000 Boer women and children in British concentration camps – a contrast indeed to the aftermath of Versailles. The British may have been bad at making war; they were extremely successful in making peace. Churchill's dictum 'in victory, magnanimity', though coined for a later occasion, was triumphantly justified.

---

1. Quoted in Knightley, *The First Casualty*, London, Purnell Book Services, 1975, p. 23
2. *The Life and Letters of Edwin Laurence Godkin*, New York, Macmillan, 1907, p. 205 quoted in Knightley, *The First Casualty*, p. 21
3. Alan Hankinson, *Man of Wars*, London, Heinemann, 1982, p. 175
4. Knightley, *The First Casualty*, p. 51
5. Roy Jenkins, *Gladstone*, London, Macmillan, 1995, p. 403
6. Knightley, *The First Casualty*, p. 52
7. Woods, *Young Winston's Wars*, London, Leo Cooper, p. xviii
8. Farwell, *The Great Boer War*, London, Allen Lane, 1976, p. 220
9. Ibid., p. 353
10. Wrench, *Lord Alfred Milner*, London, Eyre and Spottiswoode, 1958, p. 230
11. Farwell, *The Great Boer War*, p. 373
12. Trevor Royle, *War Report*, London, Mainstream Publishing, 1987, p. 84

CHAPTER THREE

The Great War, 1914–1918

'Just for a word – "neutrality", a word which in war time has so often been disregarded, just for a *"scrap of paper"* [author's italics] Great Britain is going to make war.'

> Theobald von Bethman-Hollweg, German Chancellor,
> to Sir Edward Goschen, British Ambassador, 4 August 1914

The reasons why in August 1914 Europeans decided, or were inexorably impelled, to embark on a course which led to suicide on a massive scale, and to persist in the slaughter, have engaged the minds and pens of scholars ever since the cataclysm occurred. In his masterly work, *The First World War*, Martin Gilbert quotes Valentine Fleming, the father of Peter and Ian, writing to Winston Churchill, his close friend and fellow MP, in November 1914 saying how ghastly the war was:

> Imagine a broad belt, ten miles or so in width, stretching from the Channel to the German frontier near Basle, which is positively littered with the bodies of men . . . along this 'terrain of death' stretch two more or less parallel lines of trenches, some two hundred or a thousand yards apart. In these trenches crouch lines of men in brown or grey or blue, coated with mud, unshaven, hollow-eyed with the continual strain, unable to reply to the everlasting run of shells hurled at them from three, four, five or more miles away and positively welcoming an infantry attack from one side or the other as a chance of meeting and matching themselves against human assailants, and not against invisible, irresistible machines, the outcome of an ingenuity which even you and I would be in agreement in considering unproductive from every point of view.

He ended his letter: 'It's going to be a long war in spite of the fact that on both sides every single man in it wants it stopped at once.'[1]

To our modern minds the almost unanswerable conundrum is how men on both sides were prepared to undergo, as it seemed almost indefinitely, the unspeakable horrors of the Somme, Passchendaele, Gallipoli and Verdun without revolt.

In June 1917 T.S. Eliot sent *The Nation* magazine a letter he had received from an officer who had been at the front since before his nineteenth birthday.[2] The officer was angered by what he saw as a lack of understanding at home of conditions at the front: 'The leprous earth, scattered with the swollen and blackened corpses of hundreds of young men. The appalling stench of rotten carrion.' His description continued:

> Mud like porridge, trenches like shallow and sloping cracks in the porridge, porridge that stinks in the sun. Swarms of flies and bluebottles clustering on pits of offal. Wounded men lying in the shell holes amongst the decaying corpses: helpless under the scorching sun and bitter nights, under repeated shelling. Men with bowels dropping out, lungs shot away, with blinded smashed faces or limbs blown into space. Men screaming and gibbering. Wounded men hanging in agony on the barbed wire, until a friendly spout of liquid fire shrivels them up like a fly in a candle . . . but these are only words and probably convey only a fraction of their meaning to the hearers. They shudder and it is forgotten.

Speaking about Passchendaele, Major Alan Brooke, the future Field Marshal no less, said: 'The sights up there are beyond all description; it is a blessing to a certain extent that one becomes callous to it all and that one's mind is not able to take it all in.' At a conference addressed by Haig, the Commander-in-Chief, Brooke recalled:

> I could hardly believe that my ears were not deceiving me: he spoke in the rosiest terms of our chances of breaking through. I had been all over the ground and to my mind such an eventuality was quite impossible. I am certain he was misinformed and had never seen the ground for himself.[3]

These latter remarks were only too true. Haig's diaries[4] make it quite clear that, almost unbelievably, he never himself went to the front line at all. This was not because he lacked personal physical courage. It was because he could not face the prospect of being responsible for sending thousands, or hundreds of thousands, of men into a hell he had himself seen. This is confirmed by his son in the foreword to the diaries who said:

To picture my father as a hard unfeeling man is wrong, because I know that there was a nature full of warmth of feeling and sensibility lying behind his reserve. The sufferings of his men during the Great War caused him great anguish. I believe that he felt it was his duty to refrain from visiting the casualty clearing stations because these visits made him physically ill.[5]

Duff Cooper in his biography of Haig gives further credence to this state of affairs. Talking about the officers of Haig's GHQ, he says: 'They were not ignorant of the conditions in which the men were fighting. Six young officers of brigade major rank were deputed to visit regularly the front line and to report to the General Staff on the state of the ground as well as on other matters.'[6] Duff Cooper adds, referring to the appalling mud at Passchendaele, that liaison officers from the Commander of the Royal Artillery, the Quartermaster General and the Engineer-in-Chief also kept the chiefs informed on the state of the weather, who in turn informed Haig. To the modern military mind it is extraordinary that these leaders did not go to see for themselves.

What if television had been present with mobile cameras and satellite dishes? If the Commander-in-Chief, a soldier who should be trained to accept, if not ignore, such sights, could not bring himself personally to see what he was responsible for, what would the impact have been if these images had been projected direct into the living-rooms of Britain, France and Germany? Can one imagine it remotely possible that there would not have been such a universal demand for peace that the war would have come to an immediate end? And if the war had ended in, say, 1916 would the Russian revolution have taken place? Would Hitler have come to power? The implications are breathtaking. This is a question to be kept in the back of one's mind throughout this study, whenever the temptation to ascribe almost every ill to the media is strong. Indeed Robin Day is reported to have said at a seminar at the Royal United Services Institute on 13 October 1970: 'One wonders if in future a democracy which has uninhibited television coverage in every home will ever be able to fight a war, however just.'[7]

Before 4 August 1914, there was no certainty about Britain's participation in the war. She had not been involved in the 1870 struggle between Prussia and France. Germany hoped against hope that Britain would again remain neutral and, in spite of talks which had hesitantly taken place between the French and British military staffs, France was not at all certain of British help if Germany attacked her. *The Times* was resolute in its advocacy of coming to France's aid if she was attacked. On Friday 31 July (four days before the outbreak of war) *The Times* editorial said:

> Our duty is plain. We must make instant preparations to back our friends if they are made the subject of unjust attack. . . . The days of splendid isolation are no more. We cannot stand alone in a Europe dominated by any single power, or any single group of powers.

On the outbreak of war on 4 August 1914 *The Times* (5 August) reported that there was:

> cheering and singing in Trafalgar Square, Whitehall, Parliament Street and Parliament Square. There was a profound silence just before midnight (when the British Government's ultimatum expired). Then there were vast cheers lasting for twenty minutes. The King and Queen and the Prince of Wales appeared on the balcony of Buckingham Palace three times.

There were similar scenes in Berlin and Vienna, though not to the same extent in Paris.

The press, however, had been far from unanimous. The bulk supported the Government, but the *Manchester Guardian* had approached the whole issue with scepticism.

On 23 July a leading article said: 'Vienna is notoriously the most jumpy capital in Europe, and the talk about war between Austria and Servia is surely not to be taken very seriously.'

By 25 July, the *Manchester Guardian* had changed its tune and was talking about a 'grave European crisis'.

On 27 July it said: 'War between Austria and Servia would be very regrettable; still it would not be a European calamity and, when all is said and done, Servia would have brought it on herself.'

On 28 July: 'We have no . . . commitments. Not only are we neutral now but we could and ought to remain neutral throughout the whole course of the war.' It then made a bitter attack on *The Times* for warmongering and quoted letters from Cambridge scholars and a whole host of other figures including Keir Hardie. It mentioned a massive demonstration which would take place in Trafalgar Square and many other actions of that kind.

On 30 July it said:

Englishmen are not the guardians of Servian well-being, or even of the peace of Europe. Their first duty is to England and to the peace of England. We ought to feel ourselves out of danger, for whichever way the quarrel between Austria and Servia went it would not make a scrap of difference in England. We care as little for Belgrade as Belgrade does for Manchester. But, though our neutrality ought to be assured, it is not.

On 31 July: 'We have been specifically assured that there is no contract between us and France which impairs our freedom of action in the event of a war.'

On 1 August: 'There is an organized conspiracy to drag us into the war should the attempts of the peacemakers fail.' The newspaper went on to say that 'balance of power' arguments should lead to us joining Germany against Russia, not the other way round. It also argued that the treaty with Belgium had lapsed.

On 3 August the leading article defended the German attack on Luxembourg and France – the attack on Belgium came a few hours later. The article argued that Germany had had to pre-empt Russian mobilization. Germany was 'fighting against the odds for her very existence'. On 3 August it also published a number of letters in favour of neutrality signed by Ramsay MacDonald, Gilbert Murray, Trevelyan and other leading figures. It talked of public meetings by the Labour Party and the Free Church Federation.

On 4 August it published an advertisement by the 'Neutrality League' which read: 'Britons do your duty and keep your country out of a wicked and stupid war . . . We are not bound to join in a general European war to defend the neutrality of Belgium.'

However, after war was actually declared on 4 August the *Manchester Guardian* changed its tune:

Some time the responsibility for one of the greatest errors in our history will have to be fixed, but the time is not now. Now there is nothing for Englishmen [*sic*] to do but to stand together and help by every means in their power to the attainment of our common object – an early and decisive victory over Germany.

(Leader, 5 August)

Thus, the newspaper resolved the classic media dilemma between loyalty to country and conscience in favour of the former.

As so often has been the case in our Christian civilization, the Almighty was called in aid of both sides. *The Times* quoted an appeal by the Kaiser on 6 August: 'We have to defend our most sacred possessions – the fatherland and the home – against the ruthless assault of enemies on all sides of us . . . Remember our great and glorious past. You are Germans. God help us.'

Sporadic opposition to the war remained, but Lloyd George's total support of British action in a speech at the Queen's Hall on 19 September was important in this context, as he had passionately opposed British involvement in the Boer War. His peroration was remarkable:

> May I tell you in a simple parable what I think this war is doing for us? I know a valley in North Wales between the mountains and the sea. It is a beautiful valley, snug, comfortable, sheltered by the mountains from all the bitter blasts. But it is very enervating, and I remember how the boys were in the habit of climbing the hill above the village to have a glimpse of the great mountains in the distance, and to be stimulated and freshened by the breezes which came from the hilltops, and by the great spectacle of their grandeur. We have been living in a sheltered valley for generations. We have been too comfortable and too indulgent, many, perhaps, too selfish, and the stern hand of fate has scourged us to an elevation where we can see the great everlasting things that matter for a nation – the great peaks we had forgotten, of Honour, Duty, Patriotism and, clad in glittering white, the great pinnacle of Sacrifice pointed like a rugged finger to Heaven. We shall descend into the valleys again; but as long as the men and women of this generation last, they will carry in their hearts the image of those great mountain peaks whose foundations are not shaken, though Europe rock and sway in the convulsions of a great war.

Oratory indeed.

Earlier in the speech he had said:

> I envy you young people your opportunity. They have put up the age limit for the Army, but I am sorry to say I have marched a good many years even beyond that. It is a great opportunity that comes only

once in many centuries to the children of men. For most generations sacrifice comes in drab and weariness of spirit. It comes to you today, and comes to us all, in the form of the glow and thrill of a great movement for liberty.

There was a rush to the recruiting offices immediately after this speech. Rapturous acclaim came from all sides including the Opposition Conservatives.

As John Grigg says in his biography of Lloyd George, however, such sentiments would have come better from him had he not written to his wife a week after the war began:

They are pressing the Territorials to volunteer for the war. [Gwilym] mustn't do that just yet. We are keeping the sea for France – that ought to suffice her for the moment especially as we are sending 100,000 men to help her to bear the first brunt of the attack. That's all that counts – for Russia will come in soon. I am dead against carrying on a war of conquest to crush Germany for the benefit of Russia. Beat the German Junker but no war on the German people and I am not going to sacrifice my nice boy for that purpose. You must write Wil telling him he must on no account be bullied into volunteering abroad.'[8]

The Cabinet had been agonizing over its response to the tragedy which was unfolding inexorably after the murder of the heir to the Austrian throne at Sarajevo. There were strong arguments that, were the Germans to attack in the West, British vital interests would be threatened. Total German domination of the continent could not be tolerated in 1914, it was said, although Britain had lived with the Prussian victory in 1870. However, it was the German invasion of Belgium – an apparently clear breach of the Treaty of London of 1832 (the scrap of paper) guaranteeing Belgian independence and perpetual neutrality – in response to the dictates of the plan put forward in 1905 by Alfred von Schlieffen, a former Chief of the German General Staff,[9] which ended the matter and, galvanized press and public opinion. It was easy to appeal to the British sense of fair play in supporting 'gallant little Belgium' against the Teutonic hordes, whatever the legalities of the guarantee of Belgium's neutrality; complicated arguments of the 'balance of power in Europe' had less immediate sound bite.

Henry Kissinger argues persuasively that Britain would probably have had to fight eventually anyway in order to redress the balance of power in Europe,[10] but this was by no means certain. It was the German invasion of Belgium which brought Britain into the war as far as the people of Britain were concerned. Once the die was cast the press was virtually unanimous in support for the British action.

When considering these matters and the press reaction to them, it is important to remember the context in which the British people saw themselves. Imperialism and the British Empire were not, as is now apt to be the case, dirty words: these were aspects of the British ethos which occasioned a vast throbbing pride in British breasts. For instance, there was nothing remotely embarrassing or even faintly comic about the advertisement, which, after the outbreak of war, often appeared in the *Illustrated London News* (e.g. 28 November 1914; see pl. 3). Most of the advertisement consisted of a picture by Frank Dadd of some young men, probably some time in the eighteenth century, clearly from various walks of life, marching off to enlist, following a drummer and waving gladly to women and children who stand at the side looking rather perplexed. Above the picture the caption reads 'Not once or twice in our fair island story, the path of duty was the way to glory' – Tennyson. Then underneath that are the words in large type 'THE BRITISH EMPIRE' and under that 'The land of beauty, virtue, valour, truth. Oh! Who would not fight for such a land!' Under the picture are the words, 'Follow the drum in sad times, or glad times, and all times, remember' and then under that 'ENO'S FRUIT SALT' in large letters, 'health giving refreshing invigoration known and sold from pole to pole'.

Britain had sent military observers to the Russo-Japanese war of 1904/5 who had been impressed by the strict censorship imposed on the press by the Japanese.[11] The Committee for Imperial Defence studied the problem and recommended that rules should be agreed and embodied in an Act to impose restrictions on reports of military matters. The Act would be passed on a contingency basis only to be activated in time of war. There was, however, much opposition to this and the Bill was not in fact drafted. When war broke out a War Press Bureau was set up under F.E. Smith (later Lord Birkenhead) to control the reporting of the war in France. A Chief Censor was established at the War Office with the duty of vetting *all* telegrams and letters. As far as press reports from France were concerned, these were to be censored by army officers and passed to the

Press Bureau for further checking. Kitchener's appointment as Secretary of State for War on 5 August 1914 led to even further measures: he ordered the withdrawal of all war correspondents from France with the result that the first vital few weeks of action went largely unreported except for a series of anodyne and almost entirely misleading official communiqués.

One correspondent, Arthur Moore, however, happened to be in Brussels en route to Serbia and on 30 August 1914 a special Sunday issue of *The Times* appeared under the headline 'Broken British regiments battling against the odds', telling the dire story of the British action and subsequent retreat from Mons. This became known as the Amiens despatch. It caused a major sensation since it was at complete odds with the complacent accounts of the war which had so far appeared. Ironically enough, because of his previous forays into journalism, Winston Churchill, then First Lord of the Admiralty, joined in the initial clamour which subsequently died down when it was revealed that F.E. Smith himself had vetted the report and indeed added to it in order to stress the overwhelming need for reinforcements. The resulting debate in the House of Commons led to the appointment of a Royal Engineer officer, Colonel Swinton, to provide 'Eye Witness' reports from France for the press. These too, however, were subject to censorship both in France and in London and were, as a result, very turgid.

Eventually, partly due to pressure from the United States whose correspondents were being well treated by the Germans, a few war correspondents were allowed into France in June 1915, but only under the strict control of a number of army 'minders', conducting officers who travelled with them wherever they went and acted as mobile censors.[12]

In any event there was little, if any, thought in the minds of the war correspondents of writing anything which might redound to the discredit of the British army or spread alarm and despondency at home. In practice they were largely used for propaganda purposes. Philip Gibbs, subsequently knighted and a well-known novelist, representing the *Daily Telegraph*, wrote in 1923:

We identified ourselves absolutely with the army in the field . . . We wiped out of our minds all thoughts of personal scoops and all temptations to write one word which would make the task of the officers and men more difficult or dangerous . . . There was no need of censorship of our despatches. We were our own censors.[13]

This phenomenon of the identification of the war correspondent with the military with whom they find themselves has been a notable factor of war reporting throughout – notably in the Gulf and Falkland Island conflicts. Where should a war correspondent's loyalty lie? To his editor, to his country or to the soldiers with whom he is living? It is a serious dilemma.

Whether the main agent for this concealment of the whole gruesome truth from the British people was the imposition of censorship, or the self-imposed restrictions of the journalists themselves, or the mendacity of the official communiqués, the results were ludicrous.

For instance, in the nine days after the outbreak of war, during which time, except for the Belgian army's heroic resistance at Liège, the German army had surged forwards through Belgium apparently without let or hindrance, *The Times* leader of 13 August included the following: 'The pertinacity with which the German cavalry patrols penetrate far into the interior of Belgium is apparently only excelled by their anxiety to surrender.'

And then on 29 August the *Illustrated London News*, under the heading 'The Great War' by Charles Lowe, made the following staggering claim: 'Up to the time of writing – Wednesday morning – the war on the whole, shows a balance in favour of the nations allied against Germany and Austria.'

The truth was very different. On the Western Front the French attack on the right had failed, the Belgian army had been almost completely eliminated and the rest of the French and the British armies were in full retreat almost to the gates of Paris. It looked possible that the Germans might win a victory to rival that of Sedan in 1870. On the Eastern Front the Russians were suffering one of the greatest disasters in the whole of military history at Tannenberg, described by the historian Barbara Tuchman as follows:

It is estimated that the Russians lost over thirty thousand killed. There was no doubt that ninety-two thousand prisoners were taken (sixty trains were needed to shift them to the rear). Two corps were completely wiped out. Only fifty officers and two thousand one hundred men survived and General Samsanov, the Commander of the Russian Second Army, committed suicide on the night of August 29th. With some justification Hindenberg called it 'One of the greatest victories in history'.[14]

After the battle of the Marne, the situation did stabilize for the allies on the Western Front, but large areas of France had been ceded to the Germans, and there was no sign of improvement in the Allied position in the West or, for that matter, the East. However, on 9 January 1915 the *Illustrated London News* had the following: 'The fortunes of war, on the whole, have been decidedly against them [the Germans] all along the allied line from the Channel to the Swiss frontier . . . In the east . . . the war has been equally favourable to the Russians.'

Charles Lowe excelled himself when describing the disastrous battle of Neuve Chappelle, during which the British and Indians gained a small salient of 2,000 by 1,200 yards at the cost of 7,000 British and 4,200 Indian casualties. His article in the *Illustrated London News* included the following description: 'The signal for attack was given – the most thrilling and intoxicating of all the joys of a soldier's life.' He then went on to describe the aftermath of the battle and the arrival of the wounded: 'the cheeriest crowd of wounded ever seen with the fierce joy of strife sparkling in their eyes.' To those soldiers actually present at this action these words must have appeared obscene indeed.

Alan Clark writes of the second day of the battle of Loos (26 September 1915): 'There had been twelve battalions making the attack, a strength of just under ten thousand, and in the three and a half hours of the actual battle their casualties were 385 officers and 7,861 men. The Germans suffered no casualties at all.'[15]

The *Illustrated London News* of 2 October (page 419) covered this same disaster at Loos with a map under the heading: 'The French and British Victories: Gains on the Western Front.' It added:

Sir John French, announcing the British advance, notified the following gains up to September 28: Enemy trenches captured on a front of over five miles, our troops penetrating the German lines in places to a distance of 4000 yards, the area including the Western outskirts of Hullock, the village of Loos, with the mining works round, and Hill 70.

Said Sir John French: 'Our offensive is progressing.'

On page 442 of the same number there are the photographs and descriptions of thirty officers killed in action – similar photographs of officers killed appeared every week in the magazine.

There had been much talk of a phenomenon known as 'the Angels of

Mons' which had apparently appeared in the sky to comfort the British army in its tribulations at Mons. Many people, including the mother of one of the authors, believed this story fervently as a fact. The truth was rather different. Arthur Machen, an author and journalist, made the whole story up. As he says, after reading the Amiens despatch, he thought everyone needed cheering up:

> The tale is mere and sheer invention: [that] I made it all up out of my own head, [that] to the best of my knowledge and belief it is entirely without any foundation. It was published in the 'Evening News' – I think on September 29th. On this day is held the Feast of St Michael and All Angels, and the date seems to have had its influence on the fortunes of the story. My tale concerned the spirits of the great English bowmen of the old wars, summoned from their rest by St George's mighty command: 'Array, Array, Array.' But when people began to talk about it, they called the good bowmen – 'The Angels of Mons'.[16]

The Angels were not unique. The Almighty was often invoked in aid of the British cause. An example of this comes in the *Illustrated London News* of 2 October 1915 (the same issue quoted above). It shows a drawing of a medical orderly helping a wounded soldier to walk being comforted by a ghostly Jesus Christ wearing a crown of thorns. Underneath is printed the following poem:

> When soldiers of the Cross waged Holy War,
> With courage high, and breasts that did not quail
> Before the foe, in olden times they saw
> The blessed vision of the Holy Grail.
> Tho' Christ was gone, His pledge was with them yet,
> For, borne on wings of angels, from the skies,
> They saw the chalice that once held the wine
> An emblem of the Saviour's sacrifice
> For men, and knew that still the Master met
> With his own friends, in fellowship divine.
>
> Christ has his soldiers now. Though years have rolled
> Away, the warriors of the Cross are strong
> To fight his battles, as the saints of old
> Against oppression, tyranny and wrong.

And still, amid the conflict, they can trace
The Saviour's influence. Not the Holy Grail
Which once as His remembrance was adored
But Christ himself is with them. For a veil
Is lifted from their eyes, and face to face
They must meet the presence of the risen Lord.

Shortly after the outbreak of war a campaign was mounted about German atrocities in Belgium, later quoted by Hitler as an example of propaganda expertise to be followed by Dr Goebbels. The British press cooperated enthusiastically and details were disseminated throughout the world.

It is difficult to disentangle the truth. Affronted by the Belgian refusal to let their armies pass through the country, even with promises made not to annex any territory and to pay any damages that might arise, the Germans undoubtedly committed many atrocities in an attempt to cow resistance. Many Belgian civilians were shot. Louvain and many other towns were sacked. Indeed the Germans did not attempt to conceal their desecration of that town and library. *The Times* of 31 August quoted remarks from the *Vossicher Zeitung* talking about Louvain: 'The art treasures of the old town exist no more. Lovers of art will grieve, but there was no other way of punishing the population whose devilish women poured boiling oil over the German troops.' (The same issue of *The Times*, in the aftermath of Tannenberg, had the headline: 'Russian prowess, a week of swift success. Broken German forces.')

Barbara Tuchman quotes a whole series of atrocities documented by the Germans themselves, with priests and hostages being shot and villages completely burnt down. She quotes Moltke, the German Commander-in-Chief, writing to a friend: 'Our advance in Belgium is certainly brutal but we are fighting for our lives and all who get in the way must take the consequences.'[17]

There was undoubtedly some exaggeration. Lloyd George hinted at that in his Queen's Hall speech on 19 September:

I am not going into details of outrages. Many of them are untrue, and always are in a war. War is a grim, ghastly business at best or at worst – and I am not going to say that all that has been said in the wave of outrages must necessarily be true . . . It is enough for me to have the story which the Germans themselves avow, admit, defend and proclaim – the burning and massacring, the shooting down of harmless people. Why? Because, according to the Germans, these people fired on German soldiers. What business had the German soldiers there at all?

There was a psychological need in Britain to have a cast-iron moral justification for the appalling consequences of the war in personal terms for so many people. The Belgian atrocities provided just that and the British people soaked them up. A Dutch cartoonist, Louis Raemaeker, who had crossed from Holland to England after a price had been put on his head by the Germans, provided a very powerful series of cartoons showing German atrocities. On arrival in England he was received by the Prime Minister, Mr Asquith, who wrote from 10 Downing Street, 'He [Raemaeker] shows us our enemies as they appear to the unbiased eyes of a neutral, and whenever his pictures are seen determination will be strengthened to tolerate no end of the war save the final overthrow of the Prussian military power.'

The cartoons were published in twenty-six fortnightly parts (see pls. 5 to 8), each picture being preceded by a commentary by some well-known literary or other figure – Chesterton, Hilaire Belloc, Eden Phillpotts, Bernard Vaughan SJ, the Dean of St Paul's and others. Perhaps the most powerful was a picture of a woman's body, Nurse Cavell's, lying on the ground being eaten by a number of pigs with German military helmets on (pl. 8). Opposite that picture the Dean of St Paul's writes:

The Germans have committed many more indefensible crimes than the military execution of the kind-hearted nurse who had helped war prisoners to escape. They have murdered hundreds of women who had committed no offence whatever against their military rules. But though not the worst of their misdeeds, this has probably been the stupidest. It gained us almost as many recruits as the sinking of the *Lusitania*, and it made the whole world understand – which is unhappily the truth – that the German is wholly destitute of chivalry. He knows indeed that people of other nations are affected by this sentiment; but he despises them for it. Woman is the weaker vessel; and therefore, according to his code, she must be taught to know her place, which is to cook and sew, and produce 'cannon fodder' for the Government. Readers of Schopenhauer and Nietzsche will remember the advice given by those philosophers for the treatment of women. Nietzsche recommends a whip. It never occurred to

German officialdom that the pedantic condemnation of one obscure woman, guilty by the letter of their law, would stir the heart of England and America to the depths, and steel our soldiers to further efforts against an enemy whose moral unlikeness to ourselves becomes more apparent with every new phase in the struggle.

Father Bernard Vaughan SJ writes:

Not content to crucify Canadians, murder priests, violate nuns, mishandle women and bayonet children, the enemy torpedoes civilian-carrying liners and bombs Red Cross hospitals. More, sinning against posterity as well as antiquity, Germans stand charged before man and God with reducing to ashes some of the finest artistic output of Christian civilization. When accused of crimes such as these, Germany answers through her Generals: 'The commonest, ugliest stone put to mark the burial place of a German grenadier is a more glorious and venerable monument than all the cathedrals of Europe put together' (General von Disfurth in the *Hamburger Nachrichten*).

G.K. Chesterton spoke of 'Prussia as, for many moderns . . . their first glimpse of absolute or positive evil.' Hilaire Belloc talks of massacre upon massacre: 'Louvain, Aerschot, the wholesale butchery of Dinant, the Lorraine villages (and in particular the hell of Guebervilliers). Even at the very extremity of his tide of invasion, and in the last days of it, came the atrocities and destruction of Sermaize.'

Another cartoon was of a young Britannia kissing a young Englishman in military uniform brandishing a rifle and looking to the skies with the sub-heading: 'My son, go and fight for your motherland!' (see pl. 7) Opposite it there is a long poem by Eden Phillpotts, the last verse of which runs:

> England's your mother! When the race is run
> And you are called to leave your life and die,
> Small matter what is lost, so this be one:
> An afterglow of blessed memory,
> Gracious and pure,
> In witness sure
> 'England was this man's mother: he her son.'

The Germans tried to counter the highly effective British propaganda. For instance, the *Norddeutsche Allgemeine Zeitung* of 1 December 1914 said that Gurkha and Sikh troops liked to sneak across the lines at night to slit German throats and drink the blood.[18] A more convincing effort concerned the publication in October 1914 of a 'Manifesto to the Civilized World' signed by ninety-three German artists, poets, historians, philosophers, scientists, musicians and clergymen: 'We shall wage this fight to the very end as a civilized nation.'[19]

Einstein, who was in Berlin, refused to have anything to do with it, declared that Germany had gone mad and buried himself in his physics.

The propaganda war in the early stages of the conflict was undoubtedly won by Britain, no doubt largely because there was far more truth in the British than in the German accusations. The British public was convinced that Britain was fighting against a very great evil and that God was unequivocally on the British side. A romantic view of the British role in the world still persisted: words like 'courage', 'self-sacrifice' and 'duty' still had a powerful hold on the imagination of many British people. Partly because of the propaganda about German atrocities in Belgium which found a ready audience in the United States, much of the American public was equally certain that morality lay on the British and French side and this, when added to the effect of the sinking of the *Lusitania* and the Zimmermann telegram,[20] was no doubt a major factor in the eventual American decision, albeit under a peace-loving near-pacifist President, to declare war on Germany on 6 April 1917.

Militarily the German invasion of Belgium was highly successful (as indeed it was in the Second World War). However, politically it was a total disaster as was the deliberately harsh treatment of Belgian civilians. If ever there was an example of the pen being mightier than the sword, this was it. The British people were prepared to fight to the death in 1914–18 for a variety of reasons. Hatred of Germany, largely engendered by tales of German atrocities in Belgium, was high on the list. And, for similar causes, in 1917 America entered the war, thus sealing Germany's fate.

Later in the war there were doubts about the success of British propaganda and German efforts in this regard improved. As a result of this, and of other perhaps more Machiavellian political ploys, Lloyd George appointed Lord Beaverbrook as the first British Minister for Information in February 1918. Before this, each Service Ministry and Foreign Office had its own propaganda department. Coordination had been in the hands of Sir Edward Carson, a member of the War Cabinet, until he resigned in January 1918. Beaverbrook's rumbustious personality led him into all kinds of difficulty and rows of one sort and another. However, he persisted, appointed Northcliffe as Director of Enemy Propaganda, and was undoubtedly improving matters greatly by the end of the war. His ministry, though, was never popular in political circles and was disbanded as soon as the war ended.

During the First World War the camera, already used, sometimes with duplicity, in the Boer War, began to play a growing part in the propaganda effort. Although most of the war scenes in the *Illustrated London News* consisted of artistic impressions, photographs appeared every week in this periodical and in 1916 a film was made – *The Battle of the Somme* – which was shown to the British public in late August. Some of this film was in fact staged but there were many actual images of the fighting with British troops going over the top and pictures of piles of German dead (any similar images of British dead were censored out). This film was shown to mass audiences in Britain, having the effect, perhaps strangely to our modern mind, of stiffening patriotic fervour rather than casting any doubt on the ethics of what we were doing. Indeed, one of the authors of this study remembers being shown the film in 1936, when eleven years old, at his preparatory school, and being overcome with emotion, not of horror but of pride and a longing to take part in a heroic venture of some kind.

There is a strange anomaly about the impact of the media on the conflict of 1914–18. At the lower levels, in particular at the level of the war correspondent, the press had little influence on the conduct of the war. The reports which appeared in newspapers were mainly used for propaganda purposes to sustain the morale both of fighting troops and of the people at home in the face of the hideous casualties sustained by the British armies and the squalor of the trenches in France. This, broadly, remained the situation throughout the war. There was, however, an exception – Gallipoli. An attempt was made in this disastrous theatre of war to prevent the truth from reaching Britain: only two war correspondents, Lester Lawrence and Ellis Ashmead-Bartlett, were accredited and their despatches were heavily censored. However, the mismanagement of the campaign was such and the horrors of it so dire that the truth began to leak out. This process accelerated when an Australian journalist, Keith Murdoch, the father of Rupert Murdoch, managed to get permission to visit the battlefield on his way to England. Ashmead-Bartlett, hoping to evade censorship, gave him a highly critical despatch to take to London. This was, however, seized by the Military Police in Marseilles. Nevertheless, on his arrival in London Murdoch circulated an explosive memorandum of his own throughout Whitehall. This, together with much other material, led to the recall of General Sir Ian Hamilton, the Army Commander, which was followed not long after by a total allied withdrawal.[21]

The military correspondent of *The Times*, Colonel Reppington, played a different role. He was no war correspondent reporting from the Front. He rarely, if ever, went there himself. He had friends in high circles both in France – in the early stages of the war he used to stay with the Commander-in-Chief (General French) when in France – and in London, where he frequented society functions and picked up much gossip, often true, at the dinner tables of society hostesses. As a result of this he was well informed about general strategic matters and produced some remarkably accurate articles on strategy. However, it was at a higher level still, that of the press proprietors, that the media had an enormous influence on the course of events. Perhaps as a legacy of the fall of the Aberdeen Government, brought about largely as a result of Russell's despatches, it was widely felt in the ruling classes of Britain that the press did have considerable influence on opinion and hence, potentially, on events. This was a self-fulfilling prophecy. Politicians, with the notable exception of Asquith, therefore, deferred to the press to a remarkable extent and the press proprietors themselves entered the political fray with avid relish.

The dynamic Irishman, Lord Northcliffe, owner of *The Times* and the *Daily Mail*, was undoubtedly the most important figure in the league of press barons. His brother, Lord Rothermere, the proprietor of five important newspapers including the *Daily Mirror* and the *Sunday Pictorial*, became Secretary of State for the Air after Northcliffe had publicly rejected the post, leading to the resignation as Air Minister of another press baron, Lord Cowdray. Finally there was Sir Max Aitken, owner of the *Daily Express*, elevated to the peerage as Lord Beaverbrook in 1917 and, as we have seen, Minister of Information from February to November 1918. They were an ambitious demanding lot.

The British Army Commander in France, General French used Reppington and, through him, Northcliffe, to highlight a shortage of shells on the Western Front in May 1915, bringing about the collapse of the Liberal administration, the sacking of Churchill and Haldane and the creation of a coalition government still under Asquith.

General dissatisfaction with the conduct of the war, in part instigated and stoked up by Northcliffe and Aitken, led to the fall of the Asquith Government in December 1916 and to his succession by Lloyd George, who used the press to the best of his great ability to bring about his accession to power. Northcliffe was also a powerful factor in the battle between the soldiers (brass hats) and the politicians (frocks), in the form of Haig and Robertson on the one side and Lloyd George on the other. This concerned the question of whether all the allied effort should be centred in France (the Westerners) or some of it diverted elsewhere – Salonika/Gallipoli (the Easterners). Northcliffe supported the soldiers, occasioning a remarkable rejoinder by Churchill when he wrote:

The foolish doctrine was preached to the public through innumerable agencies that generals and admirals must be right on war matters, and civilians of all kinds must be wrong. Those erroneous conceptions were inculcated billion-fold by the newspapers under the crudest forms. The feeble or presumptuous politician is portrayed cowering in his office, intent in the crash of the world on party intrigues or personal glorification, fearful of responsibility, incapable of aught save shallow phrase-making. To him enters the calm, noble, resolute figure of the great Commander by land or sea, resplendent in uniform, glittering with decorations, irradiated with the lustre of the hero, shod with the science and armed with the panoply of war. This stately figure, devoid of the slightest thought of self, offers his clear far-sighted guidance and counsel for vehement action or artifice or wise delay. But his advice is rejected; his sound plans put aside; his courageous initiative baffled by political chatterboxes and incompetents. As well, it was suggested, might a great surgeon, about to operate with sure science and the study of a lifetime upon a desperate case, have his arm jogged or his hand impeded, or even his lancet snatched from him, by some agitated relation of the patient. Such was the picture presented to the public and such was the mood which ruled.[22]

Northcliffe thought a great deal of himself. Lord Beaverbrook quotes Northcliffe, who owned half the London newspaper market, to the effect that the press was the sole source of his power. He boasted that his position was new to the world of affairs, but that he preferred it to any other as a means of getting things done.[23] Indeed, according to Robert

Blake, Northcliffe informed Haig on one occasion that he intended to overthrow the French Government if M. Briand, the Prime Minister, did not mend his ways[24]

In the summer of 1917, it is sometimes said that, in order to get rid of him, Lloyd George sent Northcliffe on a mission to America. On his return Northcliffe paid a visit to GHQ in France, where it seems that Haig, busy with his own manifold problems, appeared to be bored with Northcliffe's American reminiscences – greatly to the latter's anger. Whether that was the reason or not, Northcliffe turned against Haig and mounted a bitter campaign against him in his newspapers. For once, however, the onslaught was a failure and Haig remained as Commander-in-Chief throughout the war. To his credit, Reppington refused to take part in this vicious campaign and resigned, joining the *Morning Post* – a diehard Conservative newspaper which was the chief critic of the Government in the winter of 1917/18.

As we shall see, the situation was very different in the Second World War where, on coming to power, Churchill installed himself as Minister of Defence and Chairman of the Joint Chiefs of Staff. There was no question of disputes arising between the political and military worlds because Churchill was at the summit of both.

To summarize, therefore, in the First World War the media, consisting almost entirely of the press, largely supported the decision, once made, to fight the war and to continue it until Germany was defeated, in spite of the tragic loss of life it entailed. Lord Lansdowne's proposals for a negotiated peace – he raised it in Cabinet in 1916 and in a letter to the *Daily Telegraph* on 19 November 1917 – were ridiculed in spite of his distinguished record as a Conservative Foreign Secretary. (Incidentally, on the same day Count Hertling, the new German Chancellor, gave his public support to the Bolshevik appeal for an armistice.) Again, the press went along with the official propaganda line both on German atrocities (many but not all of which were undoubtedly true) and on concealing from the British public the full horrors of the trenches in France.

The press owners, however, notably Lord Northcliffe, conducted a series of campaigns against military and political leaders which were in part successful. They played a major role in forcing Asquith to form a coalition government and then to resign to be replaced by Lloyd George. It is certainly true that during the four years of war there were deficiencies, errors and scandals which were usefully highlighted, leading to some improvements. A letter from General Sir Frederick Maurice, ex-Director of Military Operations, was published in several newspapers on 7 May 1918 accusing the Government of starving the army in France of manpower, a charge successfully, but probably wrongly, refuted by Lloyd George in the subsequent debate in the House of Commons. However, although Asquith loftily disdained such tactics, in general intrigue and bitterness flourished at the top military and political level throughout the war and the press barons must take a large element of blame for that state of affairs which in the long run could only have been to the benefit of the Germans.

---

1. Martin Gilbert, *The First World War*, London, Harper Collins, 1994, p. 112
2. Ibid., p. 325
3. Ibid., p. 370
4. Robert Blake (ed.), *The Private Papers of Douglas Haig (1914–1919)*, London, Eyre and Spottiswoode, 1952
5. Ibid., p. 9
6. Duff Cooper, *Haig*, London, Faber and Faber, 1936, p. 159
7. Defence and the Mass Media, Report of a Seminar held at the Royal United Services Institution on 13 October 1970, p. 6
8. John Grigg, *Lloyd George From Peace to War 1912–1916*, London, Methuen, 1985 pp. 162–9
9. The plan which was frequently amended by Schlieffen – the last time in 1912 – envisaged a vast outflanking movement through Belgium and Holland descending on Paris from the north and ending the war in the west in six weeks, thus avoiding fighting on two fronts simultaneously. Von Moltke, the German Chief of Staff in 1914, eliminated Holland from the plan (reinstated by Hitler in 1940).
10. Henry Kissinger, *Diplomacy*, New York, Simon and Schuster, 1994, p. 218
11. Trevor Royle, *War Report*, Worcester, Mainstream, 1987, p. 93
12. Knightley, *The First Casualty*, London, Purnell Book Services, 1975, p. 96
13. Ibid., p. 97
14. Barbara Tuchman, *August 1914*, London, Papermac, 1962, p. 299
15. Alan Clark, *The Donkeys*, London, Pimlico, 1961, p. 173
16. Sir John Hammerton (ed.), *The Great War, I was there*, Volume I, London, The Amalgamated Press, p. 86
17. Tuchman, *August 1914*, pp. 172, 173
18. Knightley, *The First Casualty*, p. 83
19. Gilbert, *The First World War*, p. 100

20. The British 30,000 ton passenger liner *Lusitania* was sunk by a German submarine in May 1915. Of the 1,198 passengers drowned, 128 were American.

   In January 1917 the recently appointed German Foreign Minister, Dr von Zimmermann, preparing for the eventuality that unrestricted submarine warfare might bring the United States into the war against Germany, sent a coded telegram to the German Ambassador in Mexico City. This said that in the event of war between America and Germany, with Germany's 'generous financial support', Mexico could join in alliance with Germany and recover the territories it had lost seventy years earlier – Texas, New Mexico and Arizona. This telegram was published in the United States on 1 March and had an explosive effect.

21. Hickey, *Gallipoli*, London, Murray, 1995, pp. 319–21
22. W. Churchill, *The World Crisis*, p. 100
23. Beaverbrook, *Men and Power*, New York, Duell, Sloan and Price, 1956, p. 59
24. Blake, *The Private Papers of Douglas Haig*, p. 64

CHAPTER FOUR

The Second World War, 1939–1945

'I have nothing to offer but blood, toil, sweat and tears.'

Churchill, House of Commons, 13 May 1940

Whatever the rights and wrongs of the Munich Settlement in 1938, it certainly ensured a united British nation when the Germans invaded Poland and Britain stood by its obligation to go to war if Poland was attacked. In Britain, only the Communists, until the German invasion of Russia, and a small pacifist fringe had reservations about Chamberlain's declaration of war on 3 September 1939. At the time of Munich, there certainly were some arguments against a war with Germany on the grounds that Sudetenland was overwhelmingly German-speaking anyway – why should the Germans living there not join their mother country? – that Britain was militarily unprepared and that the Dominions would not all follow our lead. In September 1939, though, the situation was very different. Hitler's intention of European, if not world, domination was clear. He had torn up the Munich agreement by invading the rest of Czechoslovakia and then set about his next victim, Poland. In spite of the comparatively recent memory of the carnage of the First World War, Britain – politicians, people and media alike – was quite certain that war it had to be.

The British Government was, however, almost totally unprepared for the massive task of dealing with the media, inherent to any armed conflict, let alone an all-out war against the formidable opposition such as faced Britain in 1939.

It was not that these problems had not been discussed: they had. On 14 October 1935 the Committee of Imperial Defence decided that a sub-committee should prepare plans for the establishment of a Ministry of Information in wartime.[1] However, there were interminable arguments as to the precise responsibilities of such a body, with the Service Ministries and the Foreign Office all vying for power and authority. It was also decided that in war the BBC should come under government control but, in this matter too, details were not agreed and in some cases were not even discussed.

The fact was that there was a legacy among many politicians, and others, of opposition to the whole idea of 'propaganda' which was seen as demeaning and alien to the smooth, urbane disinterested functioning of the Civil and other Services. There had been virtually unanimous hostility in the House of Commons, for instance, to the work of Lord Beaverbrook's Ministry of Information in 1918.[2] There had been some change of feeling in the 1930s and the British Council had been established in 1934 in order to project the British image overseas, but there were still many doubts. Nevertheless, a Ministry of Information was set up on the outbreak of war under the elderly and eminent Scottish judge Lord Macmillan, who was not even a Minister of the Government, let alone a member of the Cabinet, and who had absolutely no experience whatever of the media in any form or of Parliament. The result was chaos. After only five days of war the National Executive of the National Union of Journalists passed a resolution expressing grave concern at the failure of the Ministry of Information to provide the public with adequate news of the war.[3]

When the British Expeditionary Force landed in France and the main editions of the Fleet Street papers were already in trains en route to Scotland at 11.30 p.m. on 12 September, the War Office suddenly decided that this news was still Top Secret. Trains were halted and police rushed to the stations to seize bundles of later editions from the vans. Arrangements were made to seize newspapers from commuters on railway platforms. Then at 2.30 a.m. on the next day the policy was changed and it was decided that the news was not Top Secret after all.[4]

Lord Macmillan was succeeded by Lord Reith, no less, on 4 January 1940. Although Reith was of course highly experienced in media matters, having been the first Director General of the BBC from 1927 to 1938, the situation did not improve much, if at all. The Ministry did not have the real support of the Prime Minister, Chamberlain, let alone the other departments of state with which it had to deal. Reith went to see Chamberlain but received no proper answer. He complained:

all was most unsatisfactory. One was being told to do a job by a man who agreed that one ought to do whatever one was asked to do but who could not, or would not, tell one what one's job was; nor what if any support he would give. Not only was the Ministry in bad odour; it had no terms of reference and no authority.[5]

He went on to speak of Chamberlain's lack of enthusiasm: 'When he spoke about the BBC he said that there was a great deal of dissatisfaction with it, but he hoped I would be gentle with it, and not use my knowledge of it to do things that another minister could not do'.[6]

Although rightly extolled for his great achievement in setting up the BBC and instilling in its personnel the very high standards of integrity and deportment which pervaded the organization, Reith was a very strange man of overweening conceit and intolerant antagonisms. He and Churchill had cordially disliked each other for many years and, on assuming office as Prime Minister on 10 May 1940, Churchill immediately sacked Reith, giving the job to his friend Duff Cooper, but still without a seat in the Cabinet. He in his turn was removed in July 1941 to be replaced by Brendan Bracken, a very close associate of Churchill. He was a great success in the job, capable as he was of standing up to Churchill's frequent pestering, and supporting the media in general against its many enemies. He, and the admirable Admiral Thompson, the Chief Press Censor, who performed his extremely difficult job with tact and authority, were the largely unsung heroes of the media war.

The system of censorship adopted was complicated to say the least. In theory, within Britain, the system was voluntary in that editors only sent material to the Censorship Bureau if they required advice as to the desirability of suppressing the information in the piece concerned. However, if any printed material prejudiced the defence of the realm or might be directly or indirectly useful to an enemy, editors were liable to be prosecuted under the defence regulations. The censor's approval was a complete defence against such prosecution. In practice, on the whole, this worked well. There were problems of a lack of uniformity in the early stages, but matters gradually improved until, finally in 1941, as Thompson said: 'We cured the trouble altogether.' Foreign correspondents working from London were, however, covered by compulsory censorship, as were correspondents in the field and the BBC. The system of D-notices, under which editors were asked not to publish certain restricted matters, obtained throughout the war.

Media, politicians and officials all faced basically the same problem. Given that the objective of all was to win the war – and to be fair to the media that objective largely superseded thought of commercial success during what was seen as a war of national survival – what was the basic objective of communication? Was it solely to tell the truth to the general public? If so, how much of the truth? Was it to keep up morale? If so, what was to be done about bad news?

As in the 1914–18 conflict the early reports of the war – largely taken from official bulletins – were absurd. The journalist Claire Hollingsworth was actually on the Polish/German border when the German initial invasion took place. She told one of the authors of this book that she telephoned the British Embassy in Warsaw with the news, who passed it on to a sceptical Polish Government. On Monday 4 September, three days after the German invasion of Poland, when that country was undergoing an appalling ordeal by land and air, the *Daily Herald*'s second headline read: 'Poles smash way into E. Prussia.' The script read as follows: 'Officials in Warsaw stated late last night that the Polish army has smashed a way across the northern border into East Prussia after driving the Germans from several Polish towns in bitter fighting.'

A week later the *Daily Sketch* headline was: 'Warsaw Defiant. Nazi Line Bent', the latter referring to a French attack on the Siegfried Line. On Tuesday 12 September, under the headline: 'Nazi Army Tired Out', the *Daily Express* military correspondent reported: 'The Germans have withdrawn from Warsaw, while to the south-west of the city a battle is being waged along a 180 mile front. The German High Command had admitted a reverse.'

This over-optimism was not confined to the media. In one of the more extraordinary incidents of the entire conflict, on the night of 3/4 September, RAF aircraft dropped more than six million copies of an anti-Nazi leaflet over Germany using a phraseology which seems astonishing to us today (see pl. 13).

The same phenomenon of vast over-optimism appeared in the press at many stages throughout the war. Shortly after the battleships *Prince of Wales* and *Repulse* had been sunk off Malaya and the Japanese were advancing down the Malayan peninsula, the *Sunday Pictorial* wrote: 'The news from the Pacific was better last night – five Japanese planes were shot down.' The day before the base of Singapore fell to the Japanese the *Daily Sketch* had a headline: 'Singapore's 400 shells an hour on Japs. Lines stabilized.'

The press argued strongly, and often with justification, that the fault was not their's but lay in the bland, and often futile, optimism of official bulletins. Eleven days after the Japanese invasion of Malaya, for instance, when matters were far from well in that conflict, General Wavell, the Commander-in-Chief, announced in a communiqué on 18 December: 'Active measures are already in hand to remedy the situation in Malaya. There is no doubt that the Japanese have suffered very heavy casualties.' The problem was, of course, that on many occasions and in many theatres the press had no one on the spot and had nothing other than official communiqués to report.

The truth about the débacle of the raid on Dieppe, which was an almost total failure, was never told to the British public. The *Daily Mirror* headline on the matter read: 'Big Hun losses in nine hour Dieppe battle.'

In general, the media was, with some reservations, content in its role of supporting the war effort. There were, of course, flaws – selection, often; distortions, sometimes; but very rarely indeed was there a conscious total reversal of the truth. Quite apart from any other considerations, people involved in any incident, whether soldiers or civilians, would know what had happened, and their morale would suffer if blatant untruths were told.

The situation was very different in Germany. Hitler had written in *Mein Kampf*: 'Propaganda is not concerned with the truth in general, but the truth as interpreted in the interests of the propagandists: propaganda must not investigate the truth objectively.' He wrote that:

> The receptive powers of the masses are very restricted, and their understanding is feeble. On the other hand, they quickly forget. Such being the case, all effective propaganda must be confined to a few bare essentials and these must be expressed as far as possible in stereotyped formulas. These slogans should be persistently repeated until the very last individual has come to grasp the idea that has been put forward.[7]

In fact Hitler constantly singled out British propaganda during the First World War for praise – a doubtful accolade. In early January 1928 Goebbels made a speech on perception and propaganda. He said:

> The propaganda which produces the desired results is good and all other propaganda is bad, no matter how entertaining it may be, because it is not the task of propaganda to entertain but to produce results . . . therefore it is beside the point to say your propaganda is

too crude, too mean, or too brutal, or too unfair, for all this does not matter.

On another occasion he said: 'News policy is the sovereign function of the state which the state can never renounce. During a war news should be given out for instruction rather than for information.'[8]

With total control of the media, Goebbels was able to, and did, put his theories into practice over a prolonged period, from the accession of Hitler to power in January 1933 until the nemesis of the Berlin bunker in 1945. Clearly he was successful in convincing a great number of his fellow citizens. As one of his assistants put it with chilling if obscure, euphoria: 'Real broadcasting is true propaganda. Propaganda means fighting on all battlefields of the spirit, generating, multiplying, destroying, exterminating, building and undoing. Our propaganda is determined by what we call German race, blood and nation.'[9]

The problem for the Germans was, however, that what was largely swallowed in Germany itself, where there was no access to the truth, became useless and almost farcical outside the country. Before the United States became involved in the war, American correspondents in Berlin, notably Walter Shirer, became exasperated and bitterly resentful. William Joyce's (Lord Haw-Haw's) broadcasts from Germany to Britain were listened to avidly by very many people (including, as boys, both of the present authors), not because they were believed but as examples of ridiculous German posturing to liven up an otherwise dreary scene. There was no need to ban listening to them, even if that were possible which, of course, it was not.

At a later stage in the war, as the home front in Germany was clearly collapsing under a cascade of bombs, it was impossible for German propagandists to continue with even a façade of optimism and Goebbels went to the other extreme. Aping Churchill's 'blood, toil, sweat and tears' approach he talked of heroic resistance against enormous odds in the glorious task of saving civilization from the barbaric hordes. He went so far as to speak of 'poetic' as opposed to 'concrete' truth in his last, vain attempt to justify past Nazi tyrannies.

Of all the organs of the media in Britain during the war it was the BBC which played the leading, and eventually decisive, role in countering German propaganda and the effect on British morale of the early German and, later, Japanese successes.

The infant television service, at the time catering for 20,000 households, was shut down on the outbreak of war but in 1939 some 9 million wireless (now radio!) licences were in issue – 73 for every 100 households. As the war developed, more and more people (16 million, or half the adult population) listened to the nine o'clock or, to a lesser extent, the six o'clock news. The practice of playing all the national anthems of the occupied countries ending with 'God Save the King' before the nine o'clock news on Sundays had a great impact within Britain. Both the authors of this book remember being emotionally moved by the knowledge of how many nations were under Nazi occupation. Those who listened in occupied Europe were doubtless also affected by the realization of how many other countries were also suffering and that Britain remained free and fighting on their behalf.

War Report, first broadcast after the nine o'clock news on D-Day, 6 June 1944, was listened to daily by 10–15 million people in the British Isles.[10] Winston Churchill's speeches, without which the continuance of the war by Britain in 1940 must have been in some doubt, were heard by seven out of ten of the adult population.[11] The speech in which he rallied the nation after the fall of France is still worth reading nearly sixty years later:

> We shall go on to the end. We shall fight in France. We shall fight on the seas and oceans. We shall fight with growing confidence and growing strength in the air. We shall defend our island, whatever the cost may be. We shall fight on the beaches. We shall fight on the landing grounds. We shall fight in the fields and in the streets. We shall fight in the hills. We shall never surrender.

Even the *Daily Mirror*, not notable in the past for its support of Winston Churchill, called this: 'The greatest speech ever made by a British Prime Minister', and who would dispute it?

There had been a proposal that the Government should take over the BBC on the outbreak of war, a proposal supported by Churchill, but, although five of its governors were suspended, the BBC remained constitutionally independent throughout the war. It was, however, subject to censorship. It was 'officially guided by the Ministry of Information' – teams of BBC people were seconded as liaison officers within the Ministry. Censorship applied both to security, relating to the activities of the armed services, and, more controversially, to the morale of the nation. As regards security, there were comparatively few difficulties. As Frank Gillard, a leading BBC correspondent, said in his introduction to

War Report: 'The censors always had the last word of course, but they were on our side right up to the limits of security. None of us wanted to utter anything on the air that would put a single fighting man in peril.'[12]

But what about morale? Should the BBC be allowed to express the full horror of some of the bombing of London and of other cities? How would that affect the morale, not only of those living in Britain but also of servicemen serving abroad? The instincts of the BBC's reporters were to go ahead and tell the full story, with all its horror. After all, that is the function of the reporter. But would this damage the morale of the nation? A decision was taken, wise even in retrospect, that an event could be covered in general but without any detail since this might well help the enemy: navigation, especially at night, was at that time most inaccurate. As time went on even this rule was relaxed to a certain extent. For instance, towns which had been bombed could be named after twenty-eight days. However, all weather reports were still censored and even the reporting of a soccer match between a village and a military unit was banned.[13]

The BBC's foreign language broadcasts played a major part in the war effort. On the outbreak of war the BBC was broadcasting in seven foreign languages. At the end the number had increased to forty-five, half of which were beamed into Europe. Languages spoken varied from the obvious French and German to three dialects of Chinese. Alan Bullock explained the philosophy:

> What we have to do at this point of the war [the early days] when we're on the defensive, is to establish our credibility. If there is a disaster we broadcast it before the Germans claim it if we possibly can. And when the tide turns and victories are ours we will be believed.[14]

This policy was triumphantly justified when the occupied peoples of Europe, along with some of the Germans themselves, turned to the BBC as the only available repository of truth. German broadcasts at the time were grotesque: 'After your heroic struggle, you have been liberated today', the Belgians were informed after their defeat and, similarly Holland was told: 'Only now do the Dutch soldiers feel free and safe. They know that over there in England lives the enemy of the world.' As George Orwell wrote in 1944: 'I heard it on the BBC is almost the equivalent of saying "I know it to be true".' The historian G.M. Young, writing in *The Sunday Times* in 1943, said that the BBC's news output had given it a 'standing without rival on the European continent'. He went on: 'What they say goes, and is whispered and copied and carried by men, women and children at the risk of their lives and the lives of their families from the Arctic to the Aegean.'[15]

Frank Gillard, again, in a report to the BBC from Holland in 1945 said the following:

A few days ago Chester Wilmot had a little trouble over his typewriter and when he was sending a dispatch to London by radio he tacked on a message at the end asking Mrs Davis of our office in London to send him another typewriter. Yesterday morning, in Eindhoven, a Dutchman came running across the street to me and said – 'Is it true that you're Frank Gillard?' And I said, 'Yes', and he said, 'Well, tell me, has Mrs Davis sent out Chester Wilmot a new typewriter yet?' You really have to meet these allies of ours in France and Belgium and Holland to realise what the London radio has meant to them in the last four years. Their whole lives have revolved around it, the broadcasts from London have been everything to them. Thousands of them say that they couldn't have kept up their hopes and their resistance without it. They listen in their own languages and to a very great extent to the Home Service in English as well, for there are vast numbers of people over here who can understand English even though they can't speak it. And they turn their dial, anxious not to miss a single word, even when it's just Chester Wilmot asking for typewriter reinforcements. And they go over past broadcasts with you, that Sunday morning service when General Montgomery read the lesson while the airplanes roared overhead, and that time in *War Report* when John Snagge said 'Over to Normandy', and then there was nothing but silence because there was nobody to speak at the other end. 'We were very worried about that, you know,' they say to us, 'it was a big relief to hear some of you talking again the next night.' People crowd in upon us to express their thanks, and there's one thing they invariably say: 'We listened to the BBC, and we trusted the BBC, because it always told the truth.'

The BBC had an advantage over the press after the invasion of Europe. Whereas the newspapers were still restricted to one correspondent each in any theatre of war, no fewer than seventeen BBC correspondents sailed with the navies, flew with the bombers, jumped with the paras, landed with the gliders and hit the beaches with the US and British armies.[16]

For the first time in war, because of technological improvements in the equipment made during the war, the civilian population in Britain was able to hear, if not to see, the authentic sounds of the fighting. BBC war correspondents became household names in Britain and, indeed, sometimes almost throughout the world. Frank Gillard, Stewart MacPherson, Howard Marshall, Godfrey Talbot, Wynford Vaughan Thomas, Chester Wilmot, Richard Dimbleby and others brought the war vividly into the living-rooms of Britain, not with quite the urgency of television, but nevertheless with a new force and immediacy. On D-Day about 725 radio stations throughout the United States rebroadcast BBC invasion news.[17]

When the Germans invaded Poland they had caused confusion by imitating Polish broadcasts. It was decided, therefore, that news readers in Britain would identify themselves by name before reading the news so that in the event of a German invasion a counterfeit voice would be instantly recognized: it was later discovered that the Germans had indeed been training such potential imposters when the invasion of Britain was being planned. As a result, Alvar Liddell, Bruce Belfrage, Frank Phillips and others became well-known figures through their voices, adding to the feeling of cohesive effort engendered by the BBC. (They were no longer wearing dinner jackets when broadcasting, as Lord Reith had earlier demanded!)

Richard Dimbleby had come under criticism for his reporting of the war in the Middle East. After risking his life reporting under the noses of the enemy at Tobruk and elsewhere, he was attacked for being too easily manipulated by the High Command in Cairo when he should have been roughing it at the front. There may have been some little truth in that, but the BBC was thin on the ground at the time and it was clearly impossible for the same man to report the daily bulletins in Cairo and be at the front. Be that as it may, he could certainly not be accused of seeking an easy life on his return to Britain. He flew in no fewer than twenty combat missions, being the first correspondent to fly in a bombing raid to Berlin. His reports had the ring of truth. For instance, after the invasion, he reported:

Of enemy troop movements, there was, until noon today, little or no sign from the air, even close to the immediate battle area. Long stretches of enemy roads shining with rain, deserted, dripping woods, and damp fields – static, quiet, perhaps uncannily quiet, and possibly not to remain quiet. But here and there a movement catches the eye, as our aircraft on reconnaissance roar over a large and suspicious wood – three German soldiers running like mad across a main road to fling themselves into cover. And, nearer the battle area, much nearer the battle area than they, a solitary peasant harrowing his field, up and down behind the horses, looking nowhere but before him and at the soil.

It was not only BBC radio which made an impact on events. The American attitude to the European conflict was clearly of paramount importance. Roosevelt would not have been able to give the massive help to Britain he did, long before Pearl Harbor and Hitler's astonishing declaration of war on the United States, had America's public opinion not been supportive of the British cause. The United States had, of course, taken a vast interest in the conflict. The American News Agencies – United Press, International News Service and the Associated Press – on the outbreak of war immediately hired an additional 735 men and women to serve as war correspondents as an emergency measure.[18]

The Germans were extremely careful on the outbreak of war as to how they treated the American correspondents who attended the daily conference in the Propaganda Ministry in Berlin. As in the First World War they were a pampered breed. They were provided with special exchange rates for money, a special petrol allocation, extra rations and even the use of a holiday villa. Furthermore, to get a cable from Berlin to New York took 40 minutes; from London to New York took 8 hours.[19] But all this had little effect, particularly when the German air attacks began against Britain. The names Virginia Cowles, Ed Beattie and Quentin Reynolds became almost household words in the United States. But it was Ed Murrow, for three years head of CBS in Europe, who, with his vivid imagery and strong feelings about the evils of the Nazi regime, really caught the imagination of the American people, 30 million of whom tuned in to his Sunday night broadcasts from the basement of Broadcasting House during the Blitz. The portentous tones of his opening words, 'This . . . is London', gripped the American imagination and had a vast effect on the American conscience. In one broadcast at the height of the Blitz he said: 'The fire up the river has turned the moon blood red . . . huge pear-shaped bursts of flame would rise up into the smoke and disappear . . . the world was upside down. If Hitler and company is not stopped here, the next stop is Manhattan.'

The realities of war were also brought home to Ed Murrow on one occasion when he was on holiday in Somerset and a German aeroplane was shot down crashing on the beach near the hotel in which he was staying. He watched as three of the crew were arrested and taken away across the fields.[20]

Quentin Reynolds who broadcast both to the United States and to Britain found one particular raid: 'as exciting an ordeal as I imagine living in the Athens of Pericles must have been. The constant threat of death seems to make people really alive.' However, whatever the scale and immediacy of disaster, the reporter's obsession with scoop rather than reality continued occasionally to surface. As he watched the Battle of Britain being waged in the sky above his head, the young Whitelaw Reid, of the *New York Herald Tribune*, with chilling, if hilarious, self-revelation, hailed the apparently impending invasion as: 'The biggest story since the coming of Christ.'[21]

It was not only in its war reporting, both to Britain and, in particular, to Europe, that the BBC had an effect on the outcome of the war. If Britain was to win the war, in spite of being alone against the might of Hitler's Germany for a whole year, it was clearly vital that civilian morale should remain high. Virtually everybody listened to the radio, many for much of the day, and the night for that matter. There can be few people who were over the age of, say, twelve at the outbreak of the war and who continued to live in Britain, who did not listen on a near regular basis to at least one of the following programmes: *It's That Man Again, Band Wagon, Garrison Theatre, Hi! Gang, Workers' Playtime, Music While You Work, Monday Night at Eight* and *In Town Tonight*. These broadcasts, redolent of cheerful bonhomie and exhilarating optimism, had a vast impact on maintaining and strengthening the national will, first to resist and then to win the war. The BBC's series, *The Stones Cry Out*, dealing with famous British buildings which had been badly damaged or destroyed during the bombing, broadcast to the United States, also undoubtedly had a marked effect on American public opinion, as did the brilliant seven-minute documentary film about the Blitz, *London Can Take It*, made by Quentin Reynolds and shown widely in the United States as well as Britain.

The BBC also spread Government information and advice. In the winter and spring of 1939/40 the BBC exhorted people to save and to salvage, to avoid careless talk and nip rumour in the bud, to watch their step in the blackout, to learn first aid, to turn their wirelesses down in consideration of their neighbours, to stay put but evacuate their children, to dig for victory, to shop wisely, cook economically and keep pigs, chickens, rabbits and goats (but not, it was stipulated, rats).[22]

Sixty years later it is difficult to understand or to remember to what extent people's lives in the 1930s were influenced in one way or another by the cinema. Hollywood dominated the entertainment industry to a remarkable extent. Visual images were, and are, considerably easier to absorb than the written word. Many working people did not read books at all but would go to the cinema every week. Similar to the pop stars of today, film stars became role models, their spin-doctored personalities icons to be admired and copied. Films like *Mrs Miniver* and *In Which We Serve* projected images of dogged courage around Britain and the United States. However, it was the news reels which, to a large extent together with the BBC news broadcasts, conditioned the British people's perceptions of their fortunes in the conflict. The news reels could count on an audience of an extraordinary 20 million people each week – against daily newspaper sales of 14.5 million and 9 million radio receiving sets.[23]

There were only five news reel companies. Even the smallest, Universal News, reached an audience larger than the circulation of the largest national daily newspaper, the *Daily Express*.[24] Of all the media in the Second World War the news reels were the most tightly controlled. They were, also, more obviously propagandist than any of the other media forms. They were easy to censor – scripts and film material had to be seen in advance for the twice weekly productions. Indeed, once the initial novelty of actual war scenes appearing on the cinema screen had worn off, a certain cynical wariness of the obviously propagandist intentions and the irritatingly optimistic voices of the commentators began to appear. It was also difficult for the news reel companies to come up with new and interesting images regularly twice a week without either departing from the truth or damaging the war effort in some way. The importance of selection – always a vital element in the projection of any news story – was even more marked in news reels, which purported to tell the whole truth of any incident or event in the space of a minute or so of fleeting images.

On 23 May 1940, at the height of the battle for France, news reels covering the events of the previous three days appeared in the cinema both in Southern Ireland and in Britain. They were both produced in London by the same company, Gaumont British News, and the same editor Mr Emmett. The briefs given to the news reel company were, however, very different. The British Government wished to portray the momentous events in terms of successful and heroic endeavours by Britain and its allies. The Irish Government, on the other hand, did not wish the idea to be propagated that a life-and-death struggle was being fought by Britain or that a vast and unpredictable war was being fought in Europe. The sequences for the news reels on the same day were therefore, astonishingly, as follows:

Eire
1. Italian Royalty received by Pope Pius
2. Australian Boat Race
3. Sultan of Morocco at the Mouland Festival
4. Madame Chiang Kai Shek inspects air-raid damage at Chung King
5. Kentucky Derby
6. Dublin Great Spring Show at Ballsbridge

Britain
1. The navy on guard in the north
2. The fleet at Alexandria
3. War zone special:
   Belgian troops attacked
   Bombed hospitals
   BEF tanks blow up bridges
   Refugees hide from machine-guns
   Belgian army on the road
   Parachute troops prisoners guarded
   German wounded and prisoners arriving in Britain[25]

Although British official handling of the news reel companies improved later, in the early stages of the war there was a vast difference between the British and German performance. No photographs or film of the British Expeditionary Force leaving for France were allowed. While the Germans were flooding the cinema screens of neutral countries such as Holland, Belgium and Norway with images of vast armies moving east and taking up positions in magnificent-looking fortifications in the west, the only image of the British Empire at war available for counter-balancing

German propaganda was that of a platoon of Royal Engineers marching through a suburban street carrying shovels and pickaxes.[26]

When one considers that after the collapse of France in 1940, Britain was engaged in a struggle for her very existence and that on many occasions, even after the United States and the Soviet Union had joined the battle, the British fortunes were at an extremely low ebb – particularly during the continuing crisis in the Atlantic – it is astonishing, not that some action was taken against some organs of the press, but that this was so limited in scope. The defence regulations introduced at the beginning of the war gave the Government almost unlimited power to regulate the media, but these were very rarely used. The first problems which arose concerned the Communist newspaper, the *Daily Worker*. After the Nazi–Soviet pact the Communist Party appeared intent on sabotaging the British war effort. The Home Secretary, Morrison, a leading figure in the Labour Party, became concerned about these activities and submitted a paper on the subject to the Cabinet in December 1940. He argued, however, that although it would be perfectly possible, and in some ways desirable, to close the paper down – the *Daily Worker* had been warned in July 1940 – its efforts to disrupt the war effort were in fact having very little effect. To close it down would therefore be more trouble than it was worth. Nevertheless, the Cabinet eventually decided to suppress the *Daily Worker* on 21 January 1941. The reasons given were that the *Daily Worker* had continually: 'by every device of distortion and misrepresentation sought to make out that our people had nothing to gain by a victory, that the hardships and sufferings of warfare were unnecessary and imposed upon them by a callous Government carrying out a selfish contest in the interests of a privileged class.'

However, five months later, the Soviet Union was invaded by Germany and the Communist Party immediately changed its tune. Suppression of the newspaper was lifted on 7 September 1941. For his part, Churchill, a long-time bitter opponent of Communism, made it abundantly clear that he would support Russia to his utmost. He is reputed to have said: 'If Hitler invaded hell, I would at least make a favourable reference to the devil in the House of Commons.'

There were, however, very real problems inherent to the qualified freedom of the press in wartime. When a government is criticized it will inevitably argue that the criticism is undermining the morale of the nation and damaging the war effort. The media, on the other hand, will argue that such criticism is the only way of rectifying errors or abuses, the better to conduct a successful war. This latter argument is particularly potent in the circumstances of a grand coalition of all political parties, as obtained for most of the war in Britain. If the press cannot criticize, who will?

This problem arose in acute form with the *Daily Mirror*. On 7 October 1940 Churchill argued at a Cabinet meeting that the *Daily Mirror* and the *Sunday Pictorial* were disrupting discipline in the army and making trouble between the Government and organized labour. The Attorney General, however, said that it was not possible to prosecute and it was decided that Attlee and Beaverbrook should see representatives of the Newspaper Proprietors' Association and warn them that if these irresponsible criticisms continued the Government would introduce compulsory censorship of all news and views. Churchill met Cecil King, the proprietor of the *Daily Mirror* and the *Sunday Pictorial*, at the end of January 1941 and King agreed to behave better in future. Churchill was not wholly satisfied, but Morrison, the Home Secretary, argued strongly against any action because further regulation would, he said, unite the press in opposition and drive it into even further disruptive action.

Then, on 20 February 1942, the *Daily Mirror* reverted to its bitterly critical stance:

If this war lasts another three years this bankrupt Parliament will have lasted a decade. Everything in Britain has changed since 1935 except the management. The same old faces talking the same old bluff. The same old raddled intellects unalterably engraved with the same old prejudices and stupidities. Where is the new broom to sweep out this dusty mausoleum of dead minds?

On 6 March the *Daily Mirror* continued its violent attack:

The accepted tip for Army leadership would in plain truth be this: all who aspire to lead others in war should be brass buttoned, boneheads, socially prejudiced, arrogant and fussy. A tendency to heart disease, apoplexy, diabetes and high blood pressure is desirable in the highest posts.

On the same day in the same paper the cartoonist ZEC published a cartoon depicting a sailor clinging to a raft in the middle of the ocean and the caption read: 'The price of petrol has been increased by one penny – official.' The Cabinet discussed this whole matter, and in particular the cartoon, on 9 March 1941. Morrison confirmed that in his view the newspaper was indeed systematically fermenting opposition to the war. On 18 March the War Cabinet agreed that immediate action should be taken against the *Daily Mirror* if it published further unwarranted and malignant criticism. The director and editor of the *Daily Mirror* were warned and this was made public. In his memoirs Morrison says: 'We had no further cause for complaint about the *Mirror*.'[27]

In this, as in many other matters, the great advantage to national unity lay in the fact of coalition. If the Labour Party had been in Opposition and Morrison had been Shadow Home Secretary instead of being a Cabinet Minister with all the responsibilities of that office, it would have been almost impossible to take any action at all against the media without the most massive upheaval. Indeed, it would have been extremely difficult for Labour leaders, however sensible and patriotic, to avoid joining in partisan and often unwarranted attacks on a single-party Government. Throughout the war, Churchill made absolutely certain of the support of his fellow coalition partners before embarking on any policy likely to cause controversy. This clearly influenced the attitude of the media which on the whole supported the Government through thick and thin.

There were indeed many very difficult and daunting periods in the first two or three years of the war. The sinking of the battle cruiser HMS *Hood*, the passage through the Channel of the battle cruisers *Scharnhorst* and *Gneisenau*, the traumas of the Battle of the Atlantic, the sinking of the battleships *Prince of Wales* and *Repulse*, the loss of Malaya and Singapore, the fall of Tobruk and the Blitz, let alone the initial shattering defeat in France followed by evacuation at Dunkirk all tested the nation's resolve. Under the imposing leadership of Churchill, however, there was very rarely any serious opposition by press or public to the Government in its war-making capacity. Indeed, just after the fall of Singapore on 15 February 1942 the *Manchester Guardian*, far from an automatic supporter of Churchill in the past, put its view succinctly: 'He [Churchill] can be sure that we intend to become more formidable under his leadership since we expect through him to reach a quicker and more successful end than under anyone else.'

There were a few rumblings about social policies from left-wing journals but these never really amounted to much. After the fall of Chamberlain and the accession to power of Churchill there was only one moment of real doubt about the leadership in Britain. The fall of Tobruk on 21 June 1942 was a very heavy blow to morale in Britain. As Churchill put it:

> At Singapore 85,000 men had surrendered to inferior numbers of Japanese. Now in Tobruk a garrison of 25,000 [actually 33,000] seasoned soldiers had laid down their arms to perhaps one half of their number. If this was typical of the morale of the Desert Army, no measure could be put upon the disasters which impended in north-east Africa.[28]

For once the press in Britain was critical of the direction of the war – as Churchill put it:

> The chatter and criticisms of the press, where the sharpest pens were busy and many shrill voices raised, found its counterpart in the activities of a few score of members in the House of Commons, and a fairly glum attitude on the part of our immense majority. A party government might well have been overturned at this juncture, if not by a vote, by the kind of intensity of opinion which led Mr Chamberlain to relinquish power in May 1940. But the National Coalition Government, fortified by a reconstruction in February, was massive and overwhelming in its strength and unity. All its principal ministers stood together around me, with never a thought that was not loyal and robust. I seem to have maintained the confidence of all those who watched with full knowledge the unfolding story and shared the responsibilities. No-one fought it. There was not a whisper of intrigue. We were a strong unbreakable circle, and capable of withstanding any external political attack and of persevering in the common cause through every disappointment.[29]

A debate in the House of Commons took place on 1/2 July on a motion of no confidence put by a Conservative MP, Sir John Wardlaw-Milne. It was yet another triumph for Churchill and the motion was defeated by 475 votes to 25. If there ever was any doubt about the result, this disappeared when Wardlaw-Milne at a key moment in his speech suggested that the Duke of Gloucester should be appointed Commander-in-Chief of the British army, perhaps one of the more extraordinary suggestions in the history of the British Parliament.

There was a further problem in the late autumn of 1944 when British troops became entangled in the murky aftermath of the liberation of Greece. British policy in liberated territories was to restore legitimate governments to power where feasible, to help them to maintain law and order and to bring about free and fair elections as soon as possible. The problem in Greece was that much, but not all, of the armed resistance to the Germans had been mounted by the Communists who had the objective of making certain that when the liberation came they could take over control of the country. The exiled Greek Prime Minister, Papandreou, on his return to power managed to get some Communist representatives to join his Government but these soon resigned when General Scobie, the British general responsible for law and order, insisted that all unofficial armies should be disarmed and that only the police and the official army of the Greek Government should carry arms. Papandreou wished to resign but the King, still in exile, under the advice of the British Government, refused to allow him to do so. The situation quickly deteriorated and fighting broke out between the Communist armies and the unfortunate British troops who found themselves taking part in a vicious civil war.

For virtually the first time during the war much of the British press and indeed many parliamentarians found themselves in direct opposition to British policy. A leading article in *The Times* on 7 December 1944 said: 'The disagreeable truth revealed by the news of the past three days from Athens is that British armed forces, originally invoked in the desire to avoid bloodshed have become involved in a Greek civil war.' It went on to attack the insistence on Papandreou continuing as Prime Minister even when his coalition had failed: 'If Papandreou is maintained in power by Britain . . . British troops will have been used and British lives sacrificed fighting against Greece on behalf of a Greek Government which exists only in virtue of military force.'

After the police in Greece opened fire on a demonstration, allegedly killing some women and children, the *Manchester Guardian* said in a leader: 'We are being placed in the position of backing an unpopular Government against the parties of the resistance.' And it continued: 'We cannot continue to ignore and, worse still, to suppress the whole resistance movement.' 'If we continue our present policy in Greece the "lawful and constitutional Government" will be regarded as a British puppet and the resistance movement will be driven still further towards lawlessness and revolution' (6 December).

Most people feel (and they are right) that there must be some better way out of the troubles than to shoot down with tanks and guns and aircraft the men who fought the Germans with rifles and hand grenades.

(Manchester Guardian, 12 December)

The *Daily Mirror* was, not surprisingly, more vociferous, and widened the issue by quoting American reservations under the headline: 'United States rebuke on British policy' (5 December). The United States did indeed have great reservations about British policies. It was unfortunate that much of the American administration was being changed at the moment when all this blew up. Roosevelt had won the election but had appointed a new Secretary of State, Stettinius, who used words about British policy which, probably rightly, were construed as criticism. The British came under fire by politicians and media alike for apparently supporting right-wing politicians against more populist, if left-wing, elements not only in Greece, but also in Belgium, where it supported the Pierlot Government, and in Italy where it objected to the appointment of Count Sforza as Foreign Minister.

American opinion, however, was divided. The *New York Times* supported the British Government: 'The British have been thoroughly justified in supporting both the Pierlot Government in Belgium and the Papandreou Government in Greece. There was no alternative but to get the resistance to lay down arms.' And on 6 December it quoted with approval Churchill's words: 'The Tommy guns which were provided for use against the Germans will not be used to impose by violence a Communist dictatorship without the people being able to express their wishes.'

Matters came to a head in a debate in the House of Commons on 8 December. After a fighting and aggressive speech by Churchill, the Government won by 279 votes to 30 – a slightly hollow victory since a large number of Labour MPs abstained. However, Churchill finally silenced his critics by personally flying to Athens on 25 December, together with Eden, and in conditions of high drama getting both sides to sit down together, arranging for the appointment of a regent (Archbishop Damaskinos) and, in a situation of appalling difficulty, setting in train a process which eventually led to peace.

Churchill had come to an agreement with Stalin in Moscow that in return for the predominant Soviet influence in Rumania, Britain should have the same in Greece and in practice Stalin, very surprisingly, kept to it, at no stage supporting the Communist forces in Greece.

Churchill's power to dazzle the nation and the media in times of crisis and stress by his words and actions was shown when the *Manchester Guardian*, normally no automatic friend of his, said in a leading article on 27 December, perhaps a little ruefully:

Mr Churchill is incalculable. With one of those flashes of courage and imagination which will always cause his countrymen to forgive his occasional errors of judgement, he has flown to Athens with Mr Eden on Christmas Day to see whether he himself cannot bring to an end this sanguinary quarrel . . . it is a brave and judicious gesture.

There have been two major world wars this century (so far!). The British media has played important roles in both. How do these compare? In both wars the media fully accepted that Britain was engaged in a war of national survival. As a result there was little if any basic criticism of the fact of war. There was a consensus in the country and in the media that everything should be done to win it and that nothing the media did should help the enemy in any way. Censorship, whether direct as in the First World War or a mixture of direct and indirect as in the Second, was accepted as a necessary, indeed vital, fact of life. In both wars much of the media accepted without question that part of its function should have overtones of propaganda. But that is as far as the similarities go.

In the First World War military leaders never really accepted war correspondents as allies in the struggle. In the Second World War, the same attitude persisted in the early stages, although perhaps with less virulence. However, later – and particularly after Montgomery arrived in Egypt with his populist morale-boosting policies – the situation changed. For instance, writing in November 1945 about the campaign in north-west Europe, Montgomery said:

I think it's right to say that the keynote of this campaign was the Crusading Spirit, which inspired all ranks of the Allied Expeditionary Force, and which enabled them to face up to the great and often continuous demands which were made on their energy and enthusiasm and courage. This Spirit had many and deep sources and the BBC was one of the means by which this Spirit was fostered. In this way, these correspondents made no mean contribution to final victory.[30]

Frank Gillard, writing in retrospect about the same campaign says: 'Monty and I had many talks about the role of broadcasting in our circumstances. To him it was clearly an arm of warfare – a minor arm, of course, but valuable. That was why my colleagues and I enjoyed his strong support.'[31] Indeed, certainly after the invasion of Europe, the media was very active and, by and large, welcomed by both British and American commanders. As the war advanced beyond Paris, 150 correspondents, British and American, were filing stories to 278 million readers in 6 continents.[32]

The result of the ready acceptance of the media as friend, not foe, was that many war correspondents became household names in Britain and their reports undoubtedly improved morale because of the admiration felt for them. The cold anonymity and the anodyne prose of official communiqués was translated into reality by the human pen and voice of the independent journalist. Newspaper correspondents such as Alan Moorehead, Alexander Werth, Alexander Clifford, Noel Monks and Christopher Buckley, among many others, although sometimes hampered by the demands of censorship, were able to convey accurately to the reader the mixture of heroism, fear, discomfort and boredom of the soldiers, sailors and airmen engaged in this momentous struggle.

The new factor of radio, too, of course vastly increased the immediacy and impact of war reporting. It was not only the bombing which brought Britons together as a cohesive entity, fighting against what they believed to be the supreme evil of Nazism. It was also the feeling that, through the reports of radio and newspaper correspondents, everyone in Britain was in a sense sharing in the struggle. And, of course, the impact of the BBC on subjugated Europe was immense.

Within Britain there was less overt hatred of Germany and the Germans in the Second than in the First World War. In fact, of course, German behaviour was far worse in 1939–45 than in 1914–18. The German atrocities in Belgium and elsewhere under the leadership of the Kaiser paled into almost total insignificance when compared to the Holocaust and other demonstrations of Nazi bestiality as the Germans under Hitler rampaged through Europe. The posturing, arrogant Kaiser and his absurd strutting son were not to be compared with the supremely evil Hitler and his entourage of cringing perverts. In 1939–45 in Britain there was less overt nationalism, patriotism – call it what you will. There was less insistent rhetoric directed to Honour, Duty, Sacrifice and other words of that nature. There was no need to induce belief in the righteousness of the cause because over the previous few years this had become obvious to all. Churchill's speeches, although with their share of abuse of the Nazis, were primarily devoted to maintaining the will to fight, often in the face of apparent disaster, rather than to arousing hatred of the enemy. The British people had become more sophisticated, more reticent. They knew only too well the reality of mass slaughter: the truth about modern warfare could no longer be concealed from them. They responded more to the understated images of a 'Stiff Upper Lip' in Noel Coward's film *In Which We Serve* than to the heady rhetoric of 'Once more unto the breach dear friends'. The media had grown up, too, and reflected this mood.

There was, however, a further and important difference. The political and military scene in Britain in the First World War was beset by intrigue and quarrel. Haig (and the King) versus Lloyd George, Lloyd George versus Asquith, Frocks versus Brass Hats, Easterners versus Westerners, and so on. In much of this, the media, not only Northcliffe but also Beaverbrook and others, was heavily involved. There was little, if any, of this debilitating unpleasantness in the Second World War. The media, with very few exceptions, devoted its efforts to winning the war, not generally promoting the fortunes of individuals. That was largely due to Winston Churchill, the supreme war leader who dominated the scene in Britain, and indeed elsewhere. Perhaps remembering the bitter quarrels of the first war, he insisted on combining the three jobs of Prime Minister, Minister of Defence and Chairman of the Joint Chiefs of Staff in one person – himself. Of course he made some mistakes. But he was determined to obtain support from all sides of the political and military spectrum before embarking on any venture. He succeeded in concentrating all minds in Britain, including the media, on the single aim of winning the war. This was, perhaps, his greatest single achievement.

---

1. Bray, The Relationship between the Government and the Media in Time of War, thesis, Downing College, Cambridge, 1984, p. 19
2. Pronay and Spring, *Propaganda, Politics and Film 1918–45*, London, Philip Taylor, Macmillan, 1982, p. 25

3. Stammers, *Civil Liberties in Britain during the Second World War*, Croom Helm, p. 137
4. Collier, *The Warcos*, London, Weidenfeld and Nicholson, 1989, p. 8
5. Bray, The Relationship between the Government and the Media, p. 27
6. McIntyre, *The Expense of Glory – a life of John Reith*, London, Harper Collins, p. 251
7. Marvell and Fraenkell, *Doctor Goebbels*, London, Heinemann, 1960, p. 72
8. Ibid., p. 217
9. Ibid., p. 127
10. *War Report from D-Day to VE-Day*, London, BBC Books, 1991, p. 18
11. Hickman, *What did you do in the war Auntie?* London, BBC Books, p. 31
12. *War Report*, p. 13
13. Bray, The Relationship between the Government and the Media, p. 36
14. Hickman, *What did you do in the war Auntie?*, p. 106
15. Ibid., p. 205
16. Ibid., p. 166
17. *War Report*, p. 49
18. Collier, *The Warcos*, p. 1
19. Bray, The Relationship between the Government and the Media, p. 51
20. Conversation with Lady Graham
21. Collier, *The Warcos*, p. 49
22. Hickman, *What did you do in the war Auntie?*, p. 70
23. Pronay and Spring, *Propaganda, Politics and Film*, p. 175
24. Ibid., p. 176
25. Ibid., p. 201
26. Ibid., p. 183
27. Stammers, *Civil Liberties*, p. 152
28. W. Churchill, *The Second World War*, London, Penguin, p. 56
29. Ibid., p. 568
30. *War Report*, p. 9
31. Ibid., p. 11
32. Collier, *The Warcos*, p. 178

CHAPTER FIVE

The Asian Connection: Korea and Vietnam

KOREA

'The attack upon Korea makes it plain beyond all doubt that Communism has passed beyond the use of subversion to conquer independent nations and will now use armed invasion and war. It has defied the orders of the Security Council of the United Nations issued to preserve international peace and security.'

Statement by President Truman issued on 27 June 1950

The war of 1939–45 had one facet which was at once easy to grasp and incontrovertible: in its essence it was a simple matter of good versus evil, with few moral complications. There were, of course, moral difficulties, seen in retrospect if not at the time, in the way it was fought, for instance in the bombing of Dresden and Hiroshima. However, to those on the allied side, there was no problem in justifying fighting against the supremely evil Nazi regime and the barbaric cruelties of the aggressive Japanese. As we have seen, the media, both in Britain and the United States, was virtually unanimous in its unwavering support in principle for the governments of both countries in their determination to bring about the defeat of their enemies by force of arms.

The aftermath was not so simple. Roosevelt, at Yalta, had not seen the Russians as any great threat to the postwar world: indeed, he had been more concerned about British colonialism. As they saw it, the Americans had, twice in twenty-seven years, played a large, if not dominant, part in saving the world from barbarism. Particularly in the Second World War they had suffered considerable casualties in men and treasure and they hoped, and expected, to enjoy the fruits of peace for the indefinite future under the auspices of the United Nations organization which they had played a large part in establishing. They set up the Marshall Plan in order to help the war-ravaged Europe to recover. There was, understandably, a feeling of satisfaction in the United States and its media at the end of the war.

Then, the worst began to happen. As the United States saw it, Russian Communism began to threaten the very world stability which the Americans had hoped to create by their massive and costly efforts. The absorption of Czechoslovakia into the Soviet bloc in 1948, the threat to Berlin resulting in the Berlin airlift, a whole range of Soviet-led or inspired threats to the Western way of life and, then, above all, the success of the Communists in China led by Mao Tse-tung against the American protégé Chiang Kai-shek led to a deep fear in the United States of what they saw as a monolithic Communist conspiracy to take over the world. NATO was formed in Europe and the Truman doctrine greatly assisted stability in Greece and Turkey. There was no equivalent in Asia where it looked very possible that Chiang Kai-shek would be ousted from Formosa, the large offshore island into which he had been unceremoniously bundled. An anti-Communist hysteria began to rage in the United States, stoked by the demagogic antics of Senator McCarthy who was beginning his evil witch-hunt against those accused of Communist sympathies. Large sections of the media and public opinion felt that the Truman administration was not doing enough to counter the Communist threat in the East, although it was not clear precisely what it ought to be doing.

The crunch was to come in Korea. After a turbulent history as an area over which China, Russia and Japan vied for dominance, Korea was finally occupied by a Japanese army in 1905 and became a Japanese protectorate. At the Cairo Declaration of December 1943 Roosevelt, Churchill and Chiang Kai-shek had promised the eventual unity and independence of the country. This had been reaffirmed at the Potsdam Declaration of 26 July 1945, Russia adhering to it on entering the war against Japan on 8 August 1945. However, on the Japanese surrender the United States and Russia agreed to divide the country between them for occupation purposes and that the dividing line would be the 38th parallel. Russian troops arrived very quickly and occupied the whole of North Korea, surprisingly, in the light of subsequent events, not crossing the line to the south. American troops did not arrive until about a month later, beginning on 8 September.

All attempts to unify the country with free elections failed. The

Russians in the North installed as President Kim Il Sung, a member of the Communist underground in Korea as early as 1935, and a Red Army major. The Americans, in the South, presided over the coming to power of Dr Syngman Rhee, the best known of all Korean leaders. After a farcical election, in which 589 people were killed and 10,000 were 'processed' at police stations, Syngman Rhee was installed as President of South Korea on 15 August 1948.[1]

Both regimes were oppressive dictatorships which countenanced no opposition worth the name, with that in the North exceeding the South in efficiency and ruthlessness.

The Russians organized, trained and supplied an extremely effective North Korean army of seven divisions ready for combat, three other newly activated divisions, two independent regiments and an armoured brigade.[2] The South Korean army set up by the Americans consisted of eight divisions, but it was little more than a constabulary force with little training and it lacked artillery, tanks and aircraft. The American advisers were absurdly optimistic about its chances were war with the North to come. The *New York Times* of 30 May 1950 reported the head of the American military mission as saying that the threat of attack from North Korea was virtually eliminated because of the South Korean army.[3] The Russians withdrew their forces from North Korea by December 1948. General MacArthur was the Commander of the United States Pacific Forces and, on his advice, the Americans withdrew their occupying force by 29 June 1949. Indeed at this stage the Americans did not perceive the Korean peninsula as possessing any material strategic interest for them. In September 1947, General Eisenhower, Admiral Nimitz and General Spaatz had submitted a memorandum to the effect that, 'The joint Chiefs of Staff consider that, from the standpoint of military security, the United States has little interest in maintaining the present troops and bases in Korea'. In February 1949 MacArthur had publicly excluded Korea (and Formosa) from the American defence perimeter.

Throughout this period, not surprisingly, little interest was shown by the press, either in Britain or the United States, in the course of events in Korea. For a start, it was a very long way away from Britain and any direct British strategic interest in its affairs was difficult to discern. As far as the United States was concerned, media interest in the area was concentrated on, first, the Communist victory in China and, then, on the threat to Chiang Kai-shek in Formosa.

The shock was enormous, therefore, when North Korea invaded the

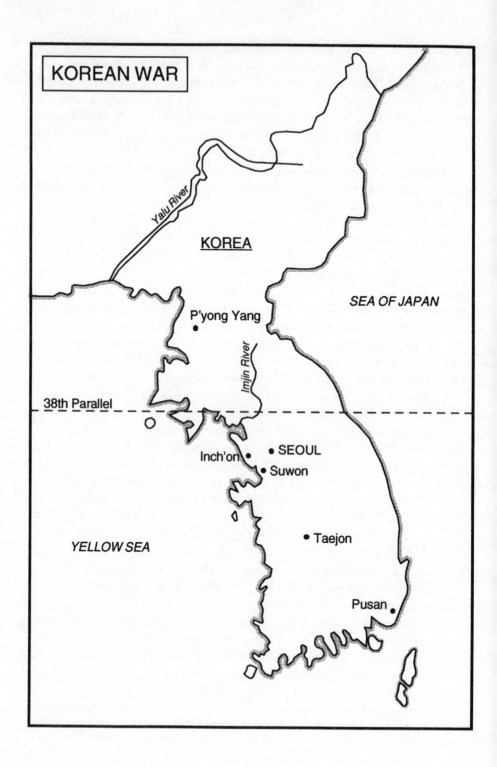

South on 25 June 1950. Predictably, the Communist world argued that the fighting was in retaliation for Southern attacks on the North and, indeed, there was evidence that Southern troops had crossed the 38th parallel on several occasions and even penetrated as far as 2½ miles into North Korean territory in May 1949.[4] However, the scale and intensity of the onslaught made it immediately clear that the North Korean intention was to take over the whole of South Korea and absorb it into a single Communist-led country. There can be no doubt that the attack was made with both Chinese and Russian acquiescence. It is also probable that neither country expected the American response which, although initially not strong in substance, was surprisingly rapid and firm in execution. In his memoirs Khrushchev makes it clear that Kim Il Sung told Stalin shortly before the attack that the whole affair would be over very quickly and that Mao Tse-tung expected the Americans to allow the Korean people to decide their future for themselves.

In fact, Truman saw the attack as a major turning-point in postwar history: if the Communists were not resisted and defeated here, their advance elsewhere would be inexorable, probably eventually leading to another world war. Having taken advice from his Secretary of State, Dean Acheson, and his Chiefs of Staff, he immediately added Formosa to MacArthur's zone of responsibility – MacArthur's headquarters was in Japan. He then moved the Seventh Fleet to the area between Formosa and China and told MacArthur to provide the maximum military supply assistance he could to the South Koreans and to evacuate all Americans from the country. Without authorization from Congress, an omission seized on by the Republicans much later, he then instructed MacArthur to use sea and air power in support of the South Koreans and, finally, to send ground troops to Korea to take part in the fighting. In parallel with these acts the Americans obtained two resolutions by the Security Council of the United Nations on 25 and 27 June, the latter calling on the members of the United Nations to: 'furnish such assistance as may be necessary to repel the armed attack and to restore the international peace and security in the area.'

Thus, for the first time in history, a worldwide international body had voted for force to be used against aggression. The voting was of some interest (*For* – the United States, Britain, France, Nationalist China, Cuba, Ecuador and Norway. *Abstaining* – Egypt and India. *Against* – Yugoslavia). Russia, which could have vetoed the resolution, was absent from the vote in protest against the presence in the United Nations of Nationalist rather than Mainland China, thus committing one of the greatest, if not *the* greatest unforced error in international politics this century. Gromyko, the Russian Foreign Minister, argued that, under the Charter of the United Nations, an absence from the vote meant that the required 'unanimity' of the Permanent Members for a Security Council resolution involving the use of force was lacking and that therefore the Russian absence was tantamount to a contrary vote, or veto. The Americans, however, were able to refute this by pointing out that the Russians had insisted to the contrary on two previous occasions. In fact Truman's order to MacArthur to fight the North Korean forces with air and naval units preceded the second Security Council resolution by a few hours.

As a result of the vote, American intervention took place under the auspices of the United Nations and a surprising number of countries provided troops of one sort and another. As well as the United States and South Korea, troops were eventually provided by Britain, Australia, Canada, New Zealand, Turkey, the Philippines, Thailand, Holland, Ethiopia, Colombia, Belgium, Greece, South Africa and France. The Indians, the Scandinavians and the Italians provided medical units. Eventually fifty-three out of fifty-nine members of the UN in 1950 approved the second Security Council resolution. The Communists had clearly miscalculated.

The American media, and nation, were immediately vastly supportive of the action. On 30 June the *New York Times* praised Truman's 'momentous and courageous act' under the headline: 'Democracy Takes Its Stand.' There were a few rumblings – the US *Daily Worker*, the *Wall Street Journal* and the *Chicago Tribune*, in a surprising alliance, opposed intervention in another foreign war. However, in general, there was great enthusiasm in the media and right across America, high, low and middle, for what was seen as overdue resistance to the Communist threat. Joseph Harsch of the *Christian Science Monitor* on the morning after the announcement of American intervention wrote: 'I have lived and worked in and out of Washington for twenty years. Never before in that time have I felt such a sense of relief and unity pass through the city.'[5] On 28 June the *New York Herald Tribune* said:

The President has acted and spoken with a magnificent courage and terse decision. This newspaper is convinced that the American people, bewildered and baffled by so many retreats, so many arguments, so many fine-spun fears and suspicions, will respond with a sense of fine relief verging on enthusiasm.

The feeling in Britain was equally near-unanimous in the media and Parliament alike. Michael Foot, no less, wrote in the left-wing journal *Tribune* that for Britain to decline to participate in United Nations' action would be 'an act of appeasement'. In a leading article on 28 June *The Times* wrote: 'After the bitter experience of the past 35 years, salvation is dependent on prompt and effective measures to resist aggression wherever it may occur.' On 29 June it went on: 'Neither side wants a major war and when the British and American moves are seen by all to be effective as well as resolute the probability of preserving the wider peace should be strengthened.'

There was some slight opposition, however; the *New Statesman*, although conceding North Korean aggression, argued that the invasion had 'given American Imperialism just the opportunity it desired'.[6] The House of Commons was almost unanimous in its enthusiastic approval of the British support of the United Nations, only four Labour left-wingers (Sydney Silverman, Tom Driberg, S.O. Davies and Emrys Hughes) opposing it. Churchill, the Leader of the Opposition, fully supported Attlee, the Prime Minister, in his decision to vote in favour of the Security Council resolution and to pledge British military aid. There was a general feeling, both in the United States and Britain, that the advance of Communism had to be checked somewhere and Korea was it.

A bizarre note was struck in the House of Commons when a Major Roberts (Conservative) asked:

> In view of the very grave situation if the North Korean Government refuses to consider this resolution [by the Security Council calling on it to withdraw] will the Prime Minister advise his representatives at the United Nations to ask for the use of the atomic bomb [loud cries of 'Oh!'] – certainly upon the capital of North Korea?

The Speaker responded: 'That is bound to be hypothetical and is therefore out of order.'

The war itself ebbed and flowed with remarkable and sometimes alarming changes of fortune. The initial North Korean onslaught swept all before it, routing the poorly led, badly equipped and unmotivated South Koreans and sweeping aside those American units which did manage to arrive on the scene, finally reaching the area of Pusan in the extreme south of the peninsula, where the Americans established an enclave. The Americans managed to hang on there, with the help of the two British battalions – the 1st Middlesex and the Argyll and Sutherland Highlanders – that had arrived from Hong Kong in time. Then MacArthur, with great skill and daring – the approaches to the beaches were extremely dangerous with a tide ranging between 23 and 32 feet – successfully landed a force at Inchon, near Seoul. This threw the North Koreans off balance. An advance from Pusan was made, Seoul was recaptured and the advance was continued until the 38th parallel was reached again at the end of September 1950.

At this point a decision had to be made whether or not to pursue the retreating North Koreans over the parallel and up to the Yalu River, the North Korean/Chinese border. In retrospect, Truman said:

> What we should have done was to stop at the neck of Korea . . . that's what the British wanted . . . we knew that the Chinese had close to a million men on the border and all that . . . but [MacArthur] was the commander in the field. You pick your man, you've got to back him up. That's the only way a military organisation can work. I got the best advice I could and the man on the spot said that was the thing to do . . . so I agreed. That was my decision – no matter what hindsight shows.[7]

The parallel with the Gulf War forty years later was in this respect almost exact. Here was a man (Kim Il Sung/Saddam Hussein) who had blatantly attacked his neighbour and had been defeated. Were his armies to be allowed to retreat behind their own lines, there to regroup under the same leadership which would suffer no penalty for the wrong that had been committed in the face of condemnation from the United Nations? President Bush in 1991 was not seduced by these arguments for a variety of reasons. He stopped the war. Under the great pressure of MacArthur's personality, however, Truman allowed the advance to continue. In the event, ignoring strong evidence that the Chinese were about to attack – on 24 November the CIA warned of 'major offensive operations' – MacArthur continued his headlong advance up to the Yalu and when the Chinese flooded over the border his armies collapsed for the second time. MacArthur's vainglorious personality had found him out and his overconfidence led to disaster. The *New York Herald Tribune* accurately called the offensive 'an invitation to disaster'. In December the Chinese again crossed the 38th parallel, retook Seoul and advanced to the south. As a result of all this the American war aim shifted, in practice if not in official terms, from the unification of Korea to the restoration of the *status quo ante.*

Before the Korean War the American army had been allowed to deteriorate to a remarkable degree. Military expenditure had been drastically reduced and combat training was slight. The troops MacArthur had available in Japan were under-strength, under-trained, under-equipped and certainly not ready to fight. This became clear in the early stages of the war. Their success in holding on to the enclave at Pusan was due as much to the extreme length of the Communist communications and the difficulties they had in resupplying their armies as it was to American military prowess, although some units did fight well. The Chinese invasion, too, catching as it did the Americans and South Koreans totally off balance, led to some discreditable actions by American units which found themselves under vicious attack by the Chinese hordes. At this stage the Commander of the American 8th Army, General Walker, who was becoming tired and dispirited, was killed in a car accident and General Ridgway was appointed as his successor, arriving on 26 December. His new and inspiring leadership changed the atmosphere as remarkably as Montgomery's had in Egypt in the past and Templer's was to in Malaya in the future. The Americans defeated the Chinese south of Seoul, recaptured the capital and advanced up to the area of the 38th parallel once more. Here they stopped when the Russians and the Chinese suggested ceasefire negotiations. Both sides dug in and a very bloody period of fighting ensued, lasting from July 1951 to 27 July 1953, when a ceasefire was eventually agreed after considerable resistance from Syngman Rhee. Indeed, even in the short period of July to November 1951 the United Nations suffered almost 60,000 casualties, 22,000 of these being American. The Chinese had procrastinated during these two years, using, mainly, the fate of the prisoners of war on both sides as a bargaining lever. There were bloody disturbances in the POW camp for North Korean prisoners in the South. Many of them refused to return to the North, leading to vicious reprisals from hardline Communist prisoners and a total loss of control by the prison guards for a period. On the other side, 38 per cent or 2,730 of the 7,190 US prisoners died in captivity. The Chinese eventually agreed to the ceasefire probably partly because of the death of Stalin and the consequent thaw of the Communist's position and partly because of the perceived threat of the American atomic bomb.

In May 1952 the Joint Chiefs of Staff recommended direct air and naval operations against China and Manchuria including the use of nuclear weapons and the Russians were told about this.[8] The Americans initiated a massive aerial bombing campaign against North Korea, destroying every worthwhile industrial target, flattening the capital Pyongyang and other cities and killing thousands of civilians in the hope that this would cripple the North Koreans both militarily and politically and make them grant concessions at the conference table – a mistake they would repeat in Vietnam. If anything the bombing strengthened rather than weakened the North Korean resolve. It certainly did not interdict the flow of North Korean supplies to their army. In spite of a massive bombing campaign on northern supply routes, by December 1952 the Communists had been able to increase and supply their forces in Korea, consisting of 1,200,000 men in seven Chinese armies and two North Korean corps.[9]

What part did the media in the United States and in Britain play in all this? The answer is – not much. There were of course periods of intense media interest, particularly in the United States during the period before and after MacArthur's dismissal (see below) and during the election campaign of 1952, and in Britain after the stand of the 'Glorious Gloucesters' in April 1951. However, in general, as was reportedly said by Hal Boyle, an American war correspondent, Korea was the worst reported war of modern times.[10]

There were various reasons for this. There was of course no universal television to bring scenes of agony or glory into the living-room. There were 10,000 sets in the United States in 1941; at the time of the Korean War television film technology was still relatively in its infancy and there were 10 million television sets in the United States in contrast to the 100 million towards the end of the Vietnam War. As far as Britain was concerned, Korea was a far-off country of which we knew very little. There were considerable difficulties for correspondents in transmitting their copy. In the first weeks of the war there were fifteen regular correspondents filing from Taejon, the temporary American headquarters south of Seoul, where there was only one telephone in the UN information office for their use. During the rest of July 1950 there was a single army radio telephone circuit shared by the army, the UN Commission and the correspondents.[11] Initially there was no censorship but correspondents were asked to prevent the North Koreans from gaining strategic or helpful information.[12] This was strictly enforced – Tom Lambert of the AP and Peter Kisher of the UP were both banished on grounds that they gave aid and comfort to the enemy in writing about an army battalion which became dubbed 'the lost battalion'. In January 1951 MacArthur resorted to actual censorship.

While the initial media reaction in Britain had been very supportive of the American action, during the autumn of 1950 this began to crumble. After Truman, on 30 November, had hinted at the possibility of using the atom bomb there was acute alarm on all sides of the British political and media spectrum and Attlee, the Prime Minister, with Churchill's support, crossed the Atlantic to see Truman in order to convey the British alarm. The British had doubts about the American attitude towards China and were worried about the intentions of the flamboyant and increasingly aggressive MacArthur. There were also grave worries, largely initiated by the media, about the behaviour of the South Korean Government, army and police toward its own people. The devastation caused by the prodigal use of American firepower at the recapture of Seoul had appalled R.W. Thompson, who covered the war for the *Daily Telegraph* in the autumn of 1950: 'The slightest resistance brought down a deluge of destruction blotting out the area.' The direct assault on the capital under the cover of massive air and artillery bombardment was seen by many correspondents to be totally unnecessary: an enveloping movement by ground troops could have produced the same result, they thought, without the devastating cost in civilian life and property. Thompson and other correspondents also drew attention to the appalling atrocities carried out by the South Korean police and army. An especially well-known correspondent, James Cameron, working for the *Picture Post*, sent a well-documented story about one particular atrocity to his editor only to have it rejected by the proprietor, Edward Hulton. This led to the resignation of the editor and much publicity. Cameron had written:

I had seen Belsen, but this was worse. This terrible mob of men – convicted of nothing – untried, South Koreans in South Korea, suspected of being 'unreliable'. There were hundreds of them; they were skeletal, puppets on string, faces translucent grey, manacled to each other with chains, cringing in the classic Oriental attitude of subjection, the squatting foetal position, in piles of garbage . . . Around this medievally gruesome market place were gathered a few knots of American soldiers photographing the scene with casual industry.[13]

The American press, too, reported Southern atrocities. One of the few cases of mass execution that reached the Western press (and was universally accepted as having been carried out by his [Rhee's] forces) took place at Kochang in the South. There some six hundred civilians, women, children and men, were herded into a ditch and mown down by machine gun fire – on the grounds solely of being suspected of being Communist.[14]

As a result of the publicity given to South Korean atrocities the killing of women and children did stop, but the execution of political prisoners continued. North Korean atrocities, which continued throughout and were probably at least as appalling as those of the South, if not more so, were hardly reported at all. Communism does not tolerate criticism.

As far as the United States was concerned, there was considerable feeling, widespread but particularly among Republicans, that the greatest power on earth should not have its hands tied behind its back. MacArthur should be allowed to use whatever means he liked, including atomic weapons and attacks on China, in order to defeat the Chinese Communists once and for all. The concept of a limited war, adopted by Truman's administration, was not popular. A bitter debate raged in the United States about policy in Korea. On 8 December 1950 a Gallup poll found 49 per cent of respondents disapproving of Truman's leadership.[15]

Although attempts were made to paper over their differences, including a heavily publicized meeting in Guam, Truman and MacArthur were in fact at loggerheads: MacArthur did not accept Truman's policy of limited war. He made this clear in private and in public to the point of challenging the Presidential authority over foreign policy and defence matters. The final touch came when MacArthur, in a letter to a Senator (Martin), publicly called for Chiang Kai-shek's forces to be allowed to land on the mainland, exactly contrary to the administration's policies. He had gone too far and, in spite of his massive prestige, Truman, the 'haberdasher's assistant', sacked him on 11 April 1951. MacArthur returned to the United States in a blaze of publicity. His speech to a joint session of Congress drew enormous media attention. A Gallup poll indicated that only 29 per cent of its sample supported the President and when MacArthur paraded through New York he was greeted by 7 million people. Previously the biggest welcome had been for Lindbergh in 1927 after his return from Paris. The amount of paper cleared up after the parades was as follows – Lindbergh 1,750 tons, MacArthur 3,249 tons.[16] However, support for MacArthur was not as strong as might have been supposed from these figures. Congress did not support him and, greatly to their credit, many newspapers, including the *New York Times* and the *Herald Tribune*, supported the President on constitutional grounds.

There was widespread relief in most of the Western world. *The Times* of 12 April 1951 said:

No general of modern times wielded the power and influence of General MacArthur. None has been stripped of his powers more suddenly or more completely. The great proconsul who yesterday had his armies in the field and held all the islands of Japan as his realm is given leave to issue one more order, and that order will be to the transport that takes him, as a retired officer, to a place of his own choosing. . . . Once again the quiet-mannered man from Missouri, the unassuming civilian who is always belittled by his critics at home, has cut his way through a grave crisis by a decisive act of political courage.

Opposition to the Democrats because of the defeats suffered by the American army, high taxation due to the war and general frustration at American impotence, however, continued at a high level. The mid-term elections in November 1950 were a disaster for Truman's administration and the Presidential election of November 1952 saw Eisenhower resoundingly victorious, in part due to his promise to end the war and to go to Korea in person.

There was one great basic difference between the criticisms by the American media of the military conduct of the Korean War and then, later, of the Vietnam War. In the case of Korea the critics attacked the administration for not being more aggressive, carrying the war to China and, even, using atomic weapons. In the case of Vietnam, as we shall see, the pressure was for less aggression and, indeed, there was a strong lobby in the latter stages of that war for the United States to cut its losses and get out. It might well be argued that the eventual outcome in Korea, the apparently permanent division of the country rather than, as in Vietnam a Communist takeover, was in part due to the different bargaining positions which the attitudes of the American media and public opinion in general gave their negotiators. The long negotiations which eventually ended each war had totally different conclusions: South Korea remained anti-Communist; South Vietnam did not. The danger to the Communists in Korea was of American escalation of the conflict; in the case of Vietnam the American people wished to get out and the Communists knew that. There were of course many other factors differentiating the Korean and Vietnam struggles but, clearly, the American *amour propre* was not to suffer such a devastating blow in Korea as it did later with the obvious defeat of its armed forces in Vietnam. Max Hastings quotes a senior American veteran of both Korea and Vietnam as saying: 'We went into Korea with a very poor army and came out with a pretty good one. We went into Vietnam with a pretty good army, and came out with a terrible one.'[17]

In the three years of hostilities 1,319,000 Americans served in the Korean theatre and 33,629 were killed. Proportionately, in terms of the length of the war, casualties were higher than in Vietnam. The British Commonwealth (Britain, Canada, New Zealand and Australia) had 1,263 killed. (The British lost three times as many dead in Korea as they did in the Falklands conflict.)

The United States did not learn much from its many mistakes in Korea. In neither Korea nor Vietnam did it bother to attempt to understand the psychology of those it sought to defend. In both cases it propped up corrupt regimes, it relied far too much on air power and it failed to understand that Nationalism, not Communism, was an important motive force of its enemies. The media also was, in general, guilty of all these errors, some of which were, perhaps, the inevitable legacies of American history with its obsession with its own, as compared to anyone else's, dream.

The British press, public opinion and Government were also, on the whole, united in their approach: support for the initial measures but worried about the dangers of the Americans finishing up by fighting a full-scale war against the Chinese, perhaps even leading to a world conflict. British press, public opinion and Government were certainly united in their relief when Truman sacked MacArthur: R.W. Thompson in the *Daily Telegraph* attacked him for his assumption of 'a kind of divinity'. The Labour left continued to oppose the Americans, the well-known left-wing intellectual, G.D.H. Cole arguing that the conflict was a civil war in which he supported the North.

However, even in retrospect, the Korean War cannot be seen as a total failure of American policy or of its armed forces. As Max Hastings puts it:

Who can doubt that if Hanoi had been defeated South Vietnam would today enjoy the same affluence as South Korea and its people at least a greater measure of freedom than they can look for under Communism. If the Korean War was a frustrating, profoundly unsatisfactory, experience, more than thirty years later it still seems a struggle that the West was right to fight.[18]

However, the stalemate in Korea was very far from being the end of the matter. Indeed it could be said that the same conflict in Asia (the Americans and their protégées versus the Communists) resumed some ten years later and this is probably how the history books of the future will see it. Certainly through the eyes of American policy-makers it was a continuation of the same struggle.

VIETNAM

Each new administration obliged to deal with Indo-China seemed to become more deeply drawn into the morass.

Henry Kissinger[19]

There can be few wars in history which have given rise to so many, often diametrically opposed, opinions as to origin, course and outcome among the pundits, political, academic and military as has Vietnam. 'Facts' can be produced to support almost any thesis. The view put forward by all six American Presidents who concerned themselves with the area (Truman, Eisenhower, Kennedy, Johnson, Nixon and Ford) and their administrations was that the United States intervened first to help the French and, later, various South Vietnamese governments in order to avert a takeover by a predatory Communist party based in the North and aided by the Russians and Chinese. In February 1950 National Security Council Document 64 had concluded that Indo-China was a 'key area of South East Asia and is under immediate threat'. The well-known Domino Theory was formalized in 1952 in a further National Security Council document which argued that the loss of even a single South-East Asian country would lead 'to relatively swift submission to or an alignment with Communism by the remainder'. The document went on to say that in the longer term an alignment with Communism would in all probability progressively follow in India and the Middle East (with the possible exception of at least Pakistan and Turkey).

In the official American Government view South Vietnam was invaded by the North, aided by guerillas in the South (the Viet Cong), subverted, armed and led by the Northern Communists.

A contrary view, held by many American intellectuals was the following:

The United States supported the French war of conquest; overturned the political settlement arranged at Geneva in 1954; established a

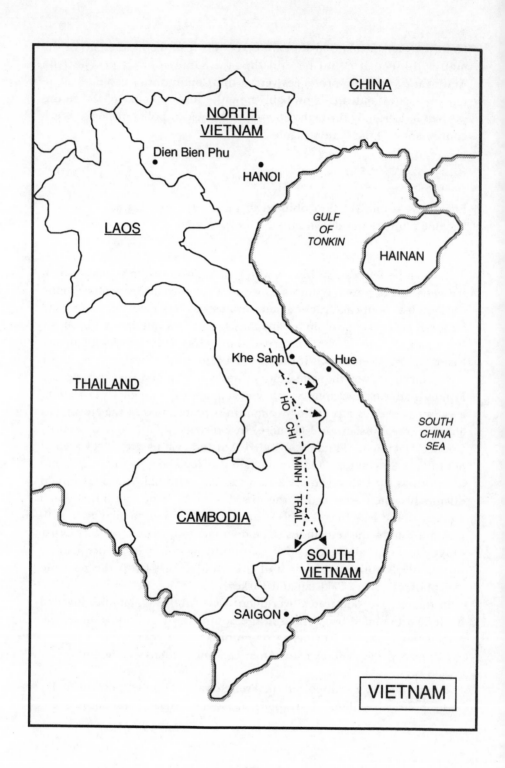

terrorist client regime in the southern sector of the country divided by foreign (i.e. US) force; moved on to open aggression against South Vietnam by 1962 and worked desperately to prevent the political settlement sought by Vietnamese on all sides; and then invaded outright in 1965, initiating an air and ground war that devastated Indo-China.[20]

In the continuing argument, figures can be and are bandied about with the utmost abandon. Kissinger states:

After the French collapse the Communists were preoccupied with establishing their system of government north of the 17th parallel, a task they pursued with characteristic savagery, killing at least fifty thousand people and putting another hundred thousand into the concentration camps. Some eighty thousand to one hundred thousand Communist guerillas moved north while one million North Vietnamese fled to South Vietnam.[21]

The American historian, Gabriel Kolko, states:

The United States in Vietnam unleashed the greatest flood of fire power against a nation known to history. The human suffering was monumental. . . . 'Enemy' killed were 850,000 minimum and a substantial part of these were civilians.[22]

Referring to the Diem regime in South Vietnam, which was established after the defeat of the French, Nixon states:

South Vietnam under Diem was substantially free, but by American standards not completely free. The mark of irresponsible reporting is that it blows events out of proportion. It achieves drama by exaggeration and its purpose is not truth but drama. The shortcomings of Diem's regime, like other aspects of the war, were blown grossly out of proportion.[23]

Kolko, on the other hand, states:

Though exact numbers are unknown, a conservative estimate (of Diem's regime) is forty thousand political prisoners in jails by the end of 1958 and twelve thousand killed during 1955/57 . . . A patina of legality for oppression was provided in August 1956 in Ordinance 47, strengthened in Law 10/59 in May 1959, which made being a 'Communist', or working with one, a capital offence.

He goes on to talk of 150,000 political prisoners by the end of 1961.[24]

Even the outcome of the war is disputed. Nearly all commentators agree that the Americans lost the war. Herman and Chomsky, on the other hand, argue that the United States, despite not reaching its 'maximal goals in Indo-China . . . did gain a partial victory'.[25] They substantiate this by making the point that the United States did avert the threat of the operation of the Domino Theory by teaching the lesson that a war of liberation is costly and dangerous.

Then, to take the state of the American army. This was recorded by John Colvin, the British Consul General in Hanoi 1965–7, in a book written after his retirement, possibly with some exaggeration. Having noted the progressive reductions of the American troop strength from January 1969 onwards he goes on to say: 'During these years (1969–72) the US military effort was further diluted by drug use, disobedience, cowardice, misconduct, desertion, murders of officers and NCOs, and confrontation between blacks and whites.'[26]

General Westmoreland, the American commander, on the other hand, talks about 'high morale of the American units in Vietnam'. He also says: 'I am convinced that the United States never fielded a more professional force than in South Vietnam during the years 1966–69.'[27] Of course, as Westmoreland says, morale suffered when it became clear that the Americans were pulling out – but could the former situation possibly have changed to the latter in so short a time?

The war in Vietnam can conveniently be divided into seven phases: first, the struggle between the French and the Communists from 1945 to the French defeat at Dien Bien Phu in May 1954; second, the Geneva Accords of July 1954 and the rule of Diem, the American-supported President of South Vietnam, until the loss of American confidence and his assassination in November 1963; third, a series of eight coups changing the leadership in the South, culminating in the accession to power of Thieu, as American involvement increased and President Johnson's decided to send American ground troops to Vietnam in March and June 1965 leading to full-scale participation by land, sea and air; fourth, the Tet Offensive by the Communists in February 1968, followed by Johnson's withdrawal from the Presidential race and a call for negotiations; fifth, Nixon installed as President in January 1969, a phased withdrawal of American troops and attempts to strengthen the South Vietnamese army which defeated a Northern attack in 1972; sixth, the escalation of the bombing including attacks on Cambodia and massive bombardment of the North while negotiations proceeded, very slowly; finally, the signing of the Paris Accords in January 1973, followed by vetoes by Congress on American aid to the South and a massive attack by the North leading to total Northern victory in April 1975.

What can observers make of all this and what impact did the American media have on the continuing tragedy, because tragedy it undoubtedly was for all concerned? There is one point of general consensus. The Vietnam War had a profound and lasting effect on the whole gamut of American life. It punctured once and for all the concept of American omnipotence. In spite of a massive economic and conventional military advantage the Americans were not able to defeat their enemy. It also added greatly to the divisions already apparent in American society – in particular the argument over the lack of racial equality. The generation of the Sixties in the United States seized on Vietnam as evidence of what they deemed to be the cynical, selfish and overbearing attitude of their parents' generation. It is often argued, plausibly, that the activities of the anti-war demonstrators on the university campuses and elsewhere had the effect, not of turning Americans against the war, but the opposite, because of the general dislike of middle America for what was seen as unpatriotic long-haired posturing and, later, blatant lawbreaking.

An American scholar put it as follows:

Common sense suggests that it is one thing to tell average Americans that their Government has made a mistake, quite another to tell them, as anti-war movement radicals did, that their lives are empty, their values criminal, and everything they cherish as worth loving and protecting is the scourge of mankind. Common sense is joined with much data, which suggests strongly if not conclusively that the war would have been more unpopular than it was, sooner than it was, among a broader and more politically salient segment of the American people had radical led protests not occurred. Public opinion data we have indicate that the antics of the anti-war movement deterred more Americans from opposing the war sooner because they were afraid of the company they would keep by so doing.

He goes on to make the point that: 'the liberal New York columnist, James Reston, argued that lawless demonstrations are not promoting peace but postponing it. They are not persuading the President or Congress to end the war but deceiving Ho Chi Minh and General Giap into prolonging it.'[28]

There are also strong arguments to the contrary, that President and Congress alike were greatly concerned about the fragmentation of American society over Vietnam and the anti-establishment bias of much of American youth, let alone the massive and near universal protest movements, peaceful and militant, which pervaded American life. It is argued that it was these protests, and the massive media coverage of them, which, through their continuing impact on every corner of American life, led to the American withdrawal from Vietnam.

Be that as it may, the alienation of the Sixties generation, whatever direct effect it had on the war itself, was certainly a factor in the developing American social scene, and its repercussions can still be seen in the greater care, certainly as regards domestic opinion, which American Presidents now evidence when approaching the possibility of armed conflict.

The overwhelming fact, of course, was that Vietnam was the first television war. The daily newspapers, weekly magazines and columnists of one sort and another undoubtedly had a great effect on public opinion. However, it was the television which brought the war, for the first time, right into the American living-room. Reading about death and destruction is one thing: actually seeing it with your own eyes is quite another. Since the Civil War the United States had not seen conflict in its own country. Unlike in Europe, war had taken place at one remove. Bombs landed not on American but on other people's towns. The cinema brought with it an air of unreality – John Wayne and, in the past, Errol Flynn – not real people and real events. But this was for real.

Comfortable middle-class America was deeply affected by the reality of pain, fear and anguish. The two best-known images, of the summary execution of a Communist by the Police Chief in Saigon in 1968, and of a little girl fleeing, naked, from a napalm attack during the 1972 Communist offensive, even though neither incident actually involved any direct American action, seared deep into the American consciousness.

The media provided the prime, and at times the only, source of information on which public opinion was formed in the first place. Of course, politicians made speeches but, apart from a few Presidential pronouncements, it was the media which decided when and how they should be presented. Returning soldiers told their stories and those who did not return were a stark and tragic reminder of the harsh realities of war. However, the vast majority of the public was conditioned day by day through the media alone.

There can be no possible doubt, for instance, that Walter Cronkite, the anchorman on *CBS News*, and other figures of his ilk, had an enormous effect on public opinion. As so much of what officialdom had said over the years was clearly not true (the constant assertion that there was light at the end of the tunnel and that the war was about to be won), the public yearned for what they saw as a disinterested sensible person who would explain to them what the truth was in a highly confused situation. Cronkite and his fellow anchormen supplied this need. When Cronkite returned from a visit to Vietnam he appeared on television on 27 February 1968. Having described the new refugees living in sheds and shanties in unbelievable squalor, estimated at 470,000 in addition to the 800,000 already officially listed as refugees, he said:

It seems now more certain than ever that the bloody experience of Vietnam is to end in a stalemate. This summer's almost certain stand off will either end in real give and take negotiations or terrible escalation; and for every means we have to escalate, the enemy can match us.

These remarks really alarmed the White House. President Johnson is reported to have said: 'If I have lost Walter, I have lost middle America.'[29]

Walter Lippman, the world famous American columnist, said on 23 September 1959 at a lunch at the National Press Club:

If the country is to be governed with the consent of the governed, then the governed must arrive at opinions about what their governors want them to consent to. How do they do this? They do it by hearing on the radio and reading in the newspapers what the corps of correspondents tell them is going on in Washington and in the country at large and in the world. Here we perform an essential service. In some field of interest we make it our business to find out what is going on under the surface and beyond the horizon, to infer, to deduce, to imagine and to guess, what is going on inside and what this meant yesterday and what it could mean tomorrow. In this we do what every sovereign citizen is supposed to do, but has not the time or the interest to do it for himself. This is our job. It is no mean calling, and we have a right to be proud of it and to be glad that it is our work.[30]

This was said, of course, before the Vietnam saga got under way as far as the United States was concerned but the point remains valid. It was the media in Vietnam whose job it was to 'find out what is going on under the surface . . . what this meant yesterday and what it could mean tomorrow'. The administration had its own problems and was certainly not going to do it for them. The questions, therefore, are: What was the corps of correspondents in Vietnam at the time? What experience did they have and how were their views formed?

There was no censorship in Vietnam. Unlike in most other wars this century there was no requirement for an official imprint before a report could be sent back to the United States or wherever and broadcast in one form or another to the world. Some correspondents actually wished that there had been some form of censorship, including Drew Middleton of the *New York Times* who said: 'On three trips to Vietnam I found generals and everyone else far more wary of talking to reporters precisely because there was no censorship.'[31] By its very nature the war was extremely difficult to report. There was no 'front line' to be visited, no clear measure of territory held or lost, no obvious gauge of success or failure. For most of the time it was very dangerous for reporters to move around (thirty were killed and twenty-three listed as missing) and in nearly every case transport could only be obtained as a favour from the military authorities. It was much easier to stay in Saigon, to go to the daily official briefing, sit on the terrace of the Hotel Continental Palace in Saigon, exchange gossip and ogle the girls passing. Even if a reporter did venture outside Saigon in an attempt to get at the action, he could not know if what he saw was typical or had any meaning outside its immediate environs. These difficulties were added to by the propensity of editors at home to tailor their stories to fit in with a line agreed on in the safety and comparative tranquility of editorial conferences thousands of miles away from the action. As far as television pictures were concerned, these had to be sent by air to Japan for onward transmission to the United States.

On top of all this many of the reporters, inevitably because of the dearth of knowledge of South-East Asia in the United States, were very inexperienced and often young. Martin Bell, for instance, later famous in

Bosnia and elsewhere said of his time in Vietnam: 'I was very inexperienced and I don't think I was getting anywhere near the reality of what was going on.'[32]

In fact in the early stages of the Vietnam saga, the American media did not take a great deal of interest in events. The battle of Dien Bien Phu, and the departure of the French, culminated in the establishment of the Diem regime in the South supported by President Kennedy's decision to increase the level of military aid and advisers (to 6,000 in May 1962, then to 16,000 by the end of 1963). Kennedy's policy of preventing South Vietnam from 'going Communist', without all out US intervention, was on the whole supported by the American press.

There was some unease at the contrast between what the press was told in official briefing about Diem's efforts against the Viet Cong and what they were able to find out on the ground but, although the administration resented what they saw as 'negative reporting', there was no major upset and there was little if any dissent from the principle of intervention, albeit at one remove. In mid-1964 there were only twenty-odd American and other foreign correspondents in Saigon.[33] However, towards the end of that year, the election (Johnson versus Goldwater) led to an intensification of political debate. The incident where American destroyers were allegedly attacked – some said that the 'attackers' were flying fish picked up on the radar – by the North Vietnamese led to the Gulf of Tonkin resolution of August 1964 where Congress accepted almost unanimously the following:

Whereas naval units of [North Vietnam] . . . in violation of international law, have deliberately and repeatedly attacked United States naval vessels lawfully present in international waters . . . and whereas these attacks are part of a deliberate and systematic campaign of aggression . . . against its neighbours . . . the United States is, therefore, prepared, as the President determines, to take all necessary steps, including the use of armed force, to assist any member or protocol state of the South East Asia Collective Defence Treaty requesting assistance in defence of its freedom.

This gave Johnson what he, unlike many others in Congress and elsewhere, saw as a carte blanche for any action against the Communists in Vietnam he chose to take at any time in the future. Johnson, throughout the affair, tried to play down the scale and intensity of

American intervention and he never really confronted Congress or public opinion with the decisions which had to be taken. He was afraid that his vision of a 'Great Society', which he hoped would be his legacy to the American people, would be subsumed or obscured in the bitterness and costs, material and human, of the full-scale war he was hoping to avoid. As Dean Rusk, his Secretary of State, said:

> Since we wanted to limit the war, we deliberately refrained from creating a war psychology in the United States. We did not try to stir up the anger of the American people in Vietnam and we did not have military troops parading through our cities or put on big war bond drives. Neither did we send movie actors across the country whipping up enthusiasm for the war . . . we tried to wage this war as calmly as possible treating it as a police action rather than as a full scale war.[34]

There were repercussions to this subterfuge. Johnson's failure to achieve unequivocal and public support for his actions, later to be much criticized by the media and politicians alike, undoubtedly led to the cautious and meticulous approach, as far as public opinion was concerned, which was shown by Bush and Clinton in the Gulf and Bosnia.

Of all the key moments in the conflict, perhaps the greatest turning-point was when President Johnson committed US ground troops to Vietnam in March 1965 – in fact originally to protect American air bases. From that moment on, the American troop commitment increased astronomically from a figure of 81,400 in July 1965 to 543,400 in April 1969.[35] At the same time of course the number of US troops killed in action escalated very roughly in proportion: totals, 509 (to July 1965), 30,568 (to 31 December 1968) and 58,191 (to January 1973). With this real American commitment came, not surprisingly, an escalation in the number of American press reporters in Vietnam. From a total of twenty-odd American and other correspondents in Saigon in mid-1964, accreditations of press correspondents accelerated to no less than 464 in January 1968, of which 179 were American.[36] Keeping even one reporter in Saigon was an expensive business by the time his or her local expenses had been paid and the reports sent to the United States. The newspapers and television channels which had sent them there clearly, therefore, expected a reward in the form of news items. There was constant pressure for correspondents to justify their expenses and to produce newsworthy reports. Particularly in the case of television there was a hunger for 'drama'. Furthermore, the drama had to be presented as in some way typical of what was happening.

An example of this was when CBS showed a film of US Marines using cigarette lighters to ignite thatched huts in the hamlet of Cam Ne in retaliation for Viet Cong fire. In his commentary on this the CBS correspondent Morley Safer said the following:

> The day's operation . . . wounded three women, killed one baby, wounded one marine, and netted these four prisoners. Four old men who could not answer questions put to them in English. Four old men who had no idea what an ID card was. Today's operation is the frustration of Vietnam in miniature. There is little doubt that American fire power can win a military victory. But to a Vietnamese peasant whose home means a lifetime of back-breaking labour it will take more than presidential promises to convince him that we are on his side.[37]

Virtually all who saw this would have concluded that it was a typical example of how the American army was behaving. Of course there were similar incidents elsewhere, but it was not a typical act at the time and even if it had been it would have been impossible for the CBS correspondent to know this: one camera cannot be everywhere in a vastly confused and confusing situation. It was the dramatic effect, not the representativeness, of the incident which attracted the news editor of CBS to show it.

There were, however, incidents of disgraceful behaviour by American servicemen. The major atrocity story of Vietnam was not in fact originally discovered or reported by the media. In April 1969 a former soldier who had served in Vietnam wrote to the Department of the Army and other officials alleging a massacre of Vietnamese civilians in March 1968 at a hamlet of the name of My Lai. Investigations were immediately started and a number of servicemen including a brigade commander were court martialled for various offences. These were all acquitted except for Lieutenant Calley who was convicted of the murder of over 100 civilians, sentenced to dismissal from the service and to hard labour for life (subsequently reduced to ten years). This story, quite rightly, occasioned great worldwide media interest and horror, adding to rising doubts about the conduct of the war.

Until mid-1967 or so there was no common media line on the war. There were doves (the *New York Times*) and hawks (*Time Magazine*) although even this is only a rough generalization of what was an ever-shifting scene in Vietnam and the United States. By the autumn of 1966 the media was producing increasingly sceptical reports about the progress of the war. Neil Sheehan wrote an article for the *New York Times Magazine*, 9 October 1966, entitled 'Not a dove but no longer a hawk', in which he said that during his first tour of Vietnam as United Press international reporter from 1962 to 1964 he had believed in basic US aims. However, after his second tour as the *New York Times* reporter in 1965–6 he realized that he had been 'naïve in believing that non-Communist Vietnam could defeat the Communist insurgency and build a decent and progressive social structure'.[38] As Barbara Tuchman put it:

Reports of American fighting methods written by correspondents in chronic antagonism to the military were reaching home. Americans who had never before seen war now saw the wounded and the helpless and the melted flesh of burning children, afflicted thus by their own countrymen.[39]

A new phenomenon appeared during the Vietnam War – to be repeated with significant differences during the conflict in the Gulf – namely, war reporting from the enemy's capital. Harrison Salisbury of the *New York Times* reported from Hanoi and was much criticized for repeating enemy propaganda, particularly during the later bombing of North Vietnam. In his book *Mauve Gloves*, after describing a particular American bombing raid, Tom Sharpe says the following:

The North Vietnamese [were] blessed with a weapon that no military device known to America could ever get a lock on. As if by magic . . . in Hanoi . . . appears . . . Harrison Salisbury writing in the *New York Times* about the atrocious American bombing of the hard scrabble folks of North Vietnam in the Iron Triangle.[40]

These reports undoubtedly added fuel to the fire of rising protest.

In fact American public opinion was, perhaps surprisingly, slow to shift. In August 1965 a Gallup poll showed there was still approval for the way Johnson was handling the situation in Vietnam by 57 per cent who approved to 27 per cent who disapproved. It was not until the end of

1967 that more Americans opposed the decision to send troops to Vietnam than supported it – a trend that increased until the troop withdrawal of January 1973, at which time the ratio was 2 to 1.

General Westmoreland, the American military commander in Vietnam, at the behest of the Government, travelled to Washington in April and July 1967 to tell Congress and the American people that progress was being made. Johnson, throughout, refused to call up the reservists, unlike Truman at the time of the Korean War, and his policy of trying to avoid the war becoming a major issue in order the better to concentrate on domestic reform was at that stage still being moderately successful in spite of the efforts of a steadily more vociferous anti-war movement.

The second, and probably the decisive major turning-point came with the Tet Offensive in February 1968. The North Vietnamese leadership decided to make a major move in the war at the time of the Chinese Lunar New Year (Tet), partly because it was hoped that the South Vietnamese would be off their guard: indeed, a ceasefire had been announced. The plan was to attack virtually all the South Vietnamese towns simultaneously with a major incursion by North Vietnamese regular troops. It was hoped to win a series of victories leading to a general uprising of Communist sympathizers in the South, particularly in the rural areas. The action began with a siege of the US military base at Khe Sanh by North Vietnamese regulars. This was followed by a simultaneous attack by the Viet Cong, helped by North Vietnamese elements, on all South Vietnamese cities and thirty-six of the forty-four provincial capitals.

In the event, the result was certainly a Communist defeat if the criterion taken is the number of combatants killed. The Communists lost something in the order of 37,000 killed and 5,800 captured, about half of those committed, whereas the Americans lost only 1,001, and the South Vietnamese and allied forces 2,082. At only one town, Hue, did the Communists hang on to any area for an appreciable time – 1,000 North Vietnamese regular soldiers captured the citadel and held it for twenty-six days. The Americans responded with heavy air and ground artillery attacks, reducing much of the city to rubble. They took similar action against two other towns, My Tho and Ben Tre, where the celebrated, but unsubstantiated, remark was reported to have been made by an American colonel: 'We had to destroy the town to save it.'

The overwhelming fact, however, was that there was no general uprising. The siege of Khe Sanh was lifted. The whole Viet Cong position in the South was crippled for a long time to come. The North Vietnamese leadership reckoned, certainly initially, that the offensive had been defeated. However, the impact of the Tet Offensive in the United States itself was vastly different: 'Before Tet editorial comments by television journalists ran nearly four to one in favour of administration policy; after Tet two to one against.'[41]

The event with the greatest impact was the showing on television of some Communist sappers actually inside the American Embassy grounds in Saigon. Television pictures and news reports of this incursion had an enormous effect in the United States. The future General Colin Powell, at the time a student at the Command and General Staff College, Fort Leavenworth, recalls:

> The morning of February 1st 1968 I came out of the bedroom, put on the coffee pot and turned on the TV news. I was stunned. There on the screen were American GIs fighting on the grounds of the US Embassy and ARVN (South Vietnamese) forces battling for the Presidential Palace in the heart of Saigon. The Viet Cong, supported by North Vietnamese army units, had launched a coordinated strike against 108 of South Vietnam's provincial and district capitals. When I went to class that day the atmosphere was one of disbelief as if we had taken a punch in the gut. Fighting over the next few days continued to be fierce and twenty-six days passed before Hue was liberated. By then, the lovely former capital where I had served lay in ruins, with at least 2,800 of its people executed by the enemy. . . . The images beamed into American living-rooms of a once faceless enemy suddenly popping up in the middle of South Vietnam's capital had a profound effect on public opinion. Tet marked a turning-point, raising doubts in the minds of moderate Americans, not just hippies and campus radicals, about the worth of this conflict, and the anti-war movement intensified.[42]

In fact, the attack on the American Embassy was a very minor affair compared with events elsewhere, but it was witnessed in one way or another by very many correspondents based in Saigon and therefore was given enormous coverage. It also had, of course, a major symbolic value – the heart of the American war effort in Vietnam was actually under physical attack. The nature of the war with its lack of a front line meant that newsmen were unable, even if they had so wished – and many did –

to present a balanced view of the offensive, certainly in the early stages. The shock was colossal. Only a short time before the American people had been told by their President, no less, that the war was approaching its end and here was concrete evidence that this assertion was simply not true. Some of the media did try, later, to put the offensive in some kind of sensible context – but by that time it was too late.

The impact was even greater because 1968 was an election year and Johnson was being challenged for the Democratic leadership not only by Senator Eugene McCarthy but also by Robert Kennedy, both on an anti-war platform. The media seized on the Tet Offensive as a potent weapon in the anti-Johnson stance that much of it had decided to take.

Many of the reports appearing in the American press were simply not true. The *Washington Post* in its first edition of 31 January 1968 carried an eight-column page 1 banner headline:

Vietcong Seize Part of US Embassy
Building Re-taken in Fight

Saigon January 31st – The Viet Cong brought their largest offensive of the war to the US Embassy in Saigon early today. Guerrillas seized part of the building and held it against attacking American military policemen and paratroops. At least ten of the policemen were killed and several more were wounded, US officials said. The Americans finally regained control of the building by launching an assault from helicopters they landed on the roof of the eight storey building. Parts of the building had been held by the enemy for six hours . . . At the Embassy, opened only months ago and said to be proof against attack, American officials said they believed that an enemy suicide squad of about twenty men were holed up in the compound on part of the first floor of the building itself . . . At 7 a.m. according to the Associated Press, the fighting was still swirling around the building. Reporters were being kept at a distance.

Almost every detail of this report was false. In fact, some Communist sappers managed to get into the Embassy grounds but never got into the Embassy itself. The report was amended slightly later but the real truth did not emerge until a few days afterwards. Many newspapers had similar reports. On television the NBC's Chet Huntley said:

The Viet Cong seized part of the United States Embassy in Saigon early Wednesday Vietnam time. Snipers are in buildings and on rooftops near the Embassy and are firing on American personnel inside the compound. Twenty suicide commandoes are reporting to be holding the first floor of the Embassy.

Reporters also sensationalized the fighting in Khe Sanh which many of them reported as another Dien Bien Phu (where the French were defeated and eventually surrendered) in the making. The two situations were in fact totally different and there was never any real danger of American defeat in Khe Sanh. The problem was that the American media had undoubtedly been misled so often in the past that it was reluctant to believe anything it was told by official sources, and denials only served to intensify speculation.

There is considerable controversy, still, about the role of the media during and after the Tet Offensive. Undoubtedly, Tet, partly because of media distortions, had a vast effect on American opinion of all shades and as a result the decision was taken, consciously or unconsciously, to withdraw American troops from Vietnam. As Colin Powell put it: 'We were in a war against an enemy who believed in his cause and was willing to pay the price, however high. Our country was not; yet it took our government five more years to get out.'[43] As Charles Douglas-Home, the Defence Correspondent of *The Times*, put it on 1 February 1968: 'The main thing which the latest Communist offensive in Vietnam seems to prove is that South Vietnam would almost certainly collapse were it not for the presence of American forces in the country.'

It was reported in *The Times* on 6 February that even the Young Conservatives came out strongly for America to withdraw: 'An elephant will never kill a mosquito.' On the next day the same newspaper reported that ninety-one Labour backbenchers had signed a motion calling on Wilson to stand by the anti-American resolution on Vietnam passed at the '67 Labour Party Conference. And on 9 February a *Times* leading article stated: 'The charge that the people, if not the President, have been misled is becoming articulate in even the blandest of journals and news media.'

Nevertheless, although the hope that the South Vietnamese would be able to fend for themselves with American material assistance remained, there was no question of the Americans sending troops back to Vietnam once they had left, whatever happened. Nixon, who came to power on the heels of Johnson's decision not to stand in 1968, hoped for what he called 'Peace with Honour', but that remained a hope rather than a viable policy. Whether the result would have been the same if the media had not greatly exaggerated the damage to the American and South Vietnamese armies will never be clearly established. (Indeed, a further thought is whether things would have been the same if the American command had instituted a policy of censorship rather than the free-for-all that existed.) One thing is certain: in a confused situation like that obtaining in Vietnam, it is too much to expect the media, and particularly the television, to produce balanced, sane and sensible reports on which sensible objective judgements can be made by the public. The temptation to dramatize, to generalize from one or two selected incidents, to criticize for the sake of criticism, or to scoop a rival by a story true or false is too great. There were many splendid correspondents, fearless seekers after truth, but the odds were stacked against them and the truth did not emerge, if at all, until long after the event – too late to correct the false impressions that were undoubtedly often given.

To say that is not to argue, as some Americans, particularly among the military, do, that the Americans might have 'won' and that it was only the media's stab in the back that turned victory into defeat. The truth is, in retrospect, that the Vietnam War was probably doomed from start to finish to end as it did, with an ignominious American withdrawal and the defeat of the South Vietnamese Government. Even if the Americans had not made the many mistakes they undoubtedly did, as spelt out by McNamara, the American Defence Secretary, in his remarkable acknowledgement of eleven major errors,[44] outside intervention was most unlikely to help in an internal struggle between an ideology, however flawed, on the one side and a series of corrupt self-seeking regimes on the other.

Nixon's victory in the election of 1968 led, as has already been stated, to a search for Peace with Honour. A series of secret and some not so secret negotiations ensued with the objective of securing a situation in which Thieu's regime would be able to retain power in the South without direct American troop involvement. By 1972, the United States had unilaterally withdrawn 500,000 troops. During Nixon's first term (1968–72) the Communists continued their attacks on the South, mainly with the use of North Vietnamese regular troops – the Viet Cong never really recovered from their losses at Tet. Nixon escalated the air war, attacking North Vietnamese bases in Cambodia and Laos, increasing the scope of his bombing of North Vietnam, including, eventually, direct attacks on Hanoi and the mining of Haiphong harbour. The very considerable air effort which included defoliation agents and napalm as well as conventional high explosives had two aims. First, to help the South Vietnamese army in its continuing struggle and to disrupt the Ho Chi Minh trail through Laos and Cambodia. This had some success. With American assistance from the air the South Vietnamese defeated a major North Vietnamese attack in 1972. And, secondly, to put pressure on North Vietnam to grant concessions at the negotiating table. This was not so successful.

The American media, by this time, was sceptical of almost any Vietnam initiative taken by the administration and continued to press for peace. Negotiations between the Americans and the North Vietnamese stuttered fitfully as the slaughter of North Vietnamese peasants and others by massive American air attacks continued, adding to the guilt-laden frustrations of large sections of American public opinion fuelled by a media most of which had come to the conclusion that the United States should never have entered the fray in the first place. Congress, which had voted for the Tonkin resolution almost unanimously, now took a very different view. In 1972 Congress voted $2 billion in aid to South Vietnam. This was cut to $1.4 billion in 1973 and it was halved again in January 1974.

The negotiations eventually led to the Paris peace accords of January 1973 which, among other matters, provided that North Vietnam would not renew infiltration of the South. Nixon had told Thieu, the South Vietnamese President, in a private letter that: 'if Hanoi fails to abide by the terms of the agreement, it is my intention to take swift and severe retaliatory action.'[45] However, the Communists took not the slightest notice of the agreement and continued these attacks without any hesitation. Nixon was unable to fulfil his pledge because Congress passed a bill setting 15 August as the date for the termination of US bombing in Cambodia, requiring Congressional approval for subsequent US military action in any area of Indo-China.

Thus, as Nixon saw it, he and his successor Ford were unable to carry out their obligations to their ally. This was undoubtedly also in part because of Nixon's problems with Watergate. The Russians poured large amounts of military supplies into the North throughout 1974, much of which found its way to the Viet Cong. When the North made a full-scale attack in 1975 the Southern army collapsed and the whole of South

Vietnam was quickly occupied by the end of April, Saigon becoming Ho Chi Minh City. The collapse was partly due to the cutting off of American military equipment but, perhaps to a greater extent, to the loss of morale of the Southern army and the increase of Northern morale occasioned by what both sides saw as the desertion of the South by the United States.

As Nixon saw it: 'Vietnam was lost, not because of a lack of power, but because of failure of skill and determination at using power.' He blamed this in part on Johnson's administration:

> They misled the public by insisting we were winning the war and thereby prepared the way for defeatism and demagoguery later on. The American people could not be expected to continue indefinitely to support a war in which they were told victory was round the corner, but which required greater and greater effort without any obvious signs of improvement. . . . The public had been so misinformed and misled by unwise Government actions and the shallow inflammatory treatment of events by the media that morale within the United States collapsed just when the North was overwhelmingly defeated on the battlefield. We won a victory after a long hard struggle, but then we threw it away. . . . The war making capacity of North Vietnam had been virtually destroyed by the bombings in December of 1972 and we had the means to make and enforce a just peace, a peace with honour. But we were denied these means when Congress prohibited military operations in or over Indo-China and cut back drastically on the aid South Vietnam needed to defend itself.[46]

Nixon adds:

> As *Newsweek* columnist Kenneth Crawford observed, this was the first war in our history during which our media were more friendly to our enemies than to our allies. American and South Vietnamese victories such as the smashing of the Tet Offensive in 1968 were portrayed as defeats. The United States whose only intent was to help South Vietnam defend itself, was condemned as an aggressor. The Soviet-supplied North Vietnamese were hailed as liberators.[47]

Be that as it may, the fact was that the American people, even if the media had not turned against continuing intervention, could not have been expected to continue indefinitely a war which was costing them so much in lives and economic resources when the connection between the security of the United States and the continuance in power of an anti-Communist regime in South Vietnam was not at all clear.

Certainly the Domino Theory did not work: other South-East Asian countries did not become Communist as a result of the 'fall' of South Vietnam. The ultimate irony is that the opposite may now be happening. The collapse of Communism in Europe may be followed by a similar metamorphosis in the new Vietnam. As the left-wing American historian, Gabriel Kolko, sadly put it:

> That a Marxist/Leninist party should extol the virtues of being rich, while ignoring the historical origins and consequences of wealth, utterly devalues the relevance and utility of its founding ideology. By 1985 its new commitments had begun to erode all that it had accomplished since 1945.

He goes on: 'The Communist party has largely capitulated to its former enemy's premises about economics and human motivations for material acquisitions. And this abdication poses the greatest dangers.'[48]

So was the whole American confrontation with Communism in Asia a tragic fuss about nothing? Certainly at the time of writing the South Koreans would not see it in those terms. Nor would the South Vietnamese boat people. Nor, probably, would most of the media which, very naturally, defends itself fiercely against those who blame it for the American defeat in Vietnam. Some bias and distortion by the media, partly engendered by reaction against vastly over-optimistic official pronouncements, there certainly was. The very nature of the beast makes this inevitable and the greater power of television to influence, if not to lead, public opinion certainly increased its impact. At the end of the fighting in Korea, the media turned out to be a hawk; in Vietnam, a dove. This undoubtedly had an effect on the interminable negotiations which eventually led to the end of each war – stalemate in Korea, defeat for the Americans in Vietnam. Why this basic change of attitude took place is not altogether clear, but it is probably something to do with the passage of those twenty or so years. Vietnam was twenty years further away from the Second World War experience. A new generation had emerged with a very different outlook on life from that of its parents.

1. Max Hastings, *The Korean War*, London, Papermac, 1993, p. 33
2. David Rees, *Korea, the Limited War*, London, MacMillan, 1964, p. 17
3. Michael Emery, Dissertation for the University of Minnesota, 1968
4. Hastings, *The Korean War*, p. 38
5. Ibid., p. 58
6. Rees, *Korea, the Limited War*, p. 143
7. Ibid., p. 151
8. Hastings, *The Korean War*, p. 393
9. Ibid., p. 279
10. Trevor Royle, *War Report*, London, Mainstream, 1987, p. 177
11. Emery, p. 335
12. Ibid., p. 336
13. Halliday and Cummins, *Korea, the Unknown War*, London, Viking, 1988, p. 92
14. Ibid., p. 146
15. Hastings, *The Korean War*, p. 222
16. Rees, *Korea, the Limited War*, p. 227
17. Hastings, *The Korean War*, p. 413
18. Ibid., p. 426
19. Kissinger, *Diplomacy*, New York, Simon and Schuster, 1994, p. 649
20. Herman and Chomsky, *Manufacturing Consent*, New York, Pantheon, 1988, p. 192
21. Kissinger, *Diplomacy*, p. 636
22. Gabriel Kolko, *Anatomy of a War*, New York, The New Press, 1994, p. 200
23. Richard Nixon, *The Real War*, London, Sidgwick and Jackson, 1980, p. 102
24. Kolko, *Anatomy of a War*, p. 89
25. Herman and Chomsky, *Manufacturing Consent*, p. 245
26. John Colvin, *Volcano under Snow* (a life of General Giap), London, Quartet, 1996, p. 256
27. Westmoreland, *A Soldier Reports*, New York, De Capo Paperback, 1976, pp. 297, 299
28. Garfinkle, *Tell-tale Hearts*, New York, St Martins Press, 1995, pp. 13, 19
29. Barbara Tuchman, *The March of Folly*, London, Cardinal, 1990, p. 440
30. *Conversations with Walter Lippman*, Boston, Little Brown, 1960, p. ix
31. Knightley, *The First Casualty*, London, Purnell, 1975, p. 423
32. Hooper, *The Military and the Media*, Gower, p. 111
33. Braestrupp, *Big Story*, New Haven, Yale University Press, 1977, p. 6
34. Summers, *A Critical Analysis of the Gulf War*, Pennsylvania, Strategic Study Institute, 1981, p. 10
35. Robert McNamara, *In Retrospect*, New York, Times Books, 1995, p. 321
36. Braestrupp, *Big Story*, p. 10
37. Ibid., p. 39
38. McNamara, *In Retrospect*, p. 259

39. Tuchman, *The March of Folly*, p. 415
40. Tom Wolfe, *Mauve Gloves*, pp. 42, 44, quoted by Summers, *On Strategy: The Vietnam War in Context*, Pennsylvania, Strategic Studies Institute, 1981, p. 24
41. Hallin, *Uncensored War*, quoted in Herman and Chomsky, *Manufacturing Consent*, p. 202
42. Colin Powell, *A Soldier's War*, London, Hutchinson, 1995, p. 122
43. Ibid., p. 128
44. McNamara, *In Retrospect*, p. 321
45. Nixon, *The Real War*, p. 116
46. Ibid., pp. 119, 120, 123
47. Ibid., p. 115
48. Kolko, *Anatomy of a War*, pp. 581, 599

CHAPTER SIX

Suez, 1956

'Ship me somewhere East of Suez, where the best is like the worst
Where there aren't no Ten Commandments, an a man can raise a thirst.'

Kipling

The Suez episode or military action – call it what you will – of autumn 1956 took place of course before the Americans became deeply embroiled in Vietnam and long before their eventual defeat there. We thought it important, though, to deal with Korea and Vietnam in one chapter since both conflicts were part of the same problem – the American confrontation with Communism in Asia. This chapter is, therefore, not in historical order.

The British experience at Suez, however, has great similarities in one important way to the American experience in Vietnam. In both countries, the actions proved to be watersheds in their people's conception of themselves and of their role in the world. At Suez, the British learnt about the limitations of their power in the postwar world. After Vietnam, the Americans had to accept precisely the same fact of life.

Anthony Nutting, the Minister of State at the Foreign Office who resigned at the time of Suez, said in a preface to his book that Kipling's lines about the Boer War were very appropriate to Suez:

Let us admit it fairly as business people should
We've had no end of a lesson, it will do us no end of good.[1]

Precisely the same could be said about the Americans and Vietnam.

Of course there were vast differences between the two affairs. In Suez the fighting lasted just a week compared to the years of the Vietnam nightmare. The casualties on both sides at Suez were minimal compared to the holocaust of Vietnam, and at Suez the East/West confrontation played only a supporting role in the drama. The levels were also very different: even after Vietnam the United States remained a superpower, able if she wished to exert her influence worldwide, whereas the British had to be content with secondary status. After Suez all dreams of Empire finally vanished.

In both cases, the victors in the 1939–45 war overestimated their capabilities and, in the end, however much it was dressed up as something else, both had to accept ignominious political, if not military, defeat.

The French, too, had hoped by their intervention to topple Nasser, who they thought was the main prop of their enemies, the rebels in Algeria. However, they learnt that their day in the Middle East was finally over. De Gaulle was not in power at the time of Suez but he supported the French action except, typically, for the French acceptance of a British Commander-in-Chief. However, on his return to power not long after the Suez debacle, he pulled France out of Algeria altogether. Had Nasser been toppled, that decision might have been very different.

At Suez, as we shall see, the Americans, under the leadership of Eisenhower and Foster Dulles, actively opposed Britain in what they believed to be an uncharacteristic and highly damaging aberration by the British Prime Minister Eden. They tried to prevent Anglo-French military action by every means at their disposal, including support for a highly critical motion in the Security Council of the United Nations which was vetoed by both Britain and France. Finally, they secured a ceasefire and the withdrawal of the Anglo-French forces by using to the full their economic muscle and forcing Britain to the verge of bankruptcy.

In the case of Vietnam, the British, although not happy with the American action did not feel able actively to oppose it in spite of the fact that during the Wilson Labour Government in Britain there was great pressure to do so. There were demonstrations in Trafalgar Square, and opposition to the American actions in Vietnam became part of the folklore of the sixties generation in Britain as elsewhere. The Americans asked Britain to send even a token military force to Vietnam and this was refused, but no governmental action was taken in Britain against the United States.

The fact of the matter was that Britain could not afford to upset the Americans: the Americans could afford to upset the British. Economic and political power may or may not corrupt; it certainly can be decisive.

The origins of the Suez crisis, like all crises, lay deep in the past. The failure to stop Hitler in his tracks long before 1939; the rise of Arab nationalism, and in particular of Egyptian nationalism after years of subordination to foreign powers; Nasser's violently anti-British propaganda in the Arab world; the bitter struggle between Israel and the Arabs; the deep American dislike and distrust of colonialism; British fading dreams of Empire; the French obsessive desire to hang on to Algeria as part of metropolitan France; Western reliance on oil for its economic survival: all these and other issues together with the existing Western–Communist worldwide antagonism came together to produce an explosive mixture waiting only for a spark to ignite it.

As Foreign Secretary to Winston Churchill, Eden had negotiated the Anglo-Egyptian agreement in October 1954 whereby the British withdrew their forces from the Canal zone. He had come under attack from the Suez group of Conservative MPs for unnecessarily abdicating British responsibilities in the area. All British troops were to leave by June 1956, and they did so. Colonel Nasser, who had assumed the office of Prime Minister of Egypt in April 1954 (he became President on 23 June 1956), had a vision of a united Arab nation under the leadership of Egypt. He initiated a highly successful propaganda campaign throughout the Arab world against Britain which he saw, rightly, as the main Western influence in the area. He needed arms to bring this about, in particular to use against Israel which he saw as an agent of imperialism and a permanent enemy of the Arab peoples. After attempting, and failing, to obtain arms from the United States he turned to the Soviet Union, signing a deal with that country in October 1955 for a considerable supply of arms (in fact they came from Czechoslovakia). This caused great alarm in Washington and London because of fears that Egypt would move inexorably into the Soviet camp. There was little the Western nations could do directly, however, and a scheme was hatched whereby a dam would be built at Aswan, a massive and very expensive undertaking of great potential economic benefit to Egypt, with American and British financial support. It was hoped thereby to wean Nasser away from Moscow and to secure him in the Western camp. Negotiations continued until 19 July 1956 when Dulles, the American Secretary of State, without consulting the British as to the timing of the move, suddenly withdrew the offer, arguing that public opinion in the United States had turned inexorably against the provision of large sums of money to a state which showed every sign of hostility towards the United States. Nasser was enraged. He retaliated on 26 July by announcing in a vitriolic speech that he was nationalizing the Universal Suez Maritime Canal Company. In fact the company was registered in France and its headquarters was in Paris. The concession under which it operated was due to expire anyway on 17 November 1968.

At that date the entire control and management of the Canal would have passed into the hands of Egypt but Nasser could not wait. He announced that the revenue from the Canal would be used to build the Aswan Dam: 'And we shall all work so that the Arab homeland may extend from the Atlantic Ocean to the Persian Gulf.' In fact at no stage did he close the Canal except to Israeli shipping.

The question of the legality of Nasser's action was, as appears often to be the case in situations of this kind, a matter for dispute by international lawyers. They argued about the exact terms of the Convention of Constantinople of 1888 between Turkey and the European powers of the day which stated: 'The Suez Maritime Canal shall always be free and open in time of war as in time of peace to every vessel of commerce or of war without distinction of flag.' In practice, however, the legalities of the matter became almost irrelevant. The action was clearly meant as a hostile blow to the Western world and, as such, it had an electric effect, particularly on the British Prime Minister, Anthony Eden, who happened to be hosting a dinner at Downing Street for King Feisal of Iraq who was on a state visit and his Prime Minister, Nuri es-Said, when the news arrived.

To a large extent the British action at Suez was the result of the state of mind of one man – Anthony Eden. A politician of great charm and enormous experience in foreign affairs dating back to his appointment in December 1935 as Foreign Secretary at the age of thirty-eight, as Prime Minister in 1956 he held a dominant position in his Cabinet. His Foreign Secretary, Selwyn Lloyd, although probably subsequently underrated, was not able to stand up to him. In the last resort, during those fateful days and weeks, what Anthony Eden said, went.

As a young man Eden had been a gallant soldier in the First World War. Like so many of his generation he was appalled at the thought of a recurrence of the horrors of Flanders as a result of the rise of Fascism in Italy and the Nazi Party in Germany. Like Churchill, but unlike many others, his reactions were not to appease but to oppose, and he resigned in February 1938 as Foreign Secretary because of Chamberlain's attempts to appease Mussolini. Later, he bitterly regretted his participation in the decision not to make a stand against Hitler's reoccupation of the Rhineland in 1936. He opposed Munich, however, and was held by Churchill as the 'one strong young figure standing up against the tides of drift and surrender'.

Churchill's insistence on remaining in office in spite of his physical and other disabilities after the election of 1951 until his eventual resignation in April 1955 resulted in a period of extreme frustration for Eden as the heir apparent. On becoming Prime Minister, Eden very quickly came under attack from the press, and particularly the Conservative press, for apparent indecisiveness. His honeymoon period was short. The Conservative *Daily Telegraph*, no less, demanded a Cabinet reshuffle in October 1955 and an article by Donald McLachlan, the paper's deputy editor, demanded the 'smack of firm government'. Eden was clearly extremely hurt by this, perhaps partly because he had the habit of smashing his fist into his open hand in order to emphasize a point and he saw the remark in acutely personal terms. *The Times* joined the attack in a leading article on 5 April 1956 under the title: 'Running In': 'In the ultimate analysis British politics is still largely the story of the success or failure of character. The Prime Minister has on occasions during the past year shown an unsureness of touch. There have been aberrations under strain.' The general ambience of prime ministerial weakness engendered by the press, combined with continued attacks by his Conservative colleagues of the Suez group, certainly had an effect on his state of mind: the Suez affair must have appeared to him to be an opportunity to show decisive leadership in the Churchillian mould. The press reaction to Eden's early record as Prime Minister, and in particular that of the *Daily Telegraph*, therefore, had a major impact on subsequent developments. When added to his deep and searing recollections of the results of appeasement in the 1930s, the apparent similarity to the situation he faced with Nasser and his belief that Nasser's whole attitude was undermining Britain's strategic position in the Middle East which was vital to our economic and political health, the mixture was explosive. His subsequent actions and their tragic denouement are, therefore, wholly explicable if not excusable.

Iverach MacDonald, the foreign editor of *The Times* who had known Eden since before the war and whom Eden clearly trusted and liked, went to see Eden at No. 10 Downing Street the day after the Nasser announcement. He reports that Eden was very calm and determined, saying that he could not tolerate Egyptian control of the Suez Canal and that Nasser must be made to disgorge it. He added that he was determined to keep in close touch with the French and, ironically as it turned out, with the Americans. He would try to solve the problem by negotiations but it might be necessary to use force as a last resort.[2]

In his memoirs Eden wrote:

In 1955, 14,666 ships passed through the canal. Three quarters of them belonged to NATO countries, and nearly one third were British. The Government determined that our essential interests in this area must be safeguarded, if necessary by military action, and that the needful preparations must be made.[3]

This is not the place to follow the complicated diplomatic manoeuvres which ensued. Eden had expected that the Americans would support tough action, but it quickly became apparent that they would do nothing of the sort. There have been suggestions that it was Foster Dulles, the American Secretary of State, who was the main influence in deciding the American line, against President Eisenhower's better judgement. However, that clearly was not the case: the President was equally opposed to the use of force by the British and French. They both saw the British action in terms of an outdated colonialism. In the earlier stages of the crisis Eisenhower left the detailed handling of the affair to Dulles, but in the later stages Eisenhower was very much in control. In fact, on 3 November, Dulles was taken to hospital suffering from cancer. Furthermore, an election was pending in the United States and Eisenhower did not wish to be involved, even as a distant supporter, in any kind of conflict when the election came. He was also worried about the possibility that the Soviet Union might become involved in hostilities leading to the danger of a Third World War. There was talk of Russian 'volunteers' appearing on the scene. His fears appeared to be justified later, when on 5 November the Russian Premier Marshal Bulganin sent a series of letters to Eden, Mollet, Ben-Gurion and Eisenhower demanding that the war be stopped and peace restored immediately. In his letter to Eden he referred to the possible use of 'modern destructive weapons' and 'rockets'. At this stage the Americans became really worried. They talked of a 'ring of steel' round Berlin. One of the authors of this book was, at the time, a member of a British Military Mission to the Soviet Army in Eastern Germany. He was sent out in a mission vehicle to find out whether the Russian army was mobilizing for war. It was not. They were securely tucked up in their barracks, probably as frightened as everyone else!

In the meantime, in August, Dulles began to produce a series of prevaricating strategies in order to postpone and eventually to avoid altogether the use of force by the British and the French. There were two conferences in London, in one of which Dulles proposed the formation of a users' association to run the Canal, a visit by Menzies, the Australian Prime Minister, to see Nasser and a series of meetings of the Security Council and the General Assembly of the United Nations in New York. Anthony Eden became more and more frustrated. It seemed to him that, like Hitler, the dictator Nasser was being allowed to get away with his illegal actions. As he saw it, this was the story of appeasement again, and it must be stopped.

Eden's worst fears were realized when Dulles finally came down in public unequivocally against the use of force. He destroyed all hope of a successful users' association when, without any consultation with Eden, he said: 'There is talk of teeth being pulled out of the plan, but I know of no teeth.'

According to Iverach MacDonald, who was in constant and close touch with Eden throughout the period, Eden reached the zenith of his fury when, on 2 October, Dulles publicly ascribed the British attitude to colonialism: 'In the NATO area Britain and France are at one with the United States. Outside, encroaching on the problem of so-called colonialism, the US is to be found playing a somewhat independent role.'[4]

When MacDonald went to see him, Eden was beside himself with rage: 'It was I who ended the so-called colonialism in Egypt' (to Churchill's misgivings and the Suez Group of Conservative MPs' fury he had abandoned the Suez base). 'And look at what Britain has done all over the world in giving the colonies independence.' MacDonald reports that Eden was angry too that Dulles should have come out publicly at such a critical time to impugn the motives of an ally: 'We have leaned over backwards to go along with him. And now look. How on earth can you work with people like that? It leaves us in an impossible position. We can't go on like this.'[5] He also drew attention to Dulles's own colonialist tendencies when, at the Geneva Conference on Vietnam after the French collapse at Dien Bien Phu, Dulles had asked Britain to join the United States in the use of force against North Vietnam and had been furious when Eden had refused to do so.

These remarks of Dulles were, according to MacDonald, the last straw for Eden and he decided that force would certainly have to be used. With the Americans in their present state of mind there was no hope of negotiating an acceptable solution. Britain and France would have to go it alone.

The rise of Arab nationalism over the years and the added impetus to this movement given by Nasser's accession to power had resulted in greatly increased resentment against Israel. Cross-border incursions were redoubled in scope and violence both from Egypt and Jordan. On 31 August 1955, an official communiqué from Egypt announced: 'Egypt has decided to despatch her heroes, the disciples of Pharaoh and the sons of Islam, and they will clean the land of Palestine.'[6] Israel had responded with venom. Tension was high and Israel had decided that some radical action was needed.

It was a great relief to Eden when two French emissaries came to see him in conditions of secrecy on 14 October and told him about a plan the Israelis had put to the French which seemed to him to offer a way out of the dilemma in which he found himself. Under this plan, if all three countries were agreed, the Israelis would attack Egypt. The British and French would immediately send an ultimatum to the Egyptians and the Israelis. The Egyptian Government would have to halt all acts of war, withdraw all its troops 10 miles from the Canal and accept temporary occupation of key points on the Canal by Anglo-French forces to guarantee freedom of passage through the Canal by vessels of all nations until a final settlement. Israel would have to halt all acts of war and withdraw all its troops 10 miles to the east of the Canal. Failing acceptance of this ultimatum by both sides Anglo-French forces would attack and seize the canal. After further meetings in Britain and France, one of which, held in great secrecy at Sèvres, a suburb of Paris, was attended by Selwyn Lloyd, this plan was agreed by all concerned and a document including precise timings and dates was signed on 24 October at Sèvres by representatives of all three nations. The British representative was Patrick Dean, the Chairman of the Joint Intelligence Committee.

Great efforts were made to keep this document, known subsequently as the Protocol of Sèvres, secret; Eden even ordered the destruction of the British copy. However, inevitably, both the French and the Israeli copies eventually leaked. There had been a danger that Israel might attack not Egypt, but Jordan, with whom Britain had a treaty by which British forces would have had to become involved. In the Sèvres document Israel agreed not to attack Jordan.[7]

The Israelis duly attacked on 29 October and, after the Anglo-French ultimatum was rejected as expected by the Egyptians, British and French air forces began to attack Egyptian airfields on 31 October. At one, much earlier, stage the plan had been to land at Alexandria and move to Cairo in order to replace Nasser,[8] but that had been changed to a landing at Port Said and the seizure of the Canal itself. Throughout, the French had been urging the British to be more aggressive. Indeed, they actively helped the Israelis: French aircraft were stationed on Israeli airfields.[9] They had, however, agreed that their forces should come under British command and the attacking force was a joint Anglo-French affair.

The nearest suitable port from which an invasion could be launched was Malta, some six days steaming away from Egypt, and there ensued a most embarrassing period after the air attacks had started before troops could actually land at Port Said. Eden explained to MacDonald that the convoy could not sail from Malta before the Anglo-French ultimatum. To do so would make it obvious that Britain and France had prior knowledge of the Israeli attack![10] During this time, opposition in the United States, the United Nations and the United Kingdom escalated in a frenzied crescendo. Parachutists landed on 5 November and the seaborne assault started on 6 November. The attack was immediately successful and British troops started to push their way down the Canal. However, succumbing to enormous pressure on all sides, including an American refusal to support the pound while the British reserves were being drained at an increasing rate, Eden and his Cabinet agreed a ceasefire as from midnight on 6 November.

The British battalion commander on his way down the Canal considered turning a Nelsonian blind eye to his orders but thought better of it. During the period leading up to the attack Eden had had some difficulties with his Cabinet, in particular with Butler and Monckton, but he had managed to avoid any overt split. Macmillan had been particularly aggressive and had supported the operation apparently without any reservations. However, it was he, as Chancellor of the Exchequer, who insisted on the ceasefire, arguing that the economic facts of life left Britain no option.

Most unfortunately, the British and French action coincided with the Russian attack on Hungary, thus adding to the general furore and giving the opponents of the operation an additional argument, to the effect that the Anglo-French action had acted as a spur, smokescreen or excuse for the far more venal and sinister Russian action. Continued American pressure succeeded in enforcing a total Anglo-French withdrawal phased with the introduction of a small United Nations force. The last British troops left on 22 December.

The Canal remained under Nasser's control. The first British ships passed through the Canal on 19 April 1957. As with the Domino Theory in Vietnam, the fears which gave rise to the action in the first place were not, in the event, realized. The Egyptians did not use their hold on the Canal to strangle the British or any other Western economy.

When the Canal was nationalized the British press reacted with almost unanimous fury. The *Daily Herald,* a Labour supporter, talked of 'No more Adolf Hitlers' and 'There is no room for appeasement'. On 30 July the *Daily Mirror* said: 'Remember Benito Mussolini? Mussolini ended hanging upside down.' The Liberal *News Chronicle* said that the British Government would be fully justified in taking retaliatory action. The *Daily Mail* suggested the immediate reoccupation of the Canal zone. The *Daily Telegraph* compared Nasser to Hitler and the *Daily Express*'s editorial included the following:

President Nasser's proposal to grab the Suez Canal should surprise nobody. It is an act of brigandage which follows naturally from what has gone on before: the scuttle from the Suez base; the American decision, supported by Britain, to give no money for the Aswan Dam; and the very nature of Nasser's Government which owes its existence to hatred of the Western Powers . . . Is Britain going to tolerate this new arrogance? With each act of surrender to Nasser the task of resistance has become harder.

The reference to Eden's 'scuttle from the Suez base' and other remarks of this nature must have strengthened his resolve not to continue to be branded with appeasement.

The Times was also vociferous. On Friday 27 July its first leader said: 'It [nationalization of the Canal] is a clear affront and threat to Western interests besides being a breach of undertakings which Egypt has freely given and received in recent years.' On 28 July, under the heading: 'Time for Decision', the first leader said: 'The truth is that Colonel Nasser's Government has such a bad record in such international dealings that it can be relied upon to use its control of the Canal as an instrument of blackmail.' And on 1 August the editorial, under the headline: 'A Hinge of History', warned of the threat to the West's interests throughout the Middle East if Nasser were allowed to get away with it. It also warned of the dangers of 'legal quibbles about the legality of Nasser's act'.

The editor of *The Times,* Sir William Haley, was on holiday with Lord Astor, the owner, on a yacht in the Mediterranean when the Canal was nationalized, and *The Times*' leading article was written by Iverach MacDonald. Haley and Astor were worried about the line MacDonald would take and were greatly relieved when they heard on the BBC World Service of *The Times*' robust line. MacDonald, too, was relieved when he received their approbation for the line he had taken.[11]

The debate in the House of Commons on 2 August 1956 confirmed this near unanimity of opinion, Gaitskell going so far as to compare Nasser to Hitler: 'Colonel Nasser's speeches . . . could only remind us of one thing – of the speeches of Hitler before the war.' Gaitskell did, however, conclude his speech with a passage reminding the House that Britain was a member of the United Nations and must not break international law.

This modification of the initial extreme position taken up by nearly all political and media opinion at the outset was maintained and strengthened in the weeks that followed. Jay and Healey, leading members of the Labour Party, sent a joint letter to *The Times* on 7 August, fully supported by Gaitskell, repudiating the use of force. Gaitskell had already written to Eden on 3 August, pointing out that in the debate he had refrained from asking certain questions because he did not wish to weaken Eden's hand, but that he was opposed to the use of force unless Nasser did something which would justify it. He could not see that he had done anything to justify the use of force as yet. Indeed by the end of July the *Daily Herald, News Chronicle, Manchester Guardian* and *Observer* had come out against the use of force unless Nasser used it first, and a front page editorial in the *Daily Mirror* on 14 August said: 'No war over Egypt.'

The Times was suffering from a sense of collective guilt over its association with appeasement during the 1930s under Dawson's editorship.[12] It was determined not to commit the same error. William Haley, the editor, who in fact was abroad for much of the crisis, wrote a trenchant leading article on 27 August headed 'Escapers' Club' arguing that there was danger that the whole affair might become shelved as one time-wasting conference succeeded another. He attacked those who questioned Eden's right to use force. It has been alleged, and it seems highly likely, that before the Anglo-French ultimatum Eden briefed MacDonald about the Anglo-French plan of collusion with Israel. MacDonald himself does not confirm or deny this allegation.[13] In the event *The Times* did not support the Government's ultimatum and the attack on Egypt to the extent that Eden clearly hoped it would. The first leader on 31 October, although stating that boldness often pays, argued that there were three reasons for deep concern – the lack of consultation with the US, the one-sidedness of the ultimatum and the fact that the Arabs were bound to say that HMG's policy helped Israel. Under the heading: 'A Lack of Candour', *The Times*' leader of 2 November 1956 quoted with approval Churchill's remark of 1942: 'I hold it perfectly justifiable to deceive the enemy, even if at the same time your own people are misled. There is one thing, however, which you must not do, and that is to mislead your ally'.

Whether or not they had advance knowledge of the collusive plot, both Haley and MacDonald were appalled at the implications. Eden's and Selwyn Lloyd's inevitable lies to the House of Commons and elsewhere were totally out of character and added to the outrage. Selwyn Lloyd had in fact been making considerable progress at the United Nations in negotiations with the Egyptian Foreign Minister, Fawzi, when he was recalled because of the impending conflict. *The Times* argued that these negotiations should have been allowed to continue.

The irony of the whole affair was compounded when Cyril Falls, the sometime Chichele Professor of the History of War at Oxford, wrote, later, on November 17, in the *Illustrated London News*: 'the two governments [Britain and France] have even been accused of collusion with Israel in bringing about a situation which would afford a justification for the use of force in Egypt. This accusation has been widely made in the United States and not withdrawn. It was made in the heat of party passion in this country at the beginning of the operation but has by now apparently been dropped.'

When the actual fighting started the press divided on party lines. The *Daily Express, Daily Mail, Daily Sketch* and *Daily Telegraph* with a combined circulation of 8,313,357 supported Eden; the *Daily Herald, Daily Mirror, News Chronicle* and *Manchester Guardian* with a circulation of 7,745,131 opposed him. Of the Sundays, Eden was supported by the *Empire News, Sunday Dispatch, Sunday Express, Sunday Graphic* and *The Sunday Times* with a circulation of 10,110,280. He was opposed by the *People, Reynolds' News, Sunday Pictorial* and *Observer* with a circulation of 11,690,072.[14]

There were of course nuances in the press handling of the crisis. Even the *Daily Telegraph*, before the invasion, warned on 30 October: 'It must be remembered that a full scale Arab–Israeli war would unite the whole Arab world against Israel.' Before hostilities started, the *Daily Mail* had been worried about the lack of American support, but on 1 November it stated: 'Britain is at war with Egypt. That is the grim inescapable overriding fact of this November morning . . . Questions and criticisms there will be and must be. We may have some to proffer ourselves. But let them wait.' The next day the tune was changed: 'A Police Action. It seems that we were wrong yesterday to head our Comment: 'Britain at War'. Britain is apparently not at war. She is engaged in a police action in the Suez area.' During the hostilities on 6 November the *Daily Mail* said:

> If the operation against Egypt is short and successful and brings the desired result, Eden's fame is secure. If it drags on, and this country is bogged down in a long, wasting guerilla war, the Prime Minister will be cast out . . . There is this, too. If Nasser remains, Eden goes.

An accurate forecast indeed! The *Daily Express* had a simple argument: 'the action is necessary to safeguard the life of the British Empire . . . and to Keep Britain great.'

The anti-Suez press was more, though not entirely, united. The *News Chronicle* began by conceding that rapid deployment of British power in the Canal zone might hold the conflicting parties apart, but later saw the action as 'folly on a grand scale'. The *Daily Herald* saw the invasion as folly from the start. The *Daily Mirror*, having initially been cautious, soon changed its view and called the action 'Eden's War'. The *Manchester Guardian* was vociferously critical from the start and the *Observer* on 4 November, the first occasion when it was able to comment, made a vicious attack on the Government: 'We had not realised that our Government was capable of such folly and such crookedness.' By that editorial and subsequent articles the *Observer* obtained the status of the leading anti-Government press campaigning organ, in the process losing some of its readership and three of its eight trustees who resigned in protest.

The American press was deeply critical, but with some reservations. Chalmers Roberts of the *Washington Post* argued that the Suez crisis: 'has destroyed the priceless ingredient of the Anglo-American alliance – America's trust in Britain's word.' The well-known columnists, the Alsop brothers, stated: 'This city [Washington], which has seen a good many extremes in political behaviour, has never seen such an exhibition of pique and anger as the Anglo/French action against Egypt has touched off.' George Kennan, on the other hand, said that: 'We have fumbled on certain past occasions; and our friends have not turned against us' (perhaps referring to past American actions in Guatemala, often quoted by Eden). 'Moreover we bear a heavy measure of responsibility for the desperation which has driven the French and the British Governments to do this ill-conceived and pathetic action.' Walter Lippman, the doyen of American columnists, said:

> The American interest is to refrain from moral judgement . . . the Franco/British actions will be judged by the outcome – in the first instance whether the military objectives are achieved in a reasonable time and at not too great a cost . . . However much we wish they had not started, we cannot now wish that they should fail.[15]

The *New York Times* of 1 November criticized the action but did not sympathize with Nasser: 'It would be ridiculous to permit Colonel Nasser to pose before the United Nations or the world as the innocent victim of aggression or to hold a protecting hand over him.'

In general, therefore, the Eisenhower–Dulles policy of opposition to the Anglo-French action, qualified by continuing antagonism to Nasser, had wide media support in the United States. The American Presidential Election which took place on 5 November may have had some effect on American policy, but this is not at all certain. Certainly Eisenhower was re-elected with an overwhelming majority of votes.

Public opinion in Britain was, as in the press, divided. Although generally in line with political affiliations, views sometimes cut across party lines. There were two resignations from the Government (Nutting and Boyle) and some Cabinet doubts in spite of Eden's subsequent denials of this[16] – notably by Monckton, Butler and Macleod. Monckton had been in the key position of Minister of Defence. He had been becoming more and more unhappy about Eden's intentions and refused to continue in the post, but accepted the job of Paymaster General on 18 October in order to preserve the appearance of solidarity. He was succeeded as Minister of Defence by Anthony Head, previously War Minister, who was in tune with Eden's thinking. Several Conservative MPs disagreed profoundly with the Government's action and many individual Conservative voters had deep reservations – General Sir Richard McCreery resigned from the British Legion in protest. During the crisis Eden's press secretary, William Clark, who had deep personal reservations about the use of force and who complained that he had been kept in the dark about what was happening, resigned. However, many working-class Labour supporters, perhaps particularly those who had served in the Middle East, supported Eden in his attack on Egypt and the opinion polls showed clearly that the Conservative Government did not lose support overall. Indeed, the British Institute of Public Opinion polls showed that Conservative fortunes took a turn for the better during the crisis itself.[17]

Gaitskell produced effective, highly partisan speeches both on 30 October in reply to Eden's initial statement and on 31 October. In the latter he mounted a root-and-branch attack on every aspect of the Government's policy: 'The speech [Eden's] represents the nadir of British fortunes, the most miserable depth to which this country has fallen.' He raised the question of collusion, which was denied by Selwyn Lloyd: 'It is quite wrong to state that Israel was incited to this action by HMG. There was no prior agreement about it.' Selwyn Lloyd, to one of the authors' personal knowledge, was tormented by guilt ever after. Eden, too, unequivocally denied collusion in the House of Commons on 20 December, also denying 'even any foreknowledge that Israel would attack Egypt'. Gaitskell remained within the constraints of the law by insisting that the Opposition would oppose the Government by every *constitutional* means.

The crisis exemplified one of the great dilemmas which often surface when armed conflict occurs. Should the Opposition, and those elements of the media identified with it, publicly attack a Government when the servicemen obeying that Government's orders are actually fighting and risking their lives? At what point, if ever, should patriotic feeling and concern for the lives of British soldiers, sailors and airmen supersede what may well be deep convictions that the action is wrong? In August 1914, the *Manchester Guardian*, as we have seen, dropped its profound opposition to Asquith's Government's policies once war was declared. Its successor, although war was never actually declared, did not follow suit at Suez. *The Economist*, which was consistently opposed to the use of force, answered the question as follows: 'For an opposition officially to oppose a war after hostilities have started is, in modern times, unprecedented; but so, too, is what Sir Anthony Eden has done.'

France had no such problems. With few exceptions the French political and media world supported military intervention, only criticizing what was seen as allied procrastination and lack of urgency.

There was no overt censorship during the Suez crisis. 'D' notices requesting editors not to publish certain matters, in particular details of the military preparations which were made, were issued and were complied with in all cases. Correspondents' access to the war front was highly restricted, but 'authoritative military sources' coordinated by a powerful multi-departmental committee based in London issued frequent bulletins. There was a dispute, which was never really settled, as to how many Egyptians, civilian and military, were killed during the invasion and there were mutterings about the inadequacies of the Services' public relations organization. Indeed, General Stockwell, the land force commander, complained bitterly in his report after the event about the lack of foresight shown in the creation and handling of the public relations service concerned with the operation. He talked of the poor quality and lack of experience of officers selected for the army PR unit.[18]

Attempts were made at psychological warfare aimed at the Egyptians under the control of Brigadier Bernard Fergusson, of Chindit (the British operation behind the Japanese lines in Burma) fame. Millions of pamphlets denigrating Nasser were produced for distribution by the RAF over Egypt, but in practice they were not dropped. Radio broadcasts from Cyprus were also aimed at the same target. However, none of these stratagems seemed to have had any effect as Nasser's prestige rose inexorably, particularly after the Anglo-French assault was seen to fail.

The BBC was faced by grave problems during the Suez crisis. Its charter gave it the responsibility of remaining independent of the Government. Part of its remit was to represent all sides of public opinion and not be used merely as one aspect of Government propaganda, particularly in a situation where war was not, and never was to be, declared. On the other hand, should it be seen to be supporting what many held to be the country's enemies? Eden found himself at loggerheads with the BBC, and in particular its Director General Sir Ian Jacob, on several occasions. At an early stage when Mr Menzies, the Australian Prime Minister, was sent to take Nasser a proposal as a result of the first London conference, there was doubt as to whether he would be allowed to appear on television. Eden was furious and on this occasion the BBC backed down, and Menzies appeared. In general, in the early stages, the BBC confined itself to factual reports of events as they occurred. Indeed, it and ITV actively restricted themselves by observing the 14-day rule invented by the BBC itself in 1944 under which discussion of issues which were to be debated in Parliament in less than fourteen days' time were barred. However, on 15 August the BBC put on a special survey of the Suez crisis which included a one-minute contribution by Major Saleh Salem, a well-known and vociferous associate of Nasser. This, predictably, led to furious accusations of near treason by Eden and other Conservative leaders. When Eden made an address to the nation on television on 7 August the question of Gaitskell's right to reply arose, but the Leader of the Opposition declined to do so on this occasion. However, later, when Eden again appeared on television in a direct talk to the nation on 3 November Gaitskell claimed the right to reply, which was resisted by Eden, in the end unsuccessfully.

The BBC also came under attack for the content of some of its external service programmes, which were far too impartial for the Government's liking. In this regard, the BBC on the whole successfully resisted governmental pressure. Indeed, it was not until 4 September that an Opposition view was first put out on the BBC except in news bulletins, when Alfred Robens, Labour's senior spokesman on foreign affairs, was interviewed in *At Home and Abroad*.

What effect, then, if any, did the media have on the onset, course and ending of the Suez crisis?

In contrast to some of the situations examined in this book the media certainly did not instigate the crisis in any way. The dispute would have occurred whatever view the media in Britain or the United States had taken. What the media in Britain and, to a certain extent in the United States, did do, however, was to stoke up the passions of those involved.

Whether Eden would have reacted as he did had it not been for the previous press attacks on his indecisiveness and the implied contrast between his and his predecessor Churchill's powers of resolution and decisive action is another matter. The answer will never be known. It is also possible that the Opposition might not have been quite so condemnatory had the anti-Suez press not been so violent in its strictures. Anti-Suez press and Opposition leaders fed on each other, raising passions to the point of hysteria.

In those hectic months between the end of July and early December 1956 it was extremely difficult for anyone in Britain to take a calm and measured view for long with the press on each side screaming for the other's blood.

Nasser, of course, had no problem with his press which was directly under his control as were all the organs of mass communication in Egypt. This exemplifies the contrast which always exists between the problems of leadership in a democracy in times of crisis and those of the leaders of totalitarian states. As far as Britain was concerned, the press certainly stoked up the controversy, outdoing itself in hyperbole and uncontrolled passion except, perhaps, for *The Times* which on the whole remained calm – perhaps partly because of its embarrassingly frank links with the Prime Minister. On the whole the BBC steered a canny and responsible course in the very difficult situation in which it found itself. Without doubt Dulles was encouraged to take the hostile line he did partly because he was able to point to the extreme division of opinion in Britain, as exemplified by the British press. Eden made this point strongly in his memoirs: 'Doubts about British national unity had its repercussions in the United States. It was constantly quoted to us by American negotiators and helped to weaken American resolution'.[19]

The contrast is most marked between the American reaction to the Falkland Islands episode, where the British press was largely united in support of the British actions and the Americans were, in the end, extremely helpful, and the American reaction to Suez where the opposite was the case. One might have expected the reverse to be true. At Suez, Eden and Eisenhower were old comrades-in-arms and Britain and the United States had a common anti-Soviet cause in the Middle East. In the Falklands, Margaret Thatcher and Reagan, although friends, were certainly not old comrades-in-arms and the United States had no conceivable interest in perpetuating a colonial link between Britain and some islands thousands of miles away in the South Atlantic, the position of which was clearly a relic of the British colonial past, and which irked many South American states with which the United States was trying to improve relations.

It is impossible to be totally precise about these matters. However, two things are certain. During the Suez crisis the Anglo-American special relationship came to a stuttering halt, happily only temporarily. Furthermore, it became clear that Britain's position as a first-rate power had finally vanished.

Lord Tyrell, the Permanent Under Secretary to the Foreign Office 1925–8 and Ambassador to Paris 1928–34, told Iverach MacDonald before the 1939–45 war that no British Government could afford to risk a war with a divided House of Commons and country. In addition, it must have at least the tacit support of the United States.[20] Anthony Eden went to war with none of these three safeguards.

1. Anthony Nutting, *No end of a lesson – The Story of Suez*, London, Constable, 1967, p. 7
2. Conversation with Iverach MacDonald, April/May 1997
3. Anthony Eden, *Full Circle*, London, Cassell, 1960, p. 426
4. MacDonald, *A Man of the Times*, London, Hamish Hamilton, 1976, p. 149
5. MacDonald, *A History of the Times*, volume 5, London, Times Books, 1984, p. 268
6. Eden, *Full Circle*, p. 515
7. Kyle, *Suez*, London, Weidenfeld and Nicholson, 1991, p. 565
8. Conversation with the late General Sir Hugh Stockwell, 1970, and Hugo Meynell, his ADC, 1997
9. Kyle, *Suez*, p. 409
10. Conversation with Iverach MacDonald, April/May 1997
11. Ibid.
12. Ibid.
13. Ibid.
14. Epstein, *British Politics in the Suez Crisis*, London, Pall Mall Press, 1964, pp. 154–63. Much of the detail given of press reactions comes from these pages.
15. Kyle, *Suez*, p. 427
16. Eden, *Full Circle*, p. 520
17. Epstein, *British Politics*, p. 149
18. Shaw, *Eden, Suez and the Mass Media*, London, Tauris, 1996, p. 83
19. Eden, *Full Circle*, p. 446
20. Conversation with Iverach MacDonald, April/May 1997

CHAPTER SEVEN

Ireland: The Longest Feud in Europe

'The Irish are a fair people; – they never speak well of one another.'

Samuel Johnson, 1775

If the people of Britain watched what had happened to the United States in Vietnam with incredulity and some self-satisfaction, it was not to be long before they themselves were faced with a situation almost as unpleasant and very much nearer home.

In the late 1960s, the dormant volcano of Northern Ireland once more erupted. The history of bitterness between Britain and Ireland predates even Tudor days, but the true seeds of these present troubles were sown in the early part of the seventeenth century. In 1608, King James I embarked on the 'plantation' of the Province of Ulster by Scottish and English settlers who were attracted by the prospect of renting land at the rate of £5 6s 8d for 1,000 acres. These settlers – known as 'undertakers' – were required to have taken the Oath of Supremacy (that is to say they were Protestants) and were required to clear their newly acquired estates of all the native Irish inhabitants. These undertakers were further required to improve their properties with stone houses, while conditions were also imposed regarding the building of towns, schools and churches. The plantation of Ulster took place at much the same time as the colonization by the British of the New England states of North America. There, however, the native population did not survive.

Since that seedtime, the discord between the Protestant settlers and the native Catholic Irish has grown into a bitter feud which has erupted into violence again and again in succeeding centuries. In the late seventeenth century, the Jacobite armies of the exiled King James II attempted to drive the Protestants out of Ireland, until they were defeated by the forces of King William, Prince of Orange (the Protestant hero 'King Billy'), at the Battle of the Boyne on 1 July 1690. The foundation of the Orange Lodges took place soon afterwards, which were and still are today the symbol of Protestant ascendancy in Ulster.

Much later, after the long and bloody strife which followed the Easter Rising of 1916, the partition of the six counties of Northern Ireland from the so-called Irish Free State was enacted at Westminster and, on 22 June 1921, King George V attended the State Opening of the Stormont Parliament. This partition, it was believed in London at the time, might finally resolve the Irish Question. However, so simple a solution was not to prove an answer.

The partition of Ireland led to some of the bitterest fighting of all, sparking off a civil war on both sides of the new border. It was not until 1923, after mass internment had been introduced both in the north and in the south, that anything approaching peace was restored.

In the ensuing years, the Stormont Parliament, dominated by the Ulster Unionists, constantly discriminated against the Catholic population, increasing further the acrimony between the two factions. There was a continued history of violence which simmered unhappily through the succeeding forty years, flaring into renewed action by the IRA during the Second World War and again in a further campaign between 1956 and 1962.

However, it was in the late 1960s that a determined campaign for civil rights by the Catholics of Northern Ireland led to a crescendo of violent rioting in the two main cities, Belfast and Londonderry. Here the Protestants insisted on their tradition of marching through the streets to recall historic events in Ireland's bloody past, while Catholics marched in protest against their loss of civil rights. These marches, pelted in both cases by the opposition with rocks, missiles and firebombs, led in August 1969 to scenes of such ferocity that the Royal Ulster Constabulary alone was unable to control them. On the afternoon of 14 August 1969, the Stormont Government requested military help from Britain to deal with the riots in Londonderry. Two companies of the Prince of Wales' Own Regiment of Yorkshire were deployed to disperse the rioters.

This was the first step in a long and terrible campaign which has lasted already for twenty-seven years and still, in 1997, sees no end. It has been a campaign which has spread from Ireland into mainland Britain, into Holland, Germany and even as far afield as Gibraltar. It has embroiled not only the governments of Britain and Ireland but also that of the United States. Into this cauldron, the world's press and television have dipped their long spoons, with differing effect on each of the warring parties. It is these effects and their impact on this bloody feud – a feud which has confounded generations of peacemakers, that we have tried to examine.

Of the factions in the feud, undoubtedly the Protestant Unionists have the clearest objectives. Northern Ireland is an integral part of the United Kingdom and so, they are determined, it shall remain. Despite the demise of the Stormont Parliament in 1972, Protestant loyalty to the British Crown remains undiminished and they have no political aspirations other than to remain a part of that kingdom. Their strength derives from their undisputed democratic position, which ensures that in any referendum or vote they still enjoy an absolute majority within the Province. Their position was made clear by the Ireland Act of June 1949, introduced by Clement Attlee's Government, which stated that: 'In no event will Northern Ireland or any part thereof cease to be a part of His Majesty's dominions and of the United Kingdom without the consent of the parliament of Northern Ireland.'[1] Nor has this assurance ever been gainsaid. Their weakness, however, lies in the arrogance of the Orange Lodges and their bigoted hatred of the Catholic population in their midst. The actions of Protestant mobs and Unionist paramilitary organizations have done much to diminish the sympathy which was felt for them by the majority of the British people.

Far more complex, however, are the objectives of the Catholic population. The recent troubles started as a clear and justifiable reaction to undoubted Unionist misrule. The preferential treatment offered to Protestant citizens and their families at the expense of the Catholics led inevitably to such a reaction, which began in 1968 as a series of comparatively peaceful demonstrations organized by the Northern Ireland Civil Rights Association (NICRA). That some of these demonstrations were seen on television to be brutally broken up by the Royal Ulster Constabulary brought home for the first time to a much wider viewing public the extent of the growing crisis in Ulster. In the NICRA march held in Londonderry on 5 October 1968, seventy-five civilians and eighteen policemen were injured, while another initially peaceful march from Belfast to Londonderry was set upon by a Unionist mob on 4 January 1969 at Burntollet Bridge and again large numbers of the marchers were injured. Many of the attacking mob were subsequently identified as special constables of the RUC in plain clothes.

It was not, however, until the arrival of the British army in Belfast and Londonderry, apparently in support of the Catholics, that the IRA began operations in earnest. In the autumn and winter of 1969, weapons and ammunition made their way into the Catholic areas of both cities from across the border, making the situation increasingly dangerous. At the same time, the Protestant paramilitaries (the Ulster Volunteer Force or UVF) were already well equipped with weapons that had been stored illegally for similar purposes. The objectives of the IRA soon became much more ambitious; reprisals against both Protestants, police and the army became their main purpose which was to harden as the years went by into a bitter determination to drive Britain out of Ireland by any means at their disposal. The ostensible aim of the IRA is a united Ireland. However, John Keegan, in a newspaper article, has described their aims as going much further:

The agencies of the Dublin government are, by its [the IRA's] reckoning, as illegal in Ireland as those of the British. Legality will be established only when the IRA acquires authority over the whole territory of the island of Ireland. It is a crazy political programme but has a powerful logic for underground extremists seeking to sustain belief in their right to victory.[2]

If this truly describes the IRA's aims, the prospects for peace in Ireland are very slender. Furthermore, as their activities remain unpleasantly newsworthy, there is another aspect of their campaign which is equally disturbing.

If, by negotiation or indeed by any other means, a binding peace agreement is reached with the IRA, there would be no further use or purpose for an organization which has remained in being for as long as any Irishman can remember and which has provided a rallying point for the bored and frequently unemployed youth of the island both north and south of the border. Sinn Fein, the political party that fronts the IRA, would become no more than a minority party among many others and the 'glory and valour' of the ancient struggle would evaporate to nothing; in recent times, the leader of Sinn Fein has been an honoured guest in the United States. The 'active service units' of the IRA have been able, almost at will, to bring the City of London to a halt. On account of these men, the pageantry of scarlet uniforms outside Buckingham Palace has on occasion been changed to combat dress. What incentive is there for them to forego this power in exchange for dull political debate? Above all, their actions are broadcast on television sets throughout the world.

The greater glory of publicity is a powerful drug. If, as we fear, IRA terrorists are now entirely addicted to that drug, there can be little hope in the future for lasting peace in Ireland.

The third and most unwilling participant in the quarrel is the British army, sent with the declared purpose of stopping the fighting and sustaining the legally elected government.[3] In the twenty-seven years that it has patrolled the streets of Northern Ireland, it has already lost more than 800 soldiers killed and a far greater number seriously injured. In that time it has learned many lessons by bitter experience and is today a very different animal from that which appeared on the streets of Londonderry in 1969. It has from time to time been vilified by each of the two factions and sometimes been brought into disrepute in the eyes of the British themselves. At other times its soldiers have been lionized for their courage and patience and, although the British media has often demanded more soldiers and tougher action, it has not once, throughout the campaign, seriously demanded the withdrawal of British troops from the Province.

Onto all these widely disparate organizations and changing policies, the world's media has shone its powerful light. Its effects are most clearly seen through the eyes of the soldiers thrown into the middle of this bitter feud.

The regiments that appeared on the streets of Northern Ireland in the autumn of 1969 were formed of young regular soldiers with plenty of self-confidence. Their officers were the first postwar generation, but were by no means lacking in experience. In the twenty-five years since the end of the Second World War, the army had seen active service in Korea, Malaya, Borneo, Palestine, Aden and Kenya, to name but a few. In Germany, the British army held a prime place among the NATO nations facing the Soviet threat in Europe, with the unique advantage at that time of having dispensed with compulsory military service. It had of course had its setbacks: the débacle at Suez, as we have seen, had been a fiasco, but this could properly be laid at the door of the politicians, whose fault it undoubtedly was.

On their arrival in Belfast, the troops were pleasantly surprised to find themselves welcomed, at least by the Catholic households, who saw them as harbingers of a better deal for the minority. However, as they patrolled the dingy streets, the soldiers, who came for the most part from the great cities of England and Scotland, were shocked at the scenes of poverty and squalor that they encountered in the Province. They found it hard to believe that these dreary towns were truly part of their own United Kingdom.

The principle of using 'minimum force' in the conduct of operations 'in aid of the civil power', as the army then called it, had been drummed into every officer from his earliest days of training. The story of the massacre at Amritsar in 1919 was a cautionary tale to be learned by every young officer. Many of the troops engaged had already had experience of dealing with riots in other theatres of war, but this presented them with the new challenge of confronting their own countrymen. Beyond the use of minimum force, however, their training for the events with which they were to be faced in Belfast and Londonderry was extremely sketchy.

Had you at that time approached these men or their officers and asked them their views about journalists and pressmen, their answer would have been unanimous: 'Keep away from them and don't talk to them.' If pressed more closely, they would probably have said: 'We have been sent here by the Government and given our orders, which we are carrying out to the best of our ability; if you want to know why we are here, go and ask the Government.' Unfortunately this easy solution did not last for long.

On 16 October 1969, on the recommendation of Lord Hunt's Special Advisory Committee on the Police in Northern Ireland, the 'B Specials', the armed Protestant special constables so much hated by the Catholics, were disbanded and the Ulster Defence Regiment, controlled by Westminster, was formed. This action so infuriated the Protestants that it was followed by an outbreak of extreme violence in the Shankill Road in Belfast in which the army was heavily engaged by Protestant gunmen. In the end, the army responded by shooting two gunmen and wounding others. This event alienated the army from the Protestants and soon similar events in the Catholic areas were to have the same effect on their relations with the other faction.

At the beginning of April 1970, attempting to quell serious rioting between the Protestants of the Highfield estate and the neighbouring Ballymurphy Catholic estate in Belfast, the army fired 104 CS gas canisters into the Catholic crowd. In the words of the journalist, Simon Winchester, who was present at the time:

it was a questionable decision to use gas that April night. It was a decision that half-united the Ballymurphy people against the army. It was a decision that ultimately brought the gunmen of the IRA to act as 'defenders of the people'. It was a decision that rendered the army

Coldstream Guards at the Crimea.
(Imperial War Museum: Q71095)

Balaklava Harbour. (Imperial War Museum: Q71108)

Lord Roberts of Kandahar with escort in South Africa. (Imperial War Museum: Q71943)

British dead after the battle of Spion Kop. (Imperial War Museum: Q82950)

Propaganda advertisement from the First World War.

'Go on Lily Whites' – Coldstreamers on the Somme.

British propaganda cartoons from the First World War by the artist Louis Raemaekers (1869–1956).

'TO YOUR HEALTH, CIVILISATION!'

'SEDUCTION: "Ain't I a lovable fellow?"'

'*MY SON, GO AND FIGHT FOR YOUR MOTHERLAND!*'

'*THROWN TO THE SWINE: The Martyred Nurse.*'

Adolf Hitler addresses a Nazi mass rally.

Wer stirbt? Wofür?

Deutsche Arbeiter
sterben für die Partei!

Deutsche Bauern
sterben für die Partei!

Deutsche Soldaten
sterben für die Partei!

Deutsche Jugend
stirbt für die Partei!

Deutsche Gottesgläubige
sterben für die Partei!

**Das Deutsche Volk stirbt
für die Partei!**

²⁹⁵

Pamphlet dropped on Germany 1939/40.

Who Dies?

What For?

German workers

die for the Party

German farmers

die for the Party

German soldiers

die for the Party

German youth

dies for the Party

German believers in God

die for the Party

The German people die

for the Party

Britain's wartime leader Winston Churchill in characteristic pose.

8th Hussars cross an American bridge in Korea. (Imperial War Museum: BF10292)

Destruction in Vietnam. (Imperial War Musuem: CT167)

THE ILLUSTRATED LONDON NEWS.

© 1968 The Illustrated London News & Sketch Ltd   World copyright of all editorial matter, both illustrations and text, is strictly reserved   No 6706   Volume 252

"WE CANNOT PROVIDE THE

SOUTH VIETNAMESE WITH THE WILL TO

SURVIVE AS AN INDEPENDENT NATION"

Mr Robert McNamara in his report to Congress, February 1, 1968.

British Navy in Port Said – the statue of De Lesseps is in the background. (Imperial War Museum: HN4209)

Port Said, Suez Crisis, 1956 – El Gami Airfield. (Imperial War Museum: HN4177)

NEWS LETTER

CITY FINAL

Telephone 44441   Monday, September 28, 1970   Price 6d (7d in Eire)

LATEST

MORNING VIEW

Bitter street battles in worst rioting for months

SHANKILL TURMOIL

Scores of arrests made and more than 200 people injured

Price Sixpence

PROTESTANT TELEGRAPH

THE TRUTH SHALL SET YOU FREE

VOL. 4, NO. 11

SATURDAY, OCT. 11, 1969

Open Air gospel services outlawed—Church services next?

Army attacks Protestant churchgoers

LOYALIST NEWS

2nd EDITION Vol 2.
30th January, 1971.   Price 6d

ARMY BRUTALITY

Ulster headlines, c. 1970.

REPUBLICAN NEWS

Vol. 1   No. 7   DECEMBER, 1970 — JANUARY, 1971   Price 9d

INTERNMENT

IMPRISONMENT, **without trial or charge has been and still is an occupational hazard for members of the Republican Movement.**

Collaboration b e t w e e n the British Government and the Free State and Stormont regimes with the resulting betrayal of Republicans, has been a prominent feature in Irish politics since Ireland was partitioned. This is nothing new . This is something that Republicans have learned to live with.

In the forties Republicans who escaped from Derry jail and crossed the border into Donegal were rounded up by Free State troops and police and imprisoned in the Curragh Concentration Camp.

On the eve of internment in 1957 the British Ambassador visited the Free State Minister of External Affairs. The next morning the introduction of internment was announced. The week before Lynch made his recent statement the present British Ambassador made two visits to Iveagh House.

Unlike the Rev. Martin Smith, County Grand Master of the Orange Order, who praised Lynch for his statement and who declared that his action was that of a statesman, we can only regard Lynch's action as another example of collaboration and betrayal.

Lynch said that internment in the South does not mean that it will follow in the Six Counties. In this he was contradicted by the Stormont puppet Prime Minister, who said that internment in the 26 Counties would strengthen the arguments for its introduction in the Six Counties. Clarke recently refused to give any assurance that there would be no internment here. In this regard he and his regime will not stand in the way of professional advice, namely, from the British Secret Service

and the R.U.C. Special Branch, who keep close in touch with the Special Branch informers in the 26 Counties.

Taylor, the Stormont "de facto"

Minister of Home Affairs, said recently: "We will not discuss internment much, but will decide and move."

There is no doubt that if and

when internment does start that Republicans will be the victims.

There can be no doubt that lists

Internment continued on Page 12

Name .... Could be you

Crime .... None

Reason for Internment ...... Being an Irishman

Owing to the increase in size of paper we are reluctantly compelled to raise the price to 9d.

BEANNACHTAI NA NODLAG DAR GCUID LEIGHTEORI GO LEIR

A policy that brought more trouble than benefit.

HMS Sheffield *struck by an Exocet missile. (Royal Navy)*

Ian MacDonald gives a press briefing at the Ministry of Defence during the Falklands War. (Press Association Photo)

US students on Grenada welcome an American serviceman. (Rex Features Ltd)

A US medical student kisses the ground on his return to the States from Grenada. (Associated Press Photo)

The road to Basra from Kuwait after air attacks by coalition forces at the end of the Gulf War. (Imperial War Musuem: GLF247)

Kate Adie interviews a British tank commander in the desert. (Royal Scots Dragoon Guards)

Douglas Hurd with UN troops in Bosnia. (Imperial War Musuem: BOS23)

A British Challenger tank with the International Force in Bosnia. (Royal Scots Dragoon Guards)

no longer a peace-keeping force but, in thousands upon thousands of Catholic eyes, an Army of Occupation.[4]

During the summer of 1970, a general election in Britain brought a Tory government to power. Many changes were made in the hierarchy of those with responsibility for controlling events, but with little apparent effect. One decision taken at this time was to make an important change in the approach of the security forces towards the media. The policy of referring comment on events up the chain of command had become quite impractical when soldiers were engaging and often shooting terrorists while television cameras and journalists looked on. It was, therefore, sensibly decided to allow any officer or soldier to make an immediate statement to the media regarding actions of which he had personal and direct knowledge. He was forbidden to speculate, to speak about other matters than his own, or to comment on the actions of others. This decision did much to help the troops who had hitherto been virtually unable to give any explanation of what they were trying to do. It was a first step in a policy which later produced some interesting and unusual developments.

Nevertheless, by the end of 1970, the army, whose arrival had been at first welcomed by the Catholics, had unwittingly but sadly alienated both parties in the Province and had achieved little in its attempt to restore peace. Worse was still to come.

The next year, 1971, saw the start of a bombing offensive launched by the IRA in Northern Ireland. In February, the first British soldier was shot dead and four others were seriously wounded by machine-gun fire during rioting in the Catholic Ballymurphy estate in West Belfast. The first soldier to die was a Gunner Curtis. His death brought a tearful expression of sympathy from a Catholic woman, Mrs McLaughlin, ending with the words: 'Please tell the people in London that we're not all savages.' This moving message was broadcast on the BBC six o'clock television news on 1 March 1971.

Three more young soldiers were lured from their barracks and shot in the back of the head by members of the IRA. During April, May and June over 130 bombing incidents took place in the Province during which a further 13 soldiers, 2 policemen and 16 civilians were killed.

In the summer, with the situation still deteriorating, the RUC, with the support of the Stormont Government, recommended to the Government in Westminster that a policy of internment should be introduced in

Northern Ireland. While the army was not much in favour of the idea, there was little doubt that police and army intelligence could identify most of the ringleaders without too much difficulty, even though it would have been impossible to convict them in court of any terrorist activity. It was therefore proposed that a swift nocturnal raid could sweep up most of them in a single operation, after which the brains and leadership behind the bombing and rioting could be kept safely behind bars. On the other hand, in a democracy, a policy of imprisonment without trial or conviction was an undertaking fraught with danger. This decision racked the Cabinet in London for a long time, but in early August 1971 the Home Secretary, Reginald Maudling, who at that time carried responsibility for the Province, authorized the operation to take place.

The policy proved to be one of the heavier millstones to be carried around the neck of the British Government for many months to come. Of the 342 men arrested in the early hours of 9 August, many were quickly released after screening; of the total number, not a single Protestant was arrested. Reaction to the policy was understandably violent, not least that voiced in the press. The internment camps became a running sore in the Government's side, while very many of the key republican figures had anyway escaped the net across the border into the south. As if that was not enough, the army in its search for intelligence embarked on a system of 'in-depth' interrogation of interned suspects which led to further outrage. While the methods involved no direct physical abuse of the suspect, it came very close indeed to mental torture. The victim was held for long periods hooded, so that he lost sense of place and time. He was also exposed to so-called 'white noise' which was a continuous and disturbing monotonous sound which deprived him of sleep and rest.

The combination of these two policies only aggravated the situation. During the autumn, the number of British troops in the Province had increased to 13,600, of whom, by the end of 1971, no fewer than 43 had been killed. The IRA's bombing campaign continued and at the end of the year a bomb placed in a bar in Belfast killed fifteen civilians outright.

Early in 1972, an event occurred which proved to be a watershed in the attitudes generated by the campaign both in Ireland and throughout the United Kingdom.

On Sunday 30 January 1972, the Civil Rights Association (NICRA) had planned to hold a major demonstration in Londonderry. The march was to be routed through the Creggan and Bogside areas of Derry, the central strongholds of the Catholic republicans; thereafter it was to move into the centre of the city, into which the police were anxious that no provocative marches should be allowed. There a number of speakers, including Lord Fenner Brockway, a well-known left-wing Labour peer, were to address the crowd. On the advice of the police and the army, the Stormont Government forbade the march to take place at all, making the whole programme illegal.

Undaunted, large crowds of reasonably good-natured Catholics gathered together on that fine sunny Sunday morning in the Creggan and started to move through the Bogside, gathering as they did so increasing numbers of demonstrators. Among the crowds were many young people for whom the opportunity to taunt and pelt the authorities with stones and missiles had become something of a standard sport. These had been classed by the security forces as 'hooligans' (or by the Army as 'yobbos'), as opposed to the more law-abiding citizens demonstrating on the matter of civil rights.

To prevent the marchers from entering the city centre, the army had set up a series of barriers at strategic positions on various streets. Its plan, if the marchers became uncontrolled, was to try to separate the demonstrators from the hooligans and then, with reinforcements, to round up and arrest large numbers of the latter, using snatch squads.

As the afternoon progressed, the confrontation became increasingly bitter with the marchers in large numbers engaging the army over the barriers with missiles and firebombs. These were answered by the army with rubber bullets, hoses and CS gas. Later, at about 4.40 p.m., when the hooligans appeared to have moved in a different direction from the mass of demonstrators, orders were given to the reinforcing battalion to move in across the barriers 'to scoop up the yobbos'. This battalion was 1st Bn The Parachute Regiment. As they rushed through the barriers, a British general was filmed on television urging them on with the cry, 'Go on the paras!'[5]

What happened thereafter has been reported in widely differing terms. The army maintained that its soldiers came under fire, which they returned, only engaging those people who were either shooting at them or attempting to bomb them. The Catholics believed that the soldiers ran amok and fired wildly into the crowds for no good reason at all. All that is certain is that at the end of the day thirteen men and youths lay dead, shot by British army bullets. No soldier was killed or wounded.

This is not the place to offer opinions about the rights and wrongs of the case. Many books have been written offering varying accounts. What is of importance in this book is to see how the media reported these events and the manner in which the two sides attempted to influence that reporting.

On that day there were a number of television camera crews recording events. There were also numerous newspaper reporters present in the thick of the rioting. Everything, however, happened so quickly that neither the cameras nor the observers managed to obtain a clear picture of what exactly occurred. Only after the firing was over was it possible to piece together with any accuracy what had happened and this was still open to varying interpretations.

The army general, who had been earlier observed on the spot, was interviewed on television and insisted that: 'there is absolutely no doubt that the Parachute battalion opened fire only after they were fired on. The soldiers fired single, aimed shots in return . . .' and he suspected that the dead: 'might not all have been killed by our troops.'[6] The army headquarters in Lisburn that evening issued a statement which was flashed to all British embassies saying that 'those shot had been suspected terrorists or bore traces of having handled weapons or bombs'. Later that night, as detailed reports emerged about the dead men from the hospitals, this statement was withdrawn, as it was clearly untrue. Throughout, army sources maintained that the soldiers had come under fire before they themselves started shooting.[7]

On the same night, the IRA held a press conference at which it informed the assembled pressmen that 'the dead men were innocent young men with no record of involvement with firearms and all of whom had been entirely uninvolved in any attempts to shoot or bomb'. None of these claims could be disproved by subsequent identification or forensic evidence.

On television in Britain and in Ireland that night, terrible spectacles were shown. One of the most harrowing showed a Catholic priest waving a bloody white handkerchief as he led the bearers of a corpse away from the scene of the shooting. The next morning the events in Derry were reported under banner headlines in Britain and around the world. *The Times* reported that: 'More than 200 heavily armed parachutists stormed into the IRA stronghold of the Bogside and a hospital officer stated tonight that 13 people had been shot dead and 17 others, including two women, wounded in a brief but fierce gun battle.'

The *Daily Mirror* went on to quote Father Denis Bradley, a Bogside priest who had been administering the last rites to the dying, as saying: 'There was a paratrooper beside me and he aimed at least eight shots indiscriminately at people running away.'

Simon Winchester, who had been in the crowd, wrote in the *Guardian*:

> Soldiers, firing into a large group of civil rights demonstrators, shot and killed thirteen civilians . . . the streets had all the appearance of the aftermath of Sharpeville . . . and, while it is impossible to be absolutely sure, one came away with the impression, reinforced by dozens of eye-witnesses, that the soldiers, men of the 1st Bn The Parachute Regiment, flown in specially from Belfast, may have fired needlessly into the large group.

Many who read the accounts concluded that the British army's discipline had finally cracked and its men had behaved as irresponsibly as soldiers in third world countries. The day was christened Bloody Sunday, a name which has come to be remembered with all the notoriety of Amritsar itself.

On the following day, a great crowd in Dublin converged on the British Embassy and burned it down; there were calls for the soldiers involved in Bloody Sunday to be charged with murder and the Irish Ambassador in London was recalled. In the Bogside and Creggan areas of Derry, barricades were raised to prevent the security forces from entering and, in the atmosphere of the moment, it did not seem wise to challenge them. A large part of Catholic Derry had become a no-go area for British troops and the RUC.

In an attempt to ease the tension, the Government in Westminster agreed to hold an inquiry into the events which had led to the deaths of these thirteen men. The matter was handed over to the judiciary and it was announced that the inquiry would be undertaken by the Lord Chief Justice sitting alone. This was scarcely likely to satisfy the republicans, as Lord Widgery, apart from being a British judge, had served in the British army during the war and attained the rank of colonel, later becoming a brigadier in the territorial army. His inquiry, when its findings were announced, exonerated the soldiers from blame in opening fire.[8] While it was some comfort to the army, it carried little weight with the rest of the world.

Contrary to the findings of the Widgery Report, the City Coroner in Londonderry, Hubert O'Neill, described the incidents, when the inquests were held, as 'unadulterated bloody murder'.[9]

In the event, whatever the truth of the events of that Sunday afternoon, the army had suffered a grievous defeat as much at the hands of the media as of the IRA. By its own incompetence in defending itself against the accusations of the IRA and the media, it had turned a misfortune into a disaster.

In the spring of 1972, the army took counsel as to how it should manage its affairs in the future. There was bitter resentment that the IRA should have succeeded in inflicting such a defeat on troops who believed they were merely trying to cope in exceptionally difficult circumstances with a quarrel that was none of their making. If it was to become a war of words and pictures, then surely they, the soldiers, should enter the lists and make sure that their side of the story too was properly told.

One of the traps into which the army's information service had fallen was its belief that it could use its service simultaneously as a psychological warfare medium. In a much later television interview, the Northern Ireland army public relations officer recounted how his service had been used by MI5 and MI6 to spread stories of doubtful truth intended to damage the IRA.[10] Psychological warfare has its place in the conduct of war and has been used widely in many different conflicts. The mistake in this case was to use what was intended to be a credible information service for the dissemination of 'black propaganda'.

To the IRA, on the other hand, the events of Bloody Sunday had been a gift which they were not slow to exploit. At the press conference which they held on that same Sunday evening, they had announced their future intention to 'murder every British soldier that they could'[11] in revenge for the killing of the thirteen innocents. Fortunately for the army, the IRA's first revenge attack went very wrong.

At about midday on 22 February 1972, a bomb planted in the Officers' Mess of the Parachute Regiment in Aldershot exploded, killing seven people. Clearly intended to kill a large number of officers at lunch, the plan misfired with terrible irony. The people killed were five women employees and a gardener; the seventh victim was, of all people, the much respected Roman Catholic Padre to the Regiment.

At his funeral, conducted by the Roman Catholic Archbishop of Liverpool, the church was packed on one side by a huge gathering of Catholic clergy and on the other by a sea of khaki, most with red berets. Outside the church were a number of other priests wearing neat macintoshes over their Roman collars and handing out excellent and well-prepared press releases to the mass of journalists present. Each sheet carried in the corner the logo of an angel blowing a trumpet.

'Even the good Lord,' remarked one military man present, 'needs a good PR service!'

On 24 March, with the situation in the Province deteriorating by the day, the British Prime Minister decided to take control of events from London. The Stormont Parliament was prorogued on that day and Direct Rule from Westminster introduced. The first Secretary of State for Northern Ireland to take his post in Stormont was William Whitelaw.

In an attempt to defuse the bitter situation which he inherited, Whitelaw tried to distance the troops from the rioting population and to lower the profile of their operations. By this time, however, the battle lines were too firmly drawn for such a policy to be successful. He tried too to negotiate a ceasefire with the IRA but this proved to be shortlived.

Within the army, new methods were needed to ensure that what it was trying to do was properly and convincingly represented to the media. It was clear that senior officers must be prepared to appear before the cameras and explain themselves and their policies. Not all were prepared for this exposure and some were much better than others. A privately run school, where training for television appearances was given, was found in Glasgow and used by the army. Here officers whose appointments might necessitate camera interviews were sent for experience of the manner in which they might be questioned and how to handle such interviews. Naturally the rule permitting soldiers on the spot to explain their actions continued and, as the months went by, the army learned a most profound truth: 'The lower the rank, the higher the credibility!'

Viewers, sitting at home, instinctively believed that, if a general appeared, he was almost certainly covering up; a colonel was probably protecting his regiment; a young officer was probably saying what he had been told to say; but, when a lance corporal appeared, of course he was telling the truth – after all, he's just an ordinary bloke like one of us!

In fairness, the GOC in Northern Ireland at the time, Lieutenant General Sir Harry Tuzo, was himself excellent on television. His transparent good humour made him instantly believable and he appeared often on the television with good effect. However, even he had his problems. On one occasion in 1972, a French television crew asked to interview him. Tuzo spoke passable French and agreed to be interviewed in that language. In the event, his grasp of the language was not good enough to enable him to speak easily and fluently and the resulting hesitancies in his answers gave the impression that he was being less than straightforward. Furthermore, the French played a shabby trick on him (which of course his staff should have spotted) by running a separate half-hidden camera which continued to film after the main interview was over. As a result, Tuzo, who had put on a cheerful relaxed face for the interview, switched back immediately afterwards to being the busy hard-pressed general officer that he was. This change of demeanour came over most unfortunately in the French programme.[12]

Another new experience that faced the army staff in those days was the effect of editing. Of course, people say, the camera cannot lie. However, in this same year two foreign camera crews (among many) came to Ulster, one American and one Russian. The Americans, as Britain's close allies in Europe, were given a fair welcome and allowed to film on the streets with comparative freedom. Naturally the Russians were much more suspect and they were only allowed to film under supervision. To do this the army staff found a bright young major in the Parachute Regiment, fluent in Russian, who had recently returned from Moscow where he had been Assistant Military Attaché.

Both films were made without trouble, the major reporting fully what the Russians had filmed and giving details of a few innocent remarks he had made to camera. Some years later the films that were made from this shooting were seen by one of the present authors. They were horrific. The Americans succeeded in showing pictures of women and children peacefully standing talking and playing in the streets when, suddenly, an armoured car sped round the corner discharging troops in riot gear who attacked the bystanders, firing rubber bullets and blinding in one eye a harmless-looking young man. The story had been skilfully woven together from a series of different shots, culminating in the extremely unfortunate incident which occurred during a particularly ferocious riot.[13]

The Russians on the other hand put together a remarkable film to show how the British had kept the downtrodden people of Ireland under a wicked military yoke for the past three centuries. They showed footage of burned-out and ruined houses which they said had been destroyed by the British soldiers in revenge for uprisings by the brave and noble proletariat of Ulster.

'Do you see prospect of a quick end to these troubles?' they asked the young major.

'No,' he replied, 'I am afraid the British army will be here for a long time to come.'

'The British have no intention of relieving the miserable lot of these unhappy citizens,' concluded the commentator.[14]

But amid these troubles, the British private soldier was, as often, the hero of the hour. Frequently, the roaming cameras found a young man who would give a clear and succinct account of what had been happening to him, which carried enormous weight with the viewers and was often spoken with resilience, good sense and great good humour.

It was not only in Ireland at this time that the media war was being conducted. The army was naturally very much in the national spotlight at home and one morning the well-known BBC interviewer, Robin Day, sought an interview with the Chief of the General Staff (CGS). In asking for a long 'in-depth' interview about the army, Day enquired: 'Who is the present CGS?'

It is an interesting reflection on the times to know that in that year (1972), the CGS had no television in his house, remarking that he had better things to do than to 'sit watching the box'. He accordingly also enquired: 'Who is Robin Day?'

On being told, he expressed himself to be quite ready to do the interview. When advised by his staff that it might be wise to get some experience of the medium before appearing, he asked what Robin Day was going to ask him about.

'About the army,' came the reply.

'Well,' replied the CGS reasonably, 'I know a lot more about the army than he does, so what is the trouble?'

He was, however, persuaded to do a practice interview at the television training school in Glasgow. Here the school prepared his training session with some care and not a little wicked intent.

When he arrived at the school, the CGS was assured that it would not take long. An interview would be set up for him; afterwards, he could watch it and if he was happy with it, there was no need to detain him longer. He strode into the studio where he was sat in a chair under the lights and before the camera. At that point the interviewer came in. He was bearded, with shoulder-length hair, and was dressed in jeans with open-toed sandals. He was not very clean. A *frisson* ran through the Chief's personal staff who had come with him and were sitting at the side of the studio.

The two men were introduced; the Chief was distinctly frigid. The cameras rolled and the interview began. It ran something like this:

Q. 'Good afternoon, you are the Head of the British army?'
CGS. 'Yes; I'm the Chief of the General Staff.'

Q. 'I see. And were you in the last war?'
(The Chief was in uniform with three or four rows of medals which included the DSO and the MC.)
CGS. (coldly) 'Yes, I was.'
Q. 'And how many men did you kill?'
CGS. (ruffled) 'How many men? I really don't know . . .'
Q. 'Or perhaps you spent the war driving a desk in Whitehall and didn't kill any?'
CGS. (cross) 'I certainly didn't spend the war in Whitehall. I spent it very differently.'
Q. 'But you do sit at a desk in Whitehall now, don't you?'
CGS. 'Yes, my office is in the Ministry of Defence, but I'm just at the moment on my way back from Ireland.'
Q. 'Ah yes, Ireland. Have you been planning the murder of some more innocent Catholics?'
CGS. (angry) 'That is an outrageous question. You know as well as I do that the army has no intention of acting remotely like that.'
Q. 'They seemed to on Bloody Sunday. Thirteen dead, wasn't it?'
CGS. 'The enquiry into the events of that day is being investigated by Lord Widgery.'
Q. 'That won't be much comfort to their wives and mothers, will it? Are you going to trust the Paras not to do it again?'
(Throughout this the Chief had become increasingly incensed. He was now rather flushed and the whites of his knuckles were beginning to show. The camera switched for a moment to a close-up of his hands.)
CGS: 'I am not prepared to talk about this while the matter is *sub judice*.'
Q. 'Ah, so you don't trust the Paras?'
CGS. (very angrily) 'That is not what I said.'
Q. 'While you were in Ireland, did you go to see the internees being interrogated?'
CGS. 'No, I did not.'
Q. 'But of course you know what they do to them, don't you? You probably ordered it.'
CGS. 'What do you mean?'
Q. 'Well, have you ever heard 'white noise'?'

And so it went on. After a few more minutes, the interview was stopped and played back. It was appalling and the staff anxiously awaited the great man's response. After a moment's silence, to his everlasting credit, a wintry smile broke out over his face and he said: 'Yes, perhaps I could do with training.'

This is not the place to go into the ways and means of handling a hostile television interview. Suffice it to say that the General, now Field Marshal Lord Carver, was a very quick learner. He soon had the interviewer (who was of course an actor) eating out of his hand.

To conclude the story, Carver gave a long and excellent interview with Robin Day, which went a long way to restoring the good image of the army in the minds of the people of this country at that very gloomy time.

Back in Northern Ireland, the spate of shootings and bombings continued through the summer of 1972. The Bogside remained a no-go area, reminding the world of the impotence of the army and the police. At the entrances to their stronghold, the Catholic inhabitants had erected heavy concrete structures to prevent any military vehicles from entering. Snipers operated from windows, looking out for unwary soldiers who came into their field of fire. For a city in a democratic country in peacetime, the situation was deplorable.

Matters came to a head on Friday 21 July, a day which the people of Belfast will never forget and which came to be christened Bloody Friday. On that day, at intervals of only a few minutes throughout the afternoon, no fewer than nineteen bombs exploded around the city. On that day, 9 people were killed, 77 women and girls were injured and 53 men and young boys. It was a turning-point, as it now became clear that some serious action had to be taken, if the Government was not to be seen to have lost control. A plan was therefore made to re-enter the no-go areas in both Londonderry and Belfast by direct military action. It was code-named 'Operation Motorman'.

The military planning was straightforward enough, given plenty of troops, but the underlying danger of a media catastrophe was immense. The military plan involved a large number of infantry battalions, which would close in on the no-go areas in the small hours of the morning and re-establish control of them. The first problem was the barricades of solid concrete; these would have to be removed quickly, if there was to be any follow up of vehicles. Secondly, what would the inhabitants do? Would they put their women and children on the barricades and bar the way? If so, how would the soldiers deal with them? And finally, and perhaps most importantly, how would the media report the operation?

This account is not concerned with the detailed planning of the military operation itself, but it was one of the very first military actions by the British army that incorporated a complete and detailed media plan.

First, the barricades. These would need to be removed by Armoured Vehicles Royal Engineers (AVREs). To the layman, these are tanks. They are tank chassis with bulldozer blades and other sapper equipment. The one story the army did not want was 'Tank battles in Derry'. The vehicles came from Ripon and were moved on transporters, heavily sheeted, to a site on the edge of the Gairloch on the west coast of Scotland. On the sides of their hulls the word 'ENGINEERS' had been painted in white paint. Beside the loch, they were unloaded and left sheeted.

By an unlucky chance, a naval officer was sailing on the Gairloch the next day and he had taken as his crew a young man who worked as a stringer for the local paper and also for the *Daily Mirror*.

'What are those tanks doing over there?' he asked.

'I don't know,' replied the helmsman, 'something the army is up to, I shouldn't wonder.'

'There aren't any exercises going on up here,' said the stringer; 'I must check on it when we get back.'

On his return ashore, he telephoned the Defence press desk and asked for information about what he had seen. The press officer knew nothing about them but undertook to make enquiries and ring back. In dealing with the press, a promise to return a call by a reputable information service is as binding as an oath. Clearly an honest answer could not be given without compromising the whole plan; equally, a lie was unacceptable. Eventually the caller was referred to HQ Scottish Command (who had not been informed in any case). By the time that the enquiry had circulated around that headquarters, the operation was under way.

When all was ready, Whitelaw, the Secretary of State and General Tuzo had a difficult decision to make. There could be no going back in this operation and if a serious firefight ensued, there could be heavy casualties. (For this eventuality, a Field Hospital had been set up outside Londonderry.) For once it was the army taking the initiative, rather than reacting to the IRA. Therefore, should the inhabitants of the Bogside not be warned beforehand?

The arguments were finely balanced. Obviously for the army, secrecy was preferable; it would make it far more likely that some of the most wanted men would be rounded up. On the other hand, if the troops had to start shooting and civilians had not been warned to stay in their houses, there was room for fearful backlash afterwards. Eventually the decision was taken to issue a Province-wide warning on television and radio for everyone to stay at home after dark.

Operation Motorman took place at 4.00 a.m. on 31 July 1972. On that night there were eighteen battalions and two Royal Marine Commandos in the Province; the whole force amounted to 21,000 men. Under cover of darkness, the navy had sent landing ships (LST) to collect the AVREs from the Gairloch. They were landed on the banks of the River Foyle on a rising tide just before midnight; they moved quickly inland and joined up with the leading troops.

In the event, the IRA made virtually no attempt to resist. The soldiers quickly occupied the areas without difficulty, although two gunmen were shot in the action. The AVREs, using their dozer blades, removed the concrete obstacles and were back on the LSTs as the tide started to fall. As daylight broke, the ships were away. It sounds, written so simply, like an anticlimax but it certainly was not. Similar operations had taken place simultaneously in Belfast, where the hard Catholic areas which had been barricaded were also occupied. The security forces sustained not a single casualty. It was a quick, clean and highly effective operation. Nowhere, in any newspaper anywhere, was there a word of criticism of the army's actions.

If Bloody Sunday had been a media defeat, Motorman was certainly a victory.

The three years from 1969 to 1972 were the learning years for the British army in confronting what could quickly become a hostile media. In earlier campaigns, the army had been accustomed to reporters who had been closely involved with their own operations and usually supportive of their activities. The reporters on the battlefield had no access to the enemy but saw it as their duty to reassure the population at home of the success of the operations being undertaken in their name. Here in Ireland, for the first time, the reporters were as ready to obtain their stories from the IRA as from government and military sources; they felt no obligation to report favourably on the actions of either ministers or soldiers, but made their judgements in the light of their own experience. In the view of General David Mostyn, who was deeply involved at the time: 'a seething anger existed throughout the Army in Northern Ireland that the British media, for the first time in history, should give the Queen's enemies a "top spot" in their reporting.'[15] Not surprisingly, such reporting engendered a bitterness between the two professions which is now hard to eradicate.

For the IRA, on the other hand, the media has proved to be a weapon of unlimited power. Quick to appreciate its value, the IRA soon realized the terrible truth that there is no such thing as bad publicity. What they needed to further their cause was as much publicity as possible. No action on their part was too terrible to undertake; indeed, as the campaign increased in violence, they realized that the more fearful the incident, the greater publicity it engendered. In 1974, their operations spread to the mainland of Britain; in November of that year a series of pub bombings in Birmingham killed 19 people and injured 182. In 1979, a series of assassinations took place which included Airey Neave outside the House of Commons, Sir Richard Sykes, the British Ambassador in The Hague and Lord Mountbatten with his grandson while on holiday in the Republic. On the same day that Mountbatten was murdered, eighteen soldiers were blown up and killed at Warrenpoint. In 1982, two bombs exploded in the London parks killing six bandsmen of the Royal Green Jackets and men and horses of the Household Cavalry (an incident which, it seemed, generated greater sympathy for the horses than the soldiers), while just before Christmas a bomb was exploded outside Harrods. In Brighton in 1984, the Conservative Party conference was bombed at the Grand Hotel, narrowly missing Margaret Thatcher and her husband. Perhaps one of their most despicable deeds was the bombing of an outdoor Armistice Day service in Enniskillen in 1987.[16] Their hope was to wear down the will of the British people to continue supporting a divided Ireland.

In an attempt to limit IRA propaganda, the Thatcher Government introduced a form of censorship by which spokesmen of proscribed organizations were not permitted to have their words broadcast on British radio or television. Although the stricture was much disliked by the terrorist organizations, it was quickly circumvented by the broadcasters who dubbed interviews with proscribed speakers with their words 'spoken by an actor'. This was perhaps the only act of peacetime censorship which has ever in recent times been introduced by a democracy on its own media.

However, despite this fearful list of bloodshed, the IRA managed to maintain a remarkable level of support in the United States. The importance of the Irish vote in American politics, coupled with the innate sympathy in the American mind toward all things Irish, enabled the IRA organizers to sustain a great well of support and goodwill in the States, not least in terms of finance raised by the so-called charitable organization NORAID. The anti-British filming quoted earlier by an American television company is only one example.

Curiously, the participants who appear to have missed out in this great media war are the Protestant Unionists. On the face of it, their situation should be the one to generate the greatest sympathy. They are after all the loyalists who wish to remain in the kingdom; they are ethnically Scots and English and the representatives of the established Church on the mainland. Yet they have never learned, it seems, to tap the sympathy that should by rights be theirs. Instead, they have often presented themselves as arrogant, unbending bigots who have never attempted to woo either the media or other allies in the same way as the republicans.

Today, in June 1997, despite a shortlived IRA ceasefire, during which the television censorship was removed and not reintroduced, the feud continues. In the run-up to the general election in May, the IRA resumed its strategy of disrupting life on the mainland. Manchester city centre was virtually destroyed by a massive explosion. Two coded telephone messages prevented the running of the Grand National at Aintree within half an hour of the off, causing the racecourse to be evacuated although no bombs were ever found. Railway stations have been closed during rush hours, motorways interrupted and airports evacuated. The ensuing publicity has magnified the power of the terrorists on each occasion, although the British public has responded with remarkable stoicism to the endless dangers and inconvenience.

All the participants in this endless feud have learned to respect the power of the media, and most have managed to find ways of turning it from time to time to their own advantage. It may be argued that the close press scrutiny of the actions of the British Government has acted as a bridle to prevent the misuse of power. The disclosure of interrogation amounting almost to torture brought such action to a speedy conclusion; equally, the presence of the media on the streets ensured that the security forces could never step across the narrow limits of the rule of law with impunity.

On the other hand, that same presence has offered the terrorists a constant platform of publicity which has spurred them on to renewed acts of violence, each more terrible and more spectacular than the last.

Finally and to the credit of the media, it has brought home to millions of its readers and viewers the bitterness and hatred that can be implanted into the hearts of men. In the plantation of Ulster, King James could have done no worse if he had sown the Province with dragons' teeth.

1. Jonathan Bardon, *History of Ulster*, Ireland, Blackstaff, 1992, p. 601
2. J. Keegan, 'The Phantom Army that threatens Britain,' *Sunday Telegraph*, 10 March 1996
3. Conversations with General Sir Harry Tuzo, 15 June 1996
4. Simon Winchester, *In Holy Terror*, London, Faber, 1974, p. 32
5. *BBC Television News*, 30 January 1972; Eamonn-McCann, *Bloody Sunday in Derry*, p. 202
6. *Daily Telegraph*, Monday 31 January 1972 (quoting Major General R.C. Ford, Commander Land Forces)
7. BBC Television documentary, *The Information War*, Michael Dewar, *British Army in Northern Ireland*, p. 60
8. *Widgery Report*, 10 April 1972: '. . . There was no general breakdown of discipline. For the most part the soldiers acted as they did because they thought their orders required it. . . .'
9. Desmond Hamill, *Pig in the Middle*, London, Methuen, 1985, p. 93
10. BBC Television documentary, *The Information War*
11. *Daily Telegraph*, 31 January 1972
12. French Television Film Record, 1972
13. American Television Film Record, 1972
14. Soviet Television Film Record, 1972
15. Conversation with General Sir David Mostyn, 28 May 1997
16. Eleven killed and sixty-three injured

CHAPTER EIGHT

The Falklands War, 1982

'I have seen the lady a second time and she really does mean it.'

Secretary of State Alexander Haig
to President Galtieri of Argentina[1]

Under the direction of the Labour Government which ruled Britain from 1974 until 1978, it had been made clear to the military that they should make no contingencies for any operations without the support of allies, other than for internal security operations in Northern Ireland. Either, it was assumed, operations would be conducted under the umbrella of NATO or as part of a United Nations force such as that in Cyprus. Any suggestion that British forces might be required to fight entirely unaided was ruled out. Nor had any specific change in directive been received on the election of a Conservative Government under the leadership of Mrs Thatcher in the spring of 1979. Indeed, under John Nott as Secretary of State for Defence in 1980, a review of the defence forces was carried out in order to reduce expenditure, which recommended swingeing cuts in the strength of the Royal Navy, primarily on the grounds that the only war in which Britain might be involved would be on the mainland of Europe.

At the same time, Britain and its economy was in a state of unrelieved gloom. Raymond Seitz, an American career diplomat who was later to become US Ambassador to Britain, recalls how, at that time: 'he couldn't find a single Brit with a good word to say about the place.'[2]

In Argentina, the leader of a military junta, General Leopoldo Galtieri, saw an opportunity to improve his deteriorating political situation in his own country by the acquisition of a group of South Atlantic islands called by him the Malvinas, but, by the British whose colony they were, the Falkland Islands. As has happened so often in the present century, he misguidedly believed that he could take this action without risk of military confrontation.

Tentative operations were begun under the cover of 'scrap metal dealers' who hoisted the Argentinian flag on the remote island of South Georgia. These were followed by a full-scale invasion of the Falkland

163

Islands on 2 April 1982. The small force of Royal Marines on the islands was quickly overpowered and the Governor, Rex Hunt, who insisted on marching out of Government House in his ceremonial uniform with plumed hat, was flown out of his islands and returned to London.

As *The Economist* pointed out, looking back on that action in its edition of 24 April:

It all seemed so easy and so right to the generals and admirals of this remote corner of the world a month ago: the Falkland Islands were there for the taking and the world would probably accept their capture as an accomplished fact. The United States had been carefully building up an excellent relationship with the pro-western Galtieri and so would probably limit itself to a lame protest; the Russians, heavily dependent on Argentine grain shipments, would make sure nothing went awry; and Argentina's friends in the third world would applaud a victory over colonialism, while Britain, deep in economic crisis, would swallow a temporary discomfort. At home, Argentinians would forget their anger with the Junta over long years of dictatorial rule and economic mismanagement.

'But,' *The Economist* concluded, 'not one of these calculations was accurate.'

So began an operation by Britain to recover the islands, which came to present the media with a host of problems almost as testing as those faced by the armed forces themselves. It proved to be an operation which confronted the media with situations such as they had very seldom encountered before and which it is unlikely will ever be repeated.

Even before the actual invasion, intelligence reports had been received by Margaret Thatcher, the British Prime Minister of still comparatively short standing, that the Argentinian forces were closing on the islands. On 31 March she sat with her advisers reviewing the situation in her office in the Houses of Parliament. With her she had no military men as none had been immediately available. Sir Antony Acland, at that time about to become Permanent Under Secretary at the Foreign Office, was present and recalls that there were a lot of long faces to be seen in the room. The Falkland Islands were 8,000 miles away; there was no air base available to the British within range of the islands and the only Royal Naval ship in the area was the Antarctic survey vessel, HMS *Endurance*, which was herself shortly to be laid up.

Suddenly, as Lady Thatcher herself recalls, the door of the room flew open and a very angry man burst in. He was Admiral Sir Henry Leach, the Chief of Naval Staff and First Sea Lord, resplendent in full naval uniform. He had come as quickly as he could from some other engagement but had been unable to make his way past the police officers guarding the entrance to the Palace of Westminster, for whom naval uniform cut little ice. After furious representations, he had finally been allowed in.[3]

'Sir Henry,' enquired Mrs Thatcher, 'how can we recover the Falkland Islands if they are invaded by Argentina?'

Without hesitation, the Admiral replied that he could despatch a naval task force to the South Atlantic to recover the islands and that it could sail in forty-eight hours. From that moment, indeed perhaps for the rest of her career, the Prime Minister never looked back.

The great distances involved and the time taken for the task force to reach the South Atlantic – even the staging post of Ascension Island, a British possession with an air base at that time leased to the Americans, was still 3,500 miles from the Falklands – gave ample time for a great deal of hectic diplomatic activity to take place in the hope of preventing a shooting war. This activity centred mainly around the United Nations and the United States. Although this diplomatic action ultimately failed in its primary aim, it is probably not too strong to say that, without the negotiations undertaken in this critical phase of the crisis, the ultimate outcome might not have been so successful for the British. They had already learned a bitter lesson of undertaking military adventures without international support at Suez in 1956.

Margaret Thatcher was fortunate to have in post in New York and Washington two of the ablest ambassadors in the British foreign service: at the United Nations in New York, Sir Anthony Parsons, and in Washington, Sir Nicholas Henderson. One of the first tasks for Parsons was to secure the support of the United Nations for the British response to the Argentine invasion. To do this he drafted a resolution for consideration by the Security Council which demanded the immediate withdrawal of the Argentine forces from the islands. The fifteen members of the Council at that time included some of fairly doubtful sympathy to the British cause. For his resolution to be approved by the Council, Sir Anthony needed the support of ten out of the fifteen members. Of the permanent members, the United States, the Soviet Union, France, Britain and China, he could only be sure in the first instance of two,

France and Britain, although he felt sure that with Henderson's help, the United States could be counted upon. A Russian veto could of course derail the whole thing.

Of the other members, he was faced with Zaïre (which held the Presidency of the Council), Guyana, Ireland, Japan, Jordan, Panama, Poland, Spain, Togo and Uganda. The vote was to be held within twenty-four hours of the draft being put forward.

After prodigious efforts, Parsons had the agreement of eight of the states. The Communist countries were beyond his diplomacy but would, he hoped, abstain, while Panama and Spain were, he knew, supportive of Argentina. Uganda was doubtful and Jordan's envoy, despite his own wish to support Britain, had instructions not to vote in favour of anything that smacked of colonialism. Shortly before the meeting, Uganda agreed to support the resolution, leaving Parsons with nine votes. In desperation he telephoned London to speak to the Foreign Secretary, but failed to find him. In a last bid he asked to speak to the Prime Minister; with only hours to spare, Margaret Thatcher telephoned King Hussein and persuaded him to change his envoy's instructions. Sir Anthony had his ten votes. Now he had only to fear a Russian veto; the matter went to the vote and only Panama voted against. Russia, Poland, China and Spain all abstained.

The resolution (No. 502), together with the principle that a sovereign state may always defend itself against aggression, which is enshrined under Article 51, served as a vital platform for the retention of world opinion in favour of Britain, without which the actions of the task force might easily have been outlawed.

In Washington a still more delicate diplomatic battle had to be fought. President Reagan's policies in Central and South America were at a difficult juncture. In an attempt to strengthen support for their activities in Central America, the United States had warmly welcomed offers of military assistance in Nicaragua and El Salvador from the Argentinians, often in operations in which the Americans preferred not to become embroiled themselves. As the Commander-in-Chief of the Argentinian forces, Galtieri had recently been generously and enthusiastically welcomed and entertained in the States. On the other hand, Britain played an important role in Europe as one of the United States' closest allies. At first, President Reagan had attempted to remain neutral in the dispute, merely extending his good offices in an attempt to find a peaceful solution. Thanks, however, to the relentless efforts of the British

Ambassador throughout the month of April, during which the American Secretary of State, Alexander Haig, carried out marathon shuttle negotiations between London and Buenos Aires, the United States Government was persuaded to forget its even-handed approach to the dispute and to side firmly with Britain. Nor was it only the administration that Henderson had carried with him; by dint of a punishing programme of television appearances and radio interviews throughout the month, the ambassador gained the support of a wide section of the American public to the British cause.

In his own words:

> I had to appear on a TV morning show at 7.30 a.m. and naturally I was asked questions about . . . our naval movements, military intentions etc. That was ABC. Half an hour later I appeared on CBS. I decided that morning to devote the next few days to public, press and congressional opinion. I undertook an uninterrupted programme of speaking engagements and interviews. My aim was to get it across to the US public that this was not an act from Gilbert and Sullivan . . . but a serious transgression of the peace that could have a direct impact on the Americans. I think it was one of the most difficult and demanding times of my life.[4]

The ambassador's remarkable achievements were elsewhere entertainingly described:

> Henderson himself became the most conspicuous expression of the British effort and performed his role to spectacular effect. A tall sparely built figure, with a relaxed and confident manner, he combined elegance with a distinct air of dishevelment. His grey hair seemed always in need of attention from the barber; his suits were expensive but sagging; his shirt collars fashionable but perpetually out of control; and his silk ties hung uneasily outside his jacket, usually with the lining on display. He fitted every American's idea of what a British gentleman should be. And he was perfectly capable of exploiting it.[5]

In the event, on 30 April the United States decided firmly to support Britain. Even before this, the British had found a powerful ally in the American Secretary of Defense, Caspar Weinberger; from the outset of

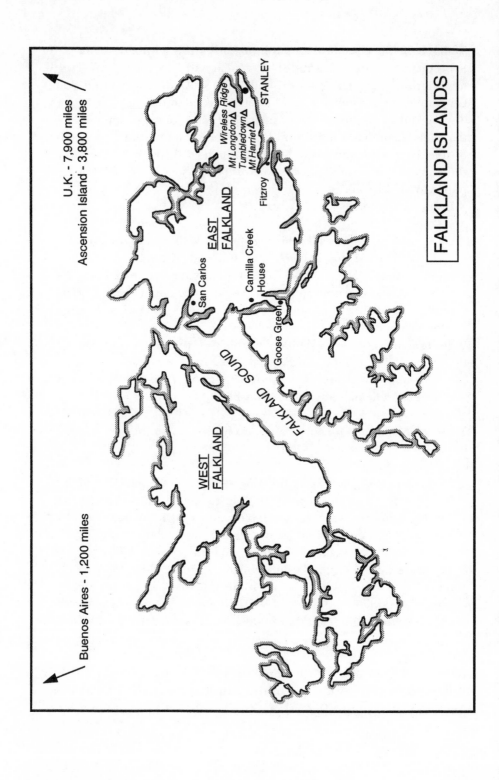

Buenos Aires - 1,200 miles

U.K. - 7,900 miles
Ascension Island - 3,800 miles

STANLEY
Wireless Ridge
Mt Longdon△
Tumbledown△
Mt Harriet△
Fitzroy

EAST
FALKLAND

San Carlos
Camilla Creek
House
Goose Green

FALKLAND SOUND

WEST
FALKLAND

FALKLAND ISLANDS

the crisis, he had taken a strong position in favour of Britain. Thanks to him and subsequently to the support given by the American administration, a flow of much critically needed equipment was made available to the British forces, including in particular the latest mark of US Sidewinder air-to-air missiles which were later to prove invaluable to the hard-pressed Sea Harriers of the Royal Navy. Weinberger's wholehearted commitment to the British cause is recorded by Henderson; he quotes an extract from Weinberger's own memoirs which reads:

> I therefore directed that all British requests were to have immediate and first priority . . . I also directed that each of these requests come directly to my desk, something that would not otherwise have happened. Finally, I directed that I be told within twenty four hours of our receipt of a British request, whether it had been granted, if not, why not and when would it be granted.[6]

Small wonder that at the end of the campaign Caspar Weinberger was honoured by the Queen with the award of a knighthood.

As the task force sailed south, two major bloodless victories had been won which would assure Britain of the support of the free world in her determination to recover her lost islands. Without the successful manipulation of diplomatic and public opinion by the two ambassadors and their staffs, much of it achieved through intelligent use of the media, the outcome of the whole affair could have been very different.

As the ships of the task force gathered to set off on their long journey down to the South Atlantic, little thought was given to facilities for the media. To the Royal Navy, the idea of embarking journalists in their ships was anathema. However, after some argument, it was at first decided to offer places to a total of six reporters. Of these none was a defence correspondent, but journalists chosen at random and in a great hurry by their editors. The man from the *Sun* arrived at Portsmouth on a motor cycle in shorts.[7] Once it became known on Fleet Street that places were available, the Ministry of Defence (MOD) and No. 10 Downing Street were besieged by other angry editors demanding places for their reporters on the ships. Not only the national press, radio and television wished to be included, but also provincial papers in large numbers. After hectic negotiations, twenty-nine all-British representatives of the media finally accompanied the task force, some on board the two aircraft carriers, *Hermes* and *Invincible*, and some with the troops in the hastily requisitioned SS *Canberra*, a white-painted cruise liner. No consideration was given to accommodating any journalists from other countries. As Lady Thatcher later recalled: 'We certainly didn't want any foreigners reporting what we were doing down there!'[8]

To each ship carrying journalists, the MOD sent a civilian public relations officer whose task was to supervise the reporters, explain to them the rules under which they were to work and to 'vet' any copy which they wished to send home. The Ministry wished to avoid use of the word 'censorship'. Nevertheless, the rules were strict, forbidding any mention of strengths, intentions or the capability of any weapon systems; even the weather could not be reported. Unbelievably, the journalists were told in their joining instructions to bring with them a 'dark suit', apparently to make sure that they were properly dressed for dinner in the wardroom.[9]

It is not too difficult to imagine the reaction of the captain of an aircraft carrier, about to sail into action, on meeting on board his own ship a group of journalists, hung about with cameras, being escorted by an MOD PR man in civilian clothes, who informs him that they will all be with him for the foreseeable future. Worse was in fact to come, as the journalists felt themselves in no way bound by naval discipline. On board HMS *Invincible*, the journalists were appointed to 'action stations' on one of the lower decks. The first time that 'action stations' was ordered, one of the pressmen wandered onto the bridge, saying that 'as he represented *The Times*, he could go where he liked'.[10] Surprisingly, the only journalist to be arrested was Simon Winchester of *The Sunday Times* and he was imprisoned by the Argentinians in Ushuaia on the mainland, where he was attempting to report from the enemy point of view.

Commenting on the problem of journalists on board warships, Admiral Sir Jeremy Black, at that time the Captain of *Invincible*, writes:

At the root of our difficulties lay one fundamental fact. The Services are taught from their earliest days to be team players and that the results of the team working together are the only results that matter, regardless of individuals who subordinate themselves to the team. Press men are the very antithesis of this. They operate as individuals, they don't understand the word team even when their lives depend on it and the only other individual in their firmament is their Editor. They will pursue their own ends at any price, having never heard of the word loyalty, and will trample on anyone or anything that stands in their way. Therefore, at a time when all concerned are experiencing pressures as great as any they have ever known, these two conflicting attitudes or disciplines are brought face to face, often for the first time. An inevitable consequence is a measure of discord and a lack of trust.[11]

There is no doubt that, at the early stages of the operation, few people believed that the task force would be required physically to drive the Argentinians off the islands. Even if no diplomatic solution was reached, it was thought probable that the Argentinians would prefer discretion to valour and not wait to fight it out. For this reason, the editors had not in every case sent their most experienced reporters, believing it likely that they would simply enjoy a cruise at Government expense, returning home within a month. Even at the highest levels there was still unwillingness to believe that a major land battle would have to be fought. Early in May, when the decision to despatch a second brigade in support of the Commando Brigade was being considered, one of the present authors was recommending this course of action to Sir Edwin Bramall, the Chief of the General Staff, when he remarked: 'You know, John, this is not going to be a second D-Day!'

Back on board the task force, the manner in which the journalists were treated varied from ship to ship. Some captains refused to meet them, others gave them briefings, while on the troopships the soldiers often welcomed them as they were able to send back stories to their own local papers. Brian Hanrahan recalls that on embarking in HMS *Hermes* he was told that his link with the Captain was to be through the Ship's Education Officer and that he should make any applications for help through him. He did not meet the Captain for some time, but on the arrival on board of the Admiral, Sandy Woodward, he was invited to a briefing with his fellow journalists at which they were informed that 'they would be told what they should and should not report'. Hanrahan commented at the time that, while the Navy might say what could *not* be reported for security reasons, it could certainly not tell him what he *should* report. Perhaps the most revealing aspect of the naval approach to the media comes from the Admiral himself. In his own account, based on his diaries, he writes: 'On this day [26 April] I also ran into trouble from an unforeseen, though probably unwitting enemy, the British Press. I should point out that I had never dealt with this phenomenon before, thus I was unsure how to handle them or what to tell them . . .'[12]

He goes on to record how the interviews that he gave were considered by the Foreign Office and others as a 'minor catastrophe'. He even reported the comment published about his television interview in the *Sunday Telegraph* which concluded: 'Seeing him on television, half sitting, half lying back, hiding his mouth behind his knuckles as he reaches hesitantly for the right words, you see what happened on the *Hermes* last week. An Admiral got out of his depth.'[13]

That an admiral whose training over some thirty-five years in the navy, which had included attendance at the Royal College of Defence Studies, the final year's training for those earmarked for high command, could say that he had had no experience of how to handle the press, is a measure of the Royal Navy's attitudes to the media at this time. What the army had been forced to learn by bitter experience in Northern Ireland a decade before was now facing the traditional 'silent service' on its own quarterdecks.

But whatever the relationships on the voyage south, matters changed considerably once it became clear that there was to be action ashore. Those journalists who had been assigned to the aircraft carriers realized that, unless their ship itself was attacked, all the action they would see would be the departure and return of the Sea Harriers and helicopters. This, incidentally, did give Brian Hanrahan the opportunity to make one of the memorable reports of the war from *Hermes*. Early on in the operations, the Argentinians had been claiming the shooting down of a number of British Sea Harriers; Hanrahan gave much needed reassurance to the people at home, as well as confirming the support of the media for the task force, with his famous report: 'I counted them all out and I counted them all back!'

However, despite the proposal by the Ministry of Defence before departure that all reports filed from the task force should be pooled, the first instinct of a good reporter is to get himself where the action is, if possible closer and sooner than any of his so-called colleagues. Those on the warships now demanded to be transferred to the landing ships, creating every sort of trouble until their wishes were met. One group, who had incensed their host captain by their demands, found themselves transferred to the deck of a Royal Fleet Auxiliary which they found to their discomfort to be loaded with ammunition.[14]

If the first duty of a reporter is to be at the scene of the action, the second and equally important requirement is to be able to file his copy. The only communications open to him in this case were those of the task force itself. While on board ship, he could do his best to persuade his hosts to transmit his messages to the Ministry of Defence for onward despatch to his editor, but, once ashore, his only hope lay in the goodwill of helicopter pilots to deliver his copy when returning to the ships. This frequently led to bitter recriminations about lost copy which never reached its destination. It seems remarkable, writing in 1997, to remember that throughout the war, no live television pictures of the operations were transmitted. To have done so was well within the state of the art at the time, but would have necessitated the use of a satellite to do so. Bernard Ingham, the Prime Minister's press secretary at the time, recalls that there were constant requests for time to be allocated on the satellites in use for communication with the task force. Lady Thatcher confirmed that 'there were far too many other important things for which the satellites were needed to justify their use for mere television pictures'.[15] Whether this was a preconceived policy decision or one arrived at in haste can only be a speculation at this distance. However, if the Falklands campaign was in any sense unique, it was the total inability of the media to reach the scene of the action or to report it, save through the good offices of the armed forces, that made it so.

Nevertheless, despite the strained relationships of the voyage, once ashore, most of the journalists earned the respect if not the admiration of the troops. They had had none of the training to prepare them for the rigours of the operation from which the marines and the soldiers benefited and yet they remained for the most part in the forefront of the events right through to the end.

It is not the purpose of this book to follow the whole sequence of events which led to the final British victory in Port Stanley. As in our earlier studies, we have tried to assess the specific effects which the presence of the media had on the outcome of the war. In the period of actual fighting, there were probably only half-a-dozen events in which the presence of the media had such an effect, but some of these left serious scars on the relationships between fighting men and journalists. Of these incidents, the most notable related to the sinking of the *Sheffield*, the landing at San Carlos, the battle for Goose Green, the fusing of Argentinian air force bombs and the events at Fitzroy and Bluff Cove. There was in addition another event which, although it had no direct effect, caused a serious upset between commanders and reporters as they began the final battle for Stanley. But first, the *Sheffield*.

Despite the shock waves that went round the world when the news of the sinking of the Argentinian cruiser *General Belgrano* was received, the impact of the sinking of HMS *Sheffield* on 4 May had far greater effect. The *Belgrano*, whatever the rights and wrongs of the case, was an elderly warship totally outclassed by the presence of nuclear submarines and it came as little surprise, certainly to the British, to hear that the Argentinian navy had taken the first casualty. The tabloid newspapers went wild with jubilation at the news, using a headline in one case which must take the prize for vulgarity.[16] But to hear, only a day later, of the demise of a destroyer of the Royal Navy at the hands of the Argentine air force put the whole operation into a different league. None of Her Majesty's ships had been sunk since 1945 and the realization of what Britain had let herself in for came as a considerable shock to her citizens. The news itself was announced dramatically in an interruption to the BBC's nine o'clock bulletin by the dry and pedantic voice of the Ministry of Defence spokesman, Ian MacDonald, of whom more later. The media did not of course play any part with regard to the attack itself, but the impact of this first spilling of British blood, carried by the media all over the world, changed attitudes to the war more sharply than any other of the many reverses which were still to come. It was soon afterwards that the first television and radio programmes began to question the wisdom and justification for embarking on this whole operation. The most outspoken of these was the BBC *Panorama* programme broadcast on 7 May, just three days after the *Sheffield* incident.

The first landings, other than clandestine operations by special forces, took place near San Carlos on 21 May on the north-west corner of East Falkland. The decision to land here was the result of long and careful study of a number of alternative sites. Not unnaturally, the choice was made in considerable secrecy and for a number of days very little news was released in London to the hungry and waiting media. Their only alternative to hard news was speculation, and this speculation led to the appearance of a new phenomenon, the armchair strategist. Numerous retired senior officers were invited to television studios and invited to suggest what they might do and where they might land, were they in charge of the operation. In many cases this was as harmless as the children's blindfold game of pinning a tail on a donkey. However, as the studies continued, with reasons provided, an intelligent Argentinian might have made a very shrewd guess as to the British choice. In fact there is no evidence of the Argentinians gaining any significant intelligence from these discussions, although they led to considerable acrimony within military and political circles. Lady Thatcher herself considers that in some cases the speculation made by these senior officers came little short of treachery.[17] It is a subject to which we shall return when we come to consider the Gulf War.

The battle for Goose Green is, however, another matter. In all that has been written about this, the first land engagement of the campaign (again other than special forces' operations), doubts have been expressed about the need or purpose of this attack on the south-west corner of East Falkland. It was carried out on 28 May with singular bravery and success by 2nd Parachute Battalion, or 2 Para as they are always known. It was, however, beyond doubt that a reasonably strong Argentinian force was deployed there which could have been expected to prove a threat to the flank of the main force as it advanced diagonally across the island towards Stanley. What was not known to the British was the true strength of the forces in Goose Green; had that been known, it is unlikely that a single battalion group would have been given the task of clearing it.

As later emerged, the Argentinian troops in Goose Green had been sent there to resist a possible landing in that part of the island. Accordingly their defensive positions were all facing seaward. As 2 Para made their way southwards towards the isthmus that leads to Goose Green, the BBC World Service in one of its hourly news bulletins reported them to be at a particular farmstead, Camilla Creek House, on the way to Goose Green. Visiting the scene of the battle a few months later, one of the authors of this book met a Falkland farmer who had heard the broadcast and had actually seen the Argentinians moving their troops to new positions facing north, where they dug in to await the arrival of the British troops.

It is difficult not to believe that, without this disclosure, it would have been a less hard fought and less bloody battle. The events that led up to the broadcast have been rigorously examined, but no definitive explanation has been given. Again speculation as to the first objectives to be attacked was rife and the name of Goose Green had been widely bandied about. Camilla Creek House in particular was mentioned in a *World at One* television programme, at the time when the battalion was in fact lying up there prior to attacking Goose Green. This speculation was repeated on the World Service. It has been suggested that the leak came from the Ministry of Defence operations centre, where it was believed that, as the attack was already under way, news of it could be released. Its exact source has never been divulged. The distinguished commanding officer of 2 Para, Lt Colonel 'H' Jones, who won a posthumous Victoria Cross while leading his battalion into the attack, had been so incensed when he heard the broadcast during his approach march, that he announced his intention to sue the BBC after the war was over. In fact it may not have been the BBC who were strictly guilty.

The fourth occasion on which the media may have affected events relates to the failure of Argentinian bombs to explode when attacking British warships. The cause of the failure has been attributed either to faulty or elderly equipment or to lack of time between launching and strike for the detonators to operate correctly. This latter cause might have been corrected by the Argentine air force, if its commanders had known. The failure of the bombs was disclosed to correspondents in a non-attributable briefing only two days after HMS *Glasgow* had been hit by a bomb which failed to explode. Such a briefing was again given to American journalists in London with speculation as to the cause.[18] It was not until after 23 May that a final clamp down on references to unexploded bombs was enforced by the Chiefs of Staff. Whether or not the Argentinians were able to benefit from this generosity of information is unclear; certainly, without this fault in their operations, the British navy would have suffered much more severely than it did.

The effects of the media in the next instance are perhaps more hypothetical. Once the second British brigade, 5 Brigade, had arrived on the islands, the land commander, Major General Jeremy Moore, planned to direct them on to Stanley on the right of the Commando Brigade. The marines and paras forming the Commando Brigade had travelled across the island on foot and were approaching the Argentinian positions on the high ground to the west of Stanley. In the absence of troop-lifting helicopters which had been lost in the Atlantic Conveyor, sunk by an Exocet attack on the same day as HMS *Coventry* was hit, the General planned to move the 5 Brigade troops by sea to a landing place at Fitzroy on the south coast of the island. It had been planned to carry out the operation under cover of darkness, but delays of one sort and another meant that the landing ships, *Sir Galahad* and *Sir Tristram*, were still at anchor in daylight on 8 June. Men of the Welsh Guards, who had had an extremely rough and unpleasant voyage around the island, were still on board *Galahad*. The weather forecast, however, was for low and thick cloud cover which would have made air attack impossible. Unfortunately, as is so often the case in the South Atlantic, a sudden and unexpected change in the weather occurred; on this particular morning the skies suddenly cleared and with equal suddenness both ships were attacked by Skyhawks and Mirages of the Argentinian air force with disastrous results.

A reporter who was actually on board *Galahad*, Mick Seamark of the *Daily Star*, saw the whole event and wrote an eyewitness account of the desperate efforts that were made to rescue the men in the burning ship. He considered it to be one of the most moving and dramatic stories that he had ever had the opportunity to cover. He despatched his piece by helicopter to one of the ships for onward transmission to London. The copy never reached its destination, nor has its disappearance ever been satisfactorily accounted for.[19] Nevertheless, news of the success of the Argentinian attack was quickly released from Buenos Aires, where it was estimated that the best part of a British battalion had been wiped out. In fact, the number of Welsh Guardsmen killed was thirty-three and the total death roll was fifty-one. The problem facing the British was whether or not to disclose the true figures; not to do so could be intensely damaging to morale, if the enemy figures were accepted; but, at the same time, the enemy, believing the British to have suffered a major setback, would think that any attack on their positions would be severely delayed. Faced with this dilemma, a decision was taken at first in the Ministry of Defence not to disclose the casualty figures. However, this policy was not followed by Bernard Ingham, the Prime Minister's press secretary, who released the figures at a press conference held in Düsseldorf without prior reference to the MOD. Whether ignorance of the true effect of the air attack would have made the Argentinian troops on the hills outside Stanley less ready to receive the 5 Brigade attacks when they came must be speculative indeed. In any case the outcome would certainly not have been different. It is worth recording that the article written by Seamark was published later, well after the war was over, described as 'the article the Ministry would not let you read at the time'.

The problems of disclosure of casualties had been met earlier when HMS *Coventry* was sunk by air attack. The navy had been loath to name the ship which had been sunk but, by acknowledging the loss of an unnamed ship, great and unnecessary anxiety was caused to the families of every ship in the task force; thereafter, in deference to the host of anxious enquiries, the ship's name was given.

The last incident occurred before the final battles were fought out grimly on the hills surrounding Stanley to the west. As the troops were preparing for these attacks, which proved to be among the fiercest battles of the war, two journalists telephoned each other on a civilian line between two of the island settlements; during the conversation, details of a forthcoming attack were disclosed. The call was overheard by a Royal Marines officer and reported to the brigade commander, who believed that the line ran through an exchange in enemy-held Stanley. In fact this was not the case so no harm was done, but, from that time, journalists were barred from attending orders groups or briefings by the commanders. Despite these anxieties, the journalists remained with the troops until the end; in fact, the first man who had sailed with the task force to walk into the town of Stanley was Max Hastings, the well-known reporter at that time for the *Standard* and the *Express*. Hastings' successful reporting of the campaign generated a good deal of ill-feeling among his colleagues, but his ability to get himself to the right place at the right time certainly earned him the respect of the troops.

Names such as Mount Longdon, Mount Harriet, Tumbledown Mountain and Wireless Ridge have now passed into the folklore of the Falklands campaign and on 14 June, General Menendez surrendered to General Moore. As a postscript and as an indication of the endless pertinacity of the reporters on the Falklands, two of them, John Witherow of *The Times* and Patrick Bishop of the *Observer*, subsequently bamboozled their way into the cabin on board HMS *Fearless* where Menendez was being held prisoner and started to interview him. They were quickly ejected by a furious naval commander.[20]

However, while the war itself was being fought out in the South Atlantic, another very different war was being fought in London between the Ministry of Defence in Whitehall and the editors of Fleet Street and the BBC.

To understand why such bitter resentment was felt by the press towards the Ministry of Defence during the Falklands War, one needs to appreciate some of the internal pressures and frictions which existed – and no doubt still exist – in that very large establishment. Until 1964 the three armed services were separately directed from the Admiralty, the War Office and the Air Ministry. Each had its own Secretary of State (in the case of the navy, he enjoyed the title of First Lord of the Admiralty), its own Permanent Secretary in the Civil Service and of course its own Chief of Staff (again in the case of the navy, the First Sea Lord). When under Peter Thorneycroft and Earl Mountbatten, all three were combined into a single ministry under a Secretary of State for Defence and a Chief of Defence

Staff (CDS), the single services retained considerable independence. Each continued to have a junior minister to represent them, a Deputy Under Secretary appointed to each service and, of course, the Chief of Staff who, together with his fellow chiefs, combined to give military advice to the government. Each Chief of Staff retained the right of direct access to the Prime Minister over the head of his Secretary of State on matters relating to his own service. The whole vast edifice was supervised at the top by the Permanent Under Secretary for Defence (PUS). This was, in principle, still the organization in place at the outset of the Falklands War.

Before the election of Margaret Thatcher's Government in 1979, the star of the Ministry of Defence was in decline. Jim Callaghan's Labour Government was little interested in defence matters; the voice of the Secretary of State (the unfortunate Fred Mulley) was not heeded in Cabinet and the urgent representations by the Chiefs of Staff for a better deal for their men went unanswered. As a result, the forces were poorly paid and some of the best of them were 'voting with their feet' and leaving. During these unhappy years for the armed forces, the position of the Civil Service became noticeably stronger in the corridors of power as the influence of the military declined.

This situation remained unchanged until Margaret Thatcher was faced with the challenge of the Falklands invasion in 1982. In an attempt to reduce defence spending, her Secretary of State, John Nott, had, only months before, introduced his proposals for expenditure reduction which included plans to sell off HMS *Invincible* and scrap the amphibious ships, *Fearless* and *Intrepid*. The navy was not unnaturally fighting a powerful rearguard action to resist these proposals, which were being financially driven by the Treasury and the Civil Service.

At the time of Galtieri's invasion, the Chief of Defence Staff, Admiral of the Fleet Sir Terence Lewin, was in New Zealand and it therefore fell to the First Sea Lord, Admiral Sir Henry Leach, to answer for the Royal Navy when asked whether it was possible to take military action. His memorable reply to the Prime Minister has already been mentioned. Doubts were immediately lodged by the Civil Service as to whether such an adventure could be afforded, but Margaret Thatcher, with the bit already between her teeth, brushed aside financial difficulties. As she recalled many years later: 'Harold Macmillan once warned me never to have a Treasury official present during operational planning. Accordingly, I never had anyone from the Treasury on my War Cabinet. The Services were to have whatever they wanted that I could give them.'[21]

From the time of his return from abroad, Admiral Lewin became a full member of the so-called War Cabinet, from which he was the direct link to the Chiefs of Staff Committee and thence to the Commander-in-Chief, Admiral Sir John Fieldhouse, at his headquarters in Northwood. Suddenly shorn of its erstwhile strength, the Civil Service cast about for what was left. The key matter which was still waiting to be snapped up was the control of information and this it grasped with both hands.

The Ministry of Defence Public Relations department was a strange animal. Headed by a civil servant of Assistant Secretary rank, its body was made up partly of military officers and partly of civilian 'information officers'. The quality of this mixed staff varied considerably. Leading the military were three senior officers from the three services – a naval captain, a brigadier and an air commodore – whose experience of running an information service was equally varied. The one belief that they all three shared (although it was by no means true) was that each was responsible to his own Chief of Staff and not to the Civil Service.

The start of operations found the PR organization in some disarray; the civilian head (CPR) had recently left and his successor, though appointed, had not yet arrived. His deputy and acting head was Ian MacDonald, who was to become in a very short time a household name. In the case of the navy, the captain had just been posted to Hong Kong and a new incumbent arrived on the day the task force sailed. He had little or no experience of public relations and was not himself a sea-going officer. The brigadier had recently commanded the Belfast brigade in Northern Ireland, had considerable experience of the media and had already made a name for himself among the defence correspondents as a highly effective communicator. Indeed, it had been he who had arranged that Max Hastings should accompany the task force.[22] The air commodore too was well regarded and thoroughly briefed by his own service. However, once the Civil Service under the powerful and very effective direction of Sir Frank Cooper, the PUS, had grabbed the reins of information control, the military PR staffs were forbidden to communicate directly to the press in any way. All press releases were to be made by the acting CPR. This apparently strange instruction had its origin a good deal earlier. During the seventies, a television film of internal security training at Sandhurst had been broadcast in which the rioters were depicted as 'Trades Unionists'. A furious senior member of the Labour Cabinet had rung up the PUS at the MOD and ordered that: 'no military man was ever to be in charge of public relations again'.[23]

Whereas the logic of a very tight control on any information release was entirely understandable, the serious omission which this system caused was the complete lack of background 'off the record' briefing for the press. Inevitably there will always arise a host of semi-technical enquiries which every reporter will need to ask in the preparation of his copy. Basic questions about the ships in the task force, details about weapon systems that were not secret, names of ship's captains and organizations of commandoes and battalions were constantly being asked and had, for the most part, to be referred to the armed services who were unable to speak for themselves. In fairness to the Civil Service, it had one overriding responsibility which was probably less readily understood by the military; this was to the Secretary of State, John Nott. Throughout the operation, he had an absolute obligation to keep Parliament informed; if news items were released to the press before Parliament, there were inevitable and powerful complaints from the House of Commons which could seriously embarrass the Government. To tread this narrow path between Westminster and Fleet Street was not easy.

It is, however, the off-record briefing that is meat and drink to the press. Background information, which enables the reporter to put flesh onto the bones of his story, was almost entirely absent from the brief, laconic statements put out by the MOD information service. MacDonald earned the *nom de guerre* of 'the I-speak-your-weight man', not without some justification because, as with the weighing machine, he did undoubtedly always speak the truth, if sometimes unpalatable and always unvarnished, in his slow, measured and maddening monotones. Some scurrilous journalists christened him 'the warm-up man for the Lutine Bell'.[24]

Pressure latterly became so great for more background briefings that Sir Frank Cooper himself eventually held a number of meetings with editors. Although these were at first welcomed, Sir Frank brought down a storm on his own head by misleading his listeners on the eve of the landings at San Carlos. Subsequently the PUS defended his actions on the grounds of the need to mislead the enemy, making his unrepentant comment that: 'I have never lost a moment's sleep on it.'[25] However, his briefings often enraged his listeners. On one occasion, after a session in which the PUS had criticized the actions of the media in forthright terms, the Deputy Head of Current Affairs at the BBC, Alan Protheroe (who also happened to be a Lieutenant Colonel in the Territorial Army), stood up and said: 'I never thought I would be called a traitor, and the last place in which I thought I would be accused of lack of patriotism was in the Ministry of Defence.'

Whereupon the editor of the *News of the World*, Derek Jameson, said: 'I can't make up my mind whether this is a conspiracy or a cock-up.'

To which the editor of *BBC Television News*, Peter Woon, replied laconically: 'Both.'

The meeting ended in disorder.[26]

The difficulties of feeding a hungry press, when the disclosure of information may endanger lives, is a continuing problem in any war. Inevitably, if it is not fed it will go to whatever source will assuage its hunger, be it to the enemy or elsewhere. In the last resort it will generate news by speculation – something which happened frequently in the Falklands campaign. However, this campaign was probably to be the last in which the media was dependent on the generosity of the government for the scraps of information thrown to it. In the event, the operation carried more glory than scars in its confrontation with the media for it obeyed the three critical requirements for a limited war: it was short, it was popularly supported and, above all, it was successful.

In all that has been written about this operation, one speculation has not been made. Suppose that after the troops were ashore, an aircraft carrier had been sunk and the fleet had been unable to provide its continued support to the troops. Suppose that, cut off from resupply and air cover, the troops had finally been forced to surrender and the remainder of the fleet had returned home ignominiously. How would the media have handled such a catastrophe? Undoubtedly the Government would have fallen and *The Downing Street Years* by Mrs Thatcher would have been a very short book. Britain's place as a military nation would have been lost once and for all and any justification for keeping armed forces capable of operating outside Europe would have evaporated for ever. Deep as the country was in recession at the time, one could be forgiven for wondering if it would have ever dragged itself out of it. Fortunately none of that happened; but while the Prime Minister never allowed herself to doubt the outcome, there were some extremely anxious moments.

This was not to be the last occasion on which the belligerents were able to control the number of journalists on the battlefield; we shall find another more extreme example in the next chapter. Yet it was unique in that the media had no means of their own to reach the scene of the fighting. Despite bitter recriminations in the early part of the operation, very strong bonds of friendship and admiration were subsequently forged with the reporters during the land battles on the Falklands. Perhaps an outstanding example was that of Robert Fox, reporting for BBC Radio, who accompanied 2 Para at Goose Green and helped Major Chris Keeble, the second-in-command, to negotiate the surrender of the Argentinians after the battle. He gave similar help to the land commander, Major General Jeremy Moore, at the time of the final surrender in Port Stanley, for which he was awarded a highly deserved MBE.

Throughout, apart from the reporting of news which originated from Argentinian sources, the Government was able to impose a heavy censorship on all the news released; that situation at least is unlikely to happen again for the British.

The credit for the winning of such an unlikely war must be given unquestionably to the courage, professionalism and determination of the armed forces. However, without equally strong leadership from the Prime Minister, those qualities would not by themselves have been enough. Similarly, without world opinion on its side, the expedition might still have failed. Although there were many mistakes made in its treatment, the British press, with some moments of uncertainty, remained on the side of its own government. Had this situation changed for any reason, is it too much to believe that the media could have brought the war to a different conclusion – a war which, in the event, lifted the hearts of the nation and enabled the British people to regain in the world so much of the respect that they had lost in the earlier decade?

Perhaps the last word should be allowed to the victor, now Baroness Thatcher: 'Don't be too hard on the media; some of their people are good. The present generation has not learnt about appeasement. Appeasement simply gives one's enemies time to to rearm. You must never, never give in to dictators!'[27]

---

1. Quoted in *The Economist*, 17 April 1982
2. Conversations with Hon Raymond Seitz, 20 February 1997
3. Conversations with Lady Thatcher, 18 March 1997
4. *Mandarin, The diaries of Nicholas Henderson*, London, Weidenfeld & Nicholson, 1994, p. 451
5. *The Falklands War*, Sunday Times Insight Team, p. 113
6. *Mandarin, Henderson*, p. 444

7. Conversations with General Sir David Ramsbotham (in 1982, Army Director of Public Relations)

8. Conversations with Lady Thatcher

9. John Witherow of *The Times*, quoted in Morrison and Tumber, *Journalists at War*, London, Sage, 1988, p. 2

10. Ibid., p. 144

11. Letter to the author from Admiral Sir Jeremy Black

12. Admiral Sandy Woodward, *One Hundred Days*, London, Collins, 1984, p. 109

13. Ibid., p. 112

14. RFA *Resource*

15. Conversations with Sir Bernard Ingham, 18 March 1997

16. 'Gotcha!', *Sun* headline, 5 May 1982

17. Conversations with Lady Thatcher

18. Morrison and Tumber, *Journalists at War*, p. 212

19. Derrik Mercer, *The Fog of War*, London, Heinemann, 1987, p. 164.

20. Morrison and Tumber, *Journalists at War*, p. 145

21. Conversations with Lady Thatcher

22. Conversations with General Ramsbotham

23. Ibid.

24. Ibid.

25. Evidence given to House of Commons Defence Committee, quoted in Mercer, *The Fog of War*, pp. 210–11

26. Conversations with General Ramsbotham

27. Conversations with Lady Thatcher

CHAPTER NINE

The Wounded Giant:
The United States, 1980–1989

'. . . Let us strive to finish the work we are in, to bind up the nation's wounds, to care for him who shall have borne the battle.'

Abraham Lincoln: Second inaugural address, 1865

THE TEHERAN HOSTAGES, 1980

The final withdrawal of the United States forces from Vietnam brought in its train effects out of all proportion to the ending of a war in a small and comparatively insignificant country in the Far East. The United States, one of only two superpowers in the world, had been seen to have failed in an enterprise undertaken to withstand the spread of Communism – a crusade which it had led in the Western world since the end of the Second World War.

Of all the many reasons adduced for the failure, the most convincing – with which the media was much involved – was the failure of support for the campaign by the American people. Preaching the importance of this lesson in November 1984, Caspar Weinberger observed that: 'before the United States commits combat forces abroad, there must be some reasonable assurance we will have the support of the American people and their elected representatives in Congress.'[1] It had become very clear in the previous decade that the American people had had little stomach for the further commitment of their combat forces anywhere in the world after the bitter experience of Vietnam. Such military undertakings as they did attempt in those years had ended in conspicuous failure. The unfortunate operation to recover the crew of the *Mayaguez* in 1975[2] was one such event, but far more damaging was the disastrous attempt to recover the American hostages from Teheran in 1980. This offered a clear example of an administration being forced into an unwise course of action under pressure from the media.

After the fall from power of the Shah of Iran in January 1979, he and his family had been offered asylum in the United States, where he had come, bringing with him, it was assumed, large sums of his country's money on his hurried flight from Teheran. In the following winter, on 4 November, a supposedly unofficial group of Iranian students overran the United States Embassy in Teheran, occupied it and took hostage fifty-three of the Embassy staff. In return for their release, the United States was required to return the Shah and his family to face trial in Iran.

For President Jimmy Carter, who was approaching the end of his first term in office, the immediate reactions of his people to this event were surprisingly supportive; led by the media, they rallied to their President. As the *Washington Post* reported:

> Americans awoke in the morning to see the menacing figure of the Ayatollah breathing hatred and preaching holy war against 'pagans' and 'heathens'. They went to bed at night after seeing mobs of Iranian demonstrators marching before the occupied US Embassy, waving their fists, shouting defiant slogans, burning the American flag and effigies of Uncle Sam and Jimmy Carter. Morning after morning, evening after evening, the TV networks showed those same scenes. Through TV, the Iranian crisis became institutionalised and a part of American daily life . . . The political impact was immense. Attacks on Carter personally by Iranian leaders, prominently reported via TV to Americans at home, gave the President a stature he had failed to achieve in three years in office. Carter became the personification of the nation, the symbol of American resolve, the rallying point for Americans at home to respond to insults from abroad.[3]

And again:

> The result was to make the Iranian story the focus of unprecedented national attention. As the networks continued to highlight the hostage story, the country became unified in opposition to Iran as it had rarely been on a single issue in the past generation. The networks discovered something else – their Iranian broadcasts were attracting enormous new audiences. Iranian coverage, and competition for new angles of it, intensified.[4]

While Carter continued to lead the international campaign to recover the hostages, he was supported by his countrymen. However, as time passed and, despite his efforts, the hostages were still not released, support started to turn to dissatisfaction. This change in the fortunes of the administration increased the pressure on the President to take some precipitate action. No matter how much the administration tried to calm the situation in the hope of conducting diplomatic negotiations, television – in the words of Secretary of State Cyrus Vance – 'magnified the pressures to the extent that it kept it on the front burner day after day in Iran and in the United States'.[5]

Walter Cronkite, the famous CBS anchorman, began signing off at the end of each *CBS Evening News*: 'And that's the way it is on such and such a day, the –th day of the hostages' capture.'[6]

Increasingly, the pressure on Carter grew. In January 1980, the *Washington Post* ran an article assessing Carter's undue caution in the face of the crisis:

It may not be fashionable to criticize President Carter while he is struggling so earnestly to cope with the Iranian crisis . . . but there is growing alarm in the backrooms of Washington about his caution and indecision . . . Ayatollah Khomeini has said tauntingly that Carter lacks the guts to take military action against Iran.[7]

Carter was faced with a terrible dilemma: it was becoming apparent that no diplomatic negotiation was likely to free the hostages. The Shah was not to be sent to certain death in response to the illegal action of Iranian students; nor did it appear that the sanctions imposed by the United Nations would cause the Ayatollah to control his students. Faced with immense pressure from the media at home to take action to recover the beleaguered diplomats, Carter took advice from his military. On 14 April, as reported in *The Times*, the President announced darkly, referring to the international diplomacy which was taking place, 'We do not have much time left.'

On the advice of the military, Carter accepted a plan which would involve the insertion of the US Delta Force (the American equivalent of the SAS) into Iran where they would overrun the Embassy, recover the hostages and fly them out to waiting ships off the coast. It was a plan fraught with difficulties, but Carter was under heavy pressure and the plan had the recommendation of the Joint Chiefs of Staff. On the other hand it was never approved by the Secretary of State, Cyrus Vance, who subsequently resigned on that account.

While there was speculation about the prospect of military action, other sections of the press had cold feet: 'Some of President Carter's aides,' wrote the *Los Angeles Times* on 22 April, 'are highly critical and apprehensive about the possibility of a military confrontation.' In *The Times* in London a day later, a White House source was quoted as saying: 'We are slipping down a slippery slope towards military confrontation.'

In the meantime trials and rehearsals for the operation were being carried out in the Nevada desert in America in circumstances of total secrecy. Before the attempt, a good working relationship had existed between Delta Force and the British SAS. A short time beforehand this link suddenly went completely silent, suggesting that something was afoot which could not be shared with allies. In the circumstances, it was not hard to guess what such an operation might be.

In the event, the operation was a disaster. Using helicopters and crews trained in anti-submarine warfare from the aircraft carrier, USS *Nimitz*, after training with land-based crews in the States, it was scarcely surprising that things went wrong in a desert environment subject to heavy dust storms. Out of eight RH53 Sea Stallion helicopters that reached the first refuelling post in the Iranian desert, only five remained serviceable. Then a manoeuvring helicopter struck one of the C130 refuelling aircraft, setting both on fire and killing eight men and injuring four others. Next onto the scene drove a bus full of Iranian peasants on their way to market. The commander asked for instructions and was told to hold them and not allow them to continue. The peasants sat wide-eyed as the astonishing events unfolded before them. Finally the commander decided to 'abort' the mission, leaving behind him in the desert eight dead, two crashed aircraft and five discarded helicopters.

Later the Iranians put the bodies of the dead Americans on display in a nauseating manner before a press conference called in Teheran.

In its leading article after the fiasco, *The Times* made the following rather surprising judgement:

> The raid failed. It strengthened the Russians, reinforced America's enemies, alarmed her friends in the Middle East and confused and weakened the alliance. It did not lead to the death of the hostages, but did not save them either . . . Of four possible outcomes of the raid, the actual one proved to be by no means the worst.

Perhaps in the event it was as well that the raid got no further than the first stop in the desert; the subsequent parts of the operation would have been far more exacting. Cyrus Vance's subsequent letter of resignation is displayed today in the Carter museum in the ex-President's home town. The calamity was undoubtedly a major contributory factor to Carter's subsequent presidential defeat.

Partly as a result of the Teheran fiasco, the years between 1975 and 1983 were perhaps the most debilitating of any for the foreign policy of the United States. Lesser countries with evil ambitions, which might in earlier years have been hesitant to act for fear of American reaction, now believed that they could move with impunity. The Cubans readily participated in the support of the Communist uprising in Angola, while Syria felt able to threaten Lebanon, both aided and abetted by the Soviet Union. Media pressure had led a United States' administration into a disastrous decision.

LEBANON AND GRENADA, 1983

In 1981, President Ronald Reagan was elected to the White House in succession to Jimmy Carter, determined to improve the tarnished prestige of his country. He must have been much encouraged by the British Prime Minister, Margaret Thatcher, who had shown only too clearly after the Falklands operation what great political dividends could be reaped from popular and successful military interventions.

His first project was an attempt to restore peace in the war-torn Levant in 1982, where in addition to the activities of Syria, Israel had marched into Lebanon from the south in an attempt to destroy the PLO bases there. Asking some of his European allies to join him, Reagan proposed the deployment of troops into Beirut, believing that they would act as a stabilizing influence in a country which had already been almost destroyed by bitter fighting. After much discussion, France, Italy and Britain agreed to send detachments of troops to patrol Beirut. It was not a task that was welcomed by the military chiefs of any one of the countries involved since it had no clear mission or prospect of conclusion. The city was divided into four parts and was to be patrolled by the participating nations. A large detachment of US marines was sent to the sector of the city close to the airport, while the British in the south sent only one armoured reconnaissance squadron from Cyprus. The French and the Italians took responsibility for sectors in the north. The multiplicity of different factions warring in and around the city made any realistic attempt at peacekeeping almost impossible, while the proximity of Soviet troops, operating with the Syrians, to the American troops in Beirut greatly increased the anxieties of the free world.

From the start of this ill-starred operation, most of the warring factions resented the presence of the allies and of the Americans in particular. On one occasion, one of the authors of this book visited the British detachment and joined the squadron leader on a routine patrol of the city in an armoured car prominently flying the Union Jack. As they passed a large building in central Beirut a burst of machine-gun fire was sprayed close over their heads. As the patrol continued round the back of the building, a Lebanese was seen running out of the house carrying a machine-gun.

'Sorry, Major,' he shouted with a broad smile, 'I thought you were the Yanks!'

The US Marines suffered a number of casualties in the city while on patrol. Angered at such a reaction to his attempts at peacekeeping, the President ordered the Second World War battleship, USS *New Jersey*, lying off Beirut, to engage assumed rebel positions in the Shouf mountains to the east of the city with her 16 in guns. This extraordinary attack almost certainly caused the terrible vengeance that was visited on the Marines on 23 October 1983. On that day, a lorry said to be delivering stores, sought entrance to the heavily sandbagged headquarters of the Marines in the city. No sooner had it been allowed in than it exploded with enormous force, killing no fewer than 241 Marines – the heaviest casualties that the US Marine Corps had suffered in a single event since the Second World War. Two days later, in a similar occurrence, 77 French soldiers were also killed. These massacres quickly brought to an end any further attempt to broker peace by military means in the Lebanon. When the US Marines finally left Beirut, Caspar Weinberger, the US Secretary of Defense, was accused by the media of a shameful retreat; he replied: 'Nothing has changed. We are not leaving Lebanon. The marines are being deployed two or three miles to the west.' 'Two or three miles to the west' just happened to be from land bases on Lebanese soil to US ships offshore.[8]

In the same year, 1983, a new threat to American interests had come to light much nearer home in the Caribbean. The operation which followed is one of the very few in recent history which was totally blanketed from press coverage. On 19 October of that year the already Marxist government in the tiny island of Grenada was forcibly and bloodily overthrown by a far more extreme revolutionary movement apparently receiving the encouragement and support of Fidel Castro in Cuba.

Grenada is situated at the southern end of the archipelago formed by the Windward Islands. It had been a British colony but was granted its independence somewhat hurriedly in 1974, when colonial governments had been under great pressure to decolonize. At the time of independence, the Prime Minister had been a strong-minded and autocratic Grenadian, Sir Eric Gairy, but only five years after independence his Government had been ousted by a Marxist coup led by a group of Communists under another Grenadian, Maurice Bishop, who had seized power in 1979 and become the new Prime Minister. The island had, however, remained part of the British Commonwealth and a Governor-General representing the Queen remained in post at the capital, St George's. It was Bishop's Government that was itself overthrown in 1983; he and his ministers were summarily shot by the revolutionaries.

Situated on Grenada was a United States medical college to which a large number of American medical students were attached, most of whom lived around two campuses in the south-west of the island. While there was no apparent threat to these students – indeed the new Revolutionary Council had specifically assured all concerned that they were in no danger and were free to leave at any time if they wished – the possibility of another hostage situation in the United States' own backyard was not something to be contemplated with equanimity. The swift and effective removal of a most unwelcome government, uncomfortably close to the United States, offered some very attractive prospects in demonstrating the renewed determination of Reagan's administration.

Even had the United States wished to, there was little or no prospect of obtaining the support of the United Nations for such an undertaking. Indeed, apart from the fact that the Soviet Union would have vetoed it, there was little if any justification for the interference by one country in the affairs of another. The only pretext for such an operation lay in the hope of a request for help coming either from the Governor-General or from Grenada's close neighbours in the Caribbean. After some negotiation, which was little short of prompting, a request was received from the Chairman of the OECS (Organization of East Caribbean States), at that time Eugenia Charles of Dominica, on 23 October. From Grenada itself, however, there was no word; a tentative approach by the United

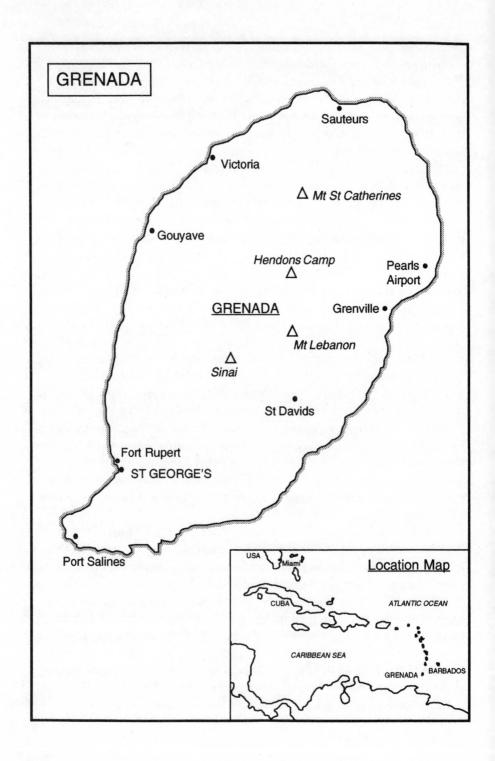

GRENADA

Sauteurs

Victoria

△ Mt St Catherines

Gouyave

Hendons Camp
△

Pearls •
Airport

GRENADA

Grenville •

△
Mt Lebanon

△
Sinai

•
St Davids

Fort Rupert
•
• ST GEORGE'S

•
Port Salines

Location Map

USA

Miami

CUBA

ATLANTIC OCEAN

CARIBBEAN SEA

GRENADA • BARBADOS

States to Britain as the ex-colonial power, proposing the removal of the revolutionary government, had been rejected out of hand and no request for help had emanated from Sir Paul Scoon, the Governor-General.

In the retrospective view of Lady Thatcher, at that time the British Prime Minister, there was no justification for the Americans to invade an island of which the Queen was monarch, and in any case there was little difference between the new revolutionary government and the earlier Marxist one. In her view, the American medical students were no more at risk from one than the other.[9] From the retrospective American view, however, expressed by Raymond Seitz, there was every need to put a stop to the spread of Communist governments in the Caribbean, readily sponsored by Fidel Castro from Cuba. The views of the United Nations, under the constant threat of Soviet veto, were simply not worth seeking.[10]

Nothing daunted, the request from the OECS provided the United States with an adequate pretext and also a forward base from which to operate on the island of Barbados, which lies only 120 nautical miles north-east of Grenada. The plan, approved by President Reagan, proposed a swift surprise invasion of the island by air and sea which would immediately secure the key points, ensure the safety of the American citizens, overpower the local forces and result in the arrest of the revolutionary government. The President's final approval was not given until shortly after he had heard the news of the bombing of the US Marines in Lebanon. Margaret Thatcher remains convinced that the disaster in Lebanon tipped the balance in the President's mind to go ahead with the invasion.[11]

There were, however, a number of difficulties to be overcome before the operation could begin: firstly, the safety of the Governor-General had to be assured, and secondly it was necessary to find out the whereabouts of the local military. Astonishingly, the information available about the island from the vast resources of the United States intelligence agencies was almost nil. As US Admiral Wesley Macdonald subsequently explained with mind-bending phraseology: 'We were not micro-managing Grenada intelligence-wise until about that time frame.'[12]

There were no maps with grid coordinates and there was no reliable information about the strength or equipment of the forces on the island. It was known that a Cuban ship had recently discharged a cargo on the island, probably much of which was arms, and also that there were a number of Cubans involved in building the runway of a large new airport at Point Salines on the south-west tip of the island. Beyond this, little was known. The operation was code-named 'Urgent Fury'.

To rescue the Governor-General, Sir Paul Scoon, himself a native Grenadian, a Special Operations team was directed to land by helicopter in the grounds of Government House by night, to collect Sir Paul and his family and fly them directly to the flagship. There the Governor would be invited to sign a prepared letter asking the President for assistance in removing the revolutionary government. A no doubt apocryphal tale went about at the time that an American agent had been sent to Government House beforehand to steal some sheets of Sir Paul's writing paper for this purpose.

This and other missions to facilitate the arrival of the main forces on the island had been assigned to various special forces. These latter were to be drawn from the US Marines from USS *Guam*, from the 82nd Airborne Division at Fort Bragg in Carolina and from the Ranger Battalions of Special Forces Command. The whole operation was under the Atlantic Command based in Norfolk, Virginia and the Force Commander was Vice Admiral Joseph Metcalf III with his headquarters aboard USS *Guam*, an amphibious assault ship.

In Barbados, there was a mass of valuable information to be had from the local forces, many of whom knew Grenada well and were only too ready to share their knowledge. Although this was dutifully passed on by the US Military Attaché in Barbados, very little of it seems to have reached the planners. Incredibly, at the outset of the operation the whereabouts on the island of at least half of the American medical students was completely unknown to any of the commanders. As it became apparent to those in Barbados that an invasion might take place, the British Deputy High Commissioner, on instructions from London, made an approach to the Americans on the island. He was curtly informed that there was nothing to tell him. Only two days before the invasion took place, the British Foreign Secretary, Geoffrey Howe, informed Parliament that he had no reason to believe that the Americans had any intention to invade Grenada.[13]

The two overriding considerations in launching this operation were to be surprise and speed. The lawful Prime Minister of Grenada, Maurice Bishop, and many of his colleagues had been murdered by the revolutionaries on 19 October. Planning had begun soon after and it was proposed to launch the invasion on 24 October. The plan had certainly been put together with commendable speed. Unfortunately, however, it was quite impossible to bring so large a force into striking distance of Grenada without sacrificing strategic surprise at least. The islanders had received warnings on their local radios of the impending attack and the revolutionary commanders were able to prepare and deploy their meagre forces in advance. Indeed the Revolutionary Council, as they called themselves, had had time to beg such friends as they had in the world to dissuade the United States from attacking them. Among the countries which they approached was Britain. Unfortunately, their telex addresses were out of date and the message was received over a weekend in London by a firm manufacturing plastic bags. On the Monday morning, the firm telephoned the Foreign and Commonwealth Office with the message. They were invited to put it in the post; by the time it arrived, so had the US invasion forces.

When the question of the media coverage of the operation was addressed, a strange decision was made by the US Government. It was simply decided that no representatives of the media would be allowed anywhere near the island until the operation had been completed. If it was believed by the administration as surely it must have been at this time that they were about to undertake a swift surgical action against minimal resistance, it would surely have been to their advantage to allow the world to witness such a success. In the light of what followed, however, their decision proved to be a wise one. Accordingly, the great concourse of the world's media was firmly held no closer than Barbados and told little or nothing of the events as they unfolded.

On the evening of 23 October (London time), the White House put a call through to No. 10 Downing Street, asking for Prime Minister Thatcher to speak to the President. She was out at a dinner given in honour of the retiring United States Ambassador at which Princess Alexandra was present. She remembers being recalled from the dinner to Downing Street, where she returned at about 10.30 p.m. There she found a message from Reagan saying that he intended to go ahead with the invasion of Grenada. Mrs Thatcher was extremely put out that her earlier advice had been disregarded and despatched an urgent message to the President:

This action will be seen as intervention by a western country in the internal affairs of a small independent nation, however unattractive its regime. I ask you to consider this in the context of our wider East–West relations and of the fact that we will be having in the next few days to present to our Parliament and people the siting of cruise missiles in this country. I must ask you to think most carefully about these points. I cannot conceal that I am deeply disturbed by your latest communication. You asked for my advice. I have set it out and hope that even at this late stage you will take it into account before events are irrevocable.[14]

Shortly afterwards she telephoned Reagan to learn his response: 'I'm sorry, Margaret,' he is said to have replied, 'but we are at zero!'[15]

There was no going back. The Prime Minister summoned the Chief of Defence Staff, Field Marshal Sir Edwin Bramall, who was fetched from his bed. It was already well past midnight.

'What can we do?' she enquired when he arrived. There was really nothing that the British could do, but there was a single British warship, HMS *Antrim*, on station in the Caribbean. A most immediate signal was therefore made to her captain, instructing him to go forthwith to the United States flagship, tell the admiral that he was the representative of the British Government and demand to be told what was happening. A more daunting instruction for a comparatively junior officer it would have been hard to imagine.

In accordance with his orders, at first light the captain took off in his small helicopter and set off for the USS *Guam*. After landing on the huge flight deck, he asked to be taken to see the flag officer commanding operations. To his surprise, he was warmly welcomed by the admiral who, surrounded by his staff officers, was cheerfully awaiting the start of the operation.

'You jes' go down to the wardroom and get yourself a good breakfast,' he was told, 'and when you get back up on the bridge, it'll all be over!'

In fact four more breakfast times were to pass before this came true.

On the night of 23/24 October, the special forces assigned to the different tasks had set off for the island. One group had the task of landing on the island to position beacons which would guide in the parachutists to seize the airfield at Point Salines. They had to parachute into the sea close to one of the navy ships, where they were to be picked up by whalers and taken ashore. In the darkness, of the sixteen men who dropped, four were lost in the sea, while those who reached the boats failed to get ashore due to the heavy swell and eventually returned with difficulty to the mother ships. As a result, H-hour for the main operation had to be delayed for twenty-four hours while the special forces repeated their attempt on the following night.

Early on the morning of 25 October, three helicopter-borne groups of special forces were to set off for different objectives on the island. One was to rescue the Governor-General, one to seize the radio station and one to capture the prison and safeguard the revolutionaries' prisoners. The helicopters to carry these missions were flown into Barbados from the United States by huge C-5A Galaxies on the night of the operation; the helicopters had to be unloaded, assembled and armed while the crews were being briefed. Delays were inevitable, making it too late to carry out their operations in darkness.

The team despatched to the radio station had no difficulty in finding their objective and quickly secured it. Unfortunately they were only lightly armed and when they were counter-attacked by one of the very few Russian APCs possessed by the revolutionaries, they were forced to withdraw. After spending the remainder of the day in hiding, they eventually made their way back to one of the ships offshore.

The team heading for Government House had great difficulty in identifying it; when they did find it and came in low, they were met with such a hail of fire from ground-based weapons that they were forced to 'abort the mission' and return to the deck of the *Guam*. Some of the team had been wounded by small arms and were off-loaded, while the remainder set out to try again. On the second attempt, the helicopters managed to drop their teams successfully in Government House garden, but then had to take off immediately to avoid the enemy fire. Sir Paul Scoon met his would-be rescuers, who told him that they would have to await the arrival of ground troops before they could leave. They remained there waiting for rescue for a further twenty-four hours. Fortunately, when they were attacked by an APC, they were able to call in air support which put paid to the counter-attack.

Far worse was the situation awaiting the five Black Hawk helicopters charged with securing the prison. Without proper maps, they were unaware that the prison was on the top of a steep sided ridge; nor did they realize that 300 metres away was an even higher ridge on which was built Fort Rupert with a garrison including anti-aircraft guns. As the aircraft searched hopelessly for somewhere to land, they were forced to come so low that they were in some cases lower in the sky than the guns on the next ridge. There was no way in which the mission could be achieved and a number of crewmen were wounded as the pilots tried to land. At last the attempt was called off, with one helicopter destroyed, some six or eight dead and some twenty men wounded.

While all this was happening, strong reactions were coming from other parts of the world; most of these were critical of the American action. The Soviet Union added further excitement to the occasion by reporting on their television news that America had invaded Granada in southern Spain, an error which fortunately they corrected fairly quickly.

While these preliminary operations were taking place, the two airfields on Grenada were being seized by Ranger battalions parachuted onto Point Salines airstrip in the south-west and by Marine units helicoptered onto the smaller airfield at Pearls on the east coast. Finally a Marine landing supported by tanks and artillery was made on the west coast and six battalions of the 82nd Airborne Division were landed at Salines. The medical students near Salines were rescued unharmed, while a further Ranger attack was launched by helicopter to rescue the remaining students on the west coast. Two more helicopters were lost in this operation.

All this time, the unfortunate Governor-General was besieged in his house at St George's, protected by a handful of American special forces. The Marines who had landed on the west coast north of St George's were charged with the task of rescuing him. Their attempts to silence the defences around the town met with similar results to those encountered by the Black Hawks; two flights each of two Cobra gunships attempted to engage the revolutionaries. They were met with intense small arms and anti-aircraft fire and two were shot down with the loss of five crewmen. Eventually the US Marines fought their way into Government House and rescued Sir Paul and Lady Scoon. Incredibly, the little party in Government House had suffered no casualties. However, even at this stage it was thought too dangerous to bring in a helicopter and the party was escorted out of the town on foot until they were able to be transported to USS *Guam*. Soon after, Sir Paul was flown back to the island and landed at Salines. Here he was presented with the urgent letter asking the Americans to come to the help of his beleaguered island. He signed it on 26 October and was invited to backdate it by two days, which he generously did.

In the meantime, back in Washington, the administration waited apprehensively for news of success. The Secretary of State, George Shultz, flew back from Europe on the same day that the first medical students were being flown home from Grenada. After receiving little or no support for the operation from the Europeans and only a sceptical response from the US Congress, Shultz was most anxious to be assured of a successful outcome at home. Raymond Seitz, who was his executive assistant at the time, recalls how, as soon as they had landed at Andrews Air Force base, they hurried to a television set showing live coverage of the arrival of the first medical students from Grenada, worried lest they expressed disapproval of what had been done.[16] They watched anxiously as the C130 taxied to a halt and the steps were run up to the door. It opened and out stepped a typical medical student. He walked down the steps where the press were waiting for him. As he stepped onto the tarmac, he fell on his knees and kissed the ground. Shultz's party heaved a vast sigh of relief; from then on they knew that the operation had been a success. On such tenuous images can success or failure hang!

By 28 October it was all over. The terrified inhabitants of the island welcomed their deliverers and were delighted at the demise of the revolutionary government. On that day, President Reagan appeared on television to give an account to his people of the successful outcome of Urgent Fury. On the island by that time were approximately nine US battalions supported by tanks and artillery on the ground, with the support of a carrier group (USS *Independence*) and an amphibious assault group at sea. All their missions had been accomplished and comparatively few lives had been lost.

The 'enemy' on the other hand had consisted of one regular Grenadian battalion supported by some mortars and anti-aircraft guns, two companies equipped with Soviet APCs (BTR-60) and a territorial militia of nominally some 1,200 men armed with machine-guns and small arms. Very many of these, however, had failed to turn up on the day. Besides the Grenadians, there were some 700 armed Cuban workmen on the island, most of whom were located at Salines. The Grenadians had no warships, no aircraft and no anti-aircraft missiles of any kind.

On that same day, Sir Paul Scoon telephoned the Queen at Buckingham Palace to report that his island was once more at peace and that a democratic government would be reinstated. So ended Operation Urgent Fury; but what of the exiled media?

The decision not to allow the media any access to Urgent Fury appears to have been taken by the United States Department of Defense on the advice of the Joint Chiefs of Staff and with the approval of the State Department. It has been suggested that this unusual decision was taken in the mistaken belief that something similar had occurred in the Falklands War which had been beneficial to the British.[17] In fact, as we have seen, the handling of the media by the British at that time was one of the least successful aspects of the war.

Subsequently, the decision was defended on the grounds of the need for speed and secrecy. Again as we have already seen, the speed of the operation was very disappointing and the secrecy was minimal. The effect of the decision on the media was naturally to infuriate them.

In a lecture given by Admiral Metcalf on the subject some years later, he made the following observation:

> At the time of the Grenada intervention, relations between the press and the US military had been eroded to an appalling state. The root of the problem was the ill will between the press and military that came out of Vietnam . . . The military brooded over the loss in Vietnam, and many blamed the press. At the same time, the media was deeply suspicious of those in authority within the military and its surrogate, the Pentagon.[18]

Despite the Government ruling, however, some seven members of the press did get ashore on the island on the first morning of the attack. Although they witnessed some of the events in St George's they were unable to file their copy because of the failure of communications between the island and the mainland. They were eventually rounded up by the US Marines and some were flown out to the *Guam*. Here one representative of the *Washington Post* succeeded in meeting the admiral and demanding that his copy should be relayed over the ship's communications. He received a very unhelpful answer and was kept below for some days.[19]

Meanwhile the combined world press fumed on the island of Barbados. CBS chartered a plane intending to fly its cameras over Grenada, but as it approached it was warned off by US fighter aircraft. This led the President of CBS to complain that 'the US media had even less access than British journalists during the Falklands War'.[20] As always, the absence of hard news led to speculation, to the reporting of news from other sources (including Cuba) and inevitably to a rash of 'military experts' invited to say what they thought was happening. When at one stage some harmless footage of military activity was released from the Pentagon, it was shown on CBS prominently labelled 'cleared by Department of Defense Censors'.[21] In another attempt to overcome the ban, the presidents of CBS and ABC News protested to Caspar Weinberger, the Secretary for Defense, that the First Amendment to the Constitution had been breached.

On the third day of the operation the way was opened for some journalists to visit the island and see for themselves what had been happening. Finally, when all the fighting was over, free access was once again given to all who wished to come. Hordes of reporters questioned the locals, the troops and the commanders. Demands for 'body-counts' were made and some went to great lengths to dig out compromising stories about the operation. Much of their thunder, however, was stolen by the wily President, Ronald Reagan, who, as mentioned earlier, appeared on television to tell the American people that a significant victory had been won, that an odious and illegitimate government had been removed and that all the American citizens were now safe. Such good news was far more appealing to the viewers than the moans of the press about why they had been excluded from the event.

This, as we have already mentioned, was one of the very few military operations by Western powers in this century from which journalists were entirely excluded. The fact that the events were confined to a small island, access to which could be entirely controlled by the US forces, made this possible. It is probably true that an efficient military operation benefits from the presence of sympathetic journalists. In this case the decision to exclude them may well have been wise. General Colin Powell, later chairman of the Joint Chiefs, went so far as to describe it as a 'messy' operation,[22] which indeed it was; but the effect on the American media was further to divorce it from its own armed forces. Not of course that the outcome of an operation of this sort was ever seriously in doubt; the worst that could have happened would have been a hostage situation, had some of the locals held the medical students to political ransom. In almost any other military undertaking that can be imagined, there is always the danger of miscalculation or of escalation. Wars that are expected to be over by Christmas often last much longer. In such circumstances, the presence of a helpful and understanding press corps must be preferable to closing the floodgates and waiting for them to burst. In Urgent Fury, the United States succeeded in the removal of a murderous and irresponsible government on a very small island; but the policy of press exclusion was, as we shall see, never attempted again.

PANAMA, 1989

If it had been President Reagan's intention to try to wipe away the bitter memories of Vietnam and its tragic aftermath, President George Bush who succeeded him was even more determined to do so. Despite the public acclaim with which Reagan's success in Grenada had been received, the military authorities at least were well aware of the shortcomings of the operation. As General Colin Powell, who was not at that time responsible for the planning, observed, 'the operation demonstrated how far cooperation among the services still had to go. The invasion of Grenada succeeded, but it was a sloppy success.'[23]

In the years that followed after Operation Urgent Fury, very great efforts had been made by the United States senior commanders to put right the evident deficiencies in their military machine. Even before Urgent Fury, the outspoken Army Chief of Staff, General Edward 'Shy' Meyer, had embarked on a great programme of retraining to put right what he had termed 'a hollow army'. Among the possible remedies which he investigated was the British army regimental system, by which soldiers remain throughout their service in a single tightly cohesive unit, led always by the same officers and NCOs. In the United States army no such organization existed and both soldiers and officers could expect to be moved from unit to unit, having no particular loyalty to one more than another. Although the development of such a system proved impractical with the size and make-up of the American army (and the reintroduction of named State regiments might have been too redolent of Civil War days), he did introduce the so-called 'cohort' system whereby recruits remained together in approximately company-size groups when they were posted to active battalions, giving an added sense of cohesion to the units.

Equally, at the highest levels, renewed thought was given to the basic principles of war and strategy which had so often been forgotten in these difficult times. The giant's wounds were healing fast and the bitter lessons of the seventies were being learned and taken to heart. As a result, the next engagement in which the US armed forces were involved ran smoothly, efficiently and successfully – with but one serious exception: the handling of the media.

From very early days, drug-running in Central and South America had been a thorn in the flesh of the United States. Countless attempts had been made to control this thriving trade, some with more success than others. The appearance of a drug baron who had also seized dictatorial powers in the strategically important but otherwise tiny state of Panama presented the administration with a new and difficult problem, once again close to its own back doorstep.

General Manuel Noriega had, in earlier days, given good service to the United States. On the payroll of the CIA, he had been a useful source of intelligence in drug-related activities in Central America. However, by the middle of 1989, his high-handed disregard of any democratic systems in his own country, coupled with every form of double dealing in his relations with the United States, had led in the first instance to his indictment for drug trafficking and money-laundering by a court in Florida, and finally to a presidential decision to remove him from power by military force.

As in Grenada, the decision to act was taken in the greatest secrecy. A prime aim of the operation was the arrest of the dictator himself and his removal to face charges in the United States. Unlike Grenada, though, the Americans had the great advantage of a large garrison of troops already stationed under treaty within the Panama Canal Zone. Thus there were air bases and logistic support readily available within the country that they were planning to invade. The local opposition was, however, of a much more significant strength than had been the case in Grenada. The Panama Defence Force (PDF), in the main loyal to Noriega, was not organized as a force capable of resisting invasion; yet it was large, well equipped and not badly trained as an internal security force. In all, both regular and paramilitary, it comprised some 30,000 men. The units of this force were spread across Panama from one coast to the other.

As for the justification for mounting an invasion of a neighbouring country, it is not easy to be convinced by the thought process. The specific events which the administration took as their reason for invasion was the shooting of a US Marine lieutenant in plain clothes when he and three fellow officers blundered into a roadblock manned by drunken PDF guards, followed shortly afterwards by the arrest of a US Navy lieutenant and his wife, both of whom were manhandled and the officer threatened with death.[24] There had been mounting pressure in Congress for action to be taken against Noriega and it appears that all that was needed was a suitable pretext. By 1989, the demise of the Soviet Union had at least removed any counter threats from that quarter and clearly any open approach to the United Nations was ruled out by the necessity for secrecy – not that it appears that such an approach was even contemplated. In fact, Raymond Seitz, at that time in the State Department, confirmed in conversation with the authors that as far as the United States were concerned, the only body that counted in matters regarding the security of the American hemisphere was Congress. The one strategic asset in Panama was the Canal, but never at any stage does it appear that its security was threatened.

It is interesting to compare the stated political objectives of the invasion of Panama with the translated aims of the military commanders. The political aims were stated to be fourfold: one, to protect American lives; two, to protect American interests and rights under the Panama Canal Treaty; three, to restore Panamanian democracy; and four, to apprehend Noriega. In planning their operation, the military were guided by the twin necessities of secrecy and speed of completion. There was no doubt in the minds of anyone that, in operations of this kind, a swift and certain success was an essential ingredient of any plan; naturally any disclosure of the American intent would result in Noriega's escape. The translation of the political objectives into military aims therefore put the priorities into a different order: one, to destroy the combat capability of the PDF and to seize the internal lines of communication; two, to seize the control points of the Panama Canal (although these were presumably already secured); and three, to apprehend Noriega and rescue his prisoners (Noriega was holding prisoner, among others, an American citizen in the employ of the CIA). If the first of these aims was to be quickly achieved, a very strong American force had to be introduced into the country in an extremely short time.

While the military plans for this operation were still being finalized, it became necessary to prepare American and world opinion for the event, without of course disclosing in advance the specific intentions. The easiest and most effective way of achieving this preparation was by demonizing Noriega. A substantial campaign against him was mounted by the United States administration which found ready listeners in the American media.

The plans for the operation had the great advantage over those for Grenada that they had been considered and worked out well in advance. The Commander of the US Southern Command (SOCOM), responsible for the planning, was a highly professional and single-minded soldier, General Max Thurman, who had previously prepared contingency plans to meet such a situation. These plans were based on the use of some 9,000 troops already stationed in Panama and the further insertion of another 10,000 from the United States. Twenty-seven objectives were to be secured almost simultaneously in a lightning operation carried out in the hours of darkness.

Every aspect of this complex operation had been carefully prepared and in many cases the troops had even rehearsed their roles under cover of routine exercises. The operation had been code-named 'Blue Spoon', which certainly carried no overtones of derring-do. When the prospect of putting the plans into effect became a probability, the Pentagon urged that a more motivating title be given to the project; it was accordingly renamed Operation 'Just Cause'.

Despite this careful preplanning, one important item slipped through the net – the handling of the media. The matter had not been overlooked by SOCOM; an outline plan for press handling had been included and this was duly passed up to the Pentagon for expansion and approval. However, the demands of secrecy had been so paramount in the planning branches of the Pentagon that all consideration of media planning was shelved in the preliminary stages. Receiving no further instructions from Washington, the staffs in Panama made no special arrangements for the media, either in the form of transportation or communications.

On 17 December 1989, the plan was put before President Bush for final approval. Among the questions that he put at the time was to ask what arrangements had been made about the media. When he was told that a pool of journalists from Washington would be given facilities in Panama, his only comment was to see that there were no leaks before the start of the operation. He approved the plan which was to be put into effect at 0100 hours on 20 December.

The airlift required to transport this great force in a single phase from widely separated bases in the States was a huge project in itself. Many of the troops were to be parachuted onto their targets while others were to be helicoptered or airlanded. A single aircraft was earmarked to fly from Andrew's Air Force Base outside Washington with the press pool on board. Editors were not approached until about 1730 hours on 19 December, offering them seats for their reporters on the plane scheduled to fly at 2300 hours. With a flying time of about five hours to Panama, there was no prospect of any of the pool arriving until well after H-hour.

In the event, the military operation went like clockwork under the direct command of another very capable officer, Lieutenant General Carl Stiner, commander of XVIII Airborne Corps based at Fort Bragg; all the objectives were successfully seized with one unfortunate exception. The *coup de main* parties of special forces despatched to capture Noriega at a number of his likely hideouts all failed to catch him. Nevertheless, every possible escape route for him had been sealed and it seemed certain that he would not escape for long. In the meantime Jose Endara, the President of Panama who had been ousted by Noriega, was reinstated by the United States and the whole country was quickly brought under the control of the military. Inevitably some fighting took place in which 23 US servicemen were killed and 394 wounded; some 400 Panamanians lost their lives, most of whom were members of the PDF. Once again the Americans were welcomed by the majority of the populace as liberators from a hated regime.

That is not to say that the American action was supported elsewhere in the world. The Russians, perhaps for the first time of any nation, employed a highly novel method of signifying diplomatic disapproval: instead of delivering a Note from their Embassy in Washington, they telephoned CNN and put up an official to broadcast their protests not just to the American Government but also to the world.[25]

Meanwhile the unfortunate Washington press correspondents had landed at the US Howard Air Force Base in Panama some five hours after most of the action had taken place. After a further delay of two hours, a helicopter was found to move the reporters. Demanding to be taken to the scene of the action, they were flown only into the base at Fort Clayton, from which they could see little and find out less. During the morning the frustrated newsmen were given a briefing by the Chargé d'Affaires at the US Embassy, John Bushnell. One reporter indignantly described the briefing as 'a history lesson'. At last the pool of reporters was taken to the centre of Panama City, where again most of the action was over, but as they flew in, they saw smoke rising from the Comandancia, the headquarters of the PDF, and demanded to be taken there. They were told that it would be 'too dangerous for them' and that even a flight around the city was too risky to be undertaken.

Late on the evening of 20 December this furious group of reporters were again briefed, this time by the US Ambassador himself. The newsmen again described this as worthless. It was not until the following morning that a proper media centre was set up, but even this was grossly lacking in adequate telephone lines to meet their needs. Furthermore, the media was now severely blocked in what it was allowed to film or report. There were to be no pictures of US casualties, no pictures of damaged helicopters and no pictures of Panamanian prisoners. No facilities were offered to fly film back to the States and none arrived until just before Christmas.

In the meantime, on 24 December, Manuel Noriega took sanctuary in the Vatican Embassy, where he was held as a much unwanted guest by the Papal Nuncio. The Nunciatura was immediately surrounded by US troops demanding his surrender by loudhailer and preventing him (or his hosts) from sleeping by playing continuous loud music over tannoys. It was not until 3 January 1990 that Noriega, in full military uniform, walked out of the Embassy and surrendered himself to a US general. He was arrested, charged and flown to Florida to face his various indictments.

The military aspects of Operation Just Cause were now over, but the inept handling of the publicity was still to have its effects. The television film that was seen all over the world in the wake of this operation did less than justice to the efficiency of its execution. Instead of shots of a well-oiled military machine carrying out a complex and imaginative plan with speed and efficiency, most viewers were treated to pictures of American soldiers running or driving up and down festively decorated Panamanian streets with buildings burning or gutted in the background, apparently wrecking Christmas for the unfortunate inhabitants. Scenes outside the Vatican Embassy gave little evidence of Peace on Earth and Goodwill to Men. Once again, despite the congratulatory interviews given by the President and his senior advisers, the success of the operation had a hollow ring about it to the viewers and listeners across the world. The giant's wounds might be healing but there was still a doubt in the minds of many as to his wisdom and judgement.

Reading even today the recollections of those directly involved in this series of military operations that spanned the 1980s, there is we believe little understanding of the dangerous messages which were sent around the world at that time due at least in part to the American mishandling of the international media. For forty years after the end of the Second World War, the so-called balance of terror which had locked the two superpowers into inaction had also prevented the outbreak of many minor hostilities among lesser nations, which had been bridled by one or other of the superpowers. The collapse of the Soviet Union in the late 1980s was to change all that. Nations within the old Soviet sphere of influence no longer felt the controlling influence of Moscow, while those that had been restrained by Washington now doubted the ability or the willingness of the United States to follow up their words with action. Yet again the world was to see the rise of that most dangerous figure, the cause of more bloodshed in this century than any other, the totalitarian dictator who believes that aggression will bring neither response nor retribution. Onto the world scene in 1990 stepped the figure of Saddam Hussein.

1. Caspar Weinberger, Speech to US National Press Club, 28 November 1984
2. In 1975, the crew of a US Merchant ship, the *Mayaguez*, was seized by the Cambodians. The US Marines carried out an assault landing on a small island where the crew was thought to be held; the Marines suffered severe casualties. In fact the crew had already been released and were not on the island at all.
3. *Washington Post*; quoted in Philip Seib, *Headline Diplomacy*, London, Praeger Publishers, 1997, p. 32
4. *Washington Post*; Ibid., p. 32
5. Ibid., p. 34
6. Ibid., p. 35
7. *Washington Post*, 7 January 1980
8. Matthew Parris and Phil Mason, *Read My Lips*, London, Robson, 1996, p. 222
9. Conversations with Lady Thatcher, 18 March 1997
10. Conversations with Hon Raymond Seitz, February 1997
11. Conversations with Lady Thatcher
12. Parris and Mason, *Read My Lips*, p. 222
13. Conversations with Lady Thatcher
14. Margaret Thatcher, *The Downing Street Years*, London, HarperCollins, 1993, p. 331
15. Recounted to the author by FM Lord Bramall shortly afterwards
16. Conversations with Hon Raymond Seitz, February 1997
17. Derrick Mercer, *The Fog of War*, London, Heinemann, 1987, p. 291
18. Lecture by Admiral Metcalf, in Peter Young (ed.), *Defence and the Media in Limited War*, Frank Cass, p. 168
19. Young (ed.), *Defence and the Media*, p. 170
20. Mercer, *The Fog of War*, p. 300
21. Ibid., p. 301
22. Mark Adkin, *Urgent Fury*, Leo Cooper, p. 321
23. Colin Powell, *A Soldier's Way*, London, Hutchinson, 1995, p. 292
24. Ibid., p. 421
25. Seib, *Headline Diplomacy*, p. 118

CHAPTER TEN

The Gulf War against Iraq, 1991

'This will not stand.'

> President George Bush on the invasion of Kuwait
> by Saddam Hussein, 6 August 1990

The war fought in the Persian Gulf against Saddam Hussein of Iraq in 1991 was the most widely and most swiftly reported war in history. Journalists from all over the world jostled with each other to follow the events as they occurred and beamed them by satellite to waiting multitudes whose hunger for news was insatiable.

Unlike the operations mentioned in the two previous chapters, there was no question of limiting media access to the scene; indeed, the war which followed proved to be arguably the greatest media event in history. There was, it is true, a half-hearted attempt by the Saudis to refuse access to their country to the foreign press, but this was quickly swept aside. Yet, despite the presence of this army of journalists, much that happened went unreported and much that was reported was only part of the whole truth.

What was reported was what the journalists saw and believed and, more importantly, what they wished their audiences to believe.

As the outbreak of hostilities grew close, so the different pressure groups increased their determination to be heard. From the militants, the demand for vengeance against an aggressor grew, while demonstrations condemning war took place in many of the world's capitals. Faced with such powerful divisions, the world leaders in the West had to tread through the minefields of public opinion with the utmost care. Perhaps more than ever before, the ubiquitous media forced those in power in the free world to measure their actions against the opinions of those they ruled.

In Britain, the Thatcher age was nearing its end. Not that the Iron Lady had any inkling that the end was near, nor had her renowned resolution in any way weakened. In the East, Mikhail Gorbachev was still seen as the brightest star that had lit up the Russian sky for decades. For the first time in living memory, there was a chance that Russia might negotiate with the rest of the world rather than prove the eternal stumbling block to international action.

Saddam Hussein, the villain of the piece, was – indeed still is in 1997 – the classic dictator. Ruling over a people for whom he appeared to have little real concern, save to demand their absolute loyalty and obedience, he made, as so many of his like had done before, serious miscalculations. Many might say that these were the fault of others for not making clear in advance their likely consequences. Once again, as we have seen on many occasions in this book before, deterrence failed.

In this chapter, we have followed the events which led up to the war and considered the media pressures brought to bear on the people who directed those events. For the first time in the reporting of war, the participants became international celebrities almost overnight. Not only the politicians treading the diplomatic stage, but the generals, the junior commanders and the soldiers and airmen themselves had to endure a limelight which had never shone so brightly on any conflict before.

In 1990, Saddam Hussein, the dictatorial ruler of Iraq, had at last brought to a conclusion a war with Iran which had dragged on indecisively for eight years, had resulted in the death and disablement of huge numbers of his people and had left his country on the verge of bankruptcy. On his southern border lay the immensely rich but tiny country of Kuwait, which could from its huge oil riches provide an instant solution to Iraq's penury. With the addition of the Kuwaiti oilwells, Saddam would find himself in control of one fifth of the world's oil. He had to assess how the remainder of that world would react if he were to seize his small neighbour's riches.

With his country already on a war footing, Saddam's military strength far outweighed that of any of his neighbours, save only for Iran which was still licking its wounds from the recent war. The Iraqi army and air force had been generously provided by the Soviet Union with modern military equipment and it was well known that Saddam had built up a powerful armoury of chemical and biological weapons, capable of being delivered by Soviet manufactured missiles. It was also not impossible that he possessed nuclear weapons. In assessing any possible reaction to his seizure of Kuwait, Saddam's main concern had to be with the United States which alone had the capability of any decisive reaction. The demise of the Soviet Union as a superpower in the late 1980s had dissipated any danger of reaction from that quarter.

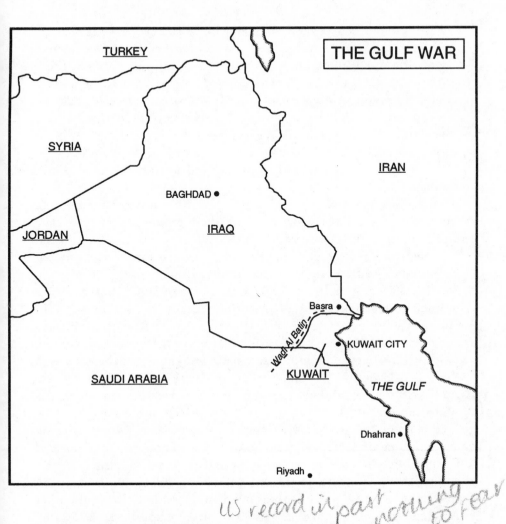

US record in past nothing to fear

It was therefore at the United States' record of the previous decade that Saddam looked to make his judgement. The unimpressive series of American military operations which we examined in the last chapter, convinced him that he had nothing to fear. As his troops started to move southwards, he watched cynically the reactions of the Western world. A series of visitors hastened to Baghdad, hoping to discover the dictator's intentions.

To the watching world press, it seemed tolerably certain that Saddam already had Kuwait in his sights. If there had been any doubt, this should soon have been dispelled by Saddam's own words broadcast on Baghdad radio on 17 July 1990:

Thanks to our new weapons, the imperialists can no longer launch a military attack against us, so they have chosen to wage an economic guerrilla war with the help of those agents of imperialism, the leaders of the Gulf states. Their policy of keeping oil prices at a low level is a poisoned dagger planted in Iraq's back . . . If words fail to protect us, we will have no choice other than to go into action to re-establish the correct state of affairs and restore our rights.[1]

On that night the first Iraqi troops moved up towards the Kuwaiti frontier.

The governments of the neighbouring Arab countries, however, were still loath to believe that Saddam truly had designs on a fellow Arab state and were unwilling to turn to the infidels to prevent him. When President George Bush, who had held office for less than a year, had sent his Secretary of Defense to Riyadh to offer support to the kingdom of Saudi Arabia in June, he had met with a curt response that there was neither need nor wish for any American troops to come to the Gulf. Similarly, President Mubarak of Egypt, after visiting Baghdad, remained convinced that Saddam had no evil intent towards Kuwait. King Hussein of Jordan was equally undisturbed. Finally, Saddam tested the water with the United States itself by summoning to his presence the United States Ambassador to Baghdad. This was the first occasion on which the Ambassador, April Glaspie, had held any private discussions with the President and the notice of the summons was too short for her to obtain any guidance from Washington. On her appearance, Saddam informed her that he wished her to transmit a message to President Bush.

The message which followed was long and rambling; it included long statements about the relationships between the United States and other Arab countries and spoke of American participation in damaging the economy of Iraq by lowering the price of oil. Commenting on America as a whole, he remarked: 'I do not belittle you, but I have taken the geography and nature of American society into account. Yours is a society that cannot accept ten thousand dead in one battle . . .' Towards the end of the message, veiled threats were made:

We know that you can harm us, although we do not threaten you. But we too could harm you. Everyone can cause damage according to his ability and size. We cannot come all the way to you in the United States, but individual Arabs may reach you.

212

[handwritten margin notes: Saddam warning us not to interfere]

You can come to Iraq with aircraft and missiles, but do not push us to the point at which we cease to care. When we feel that you want to injure our pride . . . we will cease to care and death will be our choice.[2]

So he went on at length, warning the United States not to interfere in Arab affairs and complaining of the hostility which surrounded Iraq. Finally he concluded his message and the Ambassador was able to make a reply. This too was at some length, but one part of her statement was picked upon after the war by the *New York Times* as having been an invitation to Saddam to go ahead with his plans:[3]

[handwritten margin note: arab-arab conflict?]

. . . I admire your extraordinary attempts to rebuild your country [after the Iranian war]. I know you need funds. We understand that, and our opinion is that you should have the opportunity to rebuild your country. *But we have no opinion on Arab–Arab conflicts like your border disagreement with Kuwait.* [Author's italics]

I was in the American Embassy in Kuwait during the late 1960s. The instruction that we had during that period was that we should express no opinion on this issue and that the issue was not connected with America. James Baker has directed our official spokesman to emphasize this instruction . . . All that we hope is that these issues will be solved quickly . . .

The meeting ended on a more optimistic note which must have coloured the Ambassador's report, for despite all the threats and warnings included in the main text of the message, the meeting was interpreted both by Glaspie and by the State Department as a favourable statement of Saddam's intentions. Part of her subsequent telegram to the State Department read: 'We would be well advised to ease off on public criticism [of Saddam] until we see how negotiations develop.'[4]

Saddam, on the other hand, now convinced in his own mind that he had nothing to fear from his own neighbours and that the only remaining superpower would avert its eyes from any unwelcome activity in the Middle East, followed up this meeting less than a month later by launching his armies into Kuwait City early on the morning of 2 August 1990. They met with little or no resistance and the Emir of Kuwait narrowly avoided capture as he was lifted out of his country into neighbouring Saudi Arabia by helicopter, while members of his family and court followed hurriedly by car.

[handwritten margin note: launch a Saddam armies into Kuwait city]

Saddam Hussein had rolled the dice; it remained to be seen who else would enter the game.

The immediate reaction to Saddam Hussein's seizure of Kuwait must have given the dictator great satisfaction. While the news media gave graphic descriptions of the extremely powerful Iraqi forces which had so swiftly and completely overrun the tiny state, putting 100,000 men onto the next frontier with Saudi Arabia, the remainder of the world showed little enthusiasm to do anything about it. Yet the possibility of a further invasion of Saudi Arabia by Iraq was very real as it could quickly win for Saddam control over a further fifth of the world's oil. Among the Western countries, however, there remained a marked lack of urgent response.

At a meeting of the United States National Security Council held on 2 August (when the invasion took place, it had still been 1 August in Washington), part of which was televised and broadcast, President Bush was seen hunched in his chair surrounded by his advisers, looking the very antithesis of a determined war leader. Speaking in a hesitant voice, he said, 'We're not discussing intervention.' When asked by reporters on the same day if he intended sending troops to the Gulf, he had replied that he was not contemplating such action.

General Colin Powell, the chairman of the Joint Chiefs of Staff, watching Bush carefully at the NSC meeting, did not think it was at all clear what the President was going to do or whether he would accept the loss of Kuwait.[5]

At the United Nations on the day following the Iraqi invasion, the Security Council met and approved Resolution 660 which condemned the invasion of Kuwait and demanded an immediate Iraqi withdrawal. The resolution was passed unanimously, receiving the support not only of the Western powers but also of Russia. Such a resolution, however, carried with it no threat of military action against Iraq.

Elsewhere in the Middle East, uncertainty prevailed. Saddam had shown himself to be no respecter of an Arab neighbour, yet he was still happy to receive the leaders of other Arab states and assure them of his continued goodwill towards them. At that early stage he must have been rubbing his hands with pleasure.

On the evening of 2 August, however, President Bush was scheduled to visit and speak at a symposium in Aspen, Colorado. Also present at the symposium was the British Prime Minister, Margaret Thatcher. Here the two leaders met and discussed the new situation confronting them. Margaret Thatcher recalls that when they met, Bush invited her to give her assessment first.[6] Thatcher was, as usual, uncompromising in her views: aggression could not be tolerated. By that time, as she remembers, George Bush too had reached a similar conclusion and the two leaders were of like mind. After the symposium, Bush spent the weekend at Camp David with his closest advisers and flew back to Washington on 5 August. In a BBC documentary after the war, the credit was given to Mrs Thatcher for steeling Bush's resolution for military action;[7] neither Lady Thatcher's recollection of the occasion, nor that of Sir Antony Acland, the British Ambassador who accompanied the Prime Minister to Aspen, agree with this.[8] It must, however, have been a considerable comfort to the President at that time to know that the British Prime Minister was as determined as he to put an end to Saddam Hussein's ambitions.

Meeting the world press on the White House lawn on 5 August, Bush made his intentions clear once and for all. Standing before the cameras, he made the uncompromising statement quoted at the head of this chapter:

'This will not stand,' he affirmed, stabbing the air with his fingers, 'this will not stand – this aggression against Kuwait!'[9]

A new determination was abroad in the United States. At 3.30 p.m. Eastern Standard Time on 6 August, with the agreement of King Fahd of Saudi Arabia, who had now changed his mind about the presence of foreign troops within his borders, and with full presidential approval, the first United States troops were despatched to the Middle East to deter Saddam from any further advance along the shores of the Persian Gulf.

Faced with the need to deploy a force which would deter Saddam's army at very short notice, the Pentagon's primary response was based on air power: ground-based and carrier-based fighter aircraft were the first fighting components that could be brought to bear and these were quickly followed up by airborne troops, notably the 82nd Airborne Division, and US Marines. The most serious deficiency in the early days of the deployment was in armour, with which the Iraqis were dangerously well equipped. However, while the armed forces started this massive deployment, there was still much diplomacy to attend to elsewhere in the world.

If the depressing outcome of their earlier military undertakings had done nothing else, it had taught the United States administration a number of lessons. Perhaps the most important of all was to learn the need for support in any military action that you contemplate. If you plan to undertake military operations outside your own borders, there are three aspects of support which you ignore at your peril. Firstly, you must secure the support of the country that you are planning to help; secondly, you need the support of the United Nations; but above all you require the support of your own people at home.

The first of these was already assured, although even under the threat of invasion, the Saudis were to stipulate very severe restrictions on the conduct of the foreign troops within their own borders. The United Nations, too, had made clear their disapproval of Saddam's actions, although they were not yet ready to support any armed conflict. The approval of the people of the United States to involvement in a major foreign adventure was, however, another matter; it was essential for George Bush to bring and to keep them on side. Otherwise the powerful anti-war influence across the country, still remembering Vietnam, could undermine the new-found determination of the President to resist aggression. This, he realized, must be his first and overriding task.

While these events were taking place in the United States, her European allies were as usual taking counsel of their fears. Margaret Thatcher, of course, was quick to pledge her support to the President; other countries were far less enthusiastic to become involved. After anxious negotiations, it soon appeared that only Britain, France and Italy in Europe were prepared to stand alongside America if it came to fighting. Even these three countries had difficulties in producing worthwhile contributions to the sort of forces that would be needed to deter an army of the size and strength of Saddam Hussein's.

Britain had nominally three armoured divisions deployed in West Germany for the support of NATO; during the 1980s she had been in the throes of re-equipping these divisions with a more modern tank. Under the pressures of post-Cold War economy, the new tanks had had serious teething troubles and were very slow into production. The divisions themselves were held at peacetime establishment and depended upon major reinforcement from the Territorial Army, which, if mobilized, could seriously affect Britain's economy. After much discussion in London, it was decided to contribute one armoured brigade group to the forces in Saudi Arabia. This would include two armoured regiments, each of fifty-seven Challenger tanks, and one mechanized infantry battalion equipped with the new Warrior armoured vehicles. This force would be supported by two squadrons of Tornado fighter-bombers. Apart from the aircraft, none of this force could be made available for some time, owing to the difficulty of moving the heavy equipment by sea.

The French, too, had difficulty in finding suitable units for desert warfare. They undertook to send an armoured reconnaissance brigade supported by fighter aircraft. The lack of support by many other members of the NATO alliance was dismal; even a request by the British to the Belgians to purchase from them some additional artillery ammunition was refused.

In Washington, the need to keep his people behind him continued to exercise the President. On 8 August, George Bush, who much disliked formal television appearances, addressed the people of the United States live from the White House: 'If history teaches us anything,' he said, 'it is that we must destroy aggression or it will destroy our freedom. Appeasement does not work; as in the 1930s, we see in Saddam Hussein a military dictator threatening his neighbours . . .'[10]

In the United States 61 million households tuned in to this broadcast, making it at that time the biggest event in television history. Many millions more elsewhere in the world also watched.

Again, in a televised address to an audience outside the Pentagon, he affirmed: 'When we hear of summary executions and routine torture taking place in Kuwait, America will not stand aside and allow the strong to overcome the weak.'

In the United Nations Security Council a further resolution (661) was passed unanimously to impose worldwide economic sanctions on Iraq. However, despite all this, the television cameras were soon showing pictures of anti-war demonstrators keeping noisy vigils outside the White House. 'No Blood for Oil!' read their banners, as state troopers were seen carrying the protesters away bodily.

At the outset, the task given to the military was the defence of Saudi Arabia. The prospect of driving the Iraqis out of Kuwait was still something that the military planners had not contemplated. Even with the immense American airlift and the combined forces of Saudi Arabia, Egypt, Britain and France, the prospect of taking on an army of one-third of a million men, which Saddam had now deployed into Kuwait, was more than they could hope to undertake.

In September, however, Bush, now more than ever determined to drive out the aggressor, demanded that a plan for offensive action should be put before him. What he received shocked him. If, said the military planners, we are required to attack into Kuwait, our present forces and logistic support can only undertake a direct attack into Kuwait City through the strongest part of the Iraqi defences. There are insufficient troops at present and insufficient logistic backup to enable us to swing round to the west and attack the Iraqi forces in the flank.

'And what level of casualties might you expect in such an attack?' asked the President.

'Maybe ten thousand,' came the unwelcome reply.[11]

Casualties and bodybags were the American Achilles heel. Saddam Hussein himself had said that the Americans might fight with their technological weapons but that they would never fight man to man in what he forecast to be the 'Mother of all Battles'. Certainly America in her current frame of mind would not stomach a battle leading to 10,000 casualties. In late October, the American Secretary of Defense, Richard Cheney, sent the chairman of the Joint Chiefs of Staff, General Colin Powell, to Riyadh to discuss an offensive plan with the Commander of the Coalition Forces taking part in the defensive operation known as 'Desert Shield'. This was the bluff, straight-talking American General Norman Schwarzkopf, soon to be known round the world as 'Stormin' Norman'.

Schwarzkopf set out his shopping list to transform his defensive force into one capable of driving the Iraqi army out of Kuwait. It was a formidable list, starting with the VII (US) Corps, the backbone of the American forces in Germany. He also asked for three more carrier groups, making six in all, and finally, perhaps the most demanding of all, for the mobilization of the National Guard and of reservists from all across the United States. The logistic bill was astronomical, supporting, as it would have to, some 600,000 American troops in Saudi Arabia.

To the intense surprise of the military, President George Bush, their Commander-in-Chief, accepted the list in its entirety. By this time he was in no doubt of what had to be done. A vast new movement of troops was now undertaken, greater than anything that had been seen since the Second World War. In response to this show of determination both the British and French agreed to increase their contributions to the force. Britain despatched a second armoured brigade to the scene, making the two together into a full armoured division with strong artillery, engineer and logistic support. A further two squadrons of Tornados joined the first. A similar increase was made to the French forces. In all no fewer than twenty-eight nations made a contribution to this great call to arms.

There still remained, though, a number of other hurdles to be crossed: the support of the United Nations for military action still had to be sought and, within the Security Council, a prime need was for the full support of Russia. The risk of sudden international dissension to the

President's plan had to be minimized. However, still more important for Bush was the opinion of Congress. As had never been properly done at the time of Vietnam, the President determined to seek the approval of the United States Congress to the commitment of American troops to battle against Iraq.

President Gorbachev met Bush in Helsinki in November. It was one of the most friendly meetings between the two leaders, at which the Russian pledged his support for the removal of Saddam Hussein from Kuwait. Nevertheless he made it very clear that military action must only be taken in the last resort. Every diplomatic and economic effort must first be made to persuade Saddam to withdraw his forces. To this end, Gorbachev offered to use his own good offices. As James Baker, the US Secretary of State, remarked in a later television interview: 'Without Russia on side, the whole operation could have been stalled.'

On 29 November, the United Nations Security Council passed Resolution 678, giving Iraq until 15 January to withdraw her forces from Kuwait, after which 'all necessary means' might be used to force her withdrawal. This resolution was passed by 14 votes to 2, with only Cuba and Yemen voting against and China abstaining. The United Nations had now given their approval.

Addressing Congress, George Bush made the point most strongly that this crisis was 'not about oil, but about naked aggression'. There was, however, little doubt in most people's minds that it was Saddam's control of so much of the world's oil that had driven the Western world to such extreme action. The debate in Congress lasted for three days in which many spoke eloquently for more time to be given for sanctions to work, while others attempted to frighten their listeners with renewed talk of casualties. At the conclusion, the President's request was narrowly approved by 52 votes to 47 in the Senate, and by 250 votes to 183 in the House. George Bush had his final authority to go to war.

However, before taking the final step, the President made one further move to demonstrate to the world his desire for peace – a move which disturbed his military advisers but which, with hindsight, showed an uncanny prescience of his adversary's psychology. On 9 January 1991 he despatched his Secretary of State, Jim Baker, to meet a representative of Saddam Hussein's own inner cabinet. The meeting was arranged to take place in Geneva and Saddam sent to it his Foreign Secretary, Tariq Aziz. Baker was required to make a final demand for an Iraqi withdrawal before the UN ultimatum expired. The military were worried as they foresaw the worst possible scenario: the Iraqi army and air force could withdraw the short distance back into Iraq with all their forces intact and ready to re-invade, merely waiting to see how long the enormous build-up of coalition forces would remain opposing them across the border. Raymond Seitz, who travelled with Baker to Geneva, recalls how, when they arrived at the Inter-Continental Hotel, there were raised stands outside which were thronged with the world's press. With a grim face, Baker entered the meeting. Seitz recalls that, although there seemed little prospect of any negotiation, Baker kept the meeting talking for four hours, playing it out to leave no one in any doubt of his determination.[12]

Bush had correctly read Saddam's reaction: the loss of face involved in a withdrawal under the threat of attack would have been too much for the dictator to stomach. Having received no response from Aziz, Baker handed him a letter to Saddam Hussein from President Bush; in it the latter made clear that if, at any time, Saddam were to use weapons of mass destruction – that is to say biological, chemical or nuclear – he and his whole country might expect a severe and immediate response. Tariq Aziz read the letter at the table and coldly returned it to Baker without comment.[13]

Outside the hotel, James Baker spoke to the assembled world press: 'Regrettably, during four hours of talks I have heard nothing which leads me to believe that President Saddam Hussein will meet the demands of the United Nations.'

The President of the United States had 'gone the last mile for peace'; only six days remained before the ultimatum ran out.

While this heated diplomatic manoeuvring and military preparations were continuing, the world press observed the developments and made judgements of varying wisdom. In the United States, as the discussions in Congress disclosed, the country was torn by the choice between following their President's warlike lead or joining the ranks of those who would avoid war at any price. In London, on 16 January 1991, at the time when all attempts to negotiate a peaceful settlement appeared to have failed and the UN ultimatum to Iraq to withdraw from Kuwait had expired, leading articles appearing in two British papers on the same day put into perspective the two views of the agonizing prospect that lay ahead. *The Times* was for war; the *Guardian* was for peace:

Nothing on earth is so obscene as the prospect before the armies massed in the Gulf. Days are long past when nations gloried in war.

Vast expenditure and constant effort are expended to avoid it. Rarely do they fail, but in the matter of Iraq's occupation of Kuwait, they have done so. Not since 1939 has an aggression left so clear a choice to those seeking a just international order. Blame for the failure of diplomacy since 2nd August lies squarely with Iraq. Now the only choice lies between capitulation to evil or a fight . . .

The coalition ranged against Iraq represents a step towards the collective enforcement of international law. This experiment must be made to work in the Gulf or countries must arm and ally themselves as best they can against the law of the jungle. This is a war about peace, not just in the Middle East, not just in our time, but in tomorrow's world. That is why British soldiers are rightly asked to risk their lives.

(*The Times*, 16 January 1991)

. . . The allies have pursued two policies since Saddam Hussein – misreading indolent signals from the American State Department – invaded Kuwait. The first policy was to bolster a fearful Saudi Arabia against attack and to impose the most draconian of trade embargoes on Iraq. Two months on, that policy was a success. The Saudis were safe; and the lifelines of trade for Baghdad were severed. Then the policy – for reasons which remain obscure – changed. There was a White House decision to give the defensive allied troops along the Kuwait border an offensive capability. Millions of tons of hardware poured in; troop levels doubled. The long term costs became gargantuan. A deadline for possible military action – January 15 – was set.

Well, it is now January 15; the clock stands at midnight. How does that second policy look? By its own espoused ends – 'the last chance for peace', as George Bush told Congress only three days ago – the policy stares bleak failure in the face. The combination of sanctions and offensive military build-up has not worked as the politicians who designed it hoped. It leaves, now, armed attack as the last, best chance for peace. That is bloody nonsense . . .

(*Guardian*, 16 January 1991)

Despite these differences of opinion, the President of the United States, supported by the governments of his allies, was determined to evict Saddam from the country he had seized. At 2.30 a.m., local time, on

16 January 1991, the coalition launched an air war against Iraq. The first international press report was carried on the ABC Network in the United States with a news flash which interrupted their programme *World News Tonight* exactly four minutes later.

In the preparatory period of the war, much thought had been given to the handling of the media representatives both on and off the battlefield. The experience of the previous decade had shown that attempts to prevent or limit media access to major world events seldom proved either effective or beneficial. In this case, however, where events were to take place in a country well outside the normal sphere of United States influence, there would be very limited control of the media open to the coalition. Furthermore, where there was not news, there would be speculation and, worse, where one side did not offer news, the other side might. In the event, Saddam Hussein, sensing that there might be advantage to him, even allowed 'enemy' reporters to remain in his capital, Baghdad. The reports that emanated from them had a remarkable effect as the war progressed, as we shall shortly see.

From the American point of view there were four aspects of media reporting which could prove critically damaging to their cause. Firstly and readily understandable was the need to maintain the security of their military plans; secondly, they had to continue to convince the world of the justice of their cause; thirdly, they must risk nothing being reported that might damage the precarious coalition with their allies; and finally, and perhaps most importantly of all, they must allow nothing to be seen or reported that might lose them the support of their own people at home. Their whole media plan had to be geared to the attenuation of these risks – risks that were further heightened when news releases were being made simultaneously in Riyadh, Washington and London.

Saddam Hussein, too, had a well-thought-out media policy. His priorities were not unnaturally exactly opposite to those of the coalition. His first concern was to break away from the coalition those Arab states that had joined the infidels. His second was to present himself to the world as a misjudged ruler with the determination to stand up to the combined forces of the Western world. Finally, his hope was that he could arouse the sympathy of the world by the damage inflicted on his country by a superpower and, paradoxically, to scare off the Americans at the prospect of enduring heavy military casualties themselves.

At the disposal of the world press were new technologies that had not hitherto been used to report war. Some newsmen, though by no means all at the time, were equipped with readily transportable satellite dishes which could beam reports directly from the battlefield to the studio, enabling live reports to be transmitted to world audiences in real time. Equally, opportunities existed for reporters to obtain news not only from Saudi Arabia, but from Jordan, Turkey and, as already mentioned, from Baghdad itself. Any attempt by the allies to influence the output of these massive resources was going to be a Herculean effort.

Where the direct reporting of the activities of the allied troops was concerned, the coalition authorities set up a pool system of reporting which, although frustrating to the many reporters excluded from the pools, had some great benefits to the commanders. Once given a place in a pool, the reporters were obliged to abide by the coalition rules of reporting and at the same time given the advantage of briefing and protection by the fighting troops themselves. These pool reporters in many cases forged strong links with the troops to whom they were attached and were able to file compelling stories with the cooperation of the forward commanders. On the debit side, however, they were obliged by the rules to submit their reports to military minders who, under the guise of checking for security breaches, in fact imposed a powerful censorship. The pooled reports were finally forwarded to their destinations by militarily controlled communications systems which were frequently criticized by the newsmen for their slowness.

For those not in the pools, daily briefings were given by military spokesmen in Riyadh or Dhahran, some of which could be televised for transmission to viewers around the world. Uncontrolled, however, were a number of tenacious journalists who chanced their arm in the forward areas, without submission to the 'rules' (and therefore not benefiting from the protection). These, known as 'unilaterals', were heavily distrusted by the troops, but did on a number of occasions make important contributions to the reporting of the war.

Most remarkable, though, were the journalists who, as already mentioned, remained, with Iraqi agreement, to report the war from the centre of Baghdad. Of these the best known were the CNN reporters who gave moment by moment accounts of raids on the enemy capital by smart bombs and cruise missiles, giving to their audiences breathtaking descriptions of the accuracy with which these weapons sought out and destroyed military targets within the capital. Similar fascinating accounts were reported by John Simpson of the BBC from the viewpoint of his hotel window in downtown Baghdad.

It has been estimated that during the Gulf War an average of 600 million people throughout the world watched the nightly television news reports as the events unfolded. The pattern of these news programmes was virtually identical: an 'anchorman' or news presenter who outlined the events of the day; a report of the daily military briefing from Riyadh, frequently showing film of the day's targets being struck and often featuring the craggy Commander-in-Chief or his air force deputy, General Chuck Horner; then might follow a report from one or more of the pool reporters with the fighting troops or the aircrews, after which comments were usually offered on the events reported by one of the much maligned 'pundits' or 'armchair strategists', so frequently criticized by the writers of subsequent accounts of the war.

Here it might be fair to offer some views on the role of these so-called pundits. In the Falklands War, as has already been mentioned, a number of retired service officers were severely criticized for offering suggestions of how and where they might conduct operations if they were in charge. These opinions were often much in line with the actual plans that were subsequently carried out and were thought to have helped the enemy. It came, therefore, as a rather worrying surprise to one of the authors of this book when in November 1990 he received an invitation from David Hannah, the news editor of *Channel 4 News*, asking if he would be prepared to appear, 'in the event of hostilities breaking out', as an 'expert interviewee'. Remembering only too well the indiscretions of 'experts' in the Falklands campaign, he sought advice from the Ministry of Defence Public Relations Department, making it clear that, if it was preferred, he would take no part in the programmes. In reply it was said that: 'as there would be any number of experts invited, the Ministry would prefer to have a spokesman who knew something about the subject, rather than one who did not'. With the reply came a full briefing folder of unclassified information about the British deployment, together with a list of subjects which should not be discussed.

As a result, the author participated in news programmes not only with Channel Four, but also on BBC *Newsnight* and a number of BBC early morning *Today* programmes. In the light of criticism that was once again levelled at the so-called pundits, he defended himself in a letter to *The Times*, published shortly after the end of the war. Part of this letter read:

. . . The most important rule was that nobody should ever speculate about the operations which the coalition might actually carry out.

This rule was, I think, rigidly observed throughout the war . . . I set myself three aims in anything that I said:

1. To do all that I could to encourage support for our armed forces and confidence in their ability to carry out their task.
2. To explain where possible some of the great difficulties which they faced, which might not be readily apparent to the general public.
3. To discourage over-optimism in the speed or the cost of the final outcome.

In the event, many of us were labelled prophets of doom; but how much better it was to be prepared for the worst than to make the opposite error . . .

(*The Times*, Letters page, 8 March 1991)

One aspect of such appearances does, however, merit further discussion; in the build-up to Desert Storm, much speculation took place about the likely number of casualties to be expected by the allies. On *Newsnight*, Peter Snow had his famous sandtable on which he liked to set out scenarios about which he questioned his guests and this very question often came up:

'And if the Allies chose to force their way through on the direct route from Saudi Arabia to Kuwait City, what percentage of casualties would you expect them to suffer?'

'I am not prepared to discuss any particular plan that the allies might or might not adopt.'

'Of course not, but just supposing they were to carry out a frontal attack, what about the casualties?'

'The number of casualties sustained in any military action,' one was forced to say, 'depends to a great extent on the determination shown by the opposition. As we have no idea at present how hard the Iraqis would be prepared to fight in the event of a ground war, it is impossible and valueless to speculate on the number of casualties.'

'And how about chemical weapons? If these are used by the Iraqis, there are bound to be serious casualties, are there not, irrespective of the enemy determination?'

'The United States and British armies are the best equipped in the world and the best trained to survive chemical warfare. However unpleasant it might be, I am in no doubt that they could deal with such attacks.'

Such exchanges may not have contributed much to the reporting of the war, yet it was better than walking into the minefield of speculating on casualty figures as the Commander of the British 7th Armoured Brigade discovered to his chagrin shortly before the fighting started. He describes how he held a media briefing to discuss the training of his brigade. At the end of the briefing he invited questions. David Fairhall of the *Guardian* (a very old hand as a defence correspondent) enquired:

'What sort of casualties should the British be prepared for?'
'. . . It is inconceivable," replied the brigadier, 'that if two armies of the size that are facing each other here, went to war there would not be considerable casualties.'
'What sort of figures are we talking about? What percentage? Two? Ten? Twenty?'
'We are planning on about 15 per cent,' interjected the Chief of Staff.
'15 per cent?' echoed a voice; 'that's over 1,500 men from your own brigade alone!'[14]

The fat was truly in the fire; say what he might, the Chief of Staff had given the newsmen their story.

Headlines shortly followed in London's *Evening Standard*: 'British Commander's Warning as Gulf forces go on alert: Prepare for Bloodbath.' It took a lot of work on the part of the Ministry of Defence to defuse this particular situation.

The whole subject of casualties was one in which public opinion showed itself most fickle. From the beginning, the American administration was convinced, no doubt rightly, that, while the country might support a quick and successful operation, it would soon lose heart in the event of a long drawn out struggle involving heavy bloodshed. Among the directives given to Schwarzkopf, perhaps the most imperative was the need to keep allied casualties to a minimum. Equally, world opinion would not tolerate heavy civilian casualties in the cities of Iraq. Yet, strangely one might think, there appeared to be not the least concern at the prospect of the slaughter in large numbers of Iraqi troops, even though by far the majority of these were very young conscripts. The transition from being a fifteen-year-old 'child', whose life is sacrosanct, to becoming a seventeen-year-old conscript, who can be treated as cannon-fodder, is a strange quirk of human concern which can probably be traced to the judgement of the media.

At all events, the coalition troops had to be preserved while the enemy soldiers could be cut off from their food and water supplies in the desert and then carpet-bombed with equanimity.

Thus the first stage of the war was fought from the air.

The conduct of a successful air war is a politician's dream. If the opposition is technologically inferior, great damage can be inflicted with comparatively little risk to the aircrews. It avoids the mud and blood of a ground campaign and enables wars to be fought without getting your hands dirty. The great fallacy is that, with perhaps one single and unique exception, air wars are never successful in isolation. The exception was the dropping of the atomic bombs on Japan in 1945.

The air war launched by the coalition against Iraq on 16 January 1991 had never before been matched in its intensity. Thousands of sorties were flown to destroy key targets of Saddam's war machine. His communication centres, his nuclear, biological and chemical plants, his airfields, his road and rail communications, his power stations and logistic depots were all targeted and systematically destroyed. However, the war had scarcely begun before Saddam played his first ace.

Using his Soviet-manufactured Scud missiles, operating from mobile launchers in the desert in the west of Iraq, he launched a series of attacks against Israeli cities. These missiles were known to be capable of carrying chemical warheads, so that the first television pictures to be broadcast of destruction in Tel Aviv on 18 January, showing rescuers wearing gasmasks, led the world to believe that these had been chemical attacks. In fact, they were not and the damage caused by these early generation missiles was comparatively slight. Nevertheless, there can have been no doubt whatever in Saddam's mind that these attacks would swiftly bring Israel into the war, making it impossible for the Arab members of the coalition to continue a war in alliance with the mutual and hated enemy.

Realizing the enormous damage that an Israeli response to this attack would cause, President George Bush was quickly and earnestly in touch with the Israeli leader, Yitzhak Shamir. This cannot have been an easy conversation as Bush was not on good terms with Shamir. Nor had an Arab state ever before attacked Israel with impunity. What precisely was said in those first conversations has not, we believe, ever been revealed, nor what inducements, if any, were offered to keep Israel out of the war.

Suffice it to say that, whatever did pass between them, Yitzhak Shamir was persuaded not to react to Saddam's attack. Quickly, United States' Patriot anti-missile missiles were deployed in Israel to counter the Iraqi threat. Israeli participation must surely have meant a coalition collapse and yet surprisingly, Schwarzkopf, whose political antennae were usually acute, took an unusually inept line in his television briefing on the night of the first attacks: 'Scud missiles,' he declared, 'are militarily insignificant.'

He was reportedly furious when ordered by the President, through Defense Secretary Cheney, to alter his priorities for the air war, giving the destruction of Scud missiles the highest priority. In fact, the mobile missile launchers could not be located by the air forces but many were eventually neutralized by special forces patrols operating deep in Iraqi territory.

Among the prime targets engaged in the early stages of the air war were Saddam's airfields. The allies had expected to be engaged, at least at the start of the war, by the Iraqi air force. In fact, Iraqi aircraft offered virtually no resistance and caused much speculation when large numbers of them were flown into Iran by their pilots, from where they were not heard of again. In the attacks on the airfields, the British Royal Air Force Tornados had been equipped with a new weapon system with the specific capability of destroying concrete runways. JP233, as it was code-named, released over the runways a shower of bomblets each of which was designed to break up an area of the concrete. The weapon had, however, to be dropped from a very low level. The aircrews had trained in the use of this weapon in the belief that they could approach their targets below radar cover at very high speed and escape before they could be engaged. The tactic had been designed to operate against the high technology expected of the Soviet Union in Europe. Ironically, the less advanced technology of the Iraqis was better suited to engaging low-flying aircraft and, as a result, the RAF suffered heavier casualties from this tactic than the remainder of the coalition air forces. A number of aircrews who had been forced to eject from their aircraft fell into Iraqi hands. Here again Saddam played what he believed to be a high card in his hand.

On Iraqi television, captured coalition crewmen were shown in distressed conditions, making varying 'confessions' of their own unwillingness to have participated in the war and anxiety for the war to stop. The Iraqis evidently believed that such appearances would undermine the morale of the coalition. In fact, of course, it was only too readily apparent that the crewmen had been brutalized and that their statements had been obtained under duress.

Articles in Britain in the *Sun* on 22 January read:

**THE FACES OF CAPTURED BRITISH AIRMEN ADRIAN NICHOL
AND JOHN PETERS WILL HAUNT US FOR MANY A LONG DAY.**
So brave when they went into battle, so helpless when captors
paraded them on television.

Adrian's mumbled and hollow words, like those of the two
American flyers with him, were obviously DICTATED by an Iraqi
propaganda writer.

How they must have stuck in his throat as he was forced, under
what threats we dare not even imagine, to denounce the allied
mission in which he had played such a gallant part.

No one can believe the sentiments uttered by Flight Lieutenant
Nichol, in a voice drained of emotion, were his own.

**THEY WERE THE WORDS OF AN EVIL MONSTER, SADDAM
HUSSEIN, AND THE BASTARDS OF BAGHDAD.**

The whole project backfired heavily on Saddam, whose reputation as an
unscrupulous tyrant was even further enhanced. It was a media ploy
which the Iraqis never used again.

In Baghdad itself, the Iraqis were sure that the presence of Western
reporters within their capital would, in the long run, be to their
advantage. They were in little doubt from the start of hostilities that there
would be unlimited opportunities to show these journalists scenes of
civilian slaughter as a result of the allied bombing which would be certain
to turn at least the uncommitted nations against the war. In fact their
opportunities turned out to be extremely few. One of the surprises of the
new technologies in use was the pinpoint accuracy of the allied attacks
onto military targets, even to the point of directing weapons into specific
windows of selected buildings. Inevitably, however, things did occasionally
go wrong for the allies. The most damaging single event of the air war
was undoubtedly the attack on the Amiriya shelter on the night of
13 February.

On that night, by a bitter irony the anniversary of the bombing of
Dresden, two allied bombs struck a building in Baghdad which had been
identified as a military target by American intelligence. In fact, as quickly
became apparent, it was being used as a civilian air-raid shelter. The
Iraqis were quick to take advantage of the presence of Western reporters
in the capital and all censorship restrictions were immediately lifted. The

world was soon being shown grisly pictures of the dead and wounded, captioned in harsh criticism of the Americans in those countries that remained unaligned.

The *Jordanian Times* reported the attack as: 'a living testimony to the US-led alliance's cruelty, cynicism and total disregard for human life in conducting this ugly and pointless war against Iraq.'[15]

American protests that the building had been used for military purposes and that perhaps the civilians had been persuaded to use it as a shelter in the hope of just such an event occurring, could do little to remedy the damage that the reports conveyed. In fairness to the coalition, though, the evidence of damage to civilian installations throughout the air war was remarkably small.

However, while the allies sought to carry out a swift surgical destruction of Saddam's ability to fight, the Iraqi President was himself following a different strategy. In the words of Max Hastings writing in the *Daily Telegraph* on 5 February:

> . . . But Saddam's agenda appears entirely different. Soon after the beginning of the war, I suggested that he was seeking to keep his forces in being. The key question was whether he intended to commit them to the ground battle, or was thinking further ahead.
>
> It now seems likely that Saddam is indeed looking beyond the loss of Kuwait to a scenario in which, even amid military defeat, he can claim heroic status in the Arab world for having stayed in the ring against a western-led alliance through a 'mother of wars'. Thus he has mounted a succession of headline grabbing operations, and thus his apparent confidence. Saddam is not running a war in the expectation of military victory, but a political and publicity campaign in which his weapons merely chance to be lives rather than government handouts.

However, whatever strategy was being followed by Saddam, the allies were bent on military victory. In their determination to destroy Saddam's élite Republican Guard divisions, the tanks of which were dug into the sand in the desert, the Americans had recourse to intense 'carpet bombing' by B52 heavy bombers. These unsophisticated 'iron bombs' did comparatively little damage to the dug-in tanks and, despite repeated efforts, the level of damage sustained by the Republican Guard divisions during the air war was comparatively small.

Finally, the Iraqi forward troops themselves became the target of relentless attacks, to prepare for the moment when the ground war would begin. However, while the air war continued with unabated ferocity, Norman Schwarzkopf, the allied commander, was busy moving his tanks and infantry into position for the kill.

Most of the troops deployed to Saudi Arabia to recover Kuwait had little or no experience of the desert. The bulk of the armour – the American VII Corps and the British 1st Armoured Division – had been stationed in Europe for as long as any of the soldiers could remember, planning and training to meet an attack from the Soviet Union in the east. All the training for war in the Arabian desert had to be learned in a very short time.

Of the British commanders, Lieutenant General Sir Peter de la Billiere had the advantage of considerable experience in the Middle East from his time in the SAS and had a good understanding of the Arab people. He had not, however, commanded armoured formations before. The divisional commander, Major General Rupert Smith, an officer of the Parachute Regiment, had only recently taken command of his division in Germany, while his two brigade commanders, Brigadiers Patrick Cordingley and Christopher Hammerbeck, although much experienced with armour, had little or no knowledge of the desert.

By an amusing coincidence, one of the authors of this book had been the commandant of the Army Staff College at Camberley in 1977. In that year a group of MPs asked to visit the college. They spent the day with the students who were occupied with an indoor map exercise. At the end of the day, the visitors came to see the commandant.

'That was most interesting,' said one, 'but frankly, General, I can't think why you're still teaching them that stuff! I am absolutely certain that the British army will never be asked to do that sort of thing again.'

The Commandant replied that he was required to train the officers in all kinds of warfare and that this was just one example.

In fact the students had been studying the handling of an armoured division in the desert. One of the students that year was Captain Patrick Cordingley and one of the instructors was Lieutenant Colonel de la Billiere. (By an even stranger coincidence, the exercise had originally been devised by the other author of this book when he had been an instructor at the college.)

Once fully equipped, the formations in Saudi Arabia had to carry out thorough and intense training. Apart from preparing to face a large and well-equipped army, they had to be ready to meet an enemy who might use chemical or biological weapons against them, with all the horrors that such warfare would bring. At this stage they made their first acquaintance with the pool journalists who were attached to them for the operation. Among those who established close relationships with the British troops were such well-known television reporters as Martin Bell and Kate Adie, whose reports from the units as they trained brought home vividly to the watching audiences in Britain the circumstances in which our soldiers were living and training.

In the meantime, General Schwarzkopf and his commanders were finalizing their plan of attack. This was built around a major deception plan to mislead the enemy into expecting the main thrust to be directed straight towards Kuwait City. In fact, the Commander-in-Chief planned to swing the main weight of his armour well to the west and attack northward through Iraq itself, subsequently turning east to destroy and cut off the Republican Guard Divisions – Saddam's élite forces – which were held in reserve to the north of Kuwait City.

This plan required a huge movement of troops and supplies along a single route running parallel to the Iraq–Saudi border, which must of necessity not be discovered by the enemy. Under the constant harassment of sustained air attack and highly sophisticated communications deception, there was comparatively little danger of the enemy detecting this great movement by his own means. The gravest danger of disclosure lay with the media whose worldwide reporting could readily be received in Baghdad.

Here the system of pool reporting came into its own. In fact, the pool reporters were fully briefed on the whole plan almost as soon as the troops themselves, but they were committed to the 'rules' and their copy was subject to military scrutiny. Naturally, the public briefings from headquarters never made any disclosure of allied intentions. The real danger lay with the 'unilaterals'. Some of these did speculate about allied plans, notably a report in the *Guardian* on 27 January which read: 'In the battle to free Kuwait, US armour and infantry will thrust forward across Southern Iraq.'[16]

Similarly, speculative reports suggesting that the main attack would come from the west were transmitted by CNN on more than one occasion. CNN was certainly watched avidly by the authorities in Baghdad, even if they missed the opinions of the *Guardian*.

However, the first ground operations were launched not by the coalition troops but by Saddam Hussein. Some 12 kilometres south of the Kuwaiti border with Saudi Arabia lies the small coastal village of Al-Khafji. In the first weeks of 1991, this village, so perilously close to the border and within easy range of Scud missiles had been abandoned by its inhabitants and was virtually unoccupied. On the night of 29 January – a fortnight after the start of the air war – an Iraqi force of Russian-built T-55 tanks and armoured personnel carriers amounting to some 4,000 troops attacked across the border and occupied Al-Khafji. The ensuing fighting was confused, involving Saudi and Qatari troops backed by US Marines. The town was not reoccupied for thirty-six hours. Here the official communiqués and the reports of the media varied widely.

Commenting on it subsequently in his book, de la Billiere wrote as follows:

Contrary to what CNN and other television stations reported, this was not, for the Coalition, a serious breakthrough. It was exactly what we had expected and hoped for, as it brought enemy vehicles, weapons and men out of their prepared positions and into the open . . . The screen of Allied troops near the front executed a well planned manoeuvre and let the invaders through so that the next line of Coalition forces, who were mobile, could cut them off from their supporting weapons and deal with them piecemeal. That said, the invaders came further than they were meant to.[17]

However, the news of the attack on Al-Khafji was not broken until well after midday on 30 January, when a military communiqué was picked up by a French news agency from Baghdad radio which announced that 'a massive land offensive had been launched against Al-Khafji'. In response to this, American official sources confirmed fifteen minutes later that 'a clash between Iraqi and Coalition forces had occurred' – place unspecified. During the afternoon a series of different reports were issued by news agencies and the Pentagon, most of which disagreed with each other. Baghdad radio continued to describe the operation as a major victory. It was not until the evening that a briefing in Riyadh managed to put the events into some sort of perspective and it was not until 1 February that the situation was fully recovered.

Even then, subsequent television pictures showed that the US Marines had been far more closely involved in the fighting than had been admitted by the Allied Command, who maintained, no doubt for political purposes, that the attack had been defeated by Arab coalition forces. Yet, as a correspondent of *The Times* observed, 'Whatever anyone tells you on the TV, the script for this war was not supposed to open with the Iraqis taking a town in Saudi Arabia and holding it long enough for the news to get all around the Arab world.'[18]

The first land engagement had not done much to promote confidence between the media and the allies – 'Cock-up in Khafji' it was labelled by the press.

As the great move westward of armour and supplies continued, again the activities of the unilaterals became unwelcome to the allies. From the reports of the senior officers involved in this, there appeared to be little or no difficulty encountered. Neither de la Billiere nor Cordingley find the matter worthy of report in their books. It was hardly helpful, therefore, to read in the *Independent* on 23 January a report by Robert Fisk, a notable unilateral, entitled 'Bogged Down in the Desert'.

In this piece, Fisk not only reported military units becoming lost in the desert but went on to describe the complete breakdown of convoy discipline on the supply route which he described as 'littered with the wreckage of disabled or smashed vehicles'. He described the allied plan for their principal attack as having become 'an open secret' which 'every officer' believes the Iraqis must 'long ago have acquired'.

More disturbing still from the military point of view were his reports about the medical preparations. 'Forward medical units have been instructed to give priority to battle casualties with hope of recovery,' he wrote, 'leaving terminal patients to take second place.' He reported a military doctor as saying: 'We have refrigeration trucks to take bodies to the rear but we may be overwhelmed. So we have dug two mass graves.' Finally, he commented that: 'medical staff are trained to care for gas victims but admit they could do little on coming under chemical attack to help patients undergoing operations.'[19]

Such reporting was scarcely helpful to the families of those about to be launched into battle.

As the first weeks of February slipped by, more and more of the coalition forces moved up to their assembly areas where they were to await the final order to launch the main ground attack against Saddam's forces. Very few of the allied soldiers had previous experience of battle and the uncertainty of what lay ahead filled them with anxiety. Max Hastings, himself an experienced war reporter who had accompanied the British army in the Falklands, wrote a perceptive piece for the *Daily Telegraph* which was published on 21 February. It concluded:

Focus your sympathy today, though, upon the thousands of men of the allied armoured divisions, cleaning their weapons and polishing their vehicle optics for the hundredth time, men who have not yet glimpsed an Iraqi, who know that they are at war only because they hear the crump of the guns and the bombs, and see the distant columns of smoke on the horizon they have yet to cross.

They yearn for the suspense to be ended. They do not want to risk their lives, or to kill Iraqis. But they desperately want to get on with the job . . .

Each man asks himself, in the silence of his sleeping bag in the darkness, how will he behave when the test comes.

It is the same before every battle, in every war.

It is unlikely that the allied ground forces will have long to wait before they know the answers.

Nor did they. At 4 a.m. on 24 February, the attack started. Opposite Kuwait City, the US Marines launched an attack directly into the most heavily defended part of the front; but far to the west the XVIII US Airborne Corps, supported by the French, advanced deep into Iraq, while one of its divisions, the 101st US Assault Division, the Screaming Eagles, was lifted 80 kilometres into Iraq by a vast fleet of helicopters. Shortly after midday, the 1st US Mechanized Division, the Big Red One, began to breach the minefields west of the Wadi al Batin and secure a bridgehead 25 miles deep. Through this bridgehead the British 1st Armoured Division was to pass, closely followed by the armoured divisions of the VII US Corps.

The whole operation was supported by an intense artillery barrage, as were the operations in the east by ships of the US and Royal Navy.

As is now well known, the resistance offered to this great attack was minimal. The Iraqi troops, tired, hungry and poorly led, were for the most part only too anxious to surrender after their experiences in the air war and under the artillery barrages. In a period of only four days, the Iraqi forces in Kuwait had for the most part been destroyed. The American armour had swept round to the north; the British tanks were on the outskirts of Kuwait City, as were the US Marines from the south. It was left to the Arab forces of the coalition to reoccupy the capital.

In a desperate final measure, Saddam Hussein had ordered the Kuwaiti oil wells to be torched: the whole sky was filled with towering columns of evil smelling black smoke. However, it was the events unfolding to the north of the city which dominated the world's media for the next few days.

In September 1996, five years after the end of the Gulf War, General Norman Schwarzkopf, the United States Commander-in-Chief, appeared in a BBC television documentary film which was largely about the Carthaginian general, Hannibal. The film purported to show how much Schwarzkopf had been influenced by Hannibal's tactics and compared the Gulf War to Hannibal's campaign against the Romans in 218 BC. There may well have been similarities: the long approach march made by Hannibal through France and across the Alps may have borne comparison to the wide swing across the Iraqi desert; Hannibal's elephants may perhaps be compared with the American high technology weapons available to Schwarzkopf; the final battle may have been comparable with the Roman defeat at Cannae. However, the attempted comparison between Hannibal's failure to march on Rome at the end of the campaign and the conclusion of the Gulf War was a false one. The end of the war in Kuwait has been the subject of endless discussion since 1991 and has occupied the media greatly.

As already recounted, the fighting war was over in a period of only four days, but the scenes that greeted the ground forces as they converged on the road from Kuwait City to Basra shocked them. As the Iraqis in Kuwait had realized that the war was lost, they commandeered every possible form of vehicle and tried to escape up the road back to Iraq. The great mass of fleeing vehicles provided the air forces of the coalition with an unparalleled target. The approaching ground troops were met with an appalling scene of slaughter and destruction where the mass of escaping vehicles, blocking the road, had been systematically destroyed by air attack.

With the Iraqi army in headlong flight out of Kuwait, a decision was needed about what to do next. Douglas Hurd, the British Foreign Secretary, was in Washington at the time and had called on the President in the Oval Office at the White House. He gave us the following account of events as they unfolded.[20]

While Hurd was with the President, General Colin Powell, chairman of the Joint Chiefs of Staff, entered the office where most of the President's close advisers were already. Turning to Hurd, George Bush observed that: 'as the Brits have been with us all the way, you should stay here with us now.' Accordingly, Hurd was privy to what followed. Powell outlined on the map the progress of the battle and told the President that the Iraqis had been defeated and were fleeing from Kuwait; the air forces were taking heavy toll of those escaping and the pilots were not happy to continue with the slaughter which had been described as a 'turkey shoot'. He was of the opinion that the war could be concluded within the next couple of days. After a brief discussion with his advisers, which made no mention of any further operations into Iraq, Bush, who had already seen television pictures of the slaughter of Iraqis on the Basra road, asked Powell why they could not stop fighting straight away. Powell asked for permission to consult Schwarzkopf, which he did in a neighbouring office.

In Powell's own account,[21] he subsequently obtained Schwarzkopf's agreement and the President ordered fighting to cease at midnight Washington time, 27/28 February 1991, precisely 100 hours after the start of the land war.

So ended the Gulf War. However, it left a lot of questions unanswered. In his instructions, Bush gave no direction to Schwarzkopf as to how the battle should be concluded; he demanded no surrender from Saddam, nor did he forbid the movement of enemy troops and vehicles out of Kuwait. Thus, probably two of the Republican Guard divisions were able to slip back unscathed into Iraq. (One Iraqi division opened fire while attempting to escape and was in fact almost entirely destroyed by US tanks on 2 March, some three days after the ceasefire.[22]) Having no other instructions, Schwarzkopf hastily negotiated a meeting place at Safwan just inside the Iraq border where he set up a camp-site to which he ordered the commanders of the Iraq army in Kuwait to report. He, accompanied by HRH Prince Khaled bin Sultan, representing the Saudi forces, and de la Billiere, flew up to meet them. There in the desert, three nondescript Iraqi generals (nondescript is perhaps a bad phrase as they all three looked almost exactly like Saddam Hussein in their olive-green uniforms, black berets and black moustaches) agreed to a ceasefire and a return of allied prisoners. Despite their defeat, the Iraqis were far from abject and haggled over some of the terms. Nevertheless, the recovery of Kuwait, ravaged by its occupiers, fought over by its rescuers and torched by its retreating invaders, was complete. Schwarzkopf had carried out his orders to the letter. He had driven the invader out of Kuwait in a brilliantly conceived and executed operation; he had kept his allies with him throughout, despite every attempt by Saddam to break the coalition; and he had kept allied casualties to the minimum – 147 Americans were killed in action, while the British sustained very few casualties, of which 9 were killed by so-called 'friendly fire' during the operation. But had the allies done enough?

Long after the war was over, the argument continued that the allies should have pushed on to Baghdad and destroyed Saddam's regime. His subsequent murderous attacks on the Kurds in the north of his country and on the Shias in the south have all been used as sticks with which to beat the Americans for failing to finish the job. For George Bush, however, the position was clear: he had done no more and no less than his mandate from the United Nations had required of him. Above all, he had secured a clear, undoubted and incontrovertible victory for the United States which had all the best qualities of a military operation: it was short, it was popular, it had very few casualties and it was successful.

At the final press conference held in his headquarters in Saudi Arabia on 27 February 1991, General Schwarzkopf gave his listeners an outline of how the battle had unfolded and finished by inviting questions. One question that he was asked was this: 'Would you talk about the ways in which the press contributed to the campaign?' To this, part of his reply was as follows:

> . . . I guess the one thing I would say to the press that I was delighted with is in the very very early stages of this operation, when we were over here building up, and we didn't have very much on the ground, you all were giving us the credit for a whole lot more over here. And, as a result, that gave me quite a feeling of confidence that we might not be attacked quite as quickly as I thought we were going to be attacked. Other than that, I would not like to get into the remainder of that question.[23]

With hindsight, we believe that, in that answer, he was less than just to the media. Naturally, to an anxious and harassed commander, the presence of the media is more often a hindrance than a help; however, without that extensive and instantaneous coverage of the Gulf War, the astonishing size and strength of the United States forces transported halfway round the world, the frightening efficiency of modern weapon technology and the speed and deadliness of her attacking forces would never have been so clearly and dramatically presented to the rest of the world. Indeed, without that same media, Norman Schwarzkopf himself would not today be a household name.

The media also, perhaps without realizing it, sent the world an important message: the wounded giant was now totally recovered, his strength was renewed and his spirit reawakened. If, before the Gulf War, potential aggressors had been lulled into believing that their actions might go unpunished, here was very real evidence to the contrary.

There were, of course, some parts of the media which had set their hearts against the war. In Britain, the *Guardian* constantly believed that sanctions and negotiation could have removed Saddam from Kuwait; in the *New Statesman* too, after the war was over, John Pilger wrote a scathing attack on the conduct of the war and the manner in which the military 'fed' reports to the waiting press. An extract from this piece, published on 8 March 1991, reads:

> . . . In the beginning, the Americans and the British were in the Middle East to 'defend Saudi Arabia'. This was false. Then 'all diplomacy was exhausted'. This, too, was false. Numerous, potentially successful attempts to get Saddam Hussein out of Kuwait were blocked by Washington. Then, with the bombings under way, the war became a nightly visit to Norman Schwarzkopf's video-game emporium, where it was demonstrated that missiles distinguished between good things and bad things and, of course, shed no blood. This was the 'clean fighting record' now 'stained' by the massacre on the Basra road . . .

By most, however, the need to drive Saddam out of Kuwait by military force was recognized and the war was believed to be 'just'. Indeed, in the aftermath of the war, some newspapers turned on their pacifist colleagues. Writing in *The Sunday Times* on 3 March 1991, Norman Stone commented:

> The *Guardian* speaks for a great part of the British enlightenment, and its fingernails on this subject are very raw. It did not see that the war would be over in hours. It foresaw nothing like the tiny figures for allied casualties. It expected that sanctions against Iraq would work, whereas we now see from Kuwait that the Iraqi troops, killing and looting, were supplied with everything possible while they shovelled tortured victims into alleys. In my opinion, *The Guardian*, in this respect, has let itself down.

On some of the television commentary on the war, a virulent attack was launched in the *Daily Telegraph* on 1 March 1991 by John Keegan; it was particularly directed at BBC *Newsnight*:

> It is the television opinion-makers who have aroused my ire. The Dimbleby brothers and Jeremy Paxman, in particular, seem to me to have betrayed their responsibilities to a contemptible degree. . . . On one side stood a country of 18 million Third World people, without a defence industry and with an armoury of second-hand Soviet equipment which could not be replaced if lost in combat. On the other stood three of the strongest states in the First World, with a combined population of 350 million, which are respectively the first, third and fourth international suppliers of advanced military equipment . . . The army they had assembled in the Gulf equalled in numbers that which Saddam had deployed in Kuwait, while their air forces outnumbered his by four times. The facts were so stark that the layman could conclude that once battle was joined the Iraqis would be overwhelmed in a few days of fighting. Have the television grandees told us any such thing? They have not.
>
> On the contrary: for day after day they have strung us along, turning an open-and-shut case into a cliffhanger. Sober, responsible military experts, many of them retired officers of high rank, have stated facts and opinions similar to those I have outlined, only to hear, in the familiar way, their considered advice being chipped away in the condescending, imperious, incredulous tone which is now the received style wherever the television grandees hold sway.

This anxiety to frighten, thrill or shock their audiences was an aspect of the media which was well expressed in Brigadier Patrick Cordingley's memoir of the war:

> I worry now, as I did then, about the effects of the media on modern warfare. I detected, during the initial settling-in period, the belief among reporters that they should encourage emotion. If an interview could be turned to probe fear or shock, this seemed to win favour at home. The intrusion, if challenged, was justified as caring and in the public interest. But don't the public, and indeed the armed forces, shape their behaviour to the media's demands? Did we not confess in the Gulf, under this examination, to being frightened? Well, of course, we were – but was it not unpatriotic to ask us to say

so? And then the reporting of the very clinical nature of modern weapon systems and their effects on the bunkers and buildings in Baghdad led the public, particularly the American public, to lose touch with the reality of war; a grim, ghastly and bloody affair. Such reporting also heightened the public concern over casualties. This is also a dangerous pre-occupation. I wonder if commanders can now be ruthless enough, in a television age, to pursue the enemy to the limit, if the stakes are anything less than national survival.[24]

Throughout the reporting of wars, it is to human emotions that the media makes its appeal. Pride and shame, hatred and pity, courage and fear are all ruthlessly exploited to involve the audience in the news of the day. Seldom have modern communications been used more widely to spread these emotions than in the Gulf War.

Perhaps the subject of casualties is one which deserves more careful examination. Before the battle was joined, as we have seen, the media endlessly goaded its victims into forecasting casualty figures. Once a figure could be enticed from someone in authority, slaughter could be forecast with chilling effect. The fact that the war was subsequently fought with so few casualties on the part of the allies was remarkable; but on the other hand, the fate of the Iraqi soldiers was a matter of apparent unconcern to the world. In the same press conference which we quoted earlier,[25] Schwarzkopf had no hesitation in making the following reply to this question:

'General, you said you've got all these [Iraqi] divisions along the border which were seriously attrited [*sic*: destroyed]. It figures to be about 200,000 troops maybe that were there. You've got 50,000 prisoners. Where's the rest of them?'

'There were a very very large number of dead in these units; a very very large number of dead. We even found them when we went into the units ourselves and found them in the trench lines. There were very heavy desertions . . . And so I think it's a combination of desertions; there's a combination of people that were killed; there's a combination of the people we've captured and there's a combination of some other people who are just flat still running.'

No pity for them from the victors, nor indeed from the media. Perhaps that is always the lot of the losing side. *Vae victis!*

At the time of writing, in 1997, George Bush has been denied his second term of office by his own electorate; Margaret Thatcher was removed from power by her own party before the fighting had even begun; Mikhail Gorbachev is now no more than a memory in the maelstrom of today's Russia; while Saddam Hussein remains tyrannically in power in a country which has undergone immeasurable suffering at his hands.

Since the end of the war, Saddam has appallingly mistreated the Shi'ites in the south of Iraq and has launched murderous attacks on the Kurds in the north. Here, another media-driven event took place. Pictures of Kurd families forced from their homes, cold, tired and hungry, trying to find shelter on the slopes of the inhospitable mountains of Kurdistan, once again filled the television screens. John Major, the British Prime Minister, was casting about for action which could be taken on their behalf. One of his advisers suggested 'Safe Havens for the Kurds' to be secured by UN air power. Major instantly approved and the policy was quickly supported by others. After a brief visit, James Baker urged President Bush to follow the same policy and shortly afterwards the United States deployed a military force to the area to protect and help the Kurds. As a result, Saddam Hussein was prevented from destroying more of his own people. Once more it was an action which would never have taken place had it not been for the media exposure.

In conclusion, the Gulf War received more television and press coverage than any other military event in history up to that time. In general, it gave strong support to the coalition in the conduct of an apparently just war. However, in what proved to be a totally uneven contest, the media did its best to raise anxieties about the length and cost of the war. Its preoccupation with casualties and bloodshed proved, on the allied side, almost totally without foundation. Similarly, its dismissal of concern about Iraqi suffering (except for that of civilians) showed a surprising insensitivity. Had things started to go wrong for the coalition, there is little doubt that the media would have pounced on the facts and been instrumental in damaging morale both in Britain and in the United States. For this reason, the military commanders could not afford to risk setbacks. Without the nagging fear of media criticism, the air war might have been shorter and the war ended more quickly. Equally, the fear of failure or of a prolongation of the war demanded a huge over-insurance in the coalition build-up of forces. Naturally, such criticism is easy with hindsight; however, there can be little doubt that, in the minds of today's military commanders, the hovering media can often prove more disturbing than the prospect of enemy action.

The bones of the battle continue to be picked over. Saddam's maltreatment of his own people has excited the fury of those who feel that his regime should have been destroyed at the time of the war. Others are content that the threat of aggression from Iraq has been removed. With the departure of the military, the media circus moved on to other fairgrounds, confident that it had fairly and properly reported the battle for the recapture of Kuwait from the grasp of Saddam Hussein.

---

1. Pierre Salinger, *Secret Dossier*, London, Penguin, 1992, p. 41
2. Ibid., p. 48
3. *New York Times*, comment, 13 July 1991
4. BBC documentary film, *The Gulf War*
5. Colin Powell, *A Soldier's Way*, London, Hutchinson, 1995, p. 221
6. Conversations with Lady Thatcher, 18 March 1997
7. BBC documentary film, *The Gulf War*
8. Conversations with Sir Antony Acland, January 1997
9. BBC documentary film, *The Gulf War*
10. Ibid.
11. Salinger, *Secret Dossier*, p. 174
12. Conversation with Hon Raymond Seitz, February 1997
13. Salinger, *Secret Dossier*, p. 213
14. Patrick Cordingley, *In the Eye of the Storm*, London, Hodder and Stoughton, 1996
15. Philip Taylor, *War and the Media*, Manchester, Manchester University Press, 1992, p. 188
16. The *Guardian*, article by Phil Davidson, quoted ibid., p.156
17. Peter de la Billiere, *Storm Command*, London, HarperCollins, 1992, p. 250
18. *The Times*, 1 February 1991
19. Robert Fisk in the *Independent*, 23 January 1991
20. Conversations with Douglas Hurd, February 1997
21. Powell, *A Soldier's Way*, pp. 521–2
22. de la Billiere, *Storm Command*, p. 312
23. Press conference reported in Appendix to Harry G. Summers Jr., *A Critical Analysis of the Gulf War*, New York, Dell War Series, 1992
24. Cordingley, *In the Eye of the Storm*, p. 254
25. See de la Billiere, *Storm Command*, p. 312

CHAPTER ELEVEN

Somalia, 1992–1993

'The tragedy in Somalia is the most severe any independent African state has suffered.'

Samuel Makinda, lecturer in international politics, 1993

The well-intentioned American intervention in Somalia under the auspices of the United Nations turned out to be an almost unmitigated disaster. If one was to single out one factor which led to this situation it would be the fatal consequences of the oversimplification of a series of extremely complex problems and the widespread arrogant belief that they could be solved by the use of overwhelming military power. Modern communications demand decision-making on the basis of information which by its very nature cannot possibly tell the whole truth. In its relentless quest for instant sensation the media must bear some responsibility for this state of affairs.

The story of the Somali people and their struggle for survival in the inhospitable corner of the African continent to which they are largely confined is full of complications which this chapter cannot hope to unravel. Indeed, this has been one of the difficulties about these tragic events: it has been almost impossible for any outsider fully to understand the complexities of the shifting scene and, as a result, not to commit one blunder after another in attempting to intervene.

Unlike in other countries in Africa, the people of Somalia all come from basically the same ethnic stock. They speak the same language and they are virtually all Sunni Muslims. They are proud, dignified and very intelligent. Apart from those who live in the Riverine area between the only two rivers in that vast country, they are a nomadic pastoral people who scratch a difficult living from an extremely arid and inhospitable land, moving their camels, goats and sheep around in search of pasture and water. Many of the urban dwellers have close links with their kinsmen in the countryside. Indeed, the nomadic groups like to have a family member in the capital to represent their interests and to provide an assured wage packet to assist when times are bad in the rural areas.

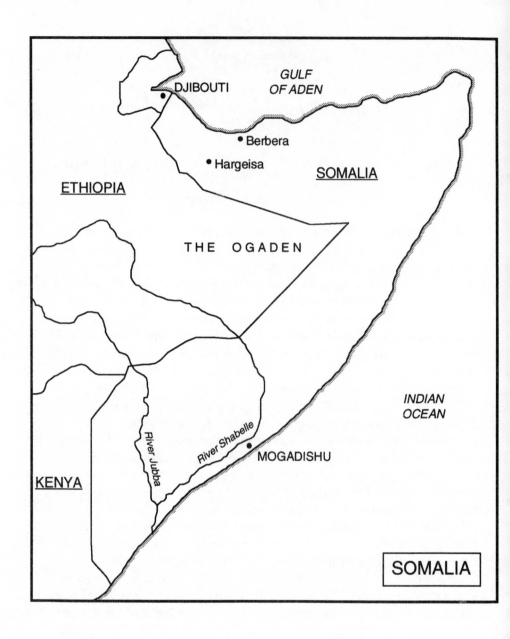

GULF
OF ADEN

DJIBOUTI

• Berbera

• Hargeisa

SOMALIA

ETHIOPIA

THE OGADEN

INDIAN
OCEAN

River Jubba

River Shabelle

MOGADISHU

KENYA

SOMALIA

Although they all come from the same ethnic stock, Somali life is dominated by a system of clans and subclans. As John Drysdale, a very experienced observer of Somalia, puts it:

> For the individual Somali family, having no financial independence, the clan or subclan is the equivalent of an insurance company, a safety net in times of stress, when life, as it often is, becomes precarious. The rain can fail, wells can dry up, pastures can turn to dust. It needs binding faith and clan loyalty to keep everyone alive.[1]

However, because there has been a perpetual need to move in search of grazing for their animals these clans and subclans have historically competed rather than cooperated as they vied for grazing and water. The clan and subclan system is, therefore, inherently schismatic. Ways of dealing with these problems have been arrived at over the years and accepted by all concerned. Yet, some conflicts have persisted, some of which would, to us, be totally unacceptable – notably the necessity for revenge. Outsiders simply do not understand their ways. Death is not the same to them as it is to us Westerners. They learn to live with, if not ignore, it. It is one of the paradoxes about Somalia that, while almost totally homogeneous in ethnic terms, it has seen as much, if not more, internecine conflict as any other African country, nearly all of which are multi-tribal.

Historically, therefore, the Somali way of life had evolved over the years, the clan and subclan system providing a cushion against the vagaries of the environment. It was the basis of the whole of their lives: for instance, all children of eight or over had to be able to recite the names of their forebears for some twenty or more generations back.[2] It was a system which neither accepted nor required a central government or administration. Each clan or subclan managed its own affairs, sometimes making alliances with other clans or subclans when necessary but in essence running its own affairs as best it could.

The colonial era led to the fragmentation of the Somali people into five separate areas – Italian, British and French Somaliland, the Somalis in Ethiopia (who had, in effect, been handed over to that country, then Abyssinia, by the British in 1897), and an area in the north of Kenya. The British, French and Italian administrations brought the rudiments of law, order and centralized authority and introduced a veneer of European culture to their areas. The Italians introduced some Italian farmers to the

Riverine area in the south-west of the country. The British did not introduce any settlers and the French area was largely confined to the town of Djibouti the population of which was only half Somali. The essential fact is, however, that most of these changes were regarded as alien, as indeed they were. In consequence, the underlying organization of Somali society was largely unaffected.

When the colonial era came to an end there was a strong impulse to create a Greater Somalia which would include all five elements mentioned above. This nationalist feeling, although understandable in the wake of colonial domination, was in fact alien to the structure of Somali life which did not easily or readily conform to centralization of any kind. Furthermore, there was no question of Kenya (still a British colony) or of Ethiopia or of French Somaliland ceding its territory to a new Greater Somalia. The result of all this was that, when independence came, the old British and Italian Somalilands which had been comparatively benevolently administered under United Nations trusteeship for the last fifteen years, merged to form the Republic of Somalia in July 1960 and French Somaliland became independent in its own right as Djibouti in 1977. Somalia was the only African state not to support the clause of the Charter of the Organization of African Unity (the OAU) which laid down that the existing colonial frontiers (of 1964) should remain unaltered.

The problem then in the Somali Republic was that it was one thing for the Somali clans or subclans to submit to British or Italian rule for a period, it was quite another for them to accept rule by one of their Somali rivals. As has already been explained, centralized control was alien to their way of life anyway and rule by one of their old rivals or even enemies was not acceptable to most Somalis. These problems were exacerbated because of the widely differing legacies left by the former colonial powers in the areas under Italian and British administration, including schools, court systems and trade focus, directed to Italy and the Gulf regions respectively. The Somalis in the old British Somaliland, in the north-west, had absorbed much of the British cultural background and found it difficult to adjust to a totally different environment particularly since the capital of the new Somalia, Mogadishu, was geographically far removed from their area and the first President came from one of the clans of the old Italian Somaliland. There were, therefore, many causes for friction.

Nevertheless, Somalia continued to live in comparative peace and harmony until a General Mohammed Siyaad Barre seized power in October 1969. At first he was widely popular, but gradually his preferment of his own clan and his failure to develop other parts of the country led to his becoming increasingly unpopular. He began to rule with despotic savagery, tried to introduce 'scientific socialism' – a system totally alien to the whole Somali way of life – attempted to ban tribalism and received support, including arms, from the Soviet Union. His one achievement was the introduction of a written Somali language, pioneered by an academic from the London School of African and Oriental Studies and Somali academics in Mogadishu. Barre also succeeded in spreading literacy to urban areas in 1973 and attempted to spread literacy to the rural areas but, because of a huge drought in 1974, this failed.

In 1977, in an attempt to gain popularity to shore up his rapidly deteriorating position in his country, he invaded Ethiopia in order to seize the Ogaden, the area where about 1 million Somalis, predominantly of his own Darod clan, lived. At this point, however, the Soviet Union, which had been heavily supporting him with money and weapons, changed sides. It ceased all help for General Barre and flew in large supplies of arms to Ethiopia, together with Russian 'advisers' and Cuban troops. The result was a catastrophic defeat for General Barre and a great loss of prestige. The Americans, however, filled the vacuum left by the Soviet Union, supplying arms and money to Somalia in return for facilities at the Port of Berbera in the old British Somaliland, including the use of the port and the further development of the military base already started by the Russians. This agreement officially terminated in 1988. The Americans, though, maintained an interest until October 1990 and vied for use of the port with Libya during much of 1990. Siyaad Barre milked both parties handsomely.

The situation in Somalia as a whole, however, continued to deteriorate. Barre was extremely clever at manipulating clan rivalries to his own advantage, but eventually more or less open warfare occurred between his forces and the north (inhabited by the Isaaq clan), culminating in 1988 in a series of totally devastating attacks on Hargeisa, the capital of the old British Somaliland, and other towns in the area by his army supported by mercenary white Rhodesians flying Hawker Hunter jets. Barre became increasingly isolated; he was maintained in office only by his Presidential Guard drawn largely from his own, Marehan, subclan. The situation in Mogadishu had disintegrated into almost total anarchic chaos by the middle of 1990, with bands of armed lawless youths rampaging around. During 1990 armed opposition also arose in the central region of Somalia in the form of General Mohammed Aideed and his United Somali Congress. Eventually, in January 1991, Barre had to escape to the south-west, the area dominated by his, Darod, clan where, supported by the Kenyan President Arap Moi, he prepared for a military comeback.

For the purposes of this book there is little point in following in detail the tortuous twists of inter-clan and subclan conflict, the many attempts at negotiations within and outside Somalia, and the involvement of other states, each with its own interests to serve – Italy, Libya, Ethiopia, Egypt, the United States, Kenya and the Soviet Union. Britain very sensibly withstood all efforts to involve her in any negotiations.

One can get some idea of the complexities of the situation in Somalia merely by listing the organizations which in March 1993 signed an agreement after a conference in Addis Ababa:

Somali African Mukti Organization (SAMO)
Somali Democratic Alliance (SDA)
Somali Democratic Movement (SDM)
Somali Democratic Movement (SDM/SNA)
Somali National Democratic Union (SNDU)
Somali National Front (SNF)
Somali National Union (SNU)
Somali People's Movement (SPM)
Somali People's Movement (SPM/SNA)
Somali Salvation Democratic Front (SSDF)
Southern Somali National Movement (SSNM)
United Somali Congress (USC/SNA)
United Somali Congress (USC)
United Somali Front (USF)
United Somali Party (USP)

Many of these organizations have been and are violently opposed to others, and this has been a great cause of continuing friction and bloodshed. There are, however, two basic issues which are relevant: firstly, the struggle for Mogadishu between Aideed and a certain Ali Mahdi, both from the Hawiye clan but from different subclans (Habar Gidir and Abgal respectively); secondly, the attempt by Barre to regain power.

The United Somali Congress (USC) had been formed in Rome in 1986. It represented the Hawiye clan in central south Somalia. General Aideed had been incarcerated in prison by General Barre, who then, for purposes of his own, made him the Somali Ambassador to India. After Barre's fall, Aideed, having sent his family to the USA where his son eventually joined the US Marines, returned and after many vicissitudes was elected as Chairman of the USC, although the election was disputed by some of his rivals. One of these was a businessman and hotel owner from Mogadishu, Ali Mahdi. When Barre fled, Mahdi announced on Radio Mogadishu that he was the interim President of Somalia. This announcement was picked up by the Western media who gave it publicity and a certain legitimacy which it did not deserve. In fact Mahdi had no legitimate claim to power whereas Aideed had signed an agreement with the two other main opposition parties whereby the three of them would hold a national meeting of reconciliation and elect an interim government following the overthrow of Barre.

Fighting broke out between the supporters of Aideed and Mahdi in Mogadishu and these problems were exacerbated when Barre's supporters of the Marehan clan invaded Somalia from Kenya, took the town and port of Kismayo and advanced towards Mogadishu. They were led by Barre's son-in-law General Mohammed Said Hersi (known as Morgan) who, as a hated governor of the north, had an unrivalled reputation for committing atrocities. Again the Western media, the United Nations and the United States, not understanding the situation, gave Morgan equal standing with that of other Somali leaders. Aideed's forces fought back and succeeded in pushing Morgan's army back to the border of Kenya. However, for the next year or so the battle flowed backwards and forwards to the complete destruction of the Riverine area whose peoples were sedentary agriculturalists and could not, therefore, up sticks and move elsewhere as could the pastoral peoples of the rest of Somalia. Barre's troops occupied the area for six months from September 1991. They plundered all the grain stores and destroyed the pumps and the implements. There was widespread starvation from mid-1992 into 1993.

The Western media had been taking a desultory interest in the happenings in Somalia for some time to the extent of arousing some opinion in the United Nations in New York that 'something should be done' by the UN to resolve the undoubtedly appalling problems caused by the series of civil wars being fought in that country and the lawlessness which pervaded Mogadishu in particular.

However, it was the starvation in the Riverine area of the country which led to the intense media interest with its tragic repercussions. It is easy to be cynical about this whole subject, but it is unfortunately true that the humanitarian and relief organizations, often for the best of motives, had the same objective of transmitting to the world pictures of acute and widening starvation, often greatly exaggerated in scope and duration, as did the media in search of a 'story'. The media needed the agencies to help them reach that area at all. It needed their transport, their interpreters, their help in many ways. The agencies needed the media in order to publicize the problems and to obtain support, political and financial, for their activities. The result was that, although there was indeed starvation in that area of Somalia and in some other areas dependent on external food supplies, it was considerably overstated.

At the end of 1991 the UN Secretary General Perez de Cuellar sent James Jonah, an Under-secretary General, to Mogadishu to negotiate a ceasefire between Aideed and Mahdi. On arrival he committed one of the very many blunders made by the United Nations. He recognized Mahdi as the interim President thus totally alienating Aideed who thereafter considered the UN and the US in particular as potential if not actual enemies. A ceasefire was not agreed at that time but it was achieved in March 1992 after the intervention of another, Canadian, UN official.

By this time food aid under the auspices of a number of non-governmental organizations such as the Save the Children Fund and the International Red Cross was arriving in large quantities at Mogadishu for transmission to the famine area in the agricultural Riverine district. However, it was being plundered, not only by the warring factions but also by the armed gangsters who roamed freely in Mogadishu and on the roads leading to the area of starvation. This was, naturally, reported by the media. According to the organization African Rights, which made a detailed investigation, it was greatly exaggerated.[3]

The United Nations under its new Secretary General Boutros-Ghali, an ex-Minister of State for Foreign Affairs in the Egyptian Government who happened to have been a friend of General Barre (an unfortunate fact used by his enemies later), decided to intervene. The Security Council established a United Nations Operation in Somalia (UNOSOM) under the control of Mohammed Sahnoun, an Algerian, the new special representative in Somalia of the Secretary General. Its purpose was to monitor the ceasefire by the immediate deployment of fifty UN observers and to introduce a UN security force in consultation 'with the parties in

Mogadishu'. Sahnoun arrived on 4 May 1992. He coped, brilliantly in the circumstances, with his manifold problems. He met virtually everyone and managed to cobble together a number of agreements which, unfortunately, did not solve the basic problems which beset the region. His relations with Boutros-Ghali deteriorated, particularly when he criticized in public, almost certainly with justification, some of the UN agencies involved in the country. He resigned in October 1992. He had, nevertheless, achieved a great deal. The death rate in the Riverine area had been greatly reduced and some political progress towards reconciliation had been made.

He was succeeded by Ismat Kittani, an Iraqi who achieved little. He did not meet many Somalis and locked himself up in his headquarters. He had an unfortunate, rather aggressive manner and suffered from insomnia. He, in his turn, was succeeded by Admiral Howe, a retired American sailor. He lacked the first-hand experience of the region and the diplomatic finesse required to gain the confidence of widely different groups with suspicions that the main intention of the United Nations was to deprive them of the power and authority to which they believed themselves, as leaders, to be entitled.

There were, perhaps not surprisingly, many clashes of personality and differences over policy within the United Nations administration in Somalia. Lansara Kouyate, the Guinean Permanent Representative to the United Nations, brought formidable negotiating skills to the post of deputy to Kittani and, later, to Admiral Howe. At one point, however, he was forced out and replaced temporarily by the American, April Glaspie, hot from her total failure in Iraq. In this situation, too, a vitally important error of judgement was made in the demonization of General Aideed with, as we shall see, tragic consequences.

One of the crucial problems faced by the UN operation in Somalia lay in the question of the basic purpose of all UN operations. Were the UN personnel there in order to monitor the delivery of humanitarian aid, able to protect themselves, but not to intervene with force? Or were they to be allowed to take military action against those trying to disrupt the free flow of aid? Or were they to be able to use force to disarm the warring factions and to bring about a ceasefire by the use of military power? Were they to keep a peace which had already been agreed by the warring factions or were they to enforce a peace which had not been agreed? The whole question of the limits of national sovereignty and the circumstances in which intervention into the internal affairs of a sovereign state could be justified arose in acute form. There were differing views about all this among those responsible for operations on the ground which were never really reconciled. Under the United Nations' Charter, in order that intervening force could be used the Security Council had to agree that there was a threat 'to international peace and security'. This was clearly not the case in Somalia, although specious arguments were produced to the contrary and generally accepted by the Security Council of the UN. Be that as it may, the media, and the very many people whom it influenced, were not impressed by such legal niceties. People were starving – women and children on television in front of their eyes – their food was being looted and it was up to the United Nations to do something concrete and immediate about it.

This was the situation which faced the outgoing President Bush in December 1992 (he had been defeated by Clinton in November). Harrowing pictures were being shown on television in the United States and the pressures on him to act were becoming irresistible. In any event he would not have wished his Presidency to have ended in a welter of accusations of incompetent callousness. He had acted with firmness and decision in the Gulf. He clearly hoped to do the same in Somalia.

On 1 December the United Nations Secretary General Boutros-Ghali, asked for the immediate launch of a major new operation to ensure that relief workers could safely bring supplies of food and medicine to Somalia. He added that he would propose that the force would be empowered to disarm the factions by force of arms if necessary. He left it open as to whether the troops would be United Nations or United States led. General Powell, the American chairman of the Joint Chiefs of Staff, insisted that if US troops were to be used they must be US led. Bush ordered what he thought would be a decisive military intervention. He was supported by the media. In an editorial on 1 December the *New York Times* said:

President Bush is right to offer as many as 20,000 US troops to a UN rescue operation. The realities there are ghastly and the choices limited . . . a thousand and more people are dying every day . . . there is no alternative to the threat or use of force if food is to reach those trapped in the chaotic clan war.

On 4 December the *New York Times* reported that the Security Council had approved the deployment of 28,000 American troops. The Americans hoped that the intervention would be short and bloodless: indeed, that was one of the premises upon which they took the decision to intervene. Success in the Gulf had clearly led to the belief that intervention was possible with comparatively few or, preferably, no body bags returning to the United States under the glare of the media and the consequent massive discomfiture of the politicians responsible. The horrors of Vietnam were in the past and, come what may, were not to be repeated.

At that time, too, the Americans were urging the Europeans to accept the use of air power in dealing with the Serbs in Bosnia and, perhaps somewhat paradoxically, hoped that this firm military action in Somalia would spur their allies on to a more forward position in Bosnia. Maximum effect with minimum casualties was the aim: overwhelming strength in Somalia, air power in Bosnia.

In practice the American intervention in Somalia was not short and it was not bloodless. The sad truth is that media coverage of incipient or actual disaster certainly does not guarantee any improvement, let alone a solution to the problem. In Somalia, if anything, it made the situation worse.

Walter Goodman pointed out some of the dangers of media coverage of human misery in a powerful article in the *New York Times* on 8 December 1992:

> The emplacement in recent days of Network News's big guns alerted the nation that something serious was afoot in Somalia. Dan Rather and scores of lesser correspondents have become certifiers of disaster. If they are on the spot, watch out!
>
> Their latest trick is especially appropriate. As the background reports to the arrival of the American troops have reminded the viewers it was television's wrenching pictures from Somalia that goaded a reluctant administration to act. Although it may have lagged behind some print journalists in taking note of mass starvation in yet another African country, once the pictures appeared of the fly tormented faces and the bloated bellies of dying babies the effect was stunning . . . the television camera is as blunt as it is powerful: it is a prisoner of its own immediacy.
>
> The pictures from Somalia cry out that something must be done, but they never help the viewer choose between doing something here and not there. Why send troops to Somalia instead of Mozambique where as many if not more people are at risk?

Programmes do relay cautions of the possible consequences of American intervention. But it remains the in-built inescapable threat and limitation of the media that the camera carries the day. The pictures . . . overwhelm analysis. How can ifs and buts compete with the image of a mother and child dying before our eyes? . . . Nearly all of Washington seems to have been converted by the pictures. Members of Congress who opposed the invasion of Iraq now come before the cameras to support the intervention in Somalia . . . When the Bush administration wanted to move on Iraq it used television to rally a divided nation to military action . . . When the war in the Persian Gulf started the Pentagon made sure that the conflict would be presented to the world as a bloodless technological triumph with no human face.

In December 1992 the American-led Operation 'Restore Hope' took place under the auspices of the United Nations. It superseded the original UNOSOM operation and was named the United Nations International Task Force (UNITAF). Its limited objective was 'To create a secure environment for the delivery of humanitarian relief'. US Marines stormed ashore at Mogadishu at night on 9 December. They found no enemy but, awaiting them, were a number of television cameras filming their assault as they landed with blackened faces and guns at the ready – a most unfortunate and embarrassing occurrence. They were joined by units from the French Foreign Legion and units from no fewer than nineteen other countries including a number of other Muslim states (the high rates of UN pay undoubtedly contributed to this enthusiasm).

UNITAF certainly made some concrete achievements in curbing anarchic violence and facilitating the flow of aid, although the famine in the Riverine area was already abating by the time the troops arrived. In fact, according to an authoritative survey, in Baidoa, the epicentre of the famine, the number of deaths fell from a peak of over 1,700 per week at the beginning of September 1992 to about 300 per week in mid-November.[4] In February twenty-four Pakistani United Nations peacekeepers were killed during a weapon search on the Aideed-controlled radio station at Mogadishu. In spite of a ceasefire which had been agreed, this led to a new cycle of violent conflict in which by mid-September 1993 fifty-six UN soldiers and several hundred Somalis had been killed.

One of the problems related to the very lax rules of engagement under which UN troops operated. In practice they seemed to be able to shoot almost at random without any real inquiries being mounted. This was particularly so when helicopter gunships were used. Clearly it was impossible for helicopters to identify in any exact way those at whom they were shooting. There were echoes of the chaos in Vietnam in the way some American and other troops operated. Undoubtedly, numbers of innocent Somali women and children were killed, the exact numbers, of course, being a matter of major contention. The consequence, predictably enough, was to cause the populace to view the United Nations not as saviours but as outside ogres, and mostly 'infidels' to boot.

In May 1993 UNITAF was succeeded by UNISOM II, a force under the command of a Turkish general. Most of the Americans had withdrawn, although logistic support remained in American hands and the deputy commander was American. For the first time in UN history the troops were given a mandate to use force not only in self-defence but also in pursuing their mission of 'creating conditions conducive to a political settlement'. American troops, as we shall see, returned, crucially, at a later date. It was over this period that General Aideed was identified by the UN and the Americans as the major villain. There were, of course, a number of reasons for this decision. There was a psychological need to find an enemy who could be attacked and defeated. It was true that interminable negotiations had taken place without success. It was also true that Aideed was no angel and that his supporters had undoubtedly been responsible for many deaths, not to speak of the looting of food aid. In these terms, however, he was no worse than a number of others. Public opinion in the West, led by the media, likes to have simple aims: on one side are the good guys; on the other the bad people. Get rid of the bad people and, hey presto, all is well, or more or less so. Of course, it was not like that in Somalia, and the more Aideed was attacked by the UN and the US, the more Somalis rallied to him. By attacking Aideed the UN gave him a status and support which transcended at least some clan and subclan boundaries and which otherwise he would not have had.

After a series of abortive and bloody affrays, the American actions against Aideed culminated in early October 1993. A plan was hatched whereby his headquarters would be attacked by crack American ranger troops flown in for the purpose. They had been trained for a snatch operation using helicopters with other gunship helicopters supporting them. The operation was a disaster. Two helicopters were shot down, one was very badly damaged, eighteen rangers were killed and dozens wounded. The American Secretary of State for Defense, Les Aspin, had to resign, partly because he had refused to supply this force with armoured vehicles. The armoured vehicles which they did use were Malaysian, full of American soldiers but with Malaysian drivers. They lost their way and at one stage drove off leaving a number of American soldiers behind. The Americans fought well and bravely, but clearly neither they nor their leaders seem to have fully realized the difficulties of operating, even with helicopters, in an urban environment against a resolute enemy. As the American Presidential candidate, Ross Perot, put it in his introduction to the book *Mogadishu, Heroism and Tragedy*: 'Television reporting of war has turned it into a spectator event that can be confused with athletic contests. Peacekeeping missions, when they become war, exact a terrible price.'[5]

As well as the dead and wounded one American was captured, who appeared on television and was subsequently released. Another dead man was shown on television being dragged through the streets of Mogadishu in front of a crowd of apparently demented Somalis. It was the latter event which led to immediate media and other calls for an American withdrawal. Clinton's decision to withdraw the American force by March 1994 effectively terminated any active UN involvement.

In any case the famine, such as it was, was already virtually over. Northern Somalia, the old British Somaliland, had declared its independence on 18 May 1991 and there was no central government over the rest of Somalia. Indeed the very word Somalia, at the time of writing – May 1997 – has little meaning. There is no such state.

It is instructive to follow the reactions of the *New York Times* and the *Washington Post* to the debacle in Mogadishu on 3 October 1993.

On 6 October the *New York Times* delivered itself of an almost classic 'sitting on the fence' editorial: 'America's national pride could be injured if the Clinton Administration decides to extricate US troops from the gathering disaster in Somalia. America's national interests could be injured if it does not.' It went on: 'If Washington can't change the goals of the mission, thus extricating itself from the quagmire the United Nations has enmeshed it in, it's time to come home.'

The *Washington Post* was also bewildered, although inclining towards a slightly more robust attitude. On 6 October an editorial said: 'Clinton should not be panicked into pulling out . . . The US has business to complete in this mission. It should do so and then get out. Mr Clinton needs to articulate much more precisely what the intentions and limits of this exercise are.'

On 8 October under the heading: 'Somalia. Time to Get Out', the *New York Times* was critical of Clinton's decision to set a target of six months before pulling out and to double the number of troops: 'Rather than make a decision either to cut American losses and withdraw now – the preferable course of action – or tough it out until [goals] are achieved, the President succumbed to the tempting illusion that he could do a little of both.' On 12 October the *Washington Post* published two articles with diametrically opposite conclusions. The first, by Richard Cohen, said: 'If we cannot save Somalia from itself, then it is best we at least save ourselves and bring the troops home.' On the other hand E.J. Dionne Jr said: 'Clinton is right to resist immediate withdrawal.' Finally, on 15 October the *Washington Post* supported the withdrawal: 'Leave it to others to build for a result in Somalia.' On 23 October the *New York Times* said: 'Mr Clinton seems finally to have realised that commando raids and the civilian deaths that result from them can't cure what is ailing Somalia.'

The overwhelming point is that both the *New York Times* and the *Washington Post* seemed to accept, without question, the view that Aideed was the villain and that the US was right in its single-minded attempts to get rid of him. They did not appear to begin to understand the complexities of the situation and the damage that the intervention had caused to a peaceful solution of Somalia's problems. Nor, for the most part, did the decision-makers in Washington as well as those of the UN in New York.

Apart from further upsetting any natural balance of power which was evolving in Somalia, the intervention brought about an enormous distrust of foreigners. Before UNISOM a white face, if not welcome was treated with a degree of respect, as a guest. After the UN/USA invasion, foreigners in Mogadishu were seen as threats to all Somalis. Thus it has been harder for relief agencies to work there.[6]

What, therefore, is now left after all these strivings and interventions? Most of the area has reverted to the pre-colonial situation with the country divided into a number of clan territories each administering itself with an element of mutual cooperation when this is found to be beneficial to both sides. There is still (May 1997) no central government, no central police force, no central banking system or any other of the normal appurtenances of a sovereign state. It is difficult for Western governments – or indeed Eastern governments – to accept this. UN organizations, for instance, can in theory only deal with sovereign states through their central administrations. The one area which does have some form of central government, the new Somaliland, paradoxically at the time of writing has not been generally recognized, certainly not by the UN, the United States or even Great Britain. At least the territory is not plagued by relics of the East–West confrontation: there is little strategic interest in the area by either the United States or anyone else for that matter, although there is talk of oil discovery.

There are few, if any, 'stories' in the Western press now about Somalia. In general the people are earning their living as they did in the pre-colonial era. There are considerable exports of meat, frankincense and myrrh (but sadly no gold!) from the north. The Riverine area is as productive as it ever was. The towns are gradually recovering their equilibrium largely unbothered by the sight of vehicles hurrying through the streets emblazoned by signs of one or other United Nations agency. There are still far too many arms about, the horrific legacy of the comparatively brief period of outside intervention and the East–West conflict. The pastoral peoples pursue their traditional way of life, adapted over the centuries to the very harsh environment in which they live their lives.

It would be wrong to discount totally the efforts made by the United States and the United Nations to help a country which was indeed in a terrible mess. A lot of lives were undoubtedly saved by humanitarian aid which did get through to the Riverine area when it was needed. How many must be a matter of conjecture, as must the number of people killed in the partisan fighting which would not have been so severe had the issue not been complicated by UN intervention and had not arms been supplied almost *ad lib* to the combatants. The motives of those nations, organizations and individuals who intervened were often far from venal, particularly in the later stages. The moral indignation which so many viewers in the United States and, indeed, throughout the world, clearly felt when confronted by scenes of imminent death by starvation was not an ignoble emotion. It is the haphazard and episodic nature of media coverage, together with the inevitable vast oversimplifications called for by the very nature of the media which led to so much tragic error. Sensational and inaccurate media reports, made by those with little or no knowledge of the area they are sent to report on, lead to a distortion of the truth. Pressures are put on governments to satisfy their public's demand for immediate action. The intervention in Somalia was undoubtedly media led. It was disastrous. There is a connection between those two statements.

1. John Drysdale, *Whatever Happened to Somalia*, London, Haan Associates, 1991, p. 70
2. Ibid., p. 70
3. African Rights, *Somalis, Operation Restore Hope – a Preliminary Assessment*, London, May 1993, pp. 2 and 3
4. Centers for Disease Control, 'Population-Based Mortality Assessment – Baidoa and Afgoi, Somalia, 1992', *Morbidity and Mortality Weekly Report* 41. 49, December 1992, pp. 913–17 quoted by African Rights, p. 9
5. Delong and Tuckey, *Mogadishu, Heroism and Tragedy*, London, Praeger, 1994
6. Conversation in January 1997 with Hamish Wilson who was in Somalia for most of the conflict, and still visits Somalia frequently

CHAPTER TWELVE

The Balkan Tragedy, 1990–1996

'As Yugoslavia disintegrated, the media of the various republics served
not to inform their respective publics but to bolster support for the
stances taken by their respective leaderships. Years before the first shots
were fired, the media were already at war and the journalists who
deliberately fanned the flames of national hatred must bear a heavy
responsibility for the carnage.'

Christopher Bennett[1]

Future military historians may well regard the Cold War as a golden age.
Those forty years of anxious peace in Europe divided the slaughter of the
two world wars from the massacres which followed the demise of the
Soviet Union. Of all the countries which prospered at the time of the
Cold War and suffered at its conclusion, few, if any, gained and lost as
much as Yugoslavia.

Under the iron rule of Josip Broz Tito, the Communist leader of the
wartime partisans, the ethnic and religious differences within the group
of republics that combined to form Yugoslavia were forcibly held in
check. Separated as a Communist country from the Soviet Union, the
country was held together by Tito with a stability which it had scarcely
known at any other time in its history. Unlike the other so-called Iron
Curtain countries, Yugoslavia opened its borders to the West and enjoyed
a thriving tourist trade based mainly on its lovely Dalmatian coastline.

The history of Yugoslavia has been one of bloodthirsty occupations and
forcible religious divisions. Serbia, Bosnia and Montenegro were
subjected to the Ottoman rule for more than three centuries; Slovenia
and most of Croatia were part of the Hapsburg empire for almost as long,
while much of the coastline was ruled by the Venetians. Even earlier, the
border between the Western and Eastern Roman Empires had divided
the Balkan peninsula, leaving the western half to be influenced by Rome
and the eastern by Constantinople. Thus the country became an
amalgam of three great religions: Roman Catholic, Greek Orthodox and,

from the Turkish occupation, Islam. Finally, the whole country had been invaded in the Second World War by German and Italian forces. Under each occupation there had been terrible records of death and destruction.

Under Tito's regime at least peace reigned. In the late 1960s, one of the present authors visited the country and travelled through most of the different republics. At that time it seemed stable and unified, with the prospect of increasing prosperity. Standing in the footprints of Gavrilo Princip, then carved out in the pavement of the street in Sarajevo to show where the disenchanted student had stood to fire his pistol at the Archduke in 1914, it was hard to believe that the same city, with its mixture of onion-domed churches and slender minarets, would soon be brought to scenes of unimaginable bloodshed.

Tito died in 1980. He left a country which was apparently at peace with itself and with every hope for the future; but it was not to be. The deathknell of Yugoslavia was rung, not at the death of Tito, but at the rise to power in Belgrade of the highly ambitious and nationalistic Serb leader, Slobodan Milošević.

Milošević, who is still in 1997 the President of Serbia, was born in 1941 and joined the Communist party as an apparatchik under Tito. Under the leadership of Ivan Stambolić, Tito's last prime minister, Milošević rose in authority until, in 1986, he was appointed the head of the so-called League of Communists in Belgrade, later to be known as the SPS – the Socialist Party of Serbia. One of his first actions in his plan for a Greater Serbia was to secure control of the Belgrade media. These included, besides TV Belgrade, the powerful and influential newspaper, *Politika*, and its lighter sister, *Politika Ekspres*. These two newspapers and their parent company, the Politika group, were together the largest media organization in Yugoslavia, controlling not only the two papers but also a radio station and a television channel. Shortly after his rise to power, Milošević dismissed and replaced with his own nominees both the director general and the editor-in-chief of this group. Once he was secure in Belgrade, he launched his first project which was to bring into the Serbian camp the smaller autonomous region of Kosovo, which adjoined the Serb Republic. To do this, he embarked on his first campaign of spreading ethnic hatred.

In making Kosovo his first target, Milošević had chosen well. That region was not only one of the poorest parts of Yugoslavia, but it also comprised a very large population of Albanians who were for the most part Muslim. Yet for the Serbs it was a place of the utmost significance; it contained two historical sites of great importance to Serbian folklore and religion. At Kosovo Polje, the great battle had taken place in 1389 between the Serbs and the Ottoman Turks after which the Serbs had been defeated and occupied by the Turks, while the town of Peć is regarded as the cradle of the Serbian Orthodox Church, where its Patriarchate was founded in 1346. By 1986, the Serb population of

Kosovo had dwindled to less than 7 per cent of the whole, while the Albanian population had continued to grow. It was not difficult, therefore, for the Serbian media, under the guidance of Milošević, to generate stories of Serbian misfortunes in an already underprivileged area.

In 1986, the Serbian Academy of Sciences and Arts, normally a much respected forum but no doubt heavily influenced by the SPS, published a memorandum on the plight of the Serbs in Kosovo. In that region, it maintained, the Albanians were guilty of waging 'open and total war' on the Serbs, who were suffering 'physical, political and legal genocide'.[2] This theme was followed by the Communist-controlled organs of the media, whipping up Serb hatred for the Albanians in Kosovo. The underlying theme was always the same: that Kosovo must be regained for Serbia. The importance of this first media campaign of ethnic hatred, launched under the leadership of Slobodan Milošević, is made clear by Mark Thompson in his book *Forging War*:

[This campaign] matters above all because it created a media model which was extended to embrace other targets of the Serbian leadership. It was a model which identified and stigmatized a national enemy, homogenized Serbs against this threat and called for resistance. After the Albanians of Kosovo, the enemies were the Slovenes and Slovenia, then Croats and Croatia, then Bosnia and its Muslim population.[3]

In Belgrade, Milošević staged huge rallies on the streets, where thousands of Serbs gathered waving nationalist flags and singing nationalist songs. This surge of nationalism spread quickly to the other autonomous region of Vojvodina and to the republic of Montenegro, in both of which the governments resigned in favour of Milošević's supporters. Finally the government in Kosovo itself, where the Albanian workers had called a national strike, was threatened by the Yugoslav National Army (JNA). Ringed by tanks and with MiG fighters flying low overhead, the Kosovo parliament had no option but to accept a new constitution which finally committed their country to union with Serbia.

The media which supported Milošević in this, his first campaign and in later campaigns designed to expand the boundaries of Serbia, was not of course a free press. The Serbian organs of the media were under the direct control of a totalitarian government and carried the messages required by that government. Nevertheless, it is significant that without the support of the media, it is unlikely that the first steps could have been taken down the long road which led to the bloody dissolution of Yugoslavia.

On 5 July 1990, the Serb Government finally removed the independence of Kosovo by closing down its only Albanian language newspaper and taking over the local radio and television services. The first steps in Milošević's plan for a greater Serbia had been taken. The Western world, however, far more occupied with the great events following the collapse of Gorbachev's Soviet empire in the east, scarcely remarked the swallowing up of Kosovo by the newly awakened Serbian dragon.

Of the remaining republics that had formed Yugoslavia, the most prosperous was the northern state of Slovenia. Insulated from the remainder by a separate language and without the disadvantage of a common border with Serbia, Slovenia had maintained a higher standard of living than the remainder of the country, higher cultural standards and a more marked independence. While in Serbia the demise of true Communism had given way to a call for nationalism, in Slovenia there was a call for democratic elections, which was given new urgency as the fate of Kosovo unfolded. At the time of the Albanian strike in Kosovo, more than a million Slovenes, almost half the entire population, joined in signing a petition condemning the state of emergency declared in Kosovo by Milošević.

Faced with this dissent from his expansionist policies, Milošević quickly turned the spotlight of his media campaigns onto Slovenia. There being virtually no Serbs in that republic, his normal complaint of Serbian maltreatment had to be changed and in this case his campaign accused the Slovenes of achieving their relative wealth at the expense of Serbia. Once again ethnic hatred was whipped up to a level of frenzy in Serbia, this time directed at Slovenes as the money-grubbers of the state. Confronted with this campaign of hatred, the Slovenes took immediate steps to plan their own independence. Numerous amendments to their constitution were passed in their parliament in September 1989 and on 20 January 1990 their delegation walked out of the Pan-Yugoslav Congress. Slovenia had set her face against integration with a nationalistic Serbia.

At the same time as Milošević had opened his media offensive against Slovenia, events had started to move in the neighbouring republic of

Croatia. While Croatia was also one of the richer republics, she suffered two great disadvantages: firstly, there were substantial Serb minorities living in parts of the republic; and secondly, she had been branded both during and in the aftermath of the Second World War with the hated name of the Ustašas. These, in origin, had been little better than terrorists – the word itself means 'insurgents' – until they were recognized by the Nazis and used to support the German occupation of Yugoslavia. After the war the Ustašas had remained in power for a short time, representing themselves as Croatian nationalists but in fact bent on the extermination of Serbs and Muslims in Croatia and neighbouring Hercegovina. Their bloody rule was finally put down by Tito's Communist regime. Not, however, before their atrocities had become a byword for horror and cruelty.

It was of course not difficult for Milošević, following his policies of Serbian aggrandizement, to recall bitter memories of Ustašas rule and to convince his listeners of the plight of the Serbs dwelling in neighbouring Croatia.

In Croatia, as in Slovenia, democratic elections had been held to replace the collapsing Communist government and they, too, had abandoned the Pan-Yugoslav Congress. Watching events in Kosovo and Slovenia and realizing the implications of remaining part of Milošević's growing empire, the Croats too planned secession from the Yugoslav union. Meanwhile, the Slovenes, under their President, Milan Kučan, prepared for a possible attack from Serbia. In addition to rearming their own militias, they set up a powerful media organization to enable them to react to Serb propaganda. Kučan planned to declare Slovenia's independence on 25 June 1991.

In Croatia, the newly elected President, Franjo Tudjman, had been with Tito's partisans in the war, subsequently joining the Yugoslav army in which he had risen to the rank of major general. He reacted bitterly to the propaganda poured out against Croatia by Belgrade, naming him and his government as Ustašas. For this he had some justification as a loyal follower of Tito. Nevertheless, the calls for nationalistic uprisings coming from Serbia soon started to destabilize those areas of Croatia with Serb populations, which were for the most part near the border with Serbia and in the southern part of the republic known as the Krajina.[4] Early in 1991, these Serb areas declared themselves separate from the rest of Croatia and set up a so-called Serb National Council in the town of Knin in the Krajina. Tudjman, after vain attempts to negotiate a peaceful settlement with Milošević and faced with the outbreak of violence between Croats and Serbs in much of his country, decided, in agreement with Slovenia, to proclaim the independence of Croatia on the same day, 25 June.

Some five days before the planned announcement of independence by the two republics, a visitor flew into Belgrade demanding to meet the leaders of Yugoslavia's federated republics. He was James Baker, the United States Secretary of State, who had been alerted to the probability of the coming secessions.

The events in Yugoslavia up to this time had been given scant regard by the nations of the West. The break-up of the Soviet empire had demanded far more attention and this in turn had been further eclipsed by Saddam Hussein's invasion of Kuwait. The troubles of Yugoslavia were seen as comparatively unimportant internal differences in a country of small significance. What was needed in Yugoslavia was a sharp rap over the knuckles, a firm instruction to settle their differences and to continue as before as a unified country. It was with this message that Baker arrived in Belgrade. He drove it home by assuring Kučan and Tudjman that the United States would not recognize Slovenia or Croatia as independent countries 'in any circumstances'.[5]

Baker flew out of Belgrade on the same day, having delivered his message. Five days later, on 25 June, the two republics declared their independence. On the morning of 27 June 1991 the JNA attacked Slovenia. The war which was to leave much of the former Yugoslavia in bloody ruins had begun.

The national army in Yugoslavia had been set up in Tito's time to meet the threat posed to the country by the Red Army. The likely approach routes for such an attack were either from Hungary in the north or from Rumania in the east. The army was therefore located in greatest strength in Serbia and was recruited largely from Serbs. Some 60 per cent of the officer strength was in fact Serbian. The army was well equipped, well trained and well led in the country's stable times, but the collapse of Communism brought with it serious problems for the military. Firmly loyal to Communist leadership, under which the senior officers had enjoyed strong and influential positions, the switch to nationalism promoted by Milošević introduced cracks in the unity of the army. Nevertheless, its Serb dominance ensured that it remained for the most part loyal to the new regime in Belgrade although, as the situation in the rest of the country deteriorated, more and more of its officers and soldiers deserted. At the time of the attack on Slovenia, however, the formations involved were commanded by a Slovene officer who still believed that the integrity of Yugoslavia was more important than the wishes of his own republic.

The JNA's attack on Slovenia, thanks to the preparations made in that country, produced a remarkable result. The army commanders had believed that a show of force was all that would be needed to bring the Slovenes to heel; they had therefore scarcely planned the operation in any detail and the troops used were for the most part newly recruited conscripts. When they were heavily and forcefully engaged by the Slovene militia, they were virtually unprepared to deal with the opposition. The Slovenes were prepared to fight for every inch of their land and for their right to secede. An outbreak of fighting on European soil shocked the world into noticing the events in the Balkans. Yugoslavia suddenly loomed large on the international map.

The first external negotiators to arrive in Yugoslavia was a 'troika' of European foreign ministers representing the European Community. Led by Minister Jacques Poos of Luxembourg, the three flew into Belgrade on 29 June and thence to Zagreb to negotiate a ceasefire in Slovenia; this proved to be the first of a line of ceasefires which would stretch away into the future, each as unsuccessful as the last. The troika was also the first of a series of foreign negotiators who tried to find, in the years that followed, a peaceful solution to the burgeoning hatred which was about to tear the country apart. Perhaps the most tantalizing aspect of the efforts of these well-meaning people was that each new team that set out to bring peace to this country in turmoil believed that they were within a hair's breadth of success before, time and again, their plans were brought to nothing by a renewed outbreak of fighting.

On this first occasion, having halted the JNA attack on Slovenia, the EC Ministers negotiated the so-called Brioni Accord, by which the parties agreed to a three-month moratorium on independence and a stop to the fighting. A group of EC 'monitors' was introduced to the country to observe the ceasefire. These men, drawn from European countries were dressed in white suits and were of course totally unarmed. We spoke to one, Jeremy Varcoe, who had at that time recently retired from the Foreign Office having previously held the post of British Ambassador in Somalia. He remembers that when he volunteered for the task, he was invited by the Foreign Office to 'fit himself out with some cricketing flannels and a white sweater' before taking up his post. He recalls with some bitterness his belief that had a firm line been taken by the EC at that time to demand the withdrawal of the JNA out of both Slovenia and Croatia, it would have been entirely possible to have put a stop to a deteriorating situation which was about to lead to anarchy and bloody strife. He strongly believed that only a credible and concerted threat of military action would have deterred the Serbs from their aggression against the other republics; without such a threat, he told us, both sides, Croats as well as Serbs, ignored the successive ceasefires which were brokered by those seeking to mediate at the time.

On 18 July, in accordance with the terms of the ceasefire, the JNA withdrew from Slovenia and it appeared to the politicians that peace had been restored. However, the events in Croatia which quickly followed soon dispelled these optimistic hopes.

Now that Yugoslavia had appeared on the media's world map, television programmes in the West started to carry background reports on what had been happening there. Foreign journalists, hitherto almost unseen, began to visit the country. Not unnaturally, the easiest stories to carry were those emanating from the capital, and the highly organized propaganda machine set up by Milošević slipped readily into business with the world's media. From its capital, Ljubljana, Slovenia too, having prepared an efficient media organization, was able to present its story to the world with some success. Not so, however, in Tudjman's Croatia; here, little attempt had been made to set up any control of the news media. As a result and thanks to the work of Milošević, the picture of Croatia presented to the outside world was still little more than that of being the only part of the country that had actively helped the Nazis.

Soon after the withdrawal of the JNA from Slovenia, the army gave its support to the Serb minorities in Croatia. Here, in the Serb-dominated areas, the activities of Serb irregular organizations began to come to light. These were led by men of fanatical purpose, trained for the most part in Serbia. Such a one was the infamous Arkan[6] whose followers, the Arkanovci, were responsible for a number of atrocities, some of which came for the first time to the notice of the world's media.

As summer passed into autumn, the fighting in Croatia grew in intensity. With the assistance of the JNA, the Serb militias in eastern Croatia started either to massacre or to drive out the non-Serbs from their territory. Similarly in the region around Knin, Croats and Muslims were either murdered or forced to flee from their homes. This policy became known as 'etničko čišćenje', the now infamous 'ethnic cleansing'.

Fighting a rearguard action in the information war, the Croatian Government addressed the handling of news. Croatian Television was renamed HRT (Hrvatska Radio-Televižija) and its Serb editor-in-chief was quickly replaced. In August 1991, a directive was sent out to all the HRT regional studios setting out the regulations for reporting the war. As an example of government-controlled television, it deserves to be quoted in full:

1. Reports must start with the latest information, and only then review the day's events.

2. Do not report future actions by the Ministry of the Interior or the National Guard.

3. Do not show people weeping or wailing.

4. Do not broadcast pictures of blown-up, badly wounded or shot Croatian soldiers.

5. Do not use the term Četniks or Extremists, but only 'Serb Terrorists'.

6. Do not use the term 'mupovci' (special police forces of the Ministry of the Interior), but only 'police'.

7. Do not report the names of owners of blown-up houses.

8. Do not call the JNA anything but 'the Serbo-communist Army of Occupation'.

9. Casualty figures of guardsmen and police must always be accompanied with: 'fell for Croatia's freedom', 'gave their lives to defend the homeland', 'heroes in defence of the homeland' etc.

10. Do not conceal defeats at the front; but stress the tremendous forces employed by the enemy and his unscrupulousness, and always finish such reports with optimistic declarations and avowals ('But we shall win back freedom' etc). Send reports of towns being successfully defended for special programmes. Failure to adhere to the above instructions will entail appropriate professional and legal consequences.

11. Footage must, in keeping with this decree, be previewed and approved by the editor before transmission.[7]

As the JNA deployed heavy weapons in Croatia the fighting became increasingly desperate. The Croats, though poorly armed, fought bitterly for their country; towns and villages were destroyed wholesale and local populations massacred. The town of Vukovar in eastern Croatia in particular was shelled and destroyed over a period of eighty-seven days. Finally, the coastline south of Dubrovnik was laid waste and the ancient city itself was shelled.

By this time, Western television crews had appeared on the scene. For the Croats, anxious above all to secure the sympathy and support of the free world, this was a most welcome arrival. Reporters were free to go where they wished and were frequently guided to where they might see evidence of Serb atrocities. The Serb leadership on the other hand preferred that such news as emanated from the country should be prepared and issued in Belgrade. On the ground, however, many Serb commanders reported openly the destruction they had wrought on Croatian towns and villages. The BBC reporter Martin Bell tells how, when crossing the River Sava into Bosnia–Hercegovina in November 1991, he met a Serb colonel who informed him, as Bell said: 'as a matter not just of record but of *pride* that they had poured down two million shells on the unhappy town of Vukovar.'[8]

The attack on Dubrovnik had a marked effect on Western opinion. Very many of the world's holidaymakers in happier times had visited the Dalmatian coast and in particular the beautiful city of Dubrovnik; to see it being destroyed before their eyes brought home to many of the world's viewers the intensity and apparent stupidity of the war unfolding before them.

It was towards the end of 1991 that a second negotiator appeared on the scene. The United Nations appointed the highly respected American senator, Cyrus Vance (who had resigned as President Carter's Secretary of State after the Iran hostage crisis), to try to negotiate a ceasefire between the Serbs and the Croats. He flew into Belgrade in November and drew up a peace plan with Presidents Milošević and Tudjman which was finally signed by both parties on 2 January 1992. Not, however, before a major step had been taken by the members of the European Community which is thought by many to have had a terrible effect on the future of Yugoslavia in the years ahead.

James Baker, the American Secretary of State, had made it clear to the presidents of the Yugoslav Republics in 1991 that the United States would not recognize their independence 'in any circumstances'. When Slovenia and Croatia announced their secession in June, the EC Foreign Ministers had persuaded them, under the terms of the Brioni Accord, to shelve the question of independence for three months; however, neither President had any intention of giving up his right to secede and it soon became clear that their recognition would be fiercely resisted by Serbia.

As a further step to restoring peace, the European Community ministers had appointed Lord Carrington, an erstwhile Secretary General of NATO, to act as their representative and negotiator in Yugoslavia. He proposed the calling of a peace conference to draw up an agreed basis for an end to the fighting, but quickly realized that the recognition of the independence of the federated republics was more likely to inflame the situation rather than restore peace. Writing on 2 December 1991 to the Chairman of the Council of Ministers, Hans van den Broek of Holland, Carrington expressed the opinion that:

> An early recognition of Croatia would undoubtedly mean the break-up of the [peace] conference . . . There is also a real danger that Bosnia–Hercegovina would ask for independence and recognition, which would be wholly unacceptable to the Serbs in the republic . . . This might well be the spark that sets Bosnia–Hercegovina alight.[9]

The peace plan, proposed by Vance to settle the Croatian war in December, involved for the first time the deployment of United Nations troops. Drawn from twelve different countries – which did not include Britain[10] – 14,000 UN soldiers were to be deployed in the Serb areas of Croatia to ensure the safety of all the inhabitants, both Croat and Serb. At the same time, the JNA would withdraw from Croatia, as would the Croatian militia from the Serb areas. Four regions to be known as UN Protected Areas (UNPAs) were identified in the southern part of Croatia. The JNA would withdraw, once the UN troops were on the ground, into the neighbouring federated republics of Bosnia and Serbia. As already mentioned, this agreement was signed by both warring parties on 2 January 1992, thereby once again raising hopes that a solution to the Balkan problems had been found.

However, despite the clear views expressed by the United States, Germany argued strongly for the recognition of the independence of Slovenia and Croatia. At the time, the German Government was under heavy pressure from its own press to recognize Croatia; this had its origins in historic ties between the two countries and was further strengthened by the presence of a large Croat minority in southern Germany. These pressures were acknowledged by the German Foreign Minister, Hans Dietrich Genscher, in conversation with Douglas Hurd.[11] Britain on the other hand, sharing Carrington's view, was firmly against such recognition.

On 16 and 17 December 1991, at a long meeting between the members of the European Community, the details of the Maastricht Treaty for European Union were hammered out. It has been widely suggested that, at that meeting, recognition of the two republics was agreed by the British as a *quid pro quo* for certain concessions in the treaty agreed by the Germans. Douglas Hurd, however, has assured us that the subject of recognition of these two republics was not in fact raised at the Maastricht meeting; he does, however, acknowledge that, at a later date, the Germans suggested that Germany was 'owed something' for her support at Maastricht and, as he put it, 'recognition would have been granted sooner or later anyway'.[12] Britain's volte-face, for which she was subsequently much blamed, was accounted for by the *Economist* in the following words:

In return for German help at the Maastricht summit on European Union, Britain's Prime Minister, John Major, gave the German Chancellor, Helmut Kohl, his word that Britain would back Germany's line on Croatia. Britain's diplomats from Douglas Hurd, the Foreign Secretary, downwards swallowed hard. Britain's switch put France on the spot. It preferred to go along rather than risk the blame for breaking ranks by holding out against recognition on her own.[13]

That there was a link between the two decisions is inescapable; the formal recognition was made one month later on 15 January 1992.

With the arrival of the first UN forces in the former Yugoslavia in the early spring of 1992, came the full weight of the Western media. That the inhabitants of Yugoslavia had decided, for their own good reasons, to start killing each other, had not, until the beginning of 1992, unduly perturbed the rest of the world. The comparatively few pictures of the Serbo-Croat war shown on television in the West, had not really caught the imagination of the public. As already mentioned, the shelling of Dubrovnik had alerted many to the apparent stupidity of the war, as had the inconvenience of the closure of the tourist trade in Yugoslavia, but the full horror of the events was yet to become widely known.

The headquarters of the first UN force to arrive was located, on the orders of the United Nations, in Sarajevo, the capital city of Bosnia–Hercegovina. This was no doubt seen as a suitably 'neutral' position from which to oversee the security of parts of Croatia. The choice, however, proved to be unfortunate. Far removed from the UN Protected Areas for which they were responsible, the commanders, without aircraft of their own, were dependent on the courtesy of the JNA for air transport. The early stages of the deployment were fraught with difficulty.

During the first three months of 1992, following the Vance ceasefire agreement, it appeared that peace had been restored. The UN forces under the Indian general, Satish Nambiar, set about the difficult task of introducing their UN battalions into the country and deploying them as instructed in Croatia. While this was happening, the European Community, having recognized the independence of Slovenia and Croatia held a referendum in Bosnia to measure public support for sovereignty for that republic too.[14]

The republic of Bosnia was quite unlike the remainder of the federation in that she had no single ethnic majority. Muslims, Croats and Serbs formed the population in almost equal numbers. The elected government, under the presidency of the Muslim, Alija Izetbegović, had indicated its wish to become independent, but the Bosnian Serbs were now pursuing the same aims in Bosnia that had already led to war in Croatia. Under the leadership of their self-styled president, Dr Radovan Karadžić, they proclaimed that certain areas of Bosnia were to be controlled by a Serb National Council. When the referendum was held, Karadžić prevented the Serbs from voting; only 63 per cent of the country voted but of those who did, 99 per cent were in favour of independence.

Early in April 1992, rumours circulated in Bosnia that the Western powers were about to recognize the independence of the republic. At once skirmishes broke out in Sarajevo which flared into open warfare when the recognition of Bosnia as a sovereign state was announced by both the United States and the European Community on 6 April. Marooned in the middle of the fighting was the headquarters of the newly arrived UN Protection Force (UNPROFOR), which had no mandate whatever for dealing with fighting in Bosnia but was merely charged with the safety of the inhabitants of the UNPAs in Croatia.

Since this was the start of a protracted war which would bring almost total destruction to one of the more lovely parts of the Balkan territories, one needs to understand the aims of the different factions involved in the war. The Bosnian Serbs, urged on by propaganda from Belgrade and again by the activities of fanatical organizations such as the Arkanovci, were determined to gain control of as much of the country as possible and then to purge it of all non-Serb inhabitants. Militarily they were the strongest of the three ethnic groups, having the backing of the JNA, although their strength lay more in the rural areas than in the towns. Declaring that the elected President of Bosnia was trying to impose a fundamentalist Islamic rule on their country, they continued to generate hatred for Muslims and Croats alike.

The Bosnian Government, on the other hand, believed, not unreasonably, that having been recognized by the outside world as a sovereign state, they might expect military support against what they deemed to be attack from Serbia. Resisting strongly with their territorial defence forces, they continued to believe that, if they could hold out long enough, they would receive, if not foreign military support, at least a lifting of the embargo which prevented them from obtaining arms for their own defence.

To the watching outside world, the picture was much different. The war was not seen as an international conflict, but as yet another Balkan civil war between peoples who were always fighting one another. The suggestion of lifting the arms embargo was at first dismissed as fuelling the fire unnecessarily. No country was anxious to become embroiled in internecine warfare in a part of the world renowned for the bitterness of its disputes. The United Nations still had no mandate for intervention in Bosnia, although the Chief of Staff of the UNPROFOR in Sarajevo, the Canadian General Lewis Mackenzie, valiantly tried to negotiate between the participants. Neither he nor any other of the UN commanders was able to assign blame for the outbreak of the fighting to either side; they were obliged merely to act as go-betweens in the hope of damping down the fighting which was going on violently around them.

Threats of diplomatic isolation against Serbia by the Americans and the Europeans had little if any effect on the war. James Baker, the American Secretary of State, 'wearied by the lies and evasions of the Serb leaders', was said at one stage to have washed his hands of further negotiation. Later, faced with mounting troubles, he warned that: 'unless Serbia backs off, it can face a freeze of diplomatic relations and the imposition of a total trade embargo.'[15] This, as may be imagined, had little effect on the participants.

The catalyst which finally compelled the world to react was the combined force of the world's press and television. Probably never before had the influence of the media been more powerfully felt by the governments of the world than in the ensuing months and years of the war in Bosnia.

During the spring and summer of 1992, the world's television screens were filled with scenes of death and destruction in Bosnia. These came for the most part from Sarajevo, a city which echoed with memories of past tragedies and could be seen as a harbinger of tragedies still to come. The sight and sounds of shelling and mortaring in a European city, with pitiful scenes of wounded citizens, excited the sympathy and anxieties of viewers throughout the free world. The television reporters and cameramen who recorded these scenes were dedicated and extremely brave men and women. Their determination to film events often led them into crossfire between the opposing sides in circumstances when little or no respect was shown to non-combatants. Their task of explaining to the watching world the truth of events in Bosnia was far from easy. For a camera crew, the key elements of their trade are transport, editing, deadlines and despatch. The first challenge is to reach the scene of the event. Once they have reached the scene and filmed it, they need to edit their footage into a presentable report which will match the space likely to be given to their subject in the programme. In his book, *In Harm's Way*, Martin Bell remarks that the average 'shooting ratio' is about ten to one; that is to say, of twenty minutes film shot, only about two minutes will be used.[16] Often the time allocated on the final news programme will be shorter still, perhaps no more than fifty seconds. In that time the reporter has to explain the circumstances to the viewers, show the event that he or she is reporting and offer some brief comment to put the situation into perspective. To explain the complex and often almost incomprehensible background to the events that were occurring in Bosnia set the journalists an impossible task. As a final challenge, the reporter has to despatch the piece by satellite to reach the studio by the deadline set for the particular news programme for which it is intended. The report when it arrives in the studio is then at the mercy of the programme editors, who may use it in its entirety, cut it or discard it completely.

The reports coming in from Sarajevo at this time built up a continuing pressure on the Western governments to take some action to stop the killing. An example of this sort published in the *Economist* in May read as follows:

Outsiders who believe that something must be done to end the cruelties of the civil war in Bosnia and Hercegovina are getting round to doing something, late in the day but more firmly than some would like. Whether it will work is another question. Mediation has failed. Armed intervention to stop the fighting, which is what 'peacekeeping' at this stage would amount to, is politically unacceptable. Attempts to get food and medicine to the besieged people in Sarajevo has failed. The remaining option is to press Serbia, through sanctions, into restraining its culpable Serb irregulars in Bosnia.[17]

On 30 May, the same day that the above article was published, the UN Security Council passed a resolution (UNSCR 757) calling for an immediate ceasefire in Bosnia, at the same time imposing sanctions on Serbia similar to those which it had earlier imposed on Iraq. As in Iraq, such a resolution had little or no effect.

The journalists in Bosnia at this time had few opportunities to move freely around the country. However, although Serb roadblocks limited access to much of the countryside, there was still plenty of action to be filmed and reported in Sarajevo itself. As a result, in the early stages of the war, there was plenty of footage of Serbs and Muslims engaging each other in the city, but comparatively little coverage of what was happening outside the capital. The mortaring of a bread queue in Sarajevo in May 1992 killing some twenty citizens provided horrific material for the news media to carry. For, as Martin Bell most tellingly admits in his book: 'people blithely imagine that journalists are where the news is. Alas, not so; the news is where the journalists are.'[18]

As we shall shortly see, the inability of the crews to penetrate the countryside hid from the world for some time a far worse picture than the murderous attacks in the capital. This was to prove a powerful example of the inability of the media to disclose the whole truth at any time but only that part of the truth which reporters are themselves able to see.

The reports from Sarajevo produced different reactions from their recipients. In the United States, which had already fought the Gulf War and carried out a less than successful intervention in Somalia, it was the year of the presidential elections. It was not a time at which the administration was anxious to involve the country in another foreign operation which offered little prospect of quick or easy solution. Indeed, the Balkans had every appearance of another quagmire of Vietnamese proportions. Britain, too, was unwilling to be drawn into the war. The

French on the other hand saw advantage in taking a European lead in the affair and, in June, President Mitterand grabbed the international headlines by flying personally into Sarajevo, landing on an airfield which was being fought over by Serbs and Muslims virtually as he landed. This brave, some might say foolhardy action by a Western head of state had a remarkable impact on the situation. After meeting both of the warring leaders, Izetbegović and Karadžić, and seeing for himself the tense and fearful situation in the capital, he flew out, promising that his visit would be followed by French aircraft bringing supplies to the beleaguered citizens. He was as good as his word and for the first time for many months Sarajevo airport was for a time reopened to humanitarian flights.

What, however, was not discovered until later in the summer was the extent of the cold-blooded horrors happening in the remainder of the country. It was the disclosure in July of the appalling events at the Omarska Mine concentration camp by a British ITV camera crew that first truly opened the eyes of the world to the extreme horrors of ethnic cleansing. A series of articles published in the American magazine *Newsweek* also unfolded in lurid detail the extent of the atrocities being practised by the Serbs:

> Banja Luka, Bosnia, July 19, 1992.
> . . . The camp is an open pit where only a third of the prisoners have shelter from the elements and most have to stand in mud, according to a witness. Six to ten people die daily.
> 'The corpses pile up. There is no food. There is no air to breathe. No medical care. Even the grass around the pit has been clawed away,' said an official of Merhamet, the Muslim relief agency, who received the account last week. 'Our hair stood up when we received the report.'
> There are mounting indications that Omarska, a town near this capital of Serb-conquered North Bosnia, houses a death camp where Serb authorities, with the backing of the army, have taken thousands of Muslims.

And again:

> July 21, 1992.
> In their zeal to 'cleanse' northern Bosnia of its Muslims and Croats, Serbs who seized control of the region have deported

thousands of unarmed civilians in sealed freight trains in the past month. Hundreds of women, children and old people have been packed into each freight car for sweltering journeys lasting three or more days into central Bosnia, according to refugees who survived the ordeal . . .

'You could only see the hands of the people in the tiny ventilation holes,' said a Muslim official who saw the first two trains. 'But we are not allowed to come close. It was like Jews being transported to Auschwitz.'[19]

In the light of such terrible news, could the world stand idle? If not, what was to be done?

On 1 August 1992, *The Economist* published a scathing article against those who pleaded ignorance of the terrible events in Bosnia:

After the Nazi holocaust, many Germans said they did not know what was going on. As whole population groups are rounded up by Serb forces and to a far lesser extent also by Muslims and Croats, no one will be able to use that excuse in Bosnia Hercegovina.

For months rumours have circulated about horrible deeds being done in parts of the country away from the spotlit Sarajevo. Now the refugees are bringing consistent stories of an evil not seen in Europe for almost fifty years.

The International Red Cross believes almost 20,000 people are being held in detention camps across Bosnia.

Terror reigns in Bosnia. Let no one claim he did not know.

And yet only a week later, the same magazine acknowledged the overwhelming difficulties involved in taking action:

Imagine that the world leaders gave some NATO general an army big enough to occupy Bosnia. That, hard and bloody enough in itself, would be the relatively easy part of the job, not the messier end. The NATO army would soon have to turn itself into a police force, posting men in every town and hamlet to stop the tribes from murdering each other. Most of the evidence is that the killing will continue with the would-be policemen as targets. The likelihood is that the outside world would quit in despair leaving the local enemies to redraw their politics by force.[20]

On the front cover of its third edition in August, *The Economist* reduced the problem to three words in its headline: 'After Pity, What?'

While there was no enthusiasm on the part of the rest of the world to become involved in this struggle, the continuing television pictures kept goading ministers into action. Whether or not to send 'troops to Bosnia' – a hopelessly unspecified generality – became a constant subject of debate in Britain and elsewhere. Long and anxious discussions were held in London, Paris and Washington, each government guided by different experiences.

In London, the Foreign Secretary, Douglas Hurd, made a speech in the Travellers' Club which was widely reported:

> There is nothing new in such misery. There is nothing new in mass rape, in the shooting of civilians, in war crimes, in ethnic cleansing, in the burning of towns and villages.
>
> What is new is that a selection of these tragedies is now visible within hours to people around the world. People reject and resent what is going on because they know it more vividly than before.[21]

However true his words may have been, they would not satisfy the need for action which was by now widely felt throughout the country.

In Washington, General Colin Powell, the chairman of the Joint Chiefs of Staff, epitomized the views of most military men, when he was interviewed by the *New York Times* and asked why the United States could not assume a 'limited' role in Bosnia:

> I had been engaged in limited military involvements before, in Vietnam for starters. I told the *Times* reporter: 'As soon as they tell me it's limited, it means they do not care whether you achieve a result or not. As soon as they tell me its surgical, I head for the bunker.' I criticized the pseudo-policy of establishing a US presence without a defined mission in trouble spots. This approach, I pointed out, had cost the lives of 241 Marines in Lebanon.

Far from being satisfied with these answers, a *New York Times* editorial accused him, with other American officials, of continuing to dither over Bosnia while thousands died; the paper referred to the $280 billion a year that the United States spent on defence, concluding that the American people were owed more on their investment in the armed forces than 'no-can-do'. 'President Bush could tell General Powell what President Lincoln once told General McClellan,' the editorial concluded, 'if you don't want to use the Army, I should like to borrow it for a while.'[22]

Despite these barbs, the US administration continued to refuse to be drawn. In London, however, in August 1992, the Prime Minister, John Major, took a hard decision. He agreed to despatch 1,800 British troops to Bosnia under UN auspices and with a very limited mandate. The French agreed at the same time to send a further 1,100 troops; they already had 2,000 in the country under the Vance Croatian agreement. Many other countries volunteered detachments at the same time.

There is little doubt in our minds, although politicians in general are reluctant to agree, that this decision and the many others that were to follow of a similar nature, were forced upon the governments of Europe by the media in general and by television in particular. Writing of the wars which he had reported, Martin Bell of the BBC observed:

The relationship between them [soldiers and journalists] in the Bosnian war was unusual and complex. Usually the soldiers got there first. This time the journalists did. And the presence of one *determined* the presence of the other. No other war – not even the Gulf war . . . – has been fought so much in public, under the eye of the camera.[23]

In retrospect neither Douglas Hurd, the then Foreign Secretary, nor Peter Carrington believe that Britain's decision to send troops was driven by the media.[24] Hurd emphasized that Britain's first priority was to prevent the war from spreading; yet the first troops deployed by the British could do little to prevent this. It is hard to believe that, without the television pictures on the screens in the United Kingdom, British troops would ever have been despatched to a part of Europe that could not, by any stretch of the imagination, be held to be a vital national interest.

The mandate from the United Nations (UNSCR 776) under which these first troops were deployed was extremely limited. There was no question whatever of peacekeeping, merely an undertaking to escort and protect convoys of humanitarian supplies to civilians in the war zones. These convoys were the responsibility of the UN High Commission for Refugees (UNHCR). In fact the first British troops did not arrive in Bosnia until October 1992.

While these decisions were being made, a major initiative was still being undertaken both by the UN and the European Community to halt the fighting. After holding his peace conference in the Hague at the end of August, where it became clear that there was little or no prospect of finding an early solution to the fighting, Lord Carrington stepped down from his post as the EC mediator and his place was taken by Lord Owen, who had been Foreign Secretary in an earlier Labour Government. Speaking to us of the frustrations of that time, Lord Carrington told us that, soon after the fighting had broken out in Bosnia, Jose Cuteleiro, his Portuguese ambassadorial colleague, had, on Carrington's instructions, negotiated with the three warring participants acceptable terms on which the fighting might have been stopped, based on a division of the country into three parts; to his great disappointment, the Muslims suddenly backed down on the agreement thanks to encouragement to continue fighting, emanating from, of all places, the Washington State Department.[25] Cyrus Vance, now working with his new co-chairman, David Owen, set about negotiating new terms under which the three ethnic groups might agree to live in peace in Bosnia. Their proposal, which came to be known as the Vance–Owen Peace Plan, turned on the division of the republic into a number of designated areas or cantons for each of the three communities (a proposal similar but more complex than the earlier division designed by Lord Carrington). Not unnaturally, the drawing of the map led to heated argument among all the participants, all of whom felt that they had been shortchanged. The Serbs, who had by this time gained control over almost 70 per cent of the country, were naturally disappointed with the mere 46 per cent they were offered, while the Muslims still harboured a secret hope that if the fighting continued long enough, the United States might come to their help and confound their enemies.

The outgoing American administration, though, had other fish to fry in Somalia and was far from enthusiastic about entering the Balkans. However, the Governor of Arkansas, Bill Clinton, campaigning in the presidential election, issued an ill-advised statement from Little Rock on 26 July, part of which read, 'The United States should take the lead in seeking United Nations Security Council authorisation for air strikes against those who are attacking the relief effort. The United States should be prepared to lend appropriate military support to that operation.'[26]

At that time Clinton had not had the benefit of Colin Powell's advice which he was to receive later in the year when he became the President-elect. Such pearls were not wasted on the ever-hopeful Muslims.

In Bosnia, in the meantime, the newly mandated UN troops arrived in the country at the start of the winter. Wearing blue helmets and transported in white vehicles, they started on their extremely delicate task. A picture of the situation which greeted them was painted in *Time Magazine*:

SARAJEVO, 21 December 1992
As the world wonders what to do about Serbia, a tour through the terrorised streets of Sarajevo shows that there is less and less to save. The war has served its barbarous purpose: a city where more than 17,000 have been killed and 110,000 wounded.

A different idea of the task which the UN troops undertook can be drawn from the following extracts from a letter received by one of the authors from a young officer with the British army in Bosnia in March 1993. It includes some significant comment about the press coverage at the same time:

TUZLA, Bosnia, 3 March 1993.
. . . The problems here are so complex that it is difficult to unravel all the facets of the situation and make sense of it all. Essentially the UN is involved in a three-sided civil war amongst people who until relatively recently were living in peaceful coexistence. However, the ugly side of nationalism has sprung up in response to the spectre of a Greater Serbia which has resulted in a war of particular viciousness and cruelty. The struggle has been taken over by numerous agitators which has inflamed the situation against the wishes of the people and given the war its own momentum; now nobody knows how to stop it.
. . . Although the Serbs are depicted as the main ogres in this conflict, no one really emerges with much credit. The Croats are by no means innocent and are perhaps the more sinister as they tend to operate in a fairly underhand manner. Although nominally they are allied with the Muslims against the Serbs, in reality they would happily divide Bosnia between themselves and the Serbs. Indeed the alliance has broken down in several areas . . . causing immense problems for our own resupply and the aid convoys moving through

the area. Thus while our mandate clearly states that the British Army's role here is to escort aid convoys in support of the UNHCR, it inevitably draws us into other implied tasks, technically outside this mandate. Thus, in order to reopen our supply lines we had to broker ceasefires and arrange for meetings between the local Croat and Muslim commanders who suddenly had become wary and distrustful of each other. Overnight they were at each other's throats and burning each other's houses. If it hadn't been for the UN, the situation there could have been far worse and whatever else we may have achieved, the fact that we have provided a degree of stability in a turbulent area more than outweighs the importance of our escorting duties.

. . . Ironically it has been the Vance–Owen Peace Plan that has sparked off difficulties between these two groups and far from being a catalyst for further discussion it has become a reason for bitter fighting in certain localities. Every single village and town is mixed between ethnic groups all intermingled together which creates endless problems in any peace agreement.

. . . In addition, although people obviously want peace, they do not appear to be war weary and are certainly not demanding peace at any price; indeed the Muslims believe that peace now would leave them at a disadvantage. They appreciate that they will never be able to defeat the Serbs politically in a peace deal and that the only way to deal with their menace permanently is to defeat them militarily (which is also certainly beyond their grasp).

. . . They [the Muslims] cannot understand why we refuse them arms and why we are here with all our armoured vehicles and do nothing to attack the Serbs. Neither the Muslims nor the Croats understand the meaning of neutrality and therefore 'if you are not for us, you must be against us'. The Serb army by comparison is extremely well equipped and trained.

. . . I think that when people first arrived here they were expecting to see some fairly horrific sights with people starving and dying in every gutter, as they had been led to believe by the media. However, the reality is very different and we have seen very few starving people, not only because of our efforts but also because food shortages just do not appear to be a problem. Obviously there are people who are genuinely desperate and in need of aid; these people are in Sarajevo, on the front line near the Serbs or in the various pockets which have been cut off ever since the war began. *For some unaccountable reason, the existence of these pockets which were known to the UN was not brought to the world's attention before it was too late to do anything to assist.* [Author's italics]

. . . Events have moved on rapidly and the Serbs are now slowly devouring each Muslim village in the pockets creating a horrific trail of havoc.[27]

The letter makes clear what limited access was possible for the journalists, whose reports in the early stages were confined to those parts of the country where they were allowed in.

If the task set to the troops was Herculean, it was equally daunting to the commanders. The United Nations in New York, under whose command UNPROFOR was expected to operate, was in no sense a military headquarters. There was very little direction offered to the commanders, there was no military infrastructure, no proper staff management, no intelligence organization and very inadequate logistic support. One of the senior officers remarked that from 5 p.m. on a Friday evening until Monday morning, it was impossible to get even an answer from New York.

In April 1993, the world was shocked by a television news report sent by Martin Bell of the BBC. He and a camera crew were accompanying the very forthright and often outspoken commander of the British detachment, Lieutenant Colonel Bob Stewart of the Cheshire Regiment. As they approached Ahmici, near Vitez where the Cheshires had their headquarters, they were confronted with a horrific scene of carnage. The Muslim village had been razed to the ground, the fallen minaret of the village mosque making a powerful image in the television pictures. Worse was to come. Bell and his crew, accompanied by the British soldiers, found a house in the village where a whole family had been massacred in the cellar. The power of this report, which did not spare the sensitivities of the viewers, shook the world. Colonel Stewart's emotional outburst to the leader of a Croat patrol that he met in the village a few moments later added to the impact of the event. It was of course by no means unique and doubtless many other such tragedies had occurred as grisly and traumatic as this one, but the immediacy of the pictures and the brutality of the killing drove home to the watching world the intensity and cold-blooded cruelty of the conflict.

Of a different kind was the impact of television pictures of a wounded child. In July of the same year, the plight of a single child who had been severely wounded in the fighting in Sarajevo was shown on television. In what can only be described as a knee-jerk reaction, the British Government sent a special aircraft to the city to fly her and some forty other casualties back to Britain for specialist treatment. In a city – indeed in a country – where tens of thousands of women and children had been wounded and murdered, this totally emotional reaction to a media report seemed to be a shallow gesture. The child named Irma was cynically referred to at UN headquarters as 'Instant Response to Media Attention'.

Earlier, in May, the new American administration had made its first move on the Bosnian chessboard. The delay in following up President Clinton's earlier forthright statements about what action should be taken was largely due to the huge changes which take place in Washington on the arrival of a new administration. Unlike the United Kingdom, where a strong civil service machine remains in place despite changes of government, in the United States most of the senior appointments in the State Department, not to mention the ambassadorial posts, are political appointments to be filled by the new President. Delay in the formulation of new foreign policy is therefore inevitable. The one unchanging pillar of the American position was their unwillingness to commit ground troops to Bosnia. They did, however, concede that, in the event of a total ceasefire, US troops would be deployed to Yugoslavia to oversee the reconstruction of the country. Air strikes against the warring parties were, as always, a politically attractive option. Early on in the year, the British Prime Minister had informed President Clinton of his unease at the prospect of any outside offensive action which could result in reprisals against the lightly armed UN troops on the ground.

To the great surprise and dismay of the British Government therefore, the proposals brought on his first visit to Britain by the new Secretary of State, Warren Christopher, intended exactly that. Raymond Seitz, at that time the United States Ambassador in London and the only career diplomat to have held that appointment, recalls that as he drove from the airport with Christopher en route to the country house of the British Foreign Secretary, Douglas Hurd, the Secretary of State asked him how he thought the British would react to a policy of 'lift and strike' – shorthand for the lifting of the arms embargo against the Bosnian Muslims coupled with air strikes against the Bosnian Serbs. Seitz did his best to point out that these two policies were both anathema to the British and indeed to the French, whose troops on the ground would almost certainly be put at risk in the increased fighting that would ensue from such policies.[28]

At Chevening, where the Prime Minister and the Defence Secretary as well as the Foreign Secretary were waiting to meet him, Christopher outlined his proposals unchanged. Douglas Hurd recalls the astonishment with which they heard him out. When he had finished, the British ministers patiently explained to him once again their reason for disquiet at such a plan. Despite the discussion which followed, Seitz recalls that some time later he was woken in the night by a call from Warren Christopher's aircraft on its way home, asking him whether he believed that the British would continue to oppose a policy of lift and strike. In the event, the arms embargo against the Muslims was never formally lifted. A resolution was, however, approved by the Security Council in June (UNSCR 836) authorizing the use of 'all necessary measures, through the use of airpower, to support UNPROFOR'.

It was this same resolution (among others) that proposed the unfortunate extension of UNPROFOR's mandate to include the protection of certain designated 'safe areas' against attack. In the same month, the Security Council approved the addition of a further 7,500 UN troops to UNPROFOR for the specific task of securing these safe areas. In the event the additional troops never materialized, leading later to one of the most damaging outcomes to any UN policy in the whole war.

The autumn and winter of 1993 was perhaps the time of greatest despondency in the whole history of the Bosnian war. The Western powers were at odds with one another as to what should be done: those that were unwilling to participate with troops on the ground, notably the United States and Germany, were demanding tougher action to stop the fighting, while those with troops committed, particularly the British and French, were understandably fractious at criticism from those unprepared to join them. The Vance–Owen Peace Plan had failed, yet because of it the three warring factions were fighting bitterly to secure as much territory as possible, believing that if the country was to be finally split up, possession would be nine points of the law. The earlier alliance between the Croats and the Muslims had broken down, leading to some of the bitterest fighting of the whole war between the two. Meanwhile Serb threats to the so-called safe areas were demonstrating the inability of the UN to protect them. The gallant General Philip Morillon, who had at one stage stood beneath a UN flag at Srebrenica, one of the so-called safe areas threatened by Serb attack, and cried out in true Gaullist fashion,

'I am Srebrenica!', stood down from command of UNPROFOR, handing the task to a Belgian, General Briquemont.

In November, Croat troops destroyed the historic bridge over the River Neretva at Mostar, presenting to the world a lasting image of senseless destruction. Small wonder that, faced with the media reports emanating from wartorn Yugoslavia, there was widespread talk of withdrawing the UN forces and leaving the country to its fate. The last lights in Bosnia seemed to be going out.

The New Year of 1994 dawned bleakly in Bosnia. General Briquemont, convinced that the task of UNPROFOR was unmanageable, resigned his appointment. Many of the UN units, drawn from a motley collection of countries, found the task beyond them; their morale was low and the incidence of black market operations indulged in by many of the UN troops was high. Command of UNPROFOR was entrusted for the first time to a British officer, Lieutenant General Sir Michael Rose.

Rose already had a distinguished career behind him, having served in the Coldstream Guards and the SAS. His experience in the Falklands and in Northern Ireland together with his more traditional commands in Germany and at the Army Staff College had prepared him well for this particularly testing appointment. Almost as soon as he had taken command, the Bosnian Serbs played into his hands by launching a 120 mm mortar bomb into a crowded market place in Sarajevo, killing almost 70 people and injuring some 200 more. The appalling scenes following this atrocity were caught in the full glare of world television and gave Rose an undisputed pretext for firm and immediate action, if necessary calling on the assistance of NATO air forces.

Commenting on the ultimatum issued to the Serbs by the UN, *The Economist* was cautious in its words:

> The ultimatum to the Bosnian Serbs – take your guns out of the hills around Sarajevo or have them blasted out – satisfies the desire to be seen to be doing something tough . . . But if the threat provokes nothing from the warring sides but a raspberry, NATO will be obliged to go ahead with air strikes that could widen the war – or risk humiliation that would doom the alliance.[29]

In fact the ultimatum had at first a salutary effect which led to the withdrawal of much of the Bosnian Serb artillery away from the city, and at the same time, in response to firm action, a number of routes which had been closed for some weeks to UN humanitarian supplies were reopened. Perhaps more importantly, the air of gloom in the country was dispelled and for the first time for many months, hopes of some solution to the war began once more to be raised. To drive home still further this new-found determination, four Serb military aircraft in breach of the UN-imposed 'no fly zone' were shot down by allied planes on 28 February in the first combat action ever undertaken by NATO in its near fifty-year existence.

By March it was reported that 'things are changing: the trams have started to run again in Sarajevo. There is calm in Mostar. Croats and Muslims are to sign a confederation agreement on 18th March.'[30] By April, there was real hope that a ceasefire might be negotiated. This hope, as were so many others, was dashed by a Bosnian Serb attack on the 'safe area' town of Gorazde. For the first time a NATO ground attack strike was ordered in which six aircraft took part. The targets were hard to locate because of poor visibility and one British Sea Harrier was shot down by a Serb anti-aircraft missile; the pilot parachuted to safety. Nevertheless, the threat to Gorazde was halted at least for a time.

Realizing the unreliability of depending on air strikes, Rose demanded extra troops to protect the safe areas. Despite another resolution approving a further 3,500 troops for the UN (UNSCR 908), still very few more were forthcoming. In the absence of the necessary strength to protect the 'safe areas', the policy was soon to become impracticable; Douglas Hurd acknowledged, when we spoke to him, that the idea of safe areas had, in the event, proved disastrous. Indeed by May, rather than reinforcing, there was even renewed talk of pulling out some of those troops already there.

By this time, three important factors in the news reporting from Bosnia had become apparent, the first two of which were clearly observed by General Rose himself.[31] In the urgency and brevity in which news reports are made, the highly complex and confused situation with which the journalists were confronted had of necessity to be simplified. The presentation of war reports in a matter of minutes or even seconds, calls for very clear and simple images: in any conflict one side is 'good' and the other 'bad', and it is not helpful to muddle the situation by reporting 'bad' actions by those on the 'good' side or vice versa. As we have tried to show, all three of the warring parties in Bosnia were at different times as blameworthy as one another, but from the outset, when the war was undoubtedly sparked off by the Serbs, it was they who became the aggressors and the Muslim underdogs the victims in the eyes of the media. Even this division was further complicated by the separation of the Serbs from the Bosnian Serbs; for in 1993, Slobodan Milošević, the President of Serbia, fearing that the extension of international sanctions on Serbia might cut off supplies of oil to his country and believing that his hopes of a Greater Serbia had progressed as far as was possible, withdrew his support from the Bosnian Serbs under Radovan Karadžić. Milošević even went so far as to offer his services to the peace negotiators who were trying to conclude the war that he himself had incited. For very many of the journalists reporting the war, the complication of these different categories became too confused for simple explanation and often remained immutable. The events themselves were difficult enough for the viewers to comprehend without the added complication of finding that last week's victims are today's murderers.

Secondly, those reporters who remained for long periods in the country often became deeply and understandably involved in the horrific events that they were required to report and, equally understandably, sympathetic to one faction rather than another. After two years of war these inescapable human feelings began to colour the reporting. Too often, Rose felt, the media took sides and distorted the truth on account of emotional involvement, usually with the Muslims. Often as a result of this unbalanced support from the media, the Muslims would break a ceasefire or launch an attack, confident that the blame would be ascribed to the other faction. Not only had the Muslims realized the benefits of engaging the sympathy of the reporters in their own country; they also went to great pains to woo the sympathies of Western countries in their own capitals and of the United Nations in New York – a policy which they pursued with remarkable success.

The third factor, which is perhaps a shameful aspect of our society, is boredom. As has happened elsewhere in the reporting of prolonged fighting, the prospect of watching yet another horrific episode from abroad begins to leave the viewers and readers unmoved. As new reports of Bosnian atrocities flooded their desks, editors started to look anxiously for new stories. By 1994, the boredom factor had started to set in.

So it happened that in May 1994, the spotlight of the world media switched suddenly from Bosnia to a new and even more harrowing scene, that of Rwanda. On 16 May, the front page of *Time Magazine* proclaimed: 'THERE ARE NO DEVILS LEFT IN HELL,' the missionary said, 'THEY ARE ALL IN RWANDA!' Descriptions of these appalling events in Africa soon crowded out the reports from Bosnia.

No lasting peace was achieved in Bosnia in 1994, largely as a result of the fighting which broke out in the summer in the so-called safe areas of Gorazde and Bihac, calling the bluff of an insupportable UN policy which left the blue-helmeted troops in an impossible position, much to the fury of General Rose. In Bihac, it even appeared that although a Bosnian Serb attack had been launched against the town, the Muslims who had garrisoned it had offered no resistance, both to embarrass the UN and to encourage adverse media coverage against the attackers.

In a subsequent address to the fellows of All Souls', Oxford in 1996, General Rose defended the achievements of the United Nations in Bosnia in 1994 in these words:

> In 1992, before the UN deployed to Bosnia, some 130,000 people were killed. In 1993, as the UN started to become effective, some 30,000 people were killed. In 1994, when I was there, 3,000 people were killed; furthermore the people were sustained by the delivery of food and fuel by the UN and its agencies . . . By the end of 1994, the conditions for peace had also been achieved. The best answer to those who say that it would have been better if the UN had not involved itself in the conflict is of course provided by those millions of people whose lives were sustained throughout the conflict by the presence of the UN.[32]

Although Rose believed that the 'conditions for peace' had been achieved, there still lay a long and bloody road ahead before that peace was secured. Four days before Christmas, the indefatigable ex-President Jimmy Carter flew into Sarajevo and brokered a ceasefire between the belligerents. It was agreed that the truce should last until the following April with the hope of a continued ceasefire thereafter. In retrospect, cynical observers have referred to this truce as 'half-time', during which both sides replenished their arms and ammunition and re-entered the fray in the spring with renewed fervour.

General Rose concluded his tour of command at the start of 1995. He is a man who has compelling faith in the role of the United Nations. He believes that, while Bosnia has been an ordeal by fire for that organization, it has come through it with no little credit. That peace was ultimately not able to be brought about without the final participation in great strength by NATO should not, he believes, detract from the successes in terms of humanitarian support achieved by UNPROFOR.

Whereas there may be some truth in this view, the UN operation can scarcely be regarded as an unqualified success. Meanwhile, in Bosnia, the inhabitants entered 1995 in an atmosphere of uneasy truce.

The renewed fighting that broke out the following spring was, if anything, more vicious than anything that had gone before. The Muslims, who had managed to replenish their armouries, launched renewed attacks on the Bosnian Serbs, while the Croats embarked on a campaign to drive the Serbs out of the Krajina. Since none of the participants saw benefit in allowing Western journalists to report these activities, much of the fighting went unnoticed by the world's television, not least because – to the editors – it was little other than 'more of the same'. Much worse, however, was to come.

General Rose's successor, another British officer, Lieutenant General Sir Rupert Smith, the erstwhile commander of the British 1st Armoured Division in the Gulf War, had inherited the command at a time of extreme gloom for the UN forces. Unlike his predecessor, he kept his own counsel, appearing very infrequently before the cameras.

Martin Bell, at that time in Sarajevo, gave a bleak description of the scene:

It was May 1995. The United Nations, which had done so much and saved so many through thirty-seven months of war, was now becalmed and rudderless and had lost its map. Its Protection Force wasn't protecting, its safe areas weren't safe. The Serbs were not only roaming the heavy weapons exclusion zones at will with their tanks and artillery, but firing them from the UN's own collection points . . . One of its disillusioned officials concluded that it had chosen the 'WIN' option: Weak, Ineffective and Negative.[33]

If the future was not to lie in a humiliating withdrawal of the United Nations from Bosnia, some firm action had to be taken. Accordingly Smith issued an ultimatum that all heavy weapons around Sarajevo were either to be removed or handed over to the UN. Failure to meet the terms of the ultimatum, which expired at midday on 25 May, would be answered by air attack. Predictably, the ultimatum was ignored. Accordingly, an air strike was called in on the Bosnian Serb ammunition depot near Pale. In response the Serbs launched a heavy artillery attack on the town of Tuzla in which some seventy people were killed outright. The world, still bored by the news from Bosnia, remained unmoved.

On the next day, the ammunition depot was attacked again by NATO. This time, however, there was a new response which hurriedly reawakened world interest in the events. On Serb television there appeared pictures of captured UN officers chained to posts in the vicinity of the ammunition depot, coupled with a demand directed at the UN to stop the bombing. Not content with these human shields, the Bosnian Serbs rounded up other UN hostages which included not only French troops but, to British horror, twenty-two soldiers of the Royal Welsh Fusiliers who had been deployed at Gorazde. Not unnaturally such news put new life into the media reporting of Bosnia.

Here was the nightmare situation which had been forecast by the British and French Governments at the time of American enthusiasm for a 'lift and strike' policy. This development which led to the collapse of the UN peacekeeping operation probably marked the watershed in the final handling of the Bosnian crisis. The UN, unable to find an answer to the Serb action, insisted on calling off the air strikes, while negotiations were put in hand to release the hostages. Britain and France on the other hand, at the insistence of Rupert Smith, decided unilaterally that the time had come to face up to the worsening crisis. The two countries decided to reinforce their commitment to Bosnia, this time not with soldiers in blue helmets and white vehicles but with two new brigades in fighting camouflage supported for the first time by artillery. To the cynics, however, it appeared that this so-called Rapid Reaction Force had an additional role of conducting a fighting withdrawal, if it was decided to leave Bosnia finally to its fate. There was no shortage of enthusiasm for such a withdrawal being echoed in the British press.

Ironically, the negotiator who finally secured the freedom of the hostages was President Milošević, the source of so much of the original enmity in Yugoslavia. Having broken with Karadžić and his General, Mladić, who had now lost the last vestiges of world sympathy for their cause, Milošević acted as an intermediary and negotiated the release of all the hostages by the middle of June.

By this time, it was apparent that the United Nations had finally shot its bolt. Two of the eastern 'safe areas', Zepa and Srebrenica had been overrun and their inhabitants had been humiliatingly driven out or killed. Only Gorazde remained, and that hanging by a thread.

On 21 July, at a conference held in London, it was decided that any further attacks on Gorazde would now be strongly resisted and that the Rapid Reaction Force would move onto Mount Igman, above Sarajevo, and defend the convoys using this route. The Americans, too, had realized that the situation was fast degenerating into open war. The final straw that spelled the end of UN negotiation was yet another heavy mortar attack by the Serbs which fell on the market place in Sarajevo on 28 August killing thirty-seven people. From that moment, NATO virtually declared war on the Bosnian Serbs. From 30 August 1995, NATO strike aircraft and guided missiles, supported by the artillery of the Rapid Reaction Force, destroyed Serb air-defence weapons, command posts, communications, ammunition depots, bridges and artillery. At the same time, a tough and vigorous American negotiator, Assistant Secretary of State Richard Holbrooke, embarked on a round of negotiations, speaking for the first time from a position of strength. The Muslims and the Croats had at the same time taken advantage of this new turn of events and advanced into western Bosnia, recapturing much of the country which the Bosnian Serbs had earlier invaded.

On 14 September, the NATO air strikes were halted and negotiations continued in earnest. Fighting was still going on between all three of the warring factions, but the confidence of the Bosnian Serbs had been destroyed and the readiness of all three to bring the war to an end was becoming apparent. A final ceasefire was announced by President Clinton to come into force on 12 October, which was to be followed by detailed agreements to be hammered out between the parties concerned at the little known Wright-Patterson Air Force Base in Dayton, Ohio. On 14 December 1995, a General Framework Agreement for Peace in Bosnia–Hercegovina, known generally as the Dayton Agreement, was signed by all the involved parties at a ceremony held at the Elysée Palace in Paris. Two days later the United Nations formally handed over responsibility for the maintenance of peace to a NATO-led International Force (IFOR). Within a few more days this force, 60,000 strong and including a powerful United States contingent, started to move into Bosnia to control and implement the peace agreement that had been negotiated after five long years of fighting.

The International Force which moved into Bosnia at the start of 1996, composed of fighting units from every part of the world, had a new and untried task to perform. First the armies of the three warring factions had to leave the field and return to barracks; then, far more difficult, the people who had been driven from their homes had to be urged to return to homes which had in so many cases been destroyed either in the fighting or deliberately. The huge task of repairing the country had to be

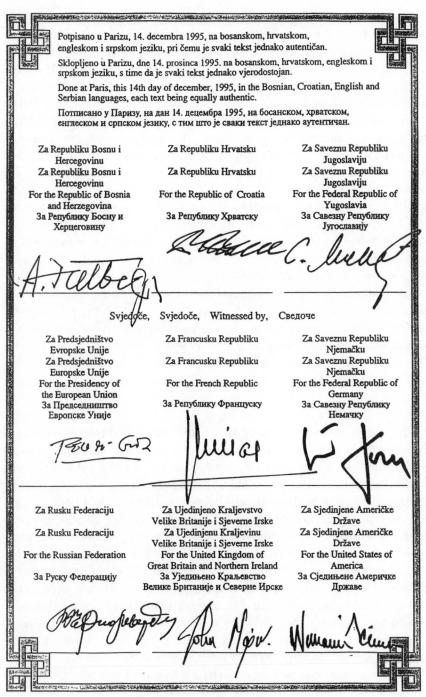

Potpisano u Parizu, 14. decembra 1995, na bosanskom, hrvatskom, engleskom i srpskom jeziku, pri čemu je svaki tekst jednako autentičan.

Sklopljeno u Parizu, dne 14. prosinca 1995. na bosanskom, hrvatskom, engleskom i srpskom jeziku, s time da je svaki tekst jednako vjerodostojan.

Done at Paris, this 14th day of december, 1995, in the Bosnian, Croatian, English and Serbian languages, each text being equally authentic.

Потписано у Паризу, на дан 14. децембра 1995, на босанском, хрватском, енглеском и српском језику, с тим што је сваки текст једнако аутентичан.

Za Republiku Bosnu i Hercegovinu
Za Republiku Bosnu i Hercegovinu
For the Republic of Bosnia and Herzegovina
За Републику Босну и Херцеговину

Za Republiku Hrvatsku
Za Republiku Hrvatsku
For the Republic of Croatia
За Републику Хрватску

Za Saveznu Republiku Jugoslaviju
Za Saveznu Republiku Jugoslaviju
For the Federal Republic of Yugoslavia
За Савезну Републику Југославију

Svjedoče, Svjedoče, Witnessed by, Сведоче

Za Predsjedništvo Evropske Unije
Za Predsjedništvo Europske Unije
For the Presidency of the European Union
За Председништво Европске Уније

Za Francusku Republiku
Za Francusku Republiku
For the French Republic
За Републику Француску

Za Saveznu Republiku Njemačku
Za Saveznu Republiku Njemačku
For the Federal Republic of Germany
За Савезну Републику Немачку

Za Rusku Federaciju
Za Rusku Federaciju
For the Russian Federation
За Руску Федерацију

Za Ujedinjeno Kraljevstvo Velike Britanije i Sjeverne Irske
Za Ujedinjenu Kraljevinu Velike Britanije i Sjeverne Irske
For the United Kingdom of Great Britain and Northern Ireland
За Уједињено Краљевство Велике Британије и Северне Ирске

Za Sjedinjene Američke Države
Za Sjedinjene Američke Države
For the United States of America
За Сједињене Америчке Државе

Signature page of the Dayton Agreement, signed in Paris on 14 December 1995.

297

addressed. Besides that, there had to be no question of any resumption of hostilities. The military force introduced into the country was immensely powerful: tanks, heavy artillery and the whole panoply of war were deployed under American, British and French command. However, it was a deployment of an unusual kind. This force had no secrets: its strength was there to be seen and understood. The Land Force Commander, Lieutenant General Sir Michael Walker, encouraged the locals to visit and see for themselves the allied strength; to make his purpose and his remit clear to all, he had a 'media-operations' staff some two hundred strong whose task it was to carry the message into every corner of Bosnia.

Although, up to the time of writing in 1997, neither IFOR nor its smaller successor (SFOR) has had to act in anger, there have been in General Walker's own words a number of 'defining moments' which have brought with them the threat of force.[34] Today peace reigns in Yugoslavia, but peace at an astronomic price.

All those that we have met, who have been involved in the terrible saga of Yugoslavia, are agreed on one thing. Of the three warring factions involved, there has been nothing to choose in terms of cruelty and double dealing. That one side, the Serbs, were responsible for the start of the war is undeniable, but once the battle was joined, none was less guilty of atrocity than another. In his book, *Balkan Odyssey*, David Owen writes:

> The duplicities of the war in Bosnia have never been better illustrated than by a conversation between a Muslim commander and his Serb counterpart picked up by intercept radios during the Muslim–Croat war. First they bargained over the price in deutschmarks of Serb shells which the Muslims wanted to buy from the Serbs to fire on the Croats in Mostar. After a price was agreed and routes for the supply in lorries arranged, the Muslim commander was heard to come back and ask if the Serbs could, for a little extra money, fire the shells themselves if they were given the cross-bearings. After a brief haggle on the number of extra deutschmarks this would involve, the Serbs duly fired on the Croats, paid for by the Muslims. When I told President Milošević about this, he was very angry and asked Karadžić in my presence whether this had happened. Karadžić confirmed that it had, but said that orders had been issued that 'it was not to happen again'.[35]

Slobodan Milošević is clearly an opportunist who has survived and managed narrowly to hold onto his presidency. Alija Izetbegović, the wily Muslim, succeeded in being cast as the innocent victim from the start of the war and has managed through thick and thin to hold on to that role. This despite one of General Walker's 'defining moments' when the Muslims were found by IFOR to be deeply involved in activities specifically forbidden by the Dayton Accord, which had involved the setting up of a terrorist training school in central Bosnia, manned by Iranians. Franjo Tudjman, the Croat leader, was described to us by one who knew him as a 'marble-eyed secret policeman'. Both Radovan Karadžić and Ratko Mladić have been indicted by the European Court in the Hague as war criminals.

Surprisingly, many may think, the United States, since the signing of the Dayton Agreement, have been re-equipping and retraining both the Bosnian and the Croatian forces. Today, in June 1997, there is no longer an arms embargo in force and the re-equipment continues apace. Whether, when the international forces are finally withdrawn, this policy will lead to a balance of power in the Balkans or to renewed enthusiasm for war can only be a matter for speculation.

The war in Bosnia has been reported to the world through all its vicissitudes by a team of brave and committed journalists who have spent longer and endured in many cases far greater danger than the soldiers who have tried to keep the peace. They have told the truth as they have seen it, but, as we know with the benefit of hindsight, it was so often only a part of the truth. The pictures of destruction and mutilation have put pressure on the leaders of the world to act, often unwisely and in haste. Many of the attempts to solve so formidable a problem were made by politicians with only a minimal understanding of the circumstances. Yet without those same pictures, there is little doubt that few if any of the attempts would have been made at all.

In his study entitled *Headline Diplomacy*, Philip Seib quotes Peter Jennings of ABC Television as saying: 'Political leadership trumps good television every time. As influential as television can be, it is most influential in the absence of decisive political leadership.'[36]

Decisive political leadership was conspicuous by its absence in the Bosnia crisis. Disagreements among European leaders were complicated by disagreements across the Atlantic. From the start, the United Nations was found wanting as a command headquarters for a military operation and its many resolutions could not be translated into practical action. Yet, with all these difficulties, the media acted as a mainspring which continually forced the inadequate clockwork to run.

It may of course be argued that without that mainspring, the affairs of Yugoslavia would have been more readily solved without outside intervention. There were many people in the world who believed that it was folly to set foot militarily in the Balkans. General Rose, on the other hand, is in no doubt that we were right to do so and that the efforts of the UN saved thousands of lives. The war was brought to an end – if indeed it has ended – by a combination of factors: a firm stand was at last taken by NATO which included the bombing of Bosnian Serb positions and tough negotiation with all three factions; the Bosnian Serbs were deserted by Milošević, leaving them isolated; and finally, a general war weariness had set in among all the participants after five years of slaughter. The thoughts of many, however, must be summed up in the closing paragraph of an article about a tour of duty in Bosnia published in a British army regimental magazine:

> In the back of our minds, however, a number of questions lurked unanswered. How artificial was the peace we had created? Could it really hope to heal six hundred years of hatred? And just how real is a peace maintained by guns and tanks?[37]

Whether the world will prove itself to be wiser when faced with another situation of this kind is impossible to say. What is certain is that when the moment comes, the media will be there to carry the demand for action to the world's leaders; they in turn must decide carefully and positively what that action is to be. If they make the right decision and hold to their course, no amount of emotional television will be strong enough to sweep them from it. However, without that leadership, who can tell where humanity and the media may not lead us?

---

1. Christopher Bennett, *Yugoslavia's Bloody Collapse*, London, Hurst & Co, 1995, p. 5
2. Mark Thompson, *Forging War*, Article XIX, International Centre against Censorship, p. 54
3. Ibid., p. 56

4. 'Krajina': literally 'frontier area'. The name dates from the Hapsburg empire: frontier areas of that empire were named Krajinas. Areas dominated by the Serbs in neighbouring republics were called by them Krajinas. The area around Knin was one such. (See map)
5. Bennett, *Yugoslavia's Bloody Collapse*, p. 154
6. 'Arkan' was the *nom de guerre* of a previous secret service operator and Belgrade ice cream parlour owner named Želko Ražnjatović, who became the leader of a notorious group of Serb fighters known as the 'Arkanovci'. See Bennett, *Yugoslavia's Bloody Collapse*, p. 150
7. Thompson, *Forging War*, p. 161
8. Martin Bell, *In Harm's Way*, London, Hamish Hamilton, 1995, p. 33
9. Ibid., p. 35
10. The twelve countries which sent troops were Argentina, Belgium, Canada, Czechoslovakia, Denmark, France, Jordan, Kenya, Nepal, Nigeria, Poland and Russia
11. Authors' conversations with Douglas Hurd, February 1997
12. Ibid.
13. *The Economist*, 24 January 1992, p. 49
14. The Badinter Commission. See Bennett, *Yugoslavia's Bloody Collapse*, p. 179
15. *The Economist*, 25 April 1992
16. Bell, *In Harm's Way*, p. 61
17. *The Economist*, 30 May 1992
18. Bell, *In Harm's Way*, p. 59
19. *Newsweek*. Quoted in Roy Gutman, *A Witness to Genocide*, Shaftesbury, Dorset, Element Books Ltd, pp. 34 and 36
20. *The Economist*, 15 August 1992
21. Quoted in Bell, *In Harm's Way*, p. 137
22. Colin Powell, *A Soldier's Way*, London, Hutchinson, 1995, p. 558
23. Bell, *In Harm's Way*, p. 137
24. Authors' conversations with Douglas Hurd and Peter Carrington, February 1997
25. Ibid.
26. David Owen, *Balkan Odyssey*, London, Gollancz, 1995, p. 13
27. Letter to the author from Captain (now Major) D.M. Bennett, 9/12 Lancers
28. Conversations with Hon Raymond Seitz, February 1997
29. *The Economist*, 12 February 1994
30. *The Economist*, 19 March 1994
31. Conversations with General Rose, March 1997
32. Address by General Sir Michael Rose to All Souls' College, Oxford, 23 February 1996
33. Bell, *In Harm's Way*, p. 257
34. Conversations with General Walker, March 1997

35. Owen, *Balkan Odyssey*, p. 350
36. Philip Seib, *Headline Diplomacy*, London, Praeger, 1997, p. 135
37. *The Delhi Spearman*, Regimental Journal of the 9/12 Royal Lancers, Vol X, p. 37 (article by Captain T.S.D. Lyle)

CHAPTER THIRTEEN

Conclusions

'Of all the unexamined assumptions of democracy none seems so strange today as the belief that public opinion is a reliable guide for a political society . . .'

Kingsley Martin, 1921[1]

Lady Thatcher addressed the subject of the media and war.[2] 'Television has changed everything,' she said with her customary conviction. However, while much has indeed changed, much has remained constant, not least human nature. During the whole of the period under review the media within democracies has influenced public opinion, which, in its turn, has influenced political decision-making in the making of war: indeed, that is partly what democracy is about.

The influence of the media is not direct. It is the perception that politicians have of its effect that can have considerable repercussions on the onset, course and ending of war. When we talked to them, Max Hastings, editor of the *Evening Standard* and ex-editor of the *Daily Telegraph*, and Simon Jenkins, ex-editor of *The Times*, were agreed in their opinion that 80 per cent of politicians in Britain live in constant fear of what the media might say, and that this fear becomes almost an obsession during times of armed conflict.

There are problems about public opinion. If one defines it as a commonly held view among the majority of a given population, a host of unanswered, or even unanswerable, questions arise. The strength of a commonly held view is clearly important, but so is its durability. Douglas Hurd has talked of the 'flash flood of emotion' often engendered by the media focusing on a particular incident or series of incidents. Furthermore, different segments of public opinion clearly have differing impacts on public policies: in spite of all efforts to create a classless society, we, like the rest of mankind, live in an élitist world.

Then, how is one to gauge what public opinion is? Surely it is primarily the media itself which determines what the public thinks since there is no other public mirror available. 'Public opinion is enraged or upset' is the headline, and by and large that is accepted to be the case. Sometimes there may be evidence of this in an opinion poll, but, more usually the media makes a statement, whether in print or on radio or television, and then itself decides that the statement represents public opinion. It is, often, advocate and jury in its own case. It is argued by some editors that experienced journalists have a 'feel' for what people in general think – a sixth sense will tell them whether what they are saying is acceptable to the public or not. However, when pressed, they will probably have to admit that their 'feel' comes from fellow journalists or others with whom they mix. The opinion of an élite can be misleading.

There are those who argue that the media reflects rather than influences public opinion, and this point is often made by the media itself. There is some truth in this assertion. Clearly, if some part of the media were continually to advocate a policy which was totally at odds with the prevailing national ethos, the public would shun the columns, wavelength or channels in question to the great commercial detriment of those concerned. The media and public opinion do in a sense feed on each other, with the media fuelling views and prejudices which may already exist, openly or latently. By and large, however, the only way in which the public learns anything at all about what is happening abroad is through the media. And in order to have an opinion about any issue it is necessary to have some information about it. The information produced by the media is of a selective nature since it is necessarily constrained by limitations of time and space. The very process of selection inevitably involves a large measure of conscious influence in a desired direction. As Walter Lippman put it:

> Every newspaper when it reaches the reader is the result of a whole series of selections as to what items should be printed, in what position, how much space each shall have, what emphasis each shall have. There are no objective standards here.[3]

It therefore seems to us to be against common sense to argue that the media does not influence public opinion, particularly where foreign affairs are concerned. With home affairs the public can bring its own experience to bear as a corrective to what it may be told by the media. Generally, this cannot happen with international matters. Whatever some academics and others may now say, the media influence on American public opinion about Vietnam was very great. President Johnson was right when he said: 'if we have lost Walter [Cronkite] we have lost middle America.'[4]

Of course the media does not speak with one voice. There may well be two or three completely different accounts of the same event or series of events and the public can choose which one to believe. That is not to argue that the media has no influence: if anything, rather the opposite. The direction of influence may vary but the fact of influence remains.

There are a number of other constant factors about the media over the period we have covered. For instance, the problem often recurs as to whether the media should be solely concerned with telling the truth or whether it should have a loyalty to its own country or, indeed, in some cases to those servicemen alongside whom the journalist may be living. This question is allied to that of censorship. There was no censorship in Vietnam. Some journalists would have welcomed it. In many ways life is far easier for the conscientious journalist when his despatches are censored: he cannot be blamed if they do harm to his own side. Once censored, he has an alibi.

A further question is whether the media should be used, consciously or unconsciously, for propaganda purposes? Or even, perhaps, without the media's knowledge, for deliberate misinformation in order to mislead the enemy? There is little doubt that few journalists would accept the latter situation. We have covered cases, both in Northern Ireland and in the Falklands where the media was deliberately used as part of a deception plan. This is wholly alien to the journalistic creed and it is clearly a mistaken policy. It leads to bitter mistrust by the media of all subsequent official pronouncements, and this happened in Vietnam after deliberate official lies. It also totally undermines media credibility which could later be most valuable to the military and political authorities in question. As we have seen, the BBC's reputation for truth was of enormous importance to the allied cause in the Second World War. As the end of the war approached, Goebbels' propaganda machine was believed by nobody: the Germans themselves were listening to the BBC in order to learn what was happening.

However, propaganda in the sense of highlighting some events or views favourable to one side with the deliberate object of inducing a desired state of mind is another matter. Throughout our study, propaganda has been a constant weapon of war. From the vilification of the Tsar before the Crimean War to the projection of German atrocities in Belgium in 1914, to the triumphal reports of British entry into Port Stanley and the success of the British armoured division in the Gulf, the media has been used, often at its own instigation, to project a favourable image of one side's efforts and the opposite of its opponent's. As Max Hastings pointed out to us this can be of great importance to the fighting soldier. The British servicemen in the Gulf knew that their fortunes were being followed day by day and night by night by their relatives and girlfriends in Britain. Unlike the 14th Army in Burma during the Second World War and to a lesser degree those fighting in Korea in 1950–1 they were not a forgotten army. Very far from it and, as a result of this, British politicians knew that they had better do the best for them they possibly could, or they would suffer later at the ballot box. Facilities for a shower of Christmas presents and home telephone calls were arranged for the servicemen in the Gulf, and this has continued in Bosnia.

There is a distinction between wars of national survival, such as the two world wars, and conflicts where national survival is clearly not at issue. We see no problem about the use of propaganda as a weapon of war in the former case. In the latter it is possible that the media may see themselves, as has sometimes been the case in Northern Ireland, as holding the ring between two equally valid ideologies. Mrs Thatcher was furious when, during the Falklands campaign, the media sometimes talked of 'the British' and 'the Argentinians' as if the media was not itself at all involved and was acting as a mere objective spectator: 'It is not "the British"; it is "we". And it is not "the Argentinians"; it is "the enemy".'[5] She used the same argument in the case of Northern Ireland where journalists would sometimes interview members of the IRA after an incident involving terrorism. There is a danger here, as some members of the media see it, that they might merely become a mouthpiece for the government of the day. Where no war had been declared and national survival was not at stake, John Simpson, for instance, thought that there would be no reason not to have interviewed the IRA man who killed Lord Mountbatten had it been possible to do so. He argued that an interview would have started from the premise that murder was wrong, that the IRA campaign of violence was wrong and that would have been made clear at the outset. The man in question would certainly have condemned himself out of his own mouth and the public in Britain would have seen the sort of person we had to deal with in the IRA. He went on to say that in any case the freedom of the press was of overriding importance and telling the truth about any issue could do no harm except when military security and the lives of British soldiers were concerned, when, of course, censorship would be acceptable. There is force in this argument and, certainly, the ban on the words of Sinn Fein leaders being broadcast on television became an absurdity when actors spoke their words for them. However, any publicity can be good publicity for terrorists and appearing to accept 'the enemy' on equal terms with our own army or police could be very demoralizing for soldiers or policemen risking their lives on behalf of their country in Northern Ireland, the Falklands or elsewhere. Journalists as a whole, and certainly John Simpson and his colleagues in the BBC, are patriots – but they can in some situations nevertheless do unwitting damage to their own country. In this case Lady Thatcher is right.

This question would certainly not have arisen in the earlier years of the period covered, which is indicative of the social revolution we have undergone. It is instructive to note that the *Manchester Guardian*, although violently opposed to a British declaration of war against Germany in 1914, decided not to continue with its criticisms and to follow the official line when war was actually declared. Its successor, the *Guardian*, however, felt no such qualms in 1956 at the time of the Suez campaign.

A consistent feature during the period of our review is the uncertainty of military commanders as how best to handle the journalists. This seems to depend on the personalities of the men concerned rather than on any hard and fast military doctrine, although recently the importance of public relations has been emphasized in training and, to an increasing extent, in practice. In Bosnia, Generals Rose and Walker talked to journalists a great deal. Indeed, they devoted much of their time to dealing with the public relations aspects of their task. General Rupert Smith on the other hand very rarely spoke to journalists on the record and did not give interviews on television, a policy he had also adopted in the Gulf. Raglan and Kitchener tried to ignore the 'luckless tribe', as Russell termed himself and his colleagues. This attitude certainly did not succeed in curbing criticism either in the Crimea or of the 'concentration camps' and farm burning in South Africa. Roberts and Montgomery, on the other hand, positively welcomed and used the media as a weapon of war – obviously a better tactic than ostracism.

There are a range of other possibilities for the authorities in dealing with the media. Outright banning, as in the case of the American invasion of Grenada, or a partial exclusion because of the impossibility of journalists getting to the scene of action other than if taken there by the military, as in the case of the Falklands, are two other scenarios. A division of journalists into those operating a 'pool system', under military supervision and with military briefing and protection, and the rest (unilaterals) as in the Gulf is another option, as is the complete free-for-all in the case of Korea, Vietnam and Bosnia. The 'D' notice system as described on pages 63 and 135 is a further option. There is one certainty: unless journalists are given official access to news, they will find it for themselves – and what they say may well not be welcome to the authorities.

There is a constant conflict between the military need for secrecy and the media demand for disclosure. This is often seen by others as a welcome and productive tension keeping both parties up to the mark. Whether welcome or not, it is inevitable and as Nik Gowing, the one-time Diplomatic Editor for *Channel 4 News*, has pointed out, the military is learning to live with it and to cope with the many problems which the ever-changing new technology brings with it.[6]

A further aspect of the impact of the media which straddles the arrival of television without essentially changing very greatly is that of motive. Journalists covering war are not, and never have been, hired because of their beautiful blue eyes but because they are thought capable of producing 'stories' which will sell the organs of the media which they serve. To be successful they need many virtues. They must be able to write or speak clearly understandable prose, to endure discomfort and danger without complaint, to overcome all kinds of difficulties in getting to the scene of the action and above all to sense where a good 'story' may lie and to persist in finding it. As Lord Deedes observed, for a journalist in the field it is the 'story' which is the Holy Grail, particularly if he is the first to find and transmit it, thereby achieving a scoop. This has not changed from the time of Russell to the present day – although Russell himself was very hesitant about the culture of the scoop which followed the invention of the telegraph. For their part, editors wish to produce a successful newspaper or news channel which people buy, listen to or watch. Proprietors also, obviously, have a considerable commercial interest in their product: indeed in some cases this is their only interest. Others, however, are mainly motivated by the power they can wield because of the influence they exert on public opinion. In the early days of the mass media, Beaverbrook, Northcliffe and the other press barons openly admitted that they were after political power and this became very apparent in the First World War. Certainly it is true that, during the early part of this century, *The Times* seemed to have little interest in making money and nearly went bankrupt as a result. Modern press owners seem to be more interested in money.

Similarly, the news has always been what is new. Whatever the carnage, and there have been examples of this in almost every war we have examined, the initial shock of the reports gradually wears off, certainly if those killed are not from one's own country. A boredom factor begins to appear, as it did, towards the end of the South African War, in Somalia, Rwanda, Chechniya, Bosnia and elsewhere.

In order really to get attention and thereby sales, the media has an obsessive need for new sensation and it always has done. It was the sensational element of McGahan's report about the Bulgarian atrocities which grabbed attention, not a scholarly discourse on the need for freedom for Bulgaria. It is no good expecting the media to produce a totally balanced view of any situation. That is not its function, however it might argue to the contrary. The essential function of the journalist, the editor and the proprietor is, and always has been, to sell the story. In wars of national survival that aspect can become obscured, or even temporarily buried, but it remains latent, to appear again as soon as it decently can. To say this is not in any way to criticize; it is merely to state a fact of life which can be obscured by wishful thinking. Of course many, perhaps most, proprietors, editors and journalists do feel a sense of responsibility for the results of their labours and will attempt, as far as they are able, to produce what they believe to be a balanced view. However, their contributions still have to be sold to someone.

Furthermore, they are all human beings with human attributes: of course they will try to project their views. They cannot be objective, any more than can the rest of us. Where the possibility or actuality of war is concerned the tendency towards subjectivity is heightened. Issues of life or death concentrate the mind wonderfully, particularly so if the observer is also a participant, as are war correspondents. Some war correspondents will admit to emotional involvement more than others. Martin Bell, among many other journalists in Bosnia, openly supported the Muslim cause. Kate Adie, on the other hand, in a recent *Face to Face* television interview said that she always tried to remain objective, the better to produce what she believed to be balanced reports: 'My emotions must not get in the way . . . my job is to deliver the facts of the matter to let people make their own judgements. I'm not there as a confessor.'

John Simpson, too, has a passionate belief, shared by Brian Hanrahan, that the job of the television journalist is not concerned with taking sides or indeed with making moral judgements. Still less is it to tell politicians what should be done about any situation. It is to find out what is happening and to tell the world about it. Decisions as to what, if anything, should be done should be left to others.

All these journalists, of course with many others, are now highly experienced war correspondents. The inexperienced journalist, however, will very easily become totally emotionally overcome by the first sight of war and its inevitable horrors and, as a result, may well fail to understand and report on the context in which he, or she, is operating. One of the reasons for the difference between the reporting of the Korean and Vietnam conflicts was the fact that the war correspondents in Korea had, in most cases, themselves been involved in some way in the 1939–45 war, and were therefore not so emotionally overcome by the sights they saw. In Vietnam, by contrast, there were many journalists who were completely new to war and, therefore, in their reports reproduced much of the shock they felt. The new presence of television also, of course, gave enormous added impetus to the searing impact on the American people of the destruction and killing.

So much for aspects of the media which have been constant over the period of our study. What changes have there been? Firstly, over the last 150 years or so Britain has gone through a vast social revolution. And, secondly, technological achievements have led to massive advances in the means of communication. To a large extent each of these two developments has fed on the other.

As far as the social revolution has been concerned one only has to imagine how Lloyd George's speech – 'The great peaks we have forgotten, of Honour, Duty, Patriotism and, clad in glittering white, the great pinnacle of Sacrifice pointing like a rugged finger to Heaven' – would be received now to realize the complete change of environment in which we all, including the media, now exist. As education has reached the whole population and the franchise has been increased (from under half a million in 1800 to over five million in 1900 to universal now) so public understanding and power have changed out of all recognition. The deference factor, one of the reasons for public acceptance of mass slaughter of 1914–18, has all but vanished. Our values, perceptions of truth, ideals and assumptions have changed radically. We do not accept leadership as we did. We question; we search for scapegoats; we refuse direction; we flout authority. Many of us listen readily, and sometimes eagerly, to the media when it criticizes the establishment and reinforces a creeping tendency to anarchy. If the Falklands campaign had lasted much longer there would undoubtedly have been media opposition to it; this had already begun to surface in a *Panorama* broadcast. The same would have happened in the Gulf. Whatever the situation, if it persists for long the feeling that 'something must be done' will surface: there must be a solution to all problems and, by definition, if this does not happen quickly the authorities are to blame. A classic example of this was when the little girl, Irma, was flown out of Sarajevo for treatment in response to a media campaign and then, later, the authorities came under media criticism for reacting so quickly to what the media itself had demanded.

Some older journalists argue that present-day journalists have less integrity than they used to and that this is in part the result of the social revolution that has occurred. We do not feel qualified to decide on this point. Certainly it would be folly for any politician now to trust the tabloid press with a highly politically sensitive secret – but it probably always was. Trust of journalists from the broadsheets is, however, another matter. Eden's total confidence in Iverach MacDonald at the time of the Suez crisis is remarkable and there is doubt as to whether that could be duplicated today, but some journalists have always been more trustworthy than others and politicians have always had to make a judgement on that. Certainly most politicians love to talk to journalists, if only to justify themselves.

There is an interesting contrast between the journalistic style of the 'serious' newspapers in the United States and in Britain. In the United States there is only one 'serious' newspaper in each city – the *New York Times*, the *Washington Post* and so on. In Britain there are at least five available everywhere. There is little competition in this area, therefore, in the United States whereas the opposite is the case in Britain. In Lord Rees-Mogg's view the lack of competition in the United States leads to 'soft' journalism as leader writers seek to impress their colleagues with safe politically correct attitudes. On the other hand the competition in Britain results in more adventurous journalism. Simon Jenkins agrees: 'American newspapers are often pompous and safe in their views, whereas British newspapers are more inclined to take risks.'

Without doubt, the greatest change has come through the advent of, first, the telegraph and photographs, then the radio, then television and now the satellite dish whereby instant pictures can be relayed from anywhere in the world to anywhere in the world. As we have seen, the telegraph revolutionized the reporting of the American Civil War and led to a hectic search for the scoop and the need for correspondents to be within daily riding reach of a telegraph office. In South Africa, the Sudan and the First World War, and indeed in the Falklands, the accepted need for quick transmission paradoxically meant that the authorities could impose censorship because it was only through their telegraph system that reports could be sent quickly to Britain. Even in Bosnia, the need to despatch television reports to a great extent anchored the newsmen to Sarajevo.

Television has undoubtedly usurped the previous role of the press and, to a certain extent, of the radio in bringing 'what's new' to the public. Having largely lost this function, the newspapers have been forced in different directions. The quality press have more of a role in explaining the background to events, although some newspapers can be, and often are, criticized for their failure to perform this function properly. The tabloids, on the other hand, have largely relapsed into garish sensation-mongering. Robin Day is quoted as saying: 'A tabloid medium is one of shock rather than information: emotion rather than intellect.'[7] Television documentaries, which could be useful as background briefing, however, cannot be studied at length as can newspapers and magazines. In a sense they are neither fish nor fowl, neither instant news, nor studied background to be carefully perused and evaluated.

The capacity for photographic reproduction did not really affect the situation much in the Crimean War in spite of Fenton's efforts. The Boer War saw an enormous increase in the public demand for pictures of the action but it was virtually impossible actually to film the battle because of the bulky nature of the equipment. There were similar problems in the First World War although the film of the Somme did play to huge audiences. Still photographs of the little napalmed girl and the execution of a Viet Cong soldier in Vietnam had a vast impact. Unlike television films they were lasting images and appeared again and again.

The advent of the radio between the two world wars had an enormous effect on public perceptions of conflict. Both authors remember as boys hearing on the radio one of Hitler's speeches to a vast Nazi rally at Nuremberg. It was a very frightening experience, the hysterical voice shouting what appeared to be demented abuse punctuated by a resounding all-pervading roar of 'Sieg Heil'. No written report could have begun to convey the acute feeling of fanatical aggression. As we have seen, the BBC played a leading role in strengthening British resolve and in keeping hope alive in Europe during the dark years. Ed Murrow's broadcasts to the United States, also, had a major, almost irreplaceable, impact. It may not be an exaggeration to say that Lord Reith in his early conditioning of the BBC ethos has had as much effect on life in Britain as almost any other figure in the last sixty-five years of the twentieth century.

Lady Thatcher, however, has a point. It is indeed the television which has changed almost everything. To see is to believe. Blood in Vietnam, starvation in Somalia and Bosnia, the repercussions of genocide in Rwanda. As Walter Goodman has pointed out, ifs and buts do not survive the sight of a dying child.[8] Any glory there may be in war for those far from the spot disintegrates under close visual scrutiny. It can well be argued that this is an enormous bonus for mankind. Politicians will not enter into conflict so readily if they know that their electorate will actually see what happens. The body bag syndrome in the United States, with the President perforce being present when the coffins arrive from abroad draped with stars and stripes to be quickly surrounded by weeping relatives, certainly has inhibited martial fervour in the United States. American actions in the Gulf and Bosnia would certainly have been different had it not been for this constraint, and the sight of the body of the American soldier being dragged through the streets of Mogadishu had an immediate and electrifying effect on American policy in Somalia. To repeat a question we have already asked – could the carnage on the Somme, Passchendaele or Verdun possibly have continued if it had been witnessed nightly in millions of European sitting rooms? The answer must be that it could not.

The student kissing the soil of America on his return from Grenada had an immediate and vastly reassuring effect on the American Secretary of State's party awaiting his verdict with great trepidation. No words, written or spoken, would have been so telling.

There are, however, a number of countervailing factors. First, there is the necessity for oversimplification on television news broadcasts, and it is the television news that overwhelmingly has the greatest effect on the public. The media has always simplified. Whatever form of communication the media has taken, it has always had a finite amount of time and space in which to explain the situation even if it understands all the nuances itself, which it seldom does because of its own inevitable limitations. As the scope of news gathering has increased and as the time available for any one item in a news broadcast has reduced, so the need for a simple 'story' has become more and more pressing for television news editors. There has always been a need for heroes and villains in order to grip the imagination of the public. Villains abound, from the Tsar, to Kruger, to the Kaiser, to Hitler, to Nasser, to General Aideed and Saddam Hussein. If heroes do not readily appear they must be invented. The American airman whose aeroplane was shot down over Bosnia, and who existed in a forest for a few days before being rescued by helicopter, had a hero's Presidential welcome on his return to the United States. There is no possibility of explaining a complex situation as nearly all events are reported in something under a couple of minutes. As Martin Bell has said, for every ten minutes filmed, only one minute is used.[9] Brian Hanrahan told us that he tries to confine his reports to 180 words: there are 480 words on this page alone.

Martin Bell covered the whole question of the mechanics of television broadcasting in some detail in a radio broadcast on 8 June 1997. He said that British television journalists have far greater freedom than do their American counterparts. Every word an American war correspondent produces is vetted before delivery. In the BBC, by contrast, there is a tradition of trust. All the editing is now performed by the journalist before transmission. The editor at home will have given the journalist some general guidelines, including length, but, with the satellite dish, the completed 'story' will arrive in London perhaps only ten minutes before air time and the only decision for the home editor may be to accept it in its entirety or to reject it. Bell went on to point out that the responsibility on the British television journalist in the field is, therefore, very great indeed. There are temptations to fabricate good 'stories' and these are, as Bell admitted, not always resisted even by the BBC. The temptation will increase, he said, as the number of channels proliferates – as is already happening.

The great responsibility on modern television journalists operating overseas is readily acknowledged by John Simpson, and no doubt by all other responsible journalists. Millions of people will, inevitably, form their perceptions about what is happening from the choices and decisions made by a small number of journalists, who will themselves be under very great pressure.

Furthermore, a film, moving or still, is inevitably only a snapshot of one particular situation. It may or may not be representative of the whole conflict. A picture of a starving child will have a very different impact from a view of normality in a village not far away. The former will be filmed; the latter will not. But both could give a false impression of the truth. The quest for sensation is endemic to the media, inevitably so, and this leads straight on to what we call 'the illusion of truth'. Although there are some exceptions, the media reports what it sees or hears and believes to be true. However, by the very nature of the media, since everything cannot be reported, the whole truth is not, nor ever can be, represented. Since people are naturally credulous they will, in general, believe what they are told. The whole process is intensified with the onset of television. What people see is infinitely more compelling than what they read or hear. 'I saw it myself' has a ring of finality to it.

Even if it were possible to explain the complexities of a situation in some depth, the public attention span is now even more limited than it was. We require instant news as we need instant food. This is partly the result of television itself with its impatient and demanding assault on the senses. Nowadays not only do we feel that we have a right to know what goes on in the entire world in short, easily understandable snippets but a right to see, at first hand, the horrors and heroisms which conflict engenders, provided that we do not see the same conflicts too often. The boredom factor soon appears to dull the senses. The television is turned off or channels are switched when similar scenes in similar locations are reported too often.

It was Lord Salisbury who complained at the turn of the century that he found out about what was going on in the world more quickly from the newspapers than from his own diplomatic service. If that was so then, how much more so now with television screens chattering away in every politician's office or, if not there, at least in an outer office to be monitored by his staff. As we have seen, it was the television screens which played a major part in bringing the Gulf War to what many thought a premature conclusion before all the Republican Guard units in Kuwait had been destroyed by showing scenes of the 'turkey shoot' of Iraqi soldiers trying to escape.

A further, and major, problem now is the pressure for instant decision which instant reporting brings with it. If the media is to be satisfied, complicated events must be met by instant official reaction. When the Berlin Wall went up President Kennedy was able to avoid making a public comment on it for eight days. He could evaluate the likely impact of his words before he uttered them. When it came down, President Bush perforce had to voice his reaction in a few hours as television cameras were brought into the Oval Office. He was, rightly in the circumstances, cautious – but he was heavily criticized for his caution.[10] We should perhaps all be grateful that Kennedy did not allow himself to be subjected to the same pressure to take instant decisions during the Cuba Missile Crisis of 1962, the closest that the world has so far come to nuclear war.

The need for rapid reactions is partly engendered by the fear of what the Opposition, primed with immediate media news and views, will do. It is expected that questions will be answered immediately. Even if Parliament or Congress is not sitting, silence is difficult to maintain when the media is in full cry and the Opposition is vociferously seeking answers. This means, often, that a position is taken up which would not have been the case if it had been possible to think it out more carefully. Major's introduction of the safe haven for Kurds, certainly in response to television pictures of suffering people in the hills, might well have been different had he not felt the need for instant action. Certainly the disastrous United Nations' so-called 'safe areas' in Bosnia would not have been established had it not been for massive media pressure. The media has in effect greatly reduced the value of the diplomatic services throughout the world. Measured despatches from ambassadors with full and detailed descriptions of the background followed by carefully evaluated options and a recommendation are now all too often a thing of the past as politicians have to react instantly to media soundbites, oversimplified and trivialized as they may be.

President Carter was clearly pressurized by the American media into the ill-fated and disastrous attempt to rescue the hostages in Teheran. His Secretary of State, Vance, who had consistently opposed any such action, resigned as a result. The President paid the penalty: he was not re-elected.

A new phenomenon has now burst on the world – military action in pursuit of humanitarian, not national, interests and this has added a further complication. Interventions in Somalia and Bosnia have both taken place as a result of scenes of destruction, killing and starvation projected on television screens and written about in newspapers. However much it may be denied, we have no doubt that these interventions would not have taken place were it not for the media. It is difficult to discern any direct interest in Somalia for the United States or in Bosnia for the British, although there are arguments here about the danger of the conflict spreading, arguments about which we are somewhat sceptical. Yet, direct military action took place in both. The media, therefore, certainly in cases of humanitarian intervention, rightly or wrongly, undoubtedly often sets the international agenda. There may well have been, and probably were, other equally or more horrific events elsewhere in the world, but because these were not reported there was no pressure to intervene. Saddam's attack on Kuwait would have been known about and reported whatever decision editors had taken about priorities. However, particularly in more recent humanitarian crises, it is the media that determines international interest and hence national concerns if not actions. It is, often, the editor's decision to send reporters to an area which leads to agonizing Cabinet decisions. At any time there may well be, and probably are, many other situations (what is going on in China, East Timor, Angola, Liberia, the South Sudan now, 1997?) which could lead to worries about what should be done and even to armed conflict, but which are ignored because they are not reported. Governments do not go around looking for areas in which they can expend their energies and money. Diplomatic despatches, the only other source of government information, are most unlikely to lead to a rush to send troops anywhere at all. It is the intensity of feeling when pictures of starving children are shown on television that leads to demands for action which can become overwhelming. Whether anything constructive can be done, of course, is another matter. In Somalia it is probably true to say that the problem would have been better sorted out without any military intervention at all. Certainly, taking sides in a civil war produces the worst of all worlds. The United Nations and NATO have in the end avoided this cardinal error in Bosnia, but only just. Douglas Hurd put the point well when he said: 'We have not been and are not willing to begin some form of military intervention which we judge useless or worse, simply because of day to day pressures from the media . . . pressures which I repeat are understandable, perhaps inevitable.'[11] Although Hurd himself has a good record in avoiding instant reaction to media pressure, in the first British intervention in Bosnia we have doubts as to whether this dictum was fully followed.

It seems that the Labour Government elected on 1 May 1997 may well make matters worse if Robin Cook, in his initial presentation of his mission statement for the Foreign Office, is to be believed. He was reported as saying: 'We are an instant witness in our sitting-rooms through the medium of television to human tragedy in distant lands, and are therefore obliged to accept moral responsibility for our response.'[12] He repeated these views on 17 July 1997 with added emphasis at a presentation at the Foreign Office with the words: 'The fact that we are witnesses in our sitting-rooms to these events *requires* (Author's italics) us to take responsibility for our reaction to such breaches of human rights.'[13] It is therefore, apparently, to be the media with all its inevitable limitations and its 'illusion of truth' which will decide what we worry about and where. Surely, democratic governments, with their accountability to Parliament, should make decisions not in reaction to the vagaries of the newsrooms with their sometimes fickle priorities but in accordance with a carefully thought out coherent and sustainable foreign policy. As Sir Michael Howard has said: 'We cannot solve the problems of the world even if CNN brings them every night into our sitting-room.'[14]

Anyway, television news organizations can only cover at the most two crises at a time because of limited money and other resources, and what the first organization chooses is followed by all the others. In practice it is generally the newspapers which first discover a crisis or disaster because they are more widely represented, often by stringers, around the world; television crews are in shorter supply and can only follow, as a pack, in pursuit of the news.

There is a recurring dilemma as to what form military intervention should take. When people are starving, should intervening soldiers have the sole task of safeguarding humanitarian convoys and, if so, to what extent should their rules of engagement allow attacks on those inhibiting that free flow? Or should they be there to make peace rather than to keep a peace already agreed? In a number of occasions both in Somalia and the former Yugoslavia soldiers had the unfortunate experience of falling between two or even three stools.

The United Nations Charter, which allows military action only in self-defence or in the case of a 'threat to international peace and security' is now wildly out of date. Although Article 2(7) clearly prohibits intervention into 'matters which are essentially within the domestic jurisdiction of any state', it has now become more or less accepted that there can be situations of such horror that the international authority has a duty to intervene. Some produce a rather spurious legal justification for such intervention by quoting Article 1(3) of the Charter which speaks of 'encouraging respect for human rights and for fundamental freedom for all'. However, the Charter clearly needs to be updated. The problem is that few countries wish to meddle with it: Britain in particular is worried about a possible loss of her status as a permanent member of the Security Council.

The media and the aid agencies often find common cause. The media, ever searching for sensation, will eagerly transmit situations of horror. The aid agencies, dependent on charitable giving, need graphic pictures of human suffering in order to garner financial and other support. A journalist sent to an area about which he knows nothing very much, needs information, transport and general assistance which the aid agencies are only too pleased to supply in the knowledge that the resulting pictures will be grist to their charitable mill. The propensity to exaggerate and to select for sensation is overwhelming and, as we have seen in Somalia, it certainly does take place.

We are, therefore, faced by a situation where the agenda is often set by the media with its own priorities and motives, which are quite different from those of the people whom we elect to perform this function. The media can, willy-nilly, usurp the democratic function of Parliament and Congress.

It is interesting to examine what politicians, journalists and officials themselves think about this apparent aberration. As a whole, politicians are apt to deny being influenced by media persuasion. Journalists, anxious about their popularity, are also very circumspect about claiming too much power. Officials have no such inhibitions and will readily argue that media pressure leads to actions which politicians would not otherwise take. In each case, as Mandy Rice-Davies observed in another context, 'They would say that, wouldn't they?'

The tragedy is that the enormous technological strides in communication have often led to less, not more, real understanding. The world is a vastly complex place. Oversimplification – and this is the inevitable result of instant communication – can lead to a mistaken and arrogant belief in the efficacy of military and other action in solving complex and deep-seated problems which are often completely misunderstood. Many problems simply do not have solutions at all, even in the long, let alone the short, term. Easy communication can lead to easy, but ignorant and dangerous, conclusions. Many situations are in practice better left alone, rather than interfered with by outsiders. The passionate plea – 'Something must be done' – may help the speaker's conscience; it may well in practice lead to a deterioration of the situation.

On the other hand, we have seen many instances where the media has achieved much needed changes, from the improvements brought about by Russell's despatches from the Crimea to Emily Hobhouse's exposure of the South African 'concentration camps' to, perhaps, after many vicissitudes, peace in Bosnia, although this last is far from certain.

Television has indeed brought about an entirely new situation. There seem to be few hard and fast rules. There are some, however. Firstly, whatever the media pressures, outsiders should not take sides in a civil war – the results are virtually certain to be disastrous. Secondly, intervention in any form, again whatever the media pressures, must have overwhelming support at home if it is to succeed – look at the outcomes of Vietnam and Suez for confirmation of this. Next, in this modern soundbite age, intervention must be quickly successful and decisive with clear, obtainable objectives. General Colin Powell was absolutely right about this and military men argue strongly against involvement in situations to which they can see no apparent solution; however, they often feel themselves threatened by defence cuts if they are unwilling to follow the wishes of politicians. They, on the other hand, can feel frustrated by the reluctance of the military to use their armed force, the whole purpose of which, as the politicians see it, is to be ready to be used when necessary.

Lastly, military commanders must learn to see the media as potential allies rather than as enemies. Often the journalists will find themselves alongside the soldiers, sailors and airmen, sharing the dangers and discomforts of war; this will draw them closer together as people but, as John Simpson reminded us, they can never regard each other as 'friends' in the conventional sense as their different duties may suddenly diverge dramatically. With modern technology, journalists cannot be excluded any longer. Public relations will be an essential, perhaps the most essential, element of any future conflict. The media *will* influence events. Surely it must be best to try to use, not antagonize, it.

What should be done, however, about the present situation where the media, and in particular television, often sets the international agenda, supersedes national diplomatic representation, produces illusions of truth, oversimplifies and can sometimes force decisions on reluctant politicians, resulting in incoherent foreign policies based on haphazard surges of public emotion? There is one certainty. No more than the internal combustion engine can the television be disinvented. Both have drawbacks and advantages. Television exists as does the satellite dish – and no doubt there will be many further innovations in communication. Short of a police state, and heaven shield us from that, journalists must and will do their job with the technology they have. In a free society editors will select what to highlight, what to investigate and where. They will continue to influence public opinion in the direction they choose. In the last resort they will not be responsible for the consequences. We cannot, and will never, have instant universal truth from our media.

Kipling replied to Beaverbrook, who was boasting about the power he had, with the following words: 'I see; power without responsibility, the prerogative of the harlot throughout the ages.' This phrase was used by Baldwin, Kipling's cousin, when talking to the press in the 1930s. He did not, however, add that the power of the harlot can only be denied by avoiding the brothel.

The truth is that any power the media has is conceded to it by the politicians. The media by itself cannot order anyone to do anything. Lord Rees-Mogg told us that there are two kinds of politician – those who, after obtaining as much information as possible, make up their own minds about a policy and then try to get the media to support them; and those who find out what the media want and then try to supply it. Our politicians must all be of the former kind. They must refuse to be rushed. They must make up their minds and stick to it. Of course they will have to persuade public opinion to their point of view, but if they have a really well-thought-out policy, in the long run they will not have much difficulty.

The parliamentary Opposition, too, has much responsibility here. In the early stages of the Suez crisis Gaitskell gave Eden the benefit of the doubt and did not press him on various sensitive points in the House of Commons. That was an act of statesmanship which other Oppositions would do well to follow. It did not inhibit him later from furiously attacking the Government, but he waited until the position became clear. His opposition was not instant and routine.

A strong government with a carefully considered policy based on the national interest, or indeed on strong moral imperatives, will be able to, and should, ignore Douglas Hurd's 'flash flood of emotion' which a 'random media searchlight' can generate.

For its part the media should continue to probe, to expose abuses, to widen horizons, to criticize when necessary and to give support where this is justified. It should try not to oversimplify. It should realize that it cannot tell the whole truth in any situation. It is not infallible. It certainly must not even approach the arrogance of William Hearst, the publisher of the *New York Journal*, in his successful instigation of the Spanish–American War in order to boost sales.[15] He sent Frederic Remington, a famous artist, to Cuba in December 1896 to record scenes of Spanish brutality and Cuban misery. An exchange of telegrams was said to have followed. Remington wired to Hearst: 'Everything is quiet. There is no trouble. There will be no war. I wish to return.' Hearst replied: 'Please remain. You furnish the pictures and I will furnish the war.'

1. Kingsley Martin, *The Triumph of Lord Palmerston*, London, George Allen and Unwin, 1924, Introduction
2. Conversation with authors, March 1997
3. Quoted by Brian McNair, *An Introduction to Political Communication*, London, Routledge, 1995, p. 27
4. Barbara Tuchman, *The March of Folly*, London, Cardinal, 1990, p. 440
5. Conversation with authors, March 1997
6. Gowing, 'Conflict, the Military and the Media', *Officer*, May/June 1997
7. Elliot, 'The Impact of the Media on the Prosecution of Contemporary Warfare', *British Army Review*, 103, April 1993
8. Walter Goodman (television critic of the *New York Times*) quoted by Philip Seib, *Headline Diplomacy*, London, Praeger, 1997, p. 45
9. Martin Bell, *In Harm's Way*, London, Hamish Hamilton, 1995, p. 61
10. Seib, *Headline Diplomacy*, pp. 104–6
11. Ibid., p. 43
12. *Daily Telegraph*, 13 May 1997
13. *The Times*, 18 July 1997
14. Quoted by Gowing, *Real Time Television Coverage of Armed Conflicts and Diplomatic Crises*, Cambridge (MS), Harvard University Press, 1994, p. 87
15. Seib, *Headline Diplomacy*, p. 5

Select Bibliography

GENERAL

Books

Azrael, J. *US and Russian Policy Making with respect to the use of force*, Washington, Rand Centre, 1996

Bailey, S. *The UN Security Council and Human Rights*, New York, St Martins Press, 1994

Bailey, S., and Daws, S. *The United Nations – a concise political guide*, London, Macmillan, 1961

Bramall, E., and Jackson, W. *The Chiefs*, London, Brasseys, 1992

Damrosch, *Enforcing Restraint*, New York, Council on Foreign Relations, 1993

Dayan, D., and Katz, E. *Media Events*, Cambridge (MS), Harvard University Press, 1992

Dilks, D. *Retreat from Power*, London, Macmillan, 1981

Fox, R. *Camera in Conflict*, Cologne, Konemann Verlagsgesellschaft, 1996

Henderson, N. *Mandarin*, London, Weidenfeld and Nicholson, 1994

Knightley, P. *The First Casualty*, London, Deutsch, 1975

Conversations with Walter Lippman, Boston, Little, Brown and Company, 1960

McDonald, I. *A History of the Times*, Vol. V, 'Struggles in War and Peace, 1939–66', London, Times Books, 1984

Macnair, B. *An Introduction to Political Communication*, London, Routledge, 1995

Mercer, D. *The Fog of War*, London, Heinemann, 1987

Messenger, C. *Century of Warfare*, London, HarperCollins, 1995

Parsons, A. *From Cold War to Hot Peace*, London, Penguin, 1995

Powell, C. *A Soldier's Way*, London, Hutchinson, 1995

Pronay, N., and Spring, D. *Propaganda, Politics and Film 1918–45*, London, Macmillan, 1982

Reid. *The Science of War*, London, Routledge, 1993

Renwick, R. *Fighting with Allies*, London, Macmillan, 1996

Royle, T. *War Report*, London, Mainstream, 1987

Seib, P. *Headline Diplomacy*, London, Praeger, 1997

Stewart, I., and Carruthers, S. *War Culture and the Media*, Trowbridge, Flicks, 1996

Thatcher, M. *The Downing Street Years*, London, HarperCollins, 1993

Young, P. *Defence and the Media in Time of Limited War*, International Conference, Brisbane, 1991

Pamphlets

Adonis, *Fostering Democracy Worldwide*, Ditchley Conference Report No. 93/6

Badsey, S. *The Impact of the Media on the Prosecution of War*, Lecture to Army Staff College, 4 April 1995

——. *Modern Military Operations and the Media*, Strategic and Combat Studies Institute, Occasional Paper No. 8, Camberley, 1994

Bray, M. *The Relationship between the Government and the Media in Time of War*, Thesis, Downing College, Cambridge University, 1984

Ditchley Conference Reports: D90/10, 'Elements of Change in International Relations'; D93/6, 'Fostering Democracy Worldwide'; D93/8, 'Human Rights and External Intervention'; D83/11, 'The Freedom and Accountability of the Media'

Duncan, A. 'Mixing with the Media: Guidelines for Operational Commanders', *British Army Review* 110, August 1994

Elliott, C. 'The Impact of the Media on the Prosecution of Contemporary Warfare', *British Army Review* 103, April 1993

——. *The Impact of the Media on Modern Warfare*, Despatches No. 4, Autumn 1993

Gowing, N. Working Paper, 1 June 1994, John Kennedy School of Government, Harvard University

Hopkinson, N. *War and the Media*, Wilton Park Paper 55, 1992

Mathias, G. Despatches No. 5, Spring 1995

Simpson, J. *The 1993 Huw Wheldon Memorial Lecture – Making News*, Royal Television Society

Wain, C. 'Television Reporting of Military Operations – a Personal View', *RUSI Journal*, March 1974

CHAPTER ONE – THE CRIMEAN WAR

Bentley, N. *Russell's Despatches from the Crimea, 1854–56*, London, Andre Deutsch, 1966

Hankinson, A. *Man of Wars*, London, Heinemann, 1982

Hibbert, C. *The Destruction of Lord Raglan*, London, Longman, 1961

Lambert, A., and Badsey, S. *The Crimean War – The War Correspondents*, Stroud, Sutton, 1994

Martin, K. *The Triumph of Lord Palmerston*, London, Allen and Unwin, 1976

Rich, N. *Why the Crimean War?* University Press of New England, 1985

Russell, W. *The British Expedition to the Crimea*, London, Routledge, 1858

Strachey, L. *Eminent Victorians*, London, Penguin, 1918

Warner, P. *The Crimean War*, London, Arthur Barker, 1972

Woodham–Smith, C. *The Reason Why*, London, Constable, 1953

——. *Florence Nightingale*, London, Constable, 1950

CHAPTER TWO – LATE VICTORIANA

Blake, R. *Disraeli*, London, Eyre and Spottiswoode, 1966
Churchill, W. *The River War*, London, Eyre and Spottiswoode, 1899
Farwell, B. *The Great Boer War*, London, Allen Lane, 1977
Fuller, J. *The Last of the Gentlemen's Wars*, London, Faber and Faber, 1937
Jenkins, R. *Gladstone*, London, Macmillan, 1995
Martin, C. *The Boer War*, London, Aberland-Schuman, 1969
Pakenham, T. *The Boer War*, London, Abacus, 1992
Woods, F. (ed.). *Young Winston's Wars*, London, Leo Cooper, 1972
Wrench, J. *Lord Alfred Milner*, London, Eyre and Spottiswoode, 1958

CHAPTER THREE – FIRST WORLD WAR 1914–18

Beaverbrook, M. *Men and Power*, New York, Duell, Sloan and Price, 1956
Berry, P., and Bostridge, M. *Vera Brittain, a Life*, London, Chatto and Windrush, 1995
Blake, R. *The Private Papers of Douglas Haig, 1914–19*, London, Eyre and Spottiswoode, 1952
Clark, A. *The Donkeys*, London, Pimlico, 1991
Duff Cooper, *Haig*, London, Faber and Faber, 1936
Gilbert, M. *The First World War*, London, HarperCollins, 1995
Grigg, J. *Lloyd George From Peace to War 1912–16*, London, Methuen, 1985
Hammerton, J. *The Great War – I was there*, Vol. 1, London, Amalgamated Press
Hickey, M. *Gallipoli*, London, Murray, 1995
Illustrated London News 1914–19
Mr Punch's History of the Great War, London, Cassell, 1919
Tuchman, B. *August 1914*, London, Papermac, 1980

CHAPTER FOUR – SECOND WORLD WAR 1939–45

Calvocoressi, P., Wint, G., and Pritchard, J. *Total War – The Causes and Courses of the Second World War*, London, Penguin, 1995
Churchill, W. *The Second World War*, London, Penguin, 1989
Collier, R. *The Warcos*, London, Weidenfeld and Nicholson, 1989
Gilbert, M. *The Second World War*, London, Phoenix Giants, 1989
Hickman, T. *What did you do in the war, Auntie?* London, BBC Books, 1995
Kennedy, L. *War Papers*, London, Fontana, 1989
Manvell, R., and Fraenkel, H. *Doctor Goebbels*, London, Heinemann, 1960
McIntyre, T. *The Expense of Glory, a Life of John Reith*, London, HarperCollins, 1994
Stammers, N. *Civil Liberties*, London, Croom Helm, 1983
War Report from D-Day to VE-Day, London, BBC Books, 1991

CHAPTER FIVE – THE ASIAN CONNECTION: KOREA/VIETNAM

Avorn, J. *Up Against the Ivy Wall*, New York, Atheneum, 1969
Braestrupp, P. *Big Story*, New Haven, Yale University Press, 1977
Colvin, J. *Volcano under Snow*, London, Quartet Books, 1996
Fitzgerald, F. *Fire in the Lake*, New York, Vintage, 1973
Garfinkle, A. *Telltale Hearts*, New York, St Martins Press, 1995
Halliday, J., and Cumings, B. *Korea the Unknown War*, London, Viking, 1988
Hastings, M. *The Korean War*, London, Joseph, 1987
Herman, E., and Chomsky, N. *Manufacturing Consent*, New York, Pantheon Books, 1988
Kissinger, H. *Diplomacy*, New York, Simon and Schuster, 1994
Kolko, G. *Anatomy of a War*, New York, The New Press, 1994
McNamara, R. *In Retrospect*, New York, Times Books, 1995
Nixon, R. *The Real War*, London, Sidgwick and Jackson, Pantheon Books, 1980
Rees, D. *Korea the Limited War*, London, Macmillan, 1964
Summers, H. *On Strategy: The Vietnam War in Context*, Pennsylvania, Strategic Study Institute, 1981
Tuchman, B. *The March of Folly*, London, Cardinal, 1990
Westmoreland, *A Soldier Reports*, New York, Da Capo Paperback, 1976

CHAPTER SIX – SUEZ

Barker, A. *Suez – the Seven Day War*, London, Faber and Faber, 1964
Beaufre, A. *The Suez Expedition 1956*, London, Faber and Faber, 1969
Childers, E. *The Road to Suez*, London, McGibbon and Kee, 1962
Eden, A. *Full Circle*, London, Cassell, 1960
Epstein, L. *British Politics in the Suez Crisis*, London, Pall Mall, 1964
Kyle, K. *Suez*, London, Weidenfeld and Nicholson, 1991
Nutting, A. *No End of a Lesson*, London, Constable, 1967
Robertson, T. *Crisis*, London, Hutchinson, 1965
Shaw, T. *Eden – Suez and the Mass Media*, London, Tauris Academic Studies, 1996
Thomas, H. *The Suez Affair*, London, Weidenfeld and Nicholson, 1966

CHAPTER SEVEN – IRELAND

Bardon, J. *History of Ulster*, Ireland, Blackstaff, 1992
Carrington, P. *Reflect on Things Past*, London, Collins, 1988
Carver, M. *Out of Step*, London, Hutchinson, 1989
Coogan, T. *The Troubles*, London, Hutchinson, 1995
Dewar, M. *British Army in Northern Ireland*, London, Alison, 1987
Hamill, D. *Pig in the Middle*, London, Methuen, 1985

McCann, E. *Bloody Sunday in Derry,* Ireland, Dingle, 1992
Miller, D. *Don't mention the war,* London, Pluto Press, 1994
Rolston and Miller, *War and Words,* Beyond the Pale Publications, 1996
Winchester, S. *In Holy Terror,* London, Faber, 1974

CHAPTER EIGHT – THE FALKLANDS

Calvert, P. *The Falklands Crisis,* London, Pinter, 1982
Hastings, M., and Jenkins, S. *The Battle for the Falklands,* London, Book Club Associates, 1983
House of Commons Defence Committee 1982–83, *Handling of Press and Public Information During the Falklands Conflict,* Volume 1, HMSO, 1982
Morrison, D., and Tumber, H. *Journalists at War,* London, Sage, 1988
The Falklands War, Sunday Times Insight Team
Woodward, A. *One Hundred Days,* London, Collins, 1984

CHAPTER NINE – THE WOUNDED GIANT

Adkin, M. *Urgent Fury,* London, Leo Cooper, 1984
Blum, W. *The CIA, a forgotten history,* New Jersey, Zed Books, 1986
Johns, C. *State Crime, the Media and the Invasion of Panama,* London, Praeger, 1990
Nadel, J. *Special Men and Special Missions,* London, Greenhill Books, 1994
Parris, M., and Mason, P. *Read My Lips,* London, Robson, 1996
Seib, P. *Headline Diplomacy,* London, Praeger, 1997
Watson, B. *Operation Just Cause,* New York, Westview Press, 1990

CHAPTER TEN – THE GULF WAR

de la Billiere, P. *Storm Command,* London, HarperCollins, 1992
Cordingley, P. *In the Eye of the Storm,* London, Hodder and Stoughton, 1996
MacArthur, B. *Despatches from the Gulf War,* London, Bloomsbury, 1991
Morrison, D. *Television and the Gulf War,* London, Libbey, 1992
Salinger, P. *Secret Dossier,* London, Penguin, 1992
Summers, H.G. *A Critical Analysis of the Gulf War,* Dell War Series, 1992
Taylor, P. *War and the Media,* Manchester, Manchester University Press, 1992

CHAPTER ELEVEN – SOMALIA

Books
Delong and Tuckey, *Mogadishu, Heroism and Tragedy,* London, Praeger, 1994
Drysdale, J. *Whatever Happened to Somalia?* London, Hoan, 1991

Pamphlets

African Rights. *Somalia – Operation Restore Hope: a Preliminary Assessment*, London, 1993

Bradbury, M. *The Somali Conflict*, Oxfam Research Paper, 1993

Clarke, W. *Somalia, Background Information for Operation Restore Hope*, Strategic Studies Institute, US Army War College, 1993

Drake, J. *The Role of the United Nations in Somalia*, UN and Conflict Programme, London, 1993

Makinda, S. *Seeking Peace from Chaos: Humanitarian Intervention in Somalia*, International Peace Academy – Occasional Paper, London, 1993

Sahnoun, M. *Somalia: The Missed Opportunities*, The United States Institute of Peace Press, Washington, 1994

Somalia, Center for Army Lessons Learned, US Army Combined Arms Command, Fort Leavenworth, 1993

CHAPTER TWELVE – THE BALKANS

Bell, M. *In Harm's Way*, London, Hamish Hamilton, 1995

Bennet, C. *Yugoslavia's Bloody Collapse*, London, Hurst & Company, 1995

Gutman, R. *A Witness to Genocide*, Shaftesbury, Element Books Ltd, 1993

Mackenzie, L. *Peacekeeper: The Road to Sarajevo*, Vancouver, Douglas and Macintyre, 1993

Owen, D. *Balkan Odyssey*, London, Gollancz, 1995

Parsons, A. *From Cold War to Hot Peace*, London, Michael Joseph, 1995

Stewart, R. *Broken Lives*, London, HarperCollins, 1993

Thompson, M. *Forging War*, Article XIX, International Centre against Censorship

Woodward, S. *Balkan Tragedy*, Washington, Brookings Institution, 1995

Index

ABC Television, 167, 200, 222, 299
Aberdeen, Lord, 42
  the fall of his government, 12, 19, 56
Acheson, Dean, 89
Acland, Sir Antony, 164, 215
Aden, 31
Adie, Kate, 232, 309
Adrianople, Treaty of, 3
Ahmici, 287
Aideed, General Mohammed, 250, 251–3
Airey, Major General, 14
Albanians, 265–7
Albert, Prince 3, 19
Aldershot, 13
Alexandra, Princess, 195
Al-Khafji, 233
All Souls' College, Oxford, 293
Alma, River 6
Alsop, brothers, 133
American Civil War, 23, 24
Amiriya, shelter, 229
Amritsar 1919, 146, 151
Antrim, HMS, 196
Argentina, 163, 165
Argyll and Sutherland Highlanders, 1st Bn,
  92
Arkan, Arkanovci, 271
Armoured Brigade, British Seventh, 226
Armoured Division, British First, 231, 235,
  294
Ascension Island, 165
Ashmead-Bartlett, Ellis, 55
Asquith, Herbert, 52, 56–9, 83
Associated Press, 71, 113
Astor, Lord, 130
Atlantic Conveyor, 176
Atlee, Clement, 91, 95, 143
Auschwitz, 281
Aziz, Tariq, 219, 220

B52, bomber, 230
B Specials, 146
Baden-Powell, Lord, 33
Badinter Commission, 301

Baker, James (US Secretary of State), 213,
  219, 220, 242, 269, 273, 277
Balaklava, Battle of, 6, 9, 12
Baldwin, Stanley, 321
Balkans, 263–302
Ballymurphy, 146, 147
Banja Luka, 280
Barbados, 194, 197
Barnes, Thomas, 5
Barre, General Mohammed, 249–51
Basra road, 236
BBC, 69–72, 176, 273, 283, 287
  Foreign Language Broadcasts, 68
  and the Gulf, 223
  Newsnight, 224, 225, 240
  Panorama, 174, 311
  Radio, 183
  and Suez, 136–8
  Television News, 182
  Today programme, 224
  War Report, 67, 69
  World at One, 175
  World Service, 175
  and World War Two, 60, 67
Beattie, Ed, 71
Beaufort, Duke of, 19
Beaverbrook, Lord (Max Aitken), 54–7, 62,
  83, 321
Beirut, 189, 190
Belfast, 142–7
Belfrage, Bruce, 70
Belgrano (Argentinian Cruiser *General
  Belgrano*), 174
Bell, Martin, 273, 278, 279, 283, 287, 294
Belloc, Hilaire, 52, 53
Ben Gurion, David, 35
Bennett, Christopher, 263
Bennett, Major David, 301
Berlin, Congress of, 26
Bethman-Hollweg, Theobald von, 39
Bihac, 293
Billiere, Lt General Sir Peter de la, 231,
  233, 234, 237
Birmingham, bombings, 160

Bishop, Maurice, 191, 194
Bishop, Patrick, 178
Black, Admiral Sir Jeremy, 170
Blake, Lord, 58
Bloemfontein, 32, 33, 35
Bloody Friday, 157
Bloody Sunday, 148–51, 156
Bluff Cove, 173
Boer War, the, 28–38
Bogside, 148, 150, 157
Borthwick, Oliver, 26, 27
Botha, General Louis, 37
Boutros Ghali, Boutros (UN Secretary
    General), 252–4
Boxer Rebellion, 37
Boyle, Edward, 134
Boyle, Hal, 94
Brachen, Brendan, 63
Bradley, Father Denis, 150
Bragg, Fort, 194, 205
Bramall, Field Marshal Lord, 171, 196
Briand, Aristide (Prime Minister of
    France), 58
Brigade, Five (British Army), 176, 177
Brioni, Accord, 270, 273
Briquemont, General, 290
Brock, Hans van den, 274
Broderick, St John, 126
Brooke, Major Alan (later Field Marshal
    Lord Alanbrooke), 40
Buckingham Palace, 144
Buenos Aires, 167, 177
Bulganin, Marshal, 126
Bulgarian Atrocities, the, 25, 26
Buller, General Sir Redvers, 29, 32, 33
Bullock, Alan, 68
Bull Run, Battle of, 24
Burdett-Coutts, W., 33
Bush, President George, 92, 107, 283, 315
    and the Gulf, 209, 212, 214–17, 219, 220,
        221, 227, 236, 238, 242
    and Panama, 201, 205
    and Somalia, 254
Bushnell, John, 206
Butler, Rab, 129, 134

Callaghan, Lord, 179
Calley, Lieutenant, 109
Cameron, James, 95
Camilla Creek House, 175
Cam Ne, 109
Campbell-Bannerman, Sir Henry, 34
Canberra, SS, 170
Cape Colony, 29, 37

Cape Town, 31, 36
Carlton Club, 19
Carrington, Lord, 274, 284
Carson, Sir Edward, 54
Carter, President, 186, 187, 189, 223, 273,
    316
Carver, Field Marshal Lord, 157
Castro, Fidel, 191, 193
Cavell, Nurse Edith, 52
CBS News, 105, 187
CBS Television, 109, 167, 200
Censorship, 307, 308
    and the Crimea, 15, 18
    and the Boer War, 18, 19, 31
    and the Great War, 46, 47
    and World War Two, 63
    and Northern Ireland, 160
    and the Falklands, 170
    and Grenada, 200
Challenger, tank, 216
Chamberlain, Joseph, 29, 35
Chamberlain, Neville, 62, 63, 77, 124
Channel 4 News, 224
Charles, Eugenia, President, 191
Chenery, Thomas, 6, 7, 10
Cheney, Richard, 218, 228
Cheshire Regiment, 287
Chesterton, G.K., 52, 53
Chevening, 289
Chiang Kai Shek, 86, 96
Chicago Times, the, 23
Chicago Tribune, the, 90
Christian Science Monitor, the, 90
Christopher, Warren (US Secretary of
    State), 288, 289
Churchill, Sir Winston, 123, 124, 127, 132,
    137
    and the Sudan, 26–8
    and the Boer War, 32, 33, 38
    and the Great War, 39, 47, 56–8
    and World War Two, 61, 63, 66, 67, 75–8,
        83
    and the Greek Civil War, 80, 81, 83
    and Korea, 86, 95
CIA, 92, 202
Clark, Alan, 49
Clark, William, 134
Clifford, Alexander, 82
Clinton, President, 108, 226, 254, 258, 259,
    284, 288
CNN, 206, 223, 232, 318
Codrington, General Sir William, 19
Cohen, Richard, 259
Colchester, 13

Coldstream Guards, 220
Cole, G.D.H., 98
Colvin, John (HM Consul General Hanoi), 102
Conan Doyle, Dr, 33
Concentration camps (Boer War), 35, 36, 38
Constantinople, Convention of 1888, 124
Cooper, Duff, 41, 63
Cooper, Sir Frank, 180, 181
Cordingley, Brigadier Patrick, 231, 234, 240
Coventry, HMS, 176, 177
Coward, Noel, 83
Cowdray, Lord, 56
Cowley, Virginia, 71
Creggan and Bogside, 148
Crimean War, the, 1–21
Croatian Television (HRT), 272
Cronkite, Walter, 105, 187, 304
Curragh, 13
Curtis, Gunner, 147
Cuteleiro, Jose, 284

Daily Chronicle, the, 29
Daily Express, the, 56, 64, 73, 130, 132, 133, 178
Daily Herald, the, 64, 130, 131, 133
Daily Mail, the, 37, 56, 130, 132, 133
Daily Mirror, the, 50, 65, 67, 76, 77, 80, 130, 131
Daily News, the, 132, 133, 150, 158
and the Crimea, 3, 7, 10, 26
Daily Sketch, the, 64, 132
Daily Star, the, 177
Daily Telegraph, the, 29, 58, 95, 125, 130, 132, 162, 230, 234, 240, 303
and the Great War, 47
Daily Worker, the, 75
Daily Worker, the (US), 90
Damaskinos, Archbishop, 80
Darod, Clan, 249
Davies, S.O., 91
Dawson, William, 131
Day, Sir Robin, 41, 155, 157, 312
Dayton Agreement, The, 296, 299
Dayton, Ohio, 296
Dean, Sir Patrick, 128
Deedes, William (Lord), 308
De Gaulle, President Charles, 122
Delane, John, 5, 7, 16, 19
and the American Civil War, 24
Delhi Spearman, The, 302
Delta Force, 187
Derby, Lord, 16

Desert Shield, Operation, 218
Desert Storm, 225
De Wet, Christiaan, 34, 38
Dickens, Charles, 7
Dickson, John, London Biograph Co., 36
Diem, President, 101, 107
Dien Bien Phu, 102, 107, 114, 127
Dieppe, 65
Dimbleby, Richard, 70
Dionne, E.J., Jnr, 259
Disraeli, Benjamin
and the Crimean War, 19
and the Bulgarian Atrocities, 25
Dodd, Frank, 46
Dominica, 191
Domino Theory, 99, 102, 118, 130
Douglas-Home, Charles, 114
Driberg, Tom, 91
Drysdale, John, 247
Duberley, Mrs Henry, 18, 19
Dublin (British Embassy), 151
Dubrovnik, 273, 275
Dulles, Foster, 122, 123, 126, 127, 134, 138
Düsseldorf, 177

Eastern Question, the, 25
Easter Rising 1916, 142
East Falklands, 174, 175
EC monitors, 270
Economist, The, 135, 164, 281, 282, 290
Eden, Anthony (Lord Avon) 80, 81, 122–9, 131–8, 321
Einstein, Albert, 54
Eisenhower, President Dwight, 87, 97, 99, 122, 126, 134, 138
Elizabeth II, Queen, 169, 193, 199
Elliot, T.S., 40
Elysée Palace, 296
Emir of Kuwait, 213
Emmet, Mr (News Reel Editor), 74
Endara, Jose, President of Panama, 205
Endurance, HMS, 164
Enniskillen, 160
Estcourt, Major General, 14
Ethnic cleansing, 271
Evening Standard, the, 178, 226, 303
Exocet, 176

Fahd, King of Saudi Arabia, 215
Fairhall, David, 226
Falklands, the, 6, 31, 138
Falklands War, the, 163–84, 199, 200, 224
Falls, Professor Cyril, 132
Fawcett, Professor, 35

Fawcett, Mrs, 35
Fawzi, Dr (Egyptian Foreign Minister), 132
Fearless, HMS, 178, 179
Feisal, King of Iraq, 124
Fenner Brockway, Lord, 149
Fenton, Roger, 19, 312
Fergusson, Brigadier Bernard, 136
Fieldhouse, Admiral Sir John, 180
Filder, Commissary General, 14
Fisk, Robert, 234
Fitzroy, 173, 176
Fleming, Valentine (Father of Ian and Peter), 39
Flynn, Errol, 104
Ford, General Sir Robert, 162
Ford, President, 99, 116
Fox, Robert, 183
French, General Sir John, 49, 56
French Foreign Legion, 256

Gairloch, 158
Gairy, Sir Eric, 191
Gaitskell, Hugh, 131, 135, 137, 321
Gallipoli, 5, 6, 40, 55
Galtieri, President Leopoldo, 163, 164, 166, 179
Gaumont British News, 74
Genscher, Hans Dietrich, 275
George V, King, 42, 142
Germany, 142, 274, 289, 290
Giap, General, 104
Gibbs, Sir Philip, 47
Gilbert, Sir Martin, 39
Gilbert and Sullivan, 167
Gillard, Frank, 67, 69, 70, 82
Gladstone, Herbert
  and the Crimean War, 19
  and the Bulgarian Atrocities, 25, 26
Glasgow, 153, 155
Gloucester, Duke of, 78
Gloucester Regiment, 94
Gneisenau (German battle cruiser), 77
Godkin, Edwin, 7, 10, 24
Goebbels, Dr, xii, 51, 65, 66, 305
Goldwater, Senator Barry, 107
Goodman, Walter, 255, 313
Goose Green, 173, 175, 183
Gorazde, 291, 293, 295
Gorbachev, Michael, 209, 219, 242, 267
Gordon, General, 27
Goschen, Sir Edward, 39
Gowing, Nik, 308
Granada, 198
Grand National, 161

Great War, the, 1914–18, 39–60
Grenada, 191–200
Grigg, John, 45
Gromyko, Andrei, 90
Guam, USS, 146, 194, 197, 200
Gulf War, the, 175, 209–43
Guardian, the, 151, 220, 226, 232, 239, 307
Gwynne, H.A. (of Reuters), 34

Hague, the, 284, 299
Haig, Field Marshal Earl, 40, 41, 57, 58, 83
Haig, Alexander, 163, 167
Haldane, Lord, 56
Haley, Sir William, 130–2
Hamilton, General Sir Ian, 56
Hammerbeck, Brigadier Christopher, 231
Hampstead Heath, 36
Hannah, David, 224
Hannibal, 171, 172, 309, 314
Hapsburg Empire, the, 263
Hardie, Keir, 42
Harmsworth, Alfred (later Lord Northcliffe), 27, 56
Harriet, Mount, 178
Harrods, 160
Harsch, Joseph, 90
Hastings, Max, 98, 178, 180, 230, 234, 303, 306
Hawiye, Clan, 250, 251
Head, Anthony, 134
Healey, Denis, 131
Hearst, William, 321
Henderson, Sir Nicholas, 165, 167, 169
Herbert, Sidney, 10
Hermes, HMS, 170–2
Hersi, General Mohammed Said (Morgan), 251
Hertling, Count, 58
Hindenberg, Graf von, 48
Hitler, Adolf, 41, 51, 65, 66, 71, 72, 82, 122, 124, 130, 131, 312
Hobhouse, Emily, 34, 35
Ho Chi Minh, 104
Holbrooke, Richard (US Assistant Secretary of State), 296
Holland, 142, 274
Hollingsworth, Claire, 64
Hood, HMS, 77
Horner, General Chuck, 224
Household Cavalry, 160
Howard, Sir Michael, 318
Howe, Geoffrey (Lord), 194
Howe, Admiral, 253
Hue, 111

Hughes, Emrys, 91
Hulton, Edward, 95
Hunt, Lord, 146
Hunt, Sir Rex, 164
Huntley, Chet, 113
Hurd, Douglas (Lord), 221, 236, 275, 282, 283, 288, 289, 317, 321
Hussein, King of Jordan, 166, 212
Hussein, Saddam, 209–18, 220, 222, 227–30, 233, 235, 239, 242, 243, 269, 317

IFOR (International Force), 296, 299
Illustrated London News, the, 46, 48, 132
Inchon, 92
Independent, the, 234
Independent, USS, 199
Ingham, Sir Bernard, 173, 177
Inkerman, Battle of, 6
International News Service, 71
International Red Cross, 281
Internment, 147, 148
Interrogation, 148
Intrepid, HMS, 179
Invincible, HMS, 170, 179
IRA (Irish Republican Army), 142, 144, 145, 147, 148, 150, 152, 153, 158, 160, 161
Iran, 273
Ireland, 141–62
  Act, June 1949, 143
Irish Free State, 142
Irma, the wounded child, 288
Islam, 264, 277
ITV, 280
Izetbegović, Alija, 276, 280, 299

Jacobs, Sir Ian, 136
James I, King, 141, 161
James II, King, 141
Jameson, Dr, 29
Jameson, Derek, 182
Jay, Lord, 131
Jenkins, Simon, 303, 311
Jennings, Peter, 299
JP233 (Weapon System) 228
Johnson, President Lyndon, 99, 103, 105, 107, 110, 113, 115, 117, 304
Johnson, Samuel, 141
Jonah, James, 252
Jones, Lt Colonel H, 176
Jordanian Times, the, 230
Joyce, William (Lord Haw Haw), 66
Just Cause, Operation, 205, 207

Kaiser, The, Wilhelm, 44, 82
Karadžić, Radovan, 276, 280, 292, 295, 298, 299
Keeble, Major Chris, 183
Keegan, John, 144, 240
Kennan, George, 133
Kennedy, President Jack, 99, 107, 315
Kennedy, Robert, 113
Khaled bin Sultan, HRH Prince, 237
Khartoum, 27
Khe Sanh, 11, 114
Khomeini, Ayatollah, 187
Kim il Sung, President, 87, 89, 92
Kimberley, Relief of, 32
King, Cecil, 76
Kingsley, Revd Charles, 3
Kipling, Rudyard, 32, 121, 321
Kisher, Peter, 94
Kissinger, Henry, 46, 99, 101
Kitchener, Lord
  and the Sudan, 23, 26, 27
  and the Boer War, 32, 34, 36, 37
  and the Great War, 47
Kittani, Ismal, 253
Knin, 268, 271
Kohl, Helmut, 275
Kolko, Gabriel, 101, 118
Komati Poort, 34
Korea, 85–99
Kosovo, 265–7
Kosovo Polje, 265, 266
Krajina, 264, 268
Kruger, President, 29
Krupp, Mauser Rifle and Field Guns, 31
Kučan, Milan, 268, 269
Kurds, the, 238, 242, 316
Kuwait, 269

Ladysmith, 27, 32, 34
Lambert, Tom, 94
Lancers, 9/12th Royal, 302
Lancers, 21st, 26
Lansdowne, Lord, 58
Lawrence, Lester, 55
Leach, Admiral Sir Henry, 165, 179
Lebanon, 189, 190
Lewin, Admiral of the Fleet Sir Terence, 179, 180
Liddell, Alvar, 70
Lift and Strike Policy, 288, 295
Lincoln, President Abraham, 24, 185, 283
Lindbergh, Charles, 96
Lipmann, Walter, 105, 134, 304

Lisburn, 150
Little Rock, Arkansas, 284
Liverpool, Lord, 15
Liverpool, Roman Catholic Archbishop of, 152
Ljubljana, 271
Lloyd George, David, 38, 44, 45, 51, 54, 57–9, 83, 310
Lloyd, Selwyn, 124, 128, 132, 135
London, City of, 144
London, Treaty of, 1832, 45
Londonderry, 142, 143, 146, 148
Longden, Mount, 178
Los Angeles Times, the, 188
Lowe, Charles, 48, 49
Lusitania, SS, 52, 54
Lutine Bell, 181
Luxembourg, 270
Lyle, Captain T., 302

Maastricht Treaty, 275
MacArthur, General Douglas, 87, 89, 90, 92–8
McCarthy, Senator Eugene, 86, 113
McClellan (US General), 283
McCreery, General Sir Richard, 134
MacDonald, Ian, 174, 180, 181
MacDonald, Iverach, 125, 127, 129, 131, 132, 138, 311
MacDonald, Ramsay, 43
Macdonald, Admiral Wesley, 193
McGowan, Januarius, 25, 26, 309
Machen, Arthur, 50
Mackenzie, General Lewis, 277
McLachlan, Donald, 125
McLaughlin, Mrs, 147
Macleod, Ian, 134
Macmillan, Harold (Lord), 129, 179
Macmillan, Lord, (Judge), 62
McNamara, Robert, 115
MacPherson, Stewart, 70
Mafeking, Relief of, 32
Mahdi, Ali, 250–2
Major, John (Prime Minister), 275, 283
Majuba Hill, Battle of, 28
Makinda, Samuel, 245
Malta, 5, 8
Malvinas Islands, 163
Manchester, bombing of, 161
Manchester Guardian, the, 307
   and the Boer War, 29, 31, 32
   and the Great War, 42, 43
   and World War Two, 77, 79–81
   and Suez, 131–3, 135

Mao Tse Tung, 86, 89
Marehan Clan, 249, 251
Marshall, Howard, 70
Martin, Kingsley, 1, 303
Martin (US Senator), 96
Maudling, Reginald, 148
Maurice, General Sir Frederick, 58
Mayaguez, 185
Menendez, General, 178
Menzies, Robert, 127, 136
Merhamet, Muslim Relief Organization, 280
Metcalf, Vice Admiral Joseph III, 194, 200
Methuen, General Lord, 36
Meyer, General Edward (Shy), 202
MI5, 152
MI6, 152
Middlesex Regiment, 1st Bn, 92
Middleton, Drew, 105
MiG fighters, 266
Milner, Lord, 29, 34
   and concentration camps, 35
   opposition to Peace Treaty, 37
   at Versailles, 38
Milošević, Slobodan, xii, 265–71, 273, 292, 295, 298–300
Minié Rifles, 7
Mirage (Argentinian fighter aircraft), 177
Mitterand, President Francois, 280
Mladić, General Ratko, 295, 299
Moi, President Daniel Arap, 250
Mollet, Guy, 126
Moltke, Field Marshal Helmuth von, 51
Monckton, Walter (Lord), 129, 134
Monks, Noel, 82
Mons, Angels of, 49, 50
Montenegro, 263, 266
Montgomery, Field Marshal Lord, 69, 81, 82, 93
Moore, Arthur, 47
Moore, Major General Jeremy, 176, 178, 183
Moorehead, Alan, 82
Morillon, General Philippe, 289
Morning Advertiser and the Crimea, 3
Morning Leader, the, 29
Morning Post, the
   and the Crimea, 3
   and the Boer War, 32, 34
   and the Sudan, 26, 27
   and the Great War, 58
Morrison, Herbert, 75–7
Moscow, 154
Mostar, 290, 291

Mostyn, General Sir David, 159
Motorman, Operation, 157
Mountbatten, Earl, 160, 178, 306
Mount Igman, 295
Mubarak, President of Egypt, 212
Mulley, Frederick (Lord), 179
Munich, 63
Murdoch, Keith (Father of Rupert), 55, 56
Murray, Gilbert, 43
Murrow, Ed, 71, 72, 312
Mussolini, Benito, 124, 130
My Lai, 109

Nambiar, General Satish, 276
Napoleon, Bonaparte, xii
Napoleon III, 2
Nasser, President Abdel Gamal, 122–5, 127–9, 131, 133, 134, 136, 137
Natal, 29
Nation, The (magazine), 40
NATO, 145, 274, 281, 290, 291, 293, 296, 300
Nazis, 268, 281
NBC Television, 113
Neave, Airey, MP, 160
Neretva, River, 290
Netley, Army Medical Board, 13
Newcastle, Duke of, 12, 14, 15
New England, 141
New Jersey, USS, 190
News Chronicle, the, 130–3
News of the World, the, 182
Newsreels, 73, 74
New Statesman, the, 91, 239
Newsweek, 117, 301
New York, 105
New York Herald Tribune, the, 70, 90, 92, 96
New York Journal, the, 321
New York Times, the, 80, 90, 96, 106, 110, 134, 243, 282
New Zealand, 179
Nicaragua, 166
Nichol, Adrian, 229
Nightingale, Florence, 10, 11
Nimitz, Admiral, 87
Nimitz, USS, 188
Nixon, President, 99, 101, 114–17
Noraid, 161
Norddeutsche Allgemeine Zeitung, 54
Norfolk, Virginia, 194
Noriega, General Manuel, 202, 203, 205–7
Northcliffe, Lord (Alfred Harmsworth), 27, 56–8, 83
Northern Ireland Civil Rights Association (NICRA), 143, 148

Nott, Sir John, 163, 179, 181
Nuri es-Said, 124
Nutting, Anthony, 121, 134

Observer, the, 131, 132, 178
Omarska Mine, 280
Omdurman, Battle of, 27
O'Neill, Hubert, Londonderry City Coroner, 151
Orange Free State, 28, 32
Orange Lodges, 142, 143
Organization of African Unity (OAU), 248
Organization of Eastern Caribbean States (OECS), 191, 193
Orwell, George, 68
Ottoman Empire, the, 263, 265
Owen, David (Lord), 284, 298

Pacifico, Don, 2
Pale, 294
Palestine Liberation Organization (PLO), 189
Palmerston, Lord, 2, 12
Panama, 201-7
Panama Canal Treaty, 204
Panama Canal Zone, 203
Panama Defence Force, 203, 204, 206
Panmure, Lord, 12
Pan-Yugoslav Congress, 267, 268
Papandreou (Greek Prime Minister), 79
Parachute Regiment, 1st Bn, Northern Ireland, 149, 151, 152, 154, 231
Parachute Regiment, 2nd Bn, 175, 176, 187
Paris, Peace of, 1856, 7
Parsons, Sir Anthony, 105
Passchendaele, 40,41
Paxman, Jeremy, 240
Pearls Airfield, 198
Peć, 265
People, the, 132
Perot, Ross, 258
Peters, John, 229
Phillips, Frank, 70
Philpotts, Eden, 52, 53
Picture Post, 95
Pierlot (Prime Minister of Belgium), 80
Politika, 265
Politika Ekspres, 265
Poos, Jacques, 270
Portsmouth, 169
Port Stanley, 32, 173, 175, 176, 187
Potsdam, Declaration of, 86
Powell, General Colin, 112, 114, 201, 202, 214, 218, 236, 237, 254, 282, 284, 320

Pretoria, 34
Princip, Gavrilo, 265
Prince of Wales (Edward VII), 7
Prince of Wales (Edward VIII), 42
Prince of Wales, HMS, 64, 77
Prince of Wales' Own Regiment of Yorkshire, 142
Prince Regent, xii
Protheroe, Alan, 181
Punch
  and the Crimea, 1
  and the South African War, 29
Pusan, 91, 92

Raemaeker, Louis, 52
Raglan, Lord, 18, 19
  and requisition to England, 8
  attacks on, 13, 14
  complaint against Russell, 15, 16
Ramsbotham, General Sir David, 184
Rapid Reaction Force, 295, 296
Reagan, President Ronald, 93, 138, 166, 189, 195, 199, 201
Red Army, 269
Rees-Mogg, Lord, 311, 321
Reith, Lord, 62, 63, 70, 313
Remington, Frederick, 321
Reppington, Colonel, 56, 58
Republican Guard (Iraqi), 230, 232, 237
Repulse, HMS, 64, 77
Reston, James, 104
Restore Hope, Operation, 256
Reuters and the Boer War, 32
Reynolds' News, 132
Reynolds, Quentin, 71, 72
Reynolds' Weekly and the Crimea, 3
Rhodes, Cecil, 29
Rice-Davies, Mandy, 319
Ridgway, General Matthew, 93
Robens, Alfred (Lord), 137
Roberts, Chalmers, 133
Roberts, Field Marshal Lord, 32–4
Roberts, Major, 91
Robertson, Field Marshal Sir William, 57
Roman Empire, the, 263
Roosevelt, President Franklin D., 71, 80, 85, 86
Rose, General Sir Michael, 290–4, 300, 307
Royal College of Defence Studies, 172
Royal Greenjackets, 160
Royal Marine Commando Brigade, 171, 176
Royal Marines, 159, 164
Royal Ulster Constabulary, 142, 143, 147

Royal Welsh Fusiliers, 295
Rumania, 269
Rupert, Fort, 197
Rusk, Dean, 107
Russell, William
  and the Crimea, 1, 5–10, 12, 17–19, 56
  and the American Civil War, 24
Rwanda, 292

'Safe Areas', 289, 291, 295
Safer, Morley, 109
Sahnoun, Mohammed, 252, 253
Saint George's 200
Saint Paul's, Dean of, 52
Salem, Major Saleh, 137
Salines, Point (Airfield), 193, 196, 198
Salisbury, Harrison, 110
Salisbury, Lord, 315
Samsonov, General, 48
San Carlos, 173, 174, 181
Sarajevo, 45, 265, 276–80, 285, 288, 290, 294, 295
SAS, 187, 231, 290
Sava River, 273
Scharnhorst (German battle cruiser), 77
Schlieffen, General Alfred von, 45
Schuyler, Eugene (US Consul General), 26
Schwarzkopf, General Norman, 218, 226, 228, 231, 232, 236–8, 241
Scobie, General Sir Ronald, 79
Scoon, Sir Paul (Governor General of Grenada), 193, 194, 197–9
Scud missiles, 227, 228, 233
Scutari, 6, 10–12
Sea Harriers, 169, 172, 291
Seamark, Mick, 177
Sebastopol, 6
Security Council
  and Korea, 89
  and the Falklands, 165, 166
  and the Gulf War, 217, 218
  and the Balkans, 279, 284, 289
Seib, Philip, 299
Seitz, Hon Raymond, 163, 193, 198, 203, 220, 288, 289
Seoul, 92, 94
Serb National Councils, 268, 276
Serbian Academy of Sciences and Arts, 266
Serbian Orthodox Church, 166
Sèvres, Protocol of, 128
SFOR (Stabilizing Force), 298
Sforza, Count, 80
Shah, the, of Iran, 186, 187
Shamir, Yitzhak, 227, 228

Shankill Road, 146
Sharpe, Tom, 110
Sharpeville, 151
Sheehan, Neil, 110
Sheerness Gunnery School, 13
Sheffield, HMS, 173, 174
Shirer, Walter, 66
Shultz, George, 198
Sidewinder missiles, 169
Silverman, Sidney, 91
Simpson, John, 223, 306, 307, 309, 314, 320
Simpson, Lt General, 14, 19
Sinn Fein, 144
Sinope, 3
Sir Galahad (landing ship), 176, 177
Sir Tristram (landing ship), 176
Skyhawks (Argentinian aircraft), 177
Smith, Dr Andrew, 11
Smith, F.E. (later Lord Birkenhead), 46, 47
Smith, Lt Gen Sir Rupert, 231, 294, 295, 307
Smuts, Jan, 34, 37
   in Lloyd George's War Cabinet, 38
Snagge, John, 69
Snow, Peter, 225
Socialist Party of Serbia (SPS), 265, 266
Somalia, 245–61, 279
Somme, the, 40, 55
South Georgia, 163
Spaatz, General, 87
Spion Kop, 32, 36
Srebrenica, 289, 290, 295
Staff College, 13, 231, 290
Stalin, Josef, 80, 89, 93
Stambolić, Ivan, 265
Star, the (newspaper), 29
Stead, W.T., 29
Steevens, George Warrington, 27
Sterling, Lt Colonel, 16
Stettinius (US Secretary of State), 80
Stewart, Colonel Bob, 287
Stiner, Lt General Carl, 205
Stockwell, General Sir Hugh, 136
Stone, Norman, 239
Storey, Wilbur, 23
Stormont Parliament, 142, 153
Strachey, Lytton, 10
Stratford, Lord, 2
Sudan, 1898, 26
Suez, 121–39, 145, 165
Sun, the (newspaper), 169, 181, 229
Sunday Dispatch, the, 132
Sunday Express, the, 132
Sunday Graphic, the, 132

Sunday Pictorial, the, 132
Sunday Telegraph, the, 162, 172
Sunday Times, The, 132, 170, 239
   and World War Two, 69
Supremacy, Oath of, 141
Swinton, Colonel, 47
Sydney Morning Herald and the Boer War, 32
Sykes, Sir Richard, 160
Syngman Rhee, 87, 93, 96

T-55, Russian tank, 233
Talbot, Godfrey, 70
Tannenberg, Battle of, 48, 51
Teheran hostages, 185–9
Tel Aviv, 227
Templer, Field Marshal Sir Gerald, 93
Tet Offensive, 102, 111–14, 117
Thackeray, William, 7
Thatcher, Baroness Margaret, 31, 138, 160, 303, 306, 307, 313
   and the Falklands, 163–6, 170, 173, 175, 179, 183
   and the Gulf, 209, 214–16, 242
   and *The Downing Street Years*, 182
Thieu, President, 102, 115, 116
Thompson, Admiral (Chief Press Censor), 63
Thompson, Mark, 266
Thompson, R.W., 95, 98
Thorneycroft, Peter (Lord), 178
Thurman, General Max, 204
Time Magazine, 110, 285, 292
Times, The, xii
   and the Crimea, 3, 5, 7, 10, 12–17, 19
   and the American Civil War, 24, 25
   and the Boer War, 31–3
   and the Great War, 42, 44, 47, 48, 51, 56
   and World War Two, 79
   and Korea, 97
   and Suez, 125, 130–2, 138
   and Vietnam, 114
   and Northern Ireland, 150
   and the Teheran hostages, 187, 188
   and the Gulf War, 220, 224, 225, 234
Tito, Josip Broz, 263, 264, 265, 267, 268
Tolstoy, Leo, 18
Tonkin, Gulf of, Resolution, 107, 116
Tornado aircraft, 216, 218, 228
Transvaal, 28, 29
Travellers' Club, 282
Trent, British Mail Packet, 24
Trevelyan, G.M., 43,
Tribune, the, 91

Truman, President Harry S., 85, 90, 92, 95–8
Tsar of Russia and the Crimean War, 2
Tuchman, Barbara, 48, 51, 110
Tudjman, Franjo, 268, 269, 271, 273, 299
Tumbledown Mountain, 178
Turkey, Sultan of, 2
Tuzla, 285, 294
Tuzo, General Sir Harry, 153, 158
Tyrell, Lord, 138

Ulster, 141–62
Ulster Defence Regiment (UDR), 146
Ulster Volunteer Force (UVF), 144
Unilaterals (Press Correspondents) 223, 232
UNHCR (UN High Commission for Refugees), 283, 286
United Nations and the Falklands, 165
United Nations Protected Areas (UNPAs), 274, 276
UNPROFOR (UN Protection Force), 276, 277, 287, 289, 290, 293
Urgent Fury, Operation, 193, 199, 201, 202
Ushuaia, 170
Ustašas, 268

Vance, Senator Cyrus, 187–9, 273, 274, 276, 283, 284, 316
Vance-Owen Peace Plan, 284, 286, 289
Varcoe, Jeremy, 270–1
Varna, 5, 6, 8
Vatican Embassy, 206, 207
Vaughan, Bernard SJ, 52, 53
Vaughan-Thomas, Wynford, 70
Venetian Empire, the, 263
Verdun, 40
Victoria, Queen and the Crimea, 3
Vietnam, 99–120, 141, 185
Vitez, 287
Vojvodina, 266
Vukovar, 273, 274, 276

Wadi al Batin, 235
Wadi Halfa, 26, 27
Walker, General (Comd US 8th Army) 93

Walker, General Sir Michael, 298, 299
Wallace, Edgar, 36, 37
Wall Street Journal, the, 90
Walter, John, 5
Wardlaw-Milne, Sir John, 78
Warrior armoured vehicles, 216
Washington, 165
Washington Post, the, 113, 133, 186, 187, 200, 258, 259, 311
Waterloo, Battle of, xii, 7, 10
Wavell, Field Marshal Lord, 65
Wayne, John, 104
Weinberger, Caspar, 167, 169, 185, 190, 200
Wellington, baggage train of, 7, 10, 15, 17
Wellington, Duke of, xii
Welsh Guards, 1st Bn, 176
Werth, Alexander, 82
Westminster Gazette, the, 35
Westmoreland, General William, 102, 111
Whitelaw, Reid, 72
Whitelaw, William (Lord), 153, 158
Widgery, Lord Chief Justice, 151
William III, King, Prince of Orange, 141
Wilmot, Chester, 69
Wilson, Harold (Lord), 122
Winchester, Simon, 146, 151, 170
Windward Islands, 191
Wingate, Major, 26
Wireless Ridge, 178
Witherow, John, 178
Wood, Field Marshal Sir Evelyn, 19
Woodward, Admiral Sir Alexander, 171
Woon, Peter, 182
World War Two, 61–84
Wright-Patterson Air Force Base, 296

Yalu River, 92
Young, G.M., 68
Yugoslav National Army (JNA) 266, 269–74, 276, 277

Zagreb, 270
ZEC (cartoonist), 76
Zepa, 295
Zimmermann, Dr Von, 54